Tennessee Zoning Boards:

Practice and Procedure

Second Edition

George A. Dean

ISBN - 10 # 0-9717208-4-3
ISBN - 13 # 978-0-9717208-4-8

GadsHill Press
Nashville, TN

PARKER, LAWRENCE, CANTRELL & DEAN
Noel Place, Suite 500
200 Fourth Avenue North,
Nashville, Tennessee 37219

gdean@plcd.com

Phone: 615-255-7500
Fax: 615-242-1515

www.tnlanduse.com

Second Edition, October 2009
First Edition, March 2002

On the cover: the AT&T Building in downtown Nashville required several variances from the Metro Board of Zoning Appeals in order to begin construction

Table of Contents

Dedicated to my wonderful and beloved daughters,

Emily Allison Scott

and

Amanda Marie Dean

Other Books by George Dean

Tennessee Zoning Board Handbook, GadsHill Press, February 2009: A short handbook (48 pages) for zoning board members to familiarize them with zoning board powers and procedures.

Legal Handbook for Tennessee Codes Officials, GadsHill Press, March 2009 (342 pages): A legal primer for codes officials.

Land Use Law: Tennessee and Beyond, GadsHill Press, October 2009 (598 pages). This is the textbook for the Land Use Planning Course at the Nashville School of Law.

Tennessee Planning Commissions: Practice and Procedure, GadsHill Press, anticipated March 2010. This will be an in-depth discussion of planning commissions here in Tennessee, their powers and responsibilities.

A Career in Briefs, 1980 to 2000; GadsHill Press, anticipated December 2009. This volume will reprint and review 25 cases that Mr. Dean handled on behalf of land use clients over the first twenty years of his career. Each section will consist of an Introduction, setting the stage for the case; a key brief filed by Mr. Dean; and the court's decision, whether in victory or defeat.

A Career in Briefs, 2000 to 2010; GadsHill Press, anticipated December 2010. A companion to the book above, focusing on more recent cases but in a similar format.

Historic Zoning in Tennessee; GadsHill Press, anticipated June 2010. A quick overview of historic zoning in Tennessee.

The Metro Board of Zoning Appeals: 2008-9; GadsHill Press, anticipated March 2010. A review of the board's decisions over the course of two years, as well as a little history about zoning and the zoning board.

Patterns of Judicial Decision-Making: The Influence of Legal Philosophy, GadsHill Press, 1976. A second printing is expected in December 2009.

Chapter One

Basic Concepts and Considerations

A. Introduction

This is the second edition of a book which is a partial realization of a goal I have had for many years. I always wanted to write a book surveying all of Tennessee land use law, but as the years have gone by, I realized that I simply couldn't write fast enough to keep up with new developments. My pesky law practice seemed to get in the way as well. As a result, this book, focusing only on the functions of the zoning board, one of the principal parts of land use regulation in Tennessee, was a compromise solution. In the years since the first edition of this book, I have finished several other volumes but still have not accomplished anything near what I'd like: to ultimately produce writings which, in total, will review much of the law of land use in Tennessee. I've made a decent start, but I have a long way to go.

The book is written with the idea that both attorneys and codes enforcement officials may find it useful. At times, the legal minutiae may be vexing for the lay reader, but hopefully the information is helpful to the codes official and will be worth the effort to work through the legal discussions. Some parts of the book, the first several sections of the first chapter, in particular, are specifically for the lawyers. An understanding by the codes official of this part of the attorney's practice might be helpful and surely, the last portions of the chapter dealing with hearings before the board will help fill in some of the gaps which have existed in the past.

We will begin with a nuts and bolts overview of practice before a local zoning board. Then we review each of the 3 major functions of a zoning board in Tennessee: administrative appeals, conditional use permits (special exceptions), and variances. The book ends with a review only a lawyer could enjoy: a brief examination of the writ of certiorari, the principal means of appealing a zoning board decision in Tennessee.

Don't underestimate the value of having a firm understanding of this from a codes perspective: since almost all zoning board cases are appealed pursuant to this old mechanism, it is useful for the codes staff to know how it works generally because it may impact the validity of the things the zoning board can do and the decisions it makes. As far as I am aware, there are no current[1] writings dealing with practice and procedure before a Tennessee zoning board.[2] Because the practice before a zoning board can be significantly different from the type of practice most lawyers are intimately familiar with, usually in the courtroom, or in a more formal administrative setting, I have long thought that an article on some of the peculiarities of procedure before a zoning board might be appropriate. This chapter attempts to fill in some of those gaps in procedure which most attorneys might not know about otherwise.

---

[1] There are however, two respected land use planning law practitioners who did write about zoning board practice some 40 to 50 years ago. See E.C. Yokley, *The Place of the Planning Commission and the Board of Zoning Appeals in Community Life*, 8 Vand. L. Rev. 794 (1955) and R. W. Phair, *Planning and Zoning: Principles and Practice*, 29 Tenn. L. Rev. 514 (1962).

[2] These local boards are known by a variety of names, including Board of Adjustment, Board of Appeals, Board of Zoning Appeals, and so on. This chapter will refer to all such administrative bodies as Boards of Zoning Appeals, and usually abbreviated as MBZA because of my municipal bias. These boards must be distinguished from planning commissions, which in general, are responsible for long-range planning and subdivision control. Compare the variance provisions of the Tennessee Public Zoning Enabling Legislation, TENN. CODE ANN. § 13-7-106 & 205 with the planning and subdivision control provisions of the Tennessee Public Planning Enabling Legislation, TENN. CODE ANN. § 13-3-101 & 13-4-101. The focus of these materials is on local boards of zoning appeals by whatever name that body might be known. Generally speaking, while there are certainly nuances to be discussed separately with regard to appearances before local legislative bodies, and other boards, such as a local planning commission, the principles discussed here are probably just as valid for those other bodies as they are for the local boards of zoning appeals.

B. Pre-Hearing Procedures

1. The Client Interview

Whether your client is a group of local citizens formed to promote the general interests of the community in which they live, or a developer of local properties, they will usually have very little understanding of the zoning system, or what technique is being employed to accomplish the client's objective.[3] As a result, they will have very little understanding of the legal criteria by which both the board of zoning appeals and a reviewing court are supposed to consider the application for relief.

For that reason, it is appropriate to meet and obtain all the documents which your client may have in his/her possession concerning the proposal. If the documents include notices from the codes department, those notices may spell out with a reasonable degree of certainty the type of relief being sought.[4] If you represent the developer, and if the developer has already visited the codes department, double-check to make sure that the avenue selected to obtain the necessary relief is the correct way of getting that relief. Also, check to make sure that there are not other ways of accomplishing the same goal; perhaps there is an easier way of getting the relief your client seeks, or perhaps there are multiple requests that might be made involving different avenues of relief. Most clients do not consider these possibilities; it should not be overlooked by legal counsel.

The initial interview is important for other reasons as well. First, while the client typically will not know or understand the legal criteria by which the zoning board is to judge the application, they usually have a common sense understanding of why he or she wants to develop,

---

[3] In fact, it may be even worse if they profess to understand because the odds are that their understanding is incorrect and the attorney will be forced to correct that as the matter progresses.

[4] The attorney should not however, depend upon the accuracy of such notices. The notices frequently are not written with great accuracy.

supports or opposes the particular project. The developer thinks that the design of his or her building is exceptionally beautiful and will enhance the property in the general location of its construction tremendously. It may fulfill an important need for low-cost housing. The opponents, neighboring property owners, ofttimes have different viewpoints concerning the same construction. The traffic congestion will increase and negatively affect the level of service on adjacent highways. Real estate values may decrease. Noise and disruptive activities will be brought into the community by virtue of the use suggested by the developer. And while these concerns may or may not find expression in the technical legal criteria which you will have to deal with, they are certainly the kinds of things that zoning boards are frequently concerned with, whether the legal guidelines require that concern or not. This "common sense" approach to land use planning decision-making is one which most board members subscribe to.[5] These intuitive concerns expressed by your client will be the same concerns that a common sense member of the board of zoning appeals will identify with as well. Thus, the attorney needs to seek an appropriate means by which to interject these concerns or considerations favorably to the needs of the client.

Secondly, the client may also have a good feel for the environment in which the project is being suggested. The developer, for example, may know or have a shrewd opinion concerning the level of support or opposition which he will get from the community surrounding the development. A neighborhood group will usually know some details concerning the development and the construction environment in the area. This information can be quite useful. When representing a developer, getting to potential members of the opposition as soon as possible may help negate the unification of the neighborhood opposition. When representing the neighbors, exploitation of weaknesses in the developer's plan or inconsistencies in the developer's plan or outright misrepresentations in the developer's presentation can be quite decisive.

[5] See Chapter Four at page 102, 221.

2. The Application

(a) Understand the Zoning Technique

The first and most important aspect of practicing land use planning law or administering a zoning ordinance is to thoroughly understand the zoning techniques which may be sought or opposed by your client or a member of the public. There are a great number of different types of zoning techniques at this time. We no longer belong to the old days of simple Euclidean zoning, although such simplicity may often be a desirable objective. Without intending to be exhaustive, your client maybe seeking (or opposing) a variance,[6] a conditional use permit,[7] a non-conforming use,[8] a planned unit development,[9] a change of zoning on his/her or a neighbor's property,[10] an administrative

---

[6] See TENN. CODE ANN. § 13-7-109(3) (relating to counties), TENN. CODE ANN. § 13-7-207(3) (relating to municipalities), and *McClurkan v Metropolitan Board of Zoning Appeals*, 565 S.W. 2d 495 (Tenn. App. 1977). See also Chapter Four at page 219.

[7] See TENN. CODE ANN. §§ 13-7-107(b), 13-7-109(2)(relating to counties), and TENN. CODE ANN. §§ 13-7-206(a), 13-7-207(2)(relating to municipalities), and *Father Ryan v City of Oak Hill*, 774 S.W. 2d 184 (Tenn. App. 1988). See also Chapter Three at page 147.

[8] See TENN. CODE ANN. §§ 13-7-208, and *City of Clarksville v Rives*, 618 S. W. 2d 502 (Tenn. App. 1981). See also Chapter Two at p. 92.

[9] See *McCallen v City of Memphis*, 786 S. W. 2d 633 (Tenn. 1990) and *Davis (MC) Group v. Metropolitan Government*, 912 SW 2d 178 (Tenn App. 1995). PUDs, as they are called, are usually considered by the local legislative body and are normally considered by the courts as an exercise of administrative power by that body.

[10] See TENN. CODE ANN. § 13-7-105 (relating to counties) and TENN. CODE ANN. § 13-7-204 (relating to municipalities); see also *Fallin v Knox County*, 656 S.W. 2d 338 (Tenn. 1983). Re-zoning is not a function of the zoning board but is rather legislative in nature and is

interpretation of the zoning ordinance,[11] some other zoning technique, or any combination of the above. It is not the purpose of this chapter to distinguish between these types of zoning relief.[12] However, it is of absolute importance to understand the legal rules which apply in order to properly represent your client before a zoning board or other administrative body.

For example, if you client is seeking (or opposing) a variance, the proof will be greatly different from that which he would present if he were seeking a conditional use permit. A variance generally requires some proof of (1) an exceptional physical or topographic condition of the property (2) causing (3) practical difficulty or undue hardship, and (4) satisfaction of the so-called negative criteria, that is, no substantial detriment to the public good, no substantial detriment to the intent and purpose of the zone plan or to the intent and purpose of the zoning ordinance.[13] An application for a conditional use permit, on the other hand, is quite different. It is necessary for counsel to ascertain the list

---

solely the domain of the local legislative body.

[11] See TENN. CODE ANN. § 13-7-109(1) (relating to counties), TENN. CODE ANN. § 13-7-207(1) (relating to municipalities), and *Qualls v City of Memphis*, 15 Tenn. App. 575 (1932). See also Chapter Two at page 73.

[12] Subsequent chapters will hopefully provide a detailed understanding of the types of relief available from a zoning board. A further understanding of the substantive law must be gleaned from the applicable Tennessee statutes, ordinances, regulations and case law. An overview of the national trends may be obtained from any of the four major treatises in the field. See P. Rohan, *Zoning and Land Use Controls*; R.M. Anderson, *American Law of Zoning* 3d; E.H. Ziegler, *Rathkoph's The Law of Zoning and Planning*; and N. Williams, *American Land Planning Law.* An excellent one volume treatise is D. Mandelker, *Zoning Law.* However, in many respects, Tennessee law differs from the majority position across the United States.

[13] See TENN. CODE ANN. § 13-7-109(3) (relating to counties) and TENN. CODE ANN. § 13-7-207(3) (relating to municipalities).

of conditions required by the municipality in order to grant the permit and produce proof concerning each of those conditions.[14]

(b) Filing the Application

If the attorney is responsible for filing the application for a permit, make sure that the request covers what is necessary and that the form is properly filed out, including the name of the applicant and his/her relationship to the land. Some local jurisdictions have made this process more and more complicated, and as a result, it usually makes sense to get the application form first, review it, attach whatever supporting documentation is required, and then file the form after completing it in the attorney's office. By the same token, if the attorney is representing the opposition, check the accuracy and completeness of the application submitted by the applicant: there may be some holes which can be exploited in front of the board.

In addition to the form itself, with many types of appeals, the preparation of a site plan for the consideration of the board is almost a necessity. If you are applying for a variance, conditional use permit, or asking that the board find the property to be legally nonconforming, most often a site plan is needed to demonstrate the location of the various aspects of the land use involved. Many zoning boards require a site plan as a part of the application process. In a sense, site plan review is part and parcel of the process undertaken by the board of zoning appeals.

Although this does not happen much here in Middle Tennessee, there are some boards which essentially require that all evidence to be considered by the board must be submitted at the time of the application, including statements of witnesses. The boards here in the Nashville area generally don't even require this, but there are a few jurisdictions which even in the absence of an adopted rule, simply insist upon filing of virtually all evidence at the time of the application. This

---

[14] See *Sexton v Anderson County*, 587 S.W. 2d 663 (Tenn. App. 1979), for example. The list of conditions in this case is quite short; the list in most ordinances for the different types of conditional uses is frequently quite lengthy.

misapprehends the nature of the application process as opposed to the hearing process. The application simply begins the process: it is not intended to force the applicant to file everything that may be worthwhile to submit to the board. While certainly there can be a cut-off date for such submissions, that should be only a few days to a week before the meeting of the board. But there should not be a requirement that all information be submitted at the time of the application.

For one thing, most applications are not filed by professionals, either legal or engineering. Most applications are filed by laymen, who don't know what is required to make out a case for relief. If the lawyer or engineer isn't free to come back later to get the case ready for a hearing, it puts the applicant in a difficult position. Of course, if the attorney is hired after the filing of the application, the first step is to check the application and make sure that it is complete and that there are no deficiencies that would cause the board to deny relief.

Most of the time, I learn more about the project after the application is submitted. There may be neighborhood meetings, changes made by virtue of other developments, and those need to be presented to the board. Trying to cut off such submissions makes little sense and is likely illegal if not specified in the rules of the board of the zoning ordinance.

(c) The Applicant and Standing Issues

One of the most important aspects of this process may be to make sure that the applicant has legal standing to file the application.[15] The particular standing requirements may vary depending on the type of relief sought and jurisdiction. As a result, this chapter probably cannot explore those issues fully. However, as a matter of practice, it is a good

---

[15] There are two important times when standing must be demonstrated: at the time of the application, and when appealing a decision of the board. See page 363 concerning the latter. Several of the important cases indicate that the legal test is the same in both situations. See *City of Brentwood v Metro Board of Zoning Appeals*, 149 SW 3d 49, 51 (Tenn. Ct. App. 2004).

idea to make sure that the application is signed by or for (in the case of an attorney or other agent[16]) the owner or other person with a legally cognizable interest in the property. For example, a lessee certainly could file an application. It is generally thought that contract vendees can also file an application. But if there is any concern about this issue, why not just make sure that the owner is the applicant? That avoids all the legal pitfalls.[17]

Must an agent demonstrate the extent of his agency? Must he submit a document indicating the consent of the owner? That would seem to eliminate the purpose of an agent in the first place, so I don't think that necessary. However, if the issue is raised at the zoning board, the applicant should be ready to demonstrate his agency. That makes for the easiest and cleanest solution. But, frankly, even if he doesn't, the board should decide whether to grant the application on the merits. There is no downside to this: if the owner(s) can't ultimately come to some agreement, the worst that will happen is that the granted relief will not be employed. There is no harm to anyone.

Many local governments set their own standing requirements. In Tennessee, it is not clear whether this is appropriate. The enabling legislation has something to say about this issue. For example, TENN.

---

[16] Most attorneys will clearly indicate their representative capacity, but that is sometimes not true of other types of agents. It is important however for an agent to specify for whom s/he is acting. Otherwise, it may be difficult or impossible to determine whether there is standing to consider the application.

[17] There are no cases in Tennessee concerning a zoning board, (although there is a subdivision case), but generally it is felt that someone with an interest in the property should be the applicant. There are some good policy reasons why that is really not necessary. For example, in the case of a variance, even if the application is filed by a third party, so long as there is no indication that the owners oppose the application, what difference does it make? The owners do not have to take advantage of the variance. It can be granted and the owners simply not use it if it is not helpful. The statutes or local ordinances may require it however.

CODE ANN. § 13-7-206 provides:[18]

> Appeals to the board of appeals may be taken by any person aggrieved or by any officer, department, board or bureau of the municipality affected by any grant or refusal of a building permit or other act or decision of the building commissioner of the municipality or other administrative official based in whole or in part upon the provisions of the ordinance enacted under this part and part 3 of this chapter.

Thus, it certainly appears that anyone "aggrieved" may appeal a decision to the local zoning board and in addition, that any officer, department, board or bureau of the local government may also file such an appeal.

What does it mean to be aggrieved within the meaning of the statute? First, the term should be construed broadly in the context of land use planning matters because it is better for the cases to be resolved on their merits rather than on "preclusive, restrictive standing rules."[19] Second, there must be some special interest in the decision or a special injury not common to the public generally.[20] In *Citizens for Collierville, Inc. v Town of Collierville*, the standing and presumably "aggrievement" was found for neighbors based on ownership of single family residential properties within 2000 feet[21] of the proposed development.[22] Further, the case is interesting in that the neighbors themselves were not petitioners, but a non-profit corporation

---

[18] TENN. CODE ANN. § 13-7-108 provides similarly with respect to the county zoning boards.

[19] *City of Brentwood v Metro Board of Zoning Appeals*, 149 SW 3d 49, 51 (Tenn. Ct. App. 2004).

[20] *Wood v Metro Government*, 196 SW 3d 152 (2005).

[21] Almost 4/10ths of a mile away.

[22] 977 SW 2d 321 (Tenn. Ct. App. 1998).

representing the neighbors was found to have standing in their stead based for the most part on the proximity of the homes.

But, let us suppose that your client is an applicant seeking either a conditional use permit, a variance, or some other zoning approval which is within the jurisdiction of the local zoning board. It would seem to make little difference whether you are the owner, lessee, or contract vendee: all three should have standing to file the appeal with the zoning board.[23] Another question that sometimes comes up, is the problem of multiple owners. Must all the owners of a tract of property sign the application? In an interesting subdivision case, *Culbert v. Carter County*,[24] the Tennessee Court of Appeals indicated that all owners should sign off. However, there is a specific statute which was interpreted in this case[25] – ordinarily, in my opinion the zoning board need not be so technical. Consider this: the board cannot resolve issues of ownership anyway; it may only consider whether there are grounds for the issuance of the requested relief. If only one owner applies, and another objects, the board should consider the case and rule based on the merits of the application. If the application is granted, and the owners can't agree on the use of the property, then most likely a judge will have to decide who has controlling interest, a job distinctly beyond

[23] Suppose that a third party who is attempting to set up a real estate transaction files the appeal on behalf of the owner but does not so state on the application. The opponents do not raise the issue at the zoning board, and on appeal, contend that the applicant lacked standing to request relief because there is no evidence in the record that the applicant had any relationship to the property. A trial court in Davidson County concluded that the opponents waived their right to raise the issue on appeal, and that since the owners of the property were clearly in attendance at the zoning board hearing in support of the application, that there was no harm even if technically the person who signed the application had no relationship to the underlying property.

[24] 1998 WL 910194

[25] Interestingly, the subdivision statute (TENN. CODE ANN. § 13-4-302(b)) considers a contract vendee, an optionee, and an attorney or authorized agent to be an appropriate applicant for its purposes.

the reach of the local zoning board.

Of course, if the attorney represents opponents to an issued permit, the standing requirements will be different and perhaps more difficult to demonstrate. If the challenge is to an interpretation of the ordinance, it would seem that anyone might appeal to the board, because that interpretation might apply anywhere in the jurisdiction. If the application is to appeal the manner in which a particular provision is applied to a particular property, then the applicant probably should have some interest in adjacent properties; as a rough rule of thumb, I always recommend that the property of a contesting neighbor be within approximately ¼ quarter of a mile of the project, and the *Collierville* case seems to justify that rule.

Regardless of the type of zoning technique being applied for, it is ofttimes useful to discuss the legal criteria with the zoning administrator or building code official who administers the code. An agreement between you, as attorney for the developer or neighborhood association, and the zoning administrator will not guarantee that you are considering all of the appropriate criteria, but will go a long way towards making sure that you have not missed anything important. Making friends of the local codes enforcement officials is important to both sides of any zoning controversy. This is a long term proposition. As an attorney, you may present many zoning applicants or opponents. A friend in the division of zoning administration is surely better than an enemy. The zoning administrator sometimes can tip the balance in a close case by the expression of his own personal feelings. It is therefore a good idea to make sure that the zoning administrator at least understands your position, or even better supports it.[26]

[26] This is difficult to do, of course, if you are appealing his interpretation of a particular provision of the zoning ordinance. But in other cases, you should strive to make him aware both of the legal and common sense reasons for proceeding as your client wishes to proceed.

3. Visits to the Site

It is usually difficult to fit in a visit to a sometimes remote parcel of property in the preparation of a zoning board case. However, a visit to the site is of great importance in making your presentation to the board. First, no matter how minutely the client details his/her description of the site, it can never replace a visit and firsthand observation on the part of the attorney. Even a photo is a poor second. Secondly, there may be some factor in which the board is interested and wanting to hear about but without having visited the site yourself, you may not be able to discuss. Most of the time, it is better for the attorney to be doing the talking about a particular aspect of the case then it is for the client or anyone else involved in the hearing, although inevitably, some help from other participants (the owner, an engineer and so on) is almost always necessary. Finally, having visited the site always gives a feeling of confidence and preparation which is difficult to develop in the absence of such a visit. In short, there are just too many details which you may pick up in a site visit which you would not get from an ordinary discussion with your client that make the site visit well worth the time and expense.[27]

4. Timetable

Because of the rapidity with which zoning board hearings approach and are heard, often within a week or two of first notice, it is important to get a timetable set in mind in smaller cases, and a written version for larger projects. It is usually best to begin from the projected date of the hearing, and work backwards to the current date.

In order to prepare the timetable, you must be familiar with the local rules and local practice, to the extent that one might be different from the other. Any rules governing the time for filing applications and other significant aspects of the process must of course be considered and built into the schedule. Generally, I prefer to: meet with my clients the day before the meeting for final preparation; file my brief on the legal issues involved one week before the hearing; have a status update

---

[27] Including the muddied shoes.

meeting with my clients sometime a day or two before that, and plan to have the draft of the brief to the clients before the status meeting so that it can be reviewed and critiqued at that meeting, with final changes going in for the final draft. This next to last meeting also allows for time to get any last minute things done that have not been done.

5. Codes Files and Local Rules

An important resource which is overlooked many times by both sides in a zoning dispute are the public records concerning the property at the local codes administration. These files are open to the public and quite often have a tremendous amount of information which is valuable in the consideration of a request to a local zoning board. For the neighborhood, it is very much worthwhile to not only review the plans submitted for the development, but also to review the history of the property. Many times something interesting will turn up. The developer also needs to know any such history. Even if it is not beneficial, it would be helpful to rebut any claims made by the opponents. Many of these records are available on the Internet.

The local rules should also be investigated.[28] A copy of the fairly simple local rules for the Metro Nashville Board are available on the Internet.[29] Notice that submission of written documents is due the Monday before the Thursday hearing and a request for the appearance of witnesses (adverse witnesses) must be made 5 days before the hearing

---

[28] From the standpoint of the administrative body, it is probably not a good idea to adopt a set of rules like Robert's of Order because they are simply too complicated. A simple description of what actually takes place should be sufficient. The attorney for the board should obviously review the rules before adoption. See "Schools of Procedure Rules," ABA Journal, July 2000 at 70.

[29] See the Metro Codes web site at: www.nashville.gov/codes/docs/public_docs/BZA_Rules_of_Procedure_080310.pdf

date.[30] These requirements must be built into the timetable developed by counsel. You may also find important procedural limitations spelled out in the local rules which would affect the manner of the presentation.

While this may go without saying, it is also important to determine the powers of the board with which you are dealing. If, for example, the board operates pursuant to the provisions of a private state act, the powers of the board may be larger or smaller than that permitted under the public enabling legislation. This obviously has an impact on the way in which a case might be presented.

While your client may not be sophisticated enough to check the file with the zoning board, you should be. On the day before the hearing (at the very least), you should visit the zoning board's office, and take a look at their entire file. First, you should be looking to see whether anyone in opposition to your position has filed a letter brief, any exhibits, or any letters in opposition which, of course, are quite frequent. Copies should be obtained if reasonably convenient so you can peruse these items at your leisure in your office and develop whatever rebuttal you may have to the points raised.

In addition, you should examine whatever file or record the zoning board has developed. Sometimes there may be an error and you may need to point it out to the zoning board staff. This is also a good time to talk with the members of the staff again to gauge how they feel about the case. You should also obtain any additional verbal information which they may have. Frequently, they receive phone calls about a particular project and they may know something as a result of those calls which you do not. The attorney needs to be quiet and listen.

6. Consultations with Experts

While there are a great number of experts who services are often instrumental in the area of presenting or opposing a land use case before a zoning board, perhaps the most important expert on a routine

[30] See §§ 6(C)(1) and 7(D) of the Metro Zoning Board Rules of Procedure on the web at the address referenced above.

basis is a transportation planner or traffic engineer. Generally speaking, from the position of the proponents, the traffic expert is retained to demonstrate that the project will not have a significant impact on traffic in the vicinity, certainly that it will not decrease the level of service on nearby streets and highways. From the standpoint of the opponents, the traffic expert hopefully can demonstrate that, in fact, a significant amount of additional traffic will be generated and, under the best case scenario, that there will actually be a decrease in the level of service provided by the surrounding streets.

Generally, the best way to present the expert is to have a written report compiled and presented to the Board of Zoning Appeals. Next, have a short segment of your oral presentation set aside so that the traffic expert can speak directly to the Board. The traffic expert's time with the Board should not be very long, but you should give the Board a chance is eyeball the expert and, to that end, you want to have an expert who makes a good appearance, speaks well, and comes across clearly to lay people when making such a presentation. Charts and graphs which have been blown up for presentation are always of great assistance in this regard.[31]

It is a mistake not to have the expert thoroughly familiar with your project. Many times experts are retained only for one section of the project, the area of their specialty, and they lack familiarity with other areas of the project. As a result, questions from the Board can catch them flatfooted or, even worse, they can give an answer which is detrimental to your cause. In an quarry case before the Metro Board of Zoning Appeals some years ago, the traffic planner retained to testify in opposition to the quarry admitted that the residential traffic that would flow from the site if the quarry approval was not forthcoming would equal or exceed the difficulties in truck traffic from such a use. This admission, while not determinative of the case, certainly took a lot of the wind out of the sails of the opponents of the quarry.

---

[31] Many boards are now using computer presentations; using a presentation manager such as PowerPoint for both the comments of the attorney and any experts makes good sense in this regard. A printed copy can be offered into evidence.

Most lawyers vigorously prepare their expert witnesses for a trial, but the same is frequently not true of a presentation before a zoning board or other administrative body. This is certainly understandable in routine cases. Where you expect to be speaking to the board for only a few moments and hope, based on your experience with the board, that the proposal will slide through without a hitch, there is little reason to go into great detail in preparation of any of your experts. On the other hand, in cases where the board has set aside a special time for a hearing and intends to give ample opportunity to both sides to make their respective presentations, it is extremely important to review the entire case with the expert, and get him/her ready for the kinds of questions which might be asked by the board. Get the expert to answer the hard questions in your office before he gets to the board room. You certainly want to hear the answer to those hard questions before he sets foot in front of the zoning board. Many times, working with the experts, you can fashion a response to the tough questions which is less detrimental to your position than his/her original, off-the-top of the head, response.

There are a large number of other experts which may be employed in order to present a case before a zoning board. Environmentalists, architects, urban planners, and others, may all be important in the context of any individual application. The attorney has to make a judgment about which ones are necessary in any particular application, and have them prepared for the hearing. Generally speaking, the rules outlined above will serve well in cases before Tennessee zoning boards.

7. Meetings with the Opposition

(a) Meetings with the Developer

When representing a neighborhood organization, it is important to get the developer to commit to precisely what type of development he is seeking in all relevant details. For that reason, it is ofttimes helpful to have a meeting with the developer or his representatives, obtain a copy of the proposals which has outlined, and try to pin him down as much as possible. This sometimes is very difficult, but too often the developers have not really solidified their own thinking, and as a result, in the latter stages of the approval process the neighborhood may learn to its dismay that the developer has changed a portion of the project in a way that it considers to be of extremely high impact to their properties, but which is not controlled by the relevant land use planning regulations. The neighborhood must seek to get all of the development package on the table for negotiations so that they can attempt to negotiate with the developer in a way to prevent those aspects of the development which are highly deleterious to the neighborhood from becoming reality, and to prevent any additions later which would also have the same impact.

The neighborhood group should also take care to investigate the background of the developer and the background of any developments which the developing company may have been responsible for in the past, either in their own city or elsewhere. Further, it is usually not hard to get details concerning the other localities where the developer has worked from both the planning commission and the local codes administration in an effort to argue that the harm to the neighborhood outweighs the benefits to the developer if the application is granted. Depending upon the type of application that may or may not be legally relevant, but it is always relevant in the common sense manner in which most boards operate.

(b) Meetings with the Neighborhood

In representing a developer, a meeting with the affected neighborhood or neighborhood organization is also important.[32] While it is doubtful that the applicant will actually be able to allay any of the concerns of the neighborhood or convert any neighbors to his position, often he will at least learn of the extent and depth of feeling amongst the opposition and the purported reasons for the opposition. Those factors can have an impact on the way in which the case is presented.

---

[32] In fact, some ordinances and even local board rules require that the applicant at least provide a contact person and offer to hold a meeting to explain the proposal. These are still in the minority, but they may increase over time. Failure to follow such requirements has at least in one case caused a reversal of the board's approval of the project.

The applicant may also learn something about why the neighbors oppose the project and, even if he cannot limit the impact of the project so as to totally remove those concerns, in so attempting, the applicant may get the respect of the zoning board. One way to do this is to carefully note the original grounds of the neighborhood's opposition. Then, at the zoning board hearing, counsel should carefully (but briefly) state each ground and the developer's response. In this fashion, the developer can demonstrate sensitivity to neighborhood concerns. The board also will give you credit for meeting with the property owners even without accomplishing anything. The board many times is concerned that developers are trying to do something behind the backs of the neighbors and by at least being forthright and straightforward about the developer's objectives, the board will give you points for your conduct.

Generally, we also send a follow-up letter to the members of the group or to all of the neighbors. There are a number of ways to make a determination as to whom to send the letter. If you have had a meeting, you can get the names and addresses of all the people who attended the meeting and send a letter to them.

Secondly, you can contact the zoning administrator and determine to whom the codes enforcement department will send notice of the application and send letters to those affected property owners. Sending a letter like this is good if for no other reason because the letter should carefully explain what the developer is actually intending to do with the property and what kind of an application is being sought. Many times the notice letters sent out by the codes enforcement department are loosely worded and generate tremendous fear on the part of the neighborhood. By sending a letter of your own which precisely details the nature of the application and the type of development, you may help minimize some of those unfounded concerns.[33] The letter usually invites phone calls to our office for further information and while such phone calls are not generally helpful in

---

[33] For example, in Nashville the notice letter sounds as though a zone change is being requested even though the board has no power to grant such relief. In our notice letter, we routinely emphasize that a zone change is not being sought and further emphasize the limited nature of the relief which the developer is actually seeking.

allaying neighborhood suspicion or opposition, again, the board may expect such information to be distributed by the developer and the developer will get the benefit of this extra work.

The developer should never lose sight of the fact that no matter how accommodating he is, neighborhood opposition can rarely ever be totally eliminated. Reasonable accommodation of neighborhood concern is smart; many times, the project will be improved as a result of such input. The neighbors, or some of them, may oppose the project even if all concerns are met. Opposition is usually motivated by emotions; reasoned responses by the developer may be met with unreasoned opposition before the board. Of course, the board may accordingly grant the application; but then and again, it may not.

8. Letter Brief to the Board

Because the amount of time which the board may be able to devote to a particular application may be limited, and because the board generally is interested more in the common sense kinds of problems presented by a development rather than the relevant legal criteria, the applicant or neighborhood group should submit a letter, informational booklet, or PowerPoint Presentation (in hard copy)[34] outlining their views. The timing of the filing is dependent upon the local rules, local practice, and the attorneys strategy about how much to reveal to opposing counsel or parties before the hearing.[35] Depending upon local custom, or board rules, it may be desirable to send copies directly to members of the board. Many board members wish an opportunity to read such material before the hearing. Further, the materials should specifically request, in the first line or slide or two, that they be made a part of the administrative record in the case.

The purpose of these informational materials is to meet the legal criteria or, in representing the neighborhood organization to show that

[34] Many zoning boards routinely use computer software for presentations at their meetings now. Take advantage of this tool.

[35] See Section B 2 above.

the developer does not meet the legal criteria, of the zoning ordinance. They should therefore analyze with precision what the legal criteria may be for the requested relief, and how each and every element of the legal requirements are met by the applicant. Conversely, if representing a neighborhood organization, the attorney should prepare materials which indicates or demonstrates that aspects of the criteria have not been met. Both parties should be alert to the possibility that in addition to whatever local legislation bears on the issue, the state enabling legislation may also add requirements which were not incorporated by the local ordinance.[36] Generally, in representing neighborhood opposition, it is best to select several elements of the requested relief which the attorney believes the development company will have the most difficulty in meeting, and focus on those rather than taking a scatter-gun approach, contesting everything.

If the attorney is submitting a letter, once completed, it should ***not*** be a blueprint of the presentation at the hearing. The legal jargon should be left at the office, not used in front of the zoning board. Some of the phrases that the board hears all the time, such as practical difficulties and unnecessary hardships are of course expected from the attorney. But when you appear before the board, forget the legal requirements; you want to demonstrate how this proposed project will benefit the public and be good for the community (or detrimental to the community if representing a neighborhood). Do not, in your oral presentation, deal with legal arguments, unless the board is interested in hearing them. Most are not.

---

[36] It is usually thought that a local ordinance cannot change the requirements for the relief sought. In the case of a variance for example, the local legislation may not include precisely the so-called negative criteria, that is, proof that the proposed variance would not have a substantial detriment on the public good, would not substantially impair the intent or purpose of the zone plan or the zoning ordinance. TENN. CODE ANN. §§ 13-7-109(3) and 207(3). If the local ordinance does not mandate these requirements in its terms, the attorney representing the proponent/opponent cannot simply ignore them. The attorney must consider them in the letter and demonstrate compliance.

On the other hand, if you are presenting a PowerPoint Presentation, it will most likely be a blueprint of the oral presentation to the board. If you have other material that you want the board to have in hand but which you won't necessarily discuss orally, add that as an attachment to the hard copy of the presentation.

The materials should include any statements by experts which you will use at the hearing. For example, you may have a traffic engineer who is going to testify concerning the level of service on the highway fronting the property. That proof, albeit in legal form, should appear in the letter (or attached to the letter in the form of a report from the expert) in order to demonstrate compliance with one or more of the legal criteria.[37] The statements of an urban planner may be helpful to demonstrate compatibility with the surrounding community. A civil engineer may be necessary for storm water management considerations, among others. And an architect may be helpful when discussing the layout of the building itself or its compatibility with the neighborhood architecturally. In any event, the letter should incorporate brief statements, giving the gist of the presentations of each of your experts so that the board knows what to expect and what you are trying to accomplish.

A flashier informational booklet may be substituted for the letter. The booklet might contain an artist's rendering of the completed development, the site plans, photographs, and so on. Naturally, compliance with the legal criteria should also be demonstrated.

A more delicate issue is whether or not a copy of these informational materials needs to be sent to opposing counsel or the opposition. Many times if you are representing the developer, you do not know who the opposition is and it is difficult to send it to every

---

[37] If you are representing the neighborhood, then the traffic engineer's position of course would be reversed and it would be attempting to show non-compliance with one or more of the legal criteria.

neighbor in the community.[38] If the local rules of the board do not require it to be sent, we do not send it to every neighbor, however we do send it to local neighborhood organizations of which we are aware. A copy of the letter is also placed on file with the zoning enforcement department or the zoning board secretary, so that if an interested neighbor wanted to look at the file of the board before the hearing, the letter would be there and could be reviewed. Typically, neighborhood associations are not sophisticated enough to review the zoning board records, and indeed, few people actually look at it, but the fact that a copy was available for inspection at the offices of the board may avert a loss based on failure to serve a copy on the opponents. Fortunately, as neighborhood organizations become more sophisticated, that is changing for the better.

If the board's local rules do require that the letter be sent, the manner of sending the letter should be in compliance with the rules, or if the rules don't specify, then a letter should at least be sent to each neighbor who has received notice of the hearing itself. A list of the neighbors to whom notice was sent can be obtained from the zoning board staff.[39] Both sides generally wish to avoid "showing their hand" before the hearing, and but it is important that copies of these letter briefs are sent to your opponents as outlined above.

9. Preparation of Other Materials

It is quite possible that other documents or exhibits need to be prepared for the hearing. The attorney should make sure that either his

---

[38] A compromise solution might be to send a copy to any neighbor who is entitled to notice under the terms of the local ordinance.

[39] The enabling statutes do not require notice of zoning board hearings (see TENN. CODE ANN. § 13-7-207), and thus, many smaller communities have no requirements for notice. Many of the larger communities, for example, Metro Nashville, have written into the zoning ordinance itself a requirement for notice to surrounding property owners. See Metro Code §§ 17.40.700, 710, 720 & 730 (general notice provisions).

staff or the experts will prepare exhibits which are appropriate to the forum. Exhibits which are too small to read or which do not accomplish the purpose for which they are intended, are not helpful at all. The use of slides, video tapes, or computer presentations should be encouraged. Professional video tape presentations can sometimes in a short time period convey more to the board than an unlimited number of attorney's words.[40]

Also, again, knowledge of the local rules of the board is important here. If the board requires that the exhibits be submitted prior to the date of the hearing, you need to know about that and comply with the rules of the board. Failure to comply can lead to the exclusion of the exhibits which may be critical to your case.

10. Ex Parte Contact

Because the board is a quasi-judicial body[41] ex parte contact by the parties or attorneys with the board members likely is inappropriate. There is no definitive court ruling on this and to the author's knowledge, no opinion by the Tennessee Board of Professional Responsibility. However, the Code of Professional Responsibility formerly provided:

> In an adversary proceeding, a lawyer shall not communicate, or cause another to communicate, as to the

---

[40] Metro Nashville now uses computerized presentations via Microsoft PowerPoint. As a result, the attorney can make a presentation in PowerPoint and request that it be uploaded to the laptop used at the hearing and run his/her own presentation using a computer. Even more important, possibly, is the ability to get an electronic copy of the materials which will be utilized by the zoning board during the presentation by the staff. In this way, the attorney can review for errors and omissions, and possibly make suggested corrections to the staff before the hearing in front of the board actually takes place.

[41] *Reddoch v. Smith*, 214 Tenn. 213, 379 S.W.2d 641 (1964).

> merits of the cause with the judge or an official before whom the proceeding is pending, except:
>
> (1) In the course of official proceedings in the cause.
>
> (2) In writing if he promptly delivers a copy of the writing to opposing counsel or to the adverse party if he is not represented by a lawyer.
>
> (3) Orally upon notice to opposing counsel or to the adverse party if he is not represented by a lawyer.
>
> (4) As otherwise authorized by law.

DR 7-110. Ethical Consideration 7-35 was similar.

The current Rules of Professional Conduct may be less clear. Rule 3.5 provides:

> A lawyer shall not:
>
> (a) seek to influence a judge, juror, a member of the jury pool, or other official by means prohibited by law;
>
> (b) communicate ex parte with a judge, juror, or a member of the jury pool, prior to or during a proceeding, except as permitted by law;

If the term "judge" is defined as is the term "tribunal," meaning a court or *other adjudicative body*,[42] then *ex parte* communication with any member of a zoning board would appear to violate RPC 3.5(b). Otherwise, this language relies on some other source ("by means prohibited by law") to render the conduct illegal and I don't know of any other provision that makes *ex parte* contact with a zoning board member

[42] RPC § 1.0(n). The term "judge" itself appears to be undefined.

(or for that matter a member of any other local administrative body) illegal. For example, TENN. CODE ANN. § 4-5-304(c) specifically provides with regard to contested case under the Uniform Administrative Procedures Act:

> . . . no party to a contested case, and no other person may communicate, directly or indirectly, in connection with any issue in that proceeding, while the proceeding is pending, with any person serving as an administrative judge, hearing officer or agency member without notice and opportunity for all parties to participate in the communication.

Thus, *ex parte* contact is prohibited by statute by any party and by any person dealing with ***state*** administrative agencies. But this provision expressly does not apply to county and municipal boards, commissions, and officers.[43] I do not know of any similar provision which does apply to local boards and commissions. It seems that an argument can be made that there is no ethical violation; however, in my view, it is nevertheless inappropriate, and members of the profession should be very careful in attempting any such contact.

This is somewhat more complicated because in other areas of planning and zoning law, *ex parte* contact is certainly appropriate because the function is legislative and hence political in nature. For example, zone changes are political and not only may you contact the members of the local legislative body, but you may also contact the members of the local planning commission because they are a part of that same legislative process in recommending approval or disapproval to the local legislative body. These differences confuse most laymen and make this area of ethical responsibility that much more difficult. [44]

On a request for a variance, a conditional use permit, or for a non-conforming use, the board must apply legal principles to a specific set

---

[43] TENN. CODE ANN. § 4-5-106.

[44] See TENN. CODE ANN. §§ 13-7-105 and 204, and *Fiser v. City of Knoxville*, 584 S.W.2d 659 (Tenn. App. 1979).

of facts and hence, lobbying with the decision-maker on an ex parte basis would appear to be inappropriate and possibly violative of the Rules of Professional Conduct in Tennessee. There is the troublesome question that laymen are not subject to the RPC inasmuch as it applies only to lawyers. In essence therefore, a layperson may have an advantage because he or she may be able to contact the board directly without running afoul of any prohibition whereas an attorney may be in violation of his/her professional rules.[45] Furthermore, there are no legislative prohibitions preventing laymen from making direct contact with any member of any local zoning board here in Tennessee. As a result, it would appear that a layperson does not violate any statutory provision by making an ex parte contact with a zoning board member.

Finally, it should be mentioned that there are several strong proponents of a contrary viewpoint with regard to contact by an attorney with members of local administrative tribunals. The argument espoused by these attorneys is that since there is no legislative prohibition of contact with a local zoning board member, the rules of professional responsibility for attorneys are not specific enough to indicate that the attorney has an obligation to refrain from such contact. While personally I disagree with this perspective, there are a number of attorneys whose opinions I value and trust who are on the other side of this argument and as a result, it seems to me, that some judicial resolution of this difficulty is necessary. There is no good case law in Tennessee on this issue yet.

11. Other Contacts

As noted immediately above, while it would appear to be inappropriate for the attorney to have *ex parte* contact with members of the board, courts in other states have held that telephone conversations with members of the board by persons interested in the proceeding are

[45] The lack of a state proviso which prohibits such contact is troublesome as we noted above.

not fatally defective.[46] However, pressure from public officers, such as the mayor, or council members, must certainly be inappropriate. This is especially true where the public officer has the power of appointment to the board.

In the interesting case *Jerrod v. Scrivener*,[47] a conditional use permit was sought for the construction of an embassy building by the United Soviet Socialist Republic in Washington, D.C. The board voted three to two to grant the permit. The court took evidence outside the board's hearing and determined that a fair and impartial hearing was denied because improper pressure was brought to bear on the members of the board by the means of letters from Dean Rusk, then Secretary of State for the United States, Charles Horsky, the advisor for National Capital Affairs, the White House and a number of other oral communications were made by other high officials in the federal government. I have been involved in cases where the local mayor, seeing and sensing that the zoning board was about to vote in a manner opposite of his wishes, gets up, gets special permission to speak to the zoning board after the public hearing has been closed, and lobbies the board to deny the application notwithstanding the fact that it apparently meet all the requirements of the zoning ordinance. Naturally, on appeal, the Chancellor took a dim view of this process.

Given the brash openness of this type of influence, it should surprise no one that such arm-twisting also goes on frequently behind closed doors in local government situations in a way so that the opposing party never has a chance to find out about it.

Very frequently, allegations are made that the mayor of the community has made telephone calls to influence the board members. Council members certainly very frequently appear in front of boards of zoning appeals within this author's experience. Unless direct proof is had of such ex parte communications by the mayor or other councilmen, the author doubts that attempting to utilize this type of information

---

[46] Anderson, § 22.48, citing *Nelson v. Zoning Board of Appeals*, 152 Conn. 120, 203 A.2d 606 (1964).

[47] 225 F. Supp. 827 (D.C. 1964).

would ordinarily be successful. For example, under the common law writ of certiorari,[48] while you certainly could present additional evidence to the court concerning ex parte phone calls by the mayor to the board members, it is most likely the case that the board members will simply deny ever receiving such phone calls. The same would apply to council members. Even if the calls are admitted, courts may be loath to invalidate board action based on a phone call that is represented by the board member as unimportant to the deliberations.

With regard to the members of the local legislative body who appear in front of the zoning board, this appearance of course is not *ex parte*, and the author believes that the Tennessee courts would ordinarily permit the introduction of such testimony during the ordinary course of the hearing. At that point, the party opposing the introduction of the evidence can cross-examine or take whatever prophylactic measures deemed necessary to discredit or otherwise insulate itself from the negative testimony. The author believes that the Tennessee courts would hold that a member of the legislative body may appear and testify just like any ordinary citizen and that the applicant is not prejudiced by the appearance of such a member of the local legislative body.[49]

---

[48] See Chapter Five.

[49] See *Fiser v City of Knoxville*, 584 S.W. 2d 659 (Tenn. App. 1979). The thought that such testimony may have only a minimal impact may be correct: in Nashville, anyway, the zoning board rarely places much credibility in the council persons who appear, understanding intuitively, that the appearance is most likely politically motivated. In smaller communities, perhaps the situation would be different. In *BMC Enterprises, Inc. v. City of Mt. Juliet*, 273 SW 3d 619 (Tenn. Ct. App. 2008) a city commissioner appeared and testified but the Court concluded There is no material evidence in the record to support the Board's decision. The Board applied an incorrect analysis to the issue of expanding BMC's nonconforming use pursuant to the Zoning Ordinance and state law, emphasizing the City Commission's intent in placing crematories in an IS zoning district, a fact not relevant to determining whether the crematory is an expansion of Plaintiff's funeral home business.

It is certainly not desirable from the opposing party's point of view to have the councilman appear in front of the zoning board. However, within the experience of the author,[50] the boards generally are not all that interested in the opinions of the local legislative members. The board members generally feel that they are the ones on the hot seat, the ones that have to make the hard decisions and they act accordingly.

C. Hearing Procedures

1. Informality

The best word to describe a hearing before a zoning board is informal.[51] The local rules of the board may specify the manner in which it conducts its hearings, but many times there are no such local rules and without checking with the staff, the lawyer, may not have any idea what process will be used by the board in considering the application. The board members frequently speak at the same time, with several conversations going on at any given point. The attorney needs to remember that the process is one governed by laymen, not familiar with the technical rules of evidence, and they are simply trying to let everybody "have their say." Within reason, this informal atmosphere is perfectly appropriate. It can go so far as to become violative of procedural due process.[52]

---

[50] The author must confess that most of his practice is before the Metropolitan Board of Zoning Appeals for the Metropolitan Government of Nashville and Davidson County and thus the practice in some of the smaller outlying counties in Tennessee may be different although, parenthetically, the author has practiced in many of the small counties here in Tennessee and in other states, and has frankly not noticed a real difference.

[51] See *Sexton v. Anderson County*, 587 S.W. 2d 663 (Tenn. App. 1979).

[52] *Sexton*, 587 S.W. 2d 663 (witnesses were not sworn and the court seemed to believe this is not proper).

It is best to have some idea of what procedure will be used by attending a prior hearing of this same board, talking with the staff, or by picking it up from the local rules.[53] The attorney should structure the presentation to accommodate the individual board's hearing process.

The informality of the hearing may be helpful. It may allow an attorney to get more into the record than otherwise would have been permitted. However, the attorney has to be careful of not pushing so had that an adverse reaction develops because while an appeal from the zoning board is possible, usually the decision n the facts by the board is final and ofttimes, determinative.

2. Notice

There are no express provisions for notice in the TPZES.[54] However, many local ordinances now require notice to affected property owners and others. The type of notice varies considerably. In Metro Nashville, for example, notice is given by newspaper, by mail, and by signs posted on the property.[55] In addition, although not legally mandated, the board posts its docket on the Internet[56] as well as the results of the hearings (within a few days of the decision). In some communities, the applicant is responsible for giving notice.

---

[53] The danger of this approach is that the rules may not have been updated for the last ten years and may now not reflect the process the board uses to determine cases.

[54] There is no requirement even for notice to the applicant. The Tennessee Public Planning Enabling Statutes at least provide that much in the subdivision context. TENN. CODE ANN. § 13-4-304(c) (notice of time and place of hearing must be sent at least 5 days beforehand to the applicant).

[55] Metro Code § 17.40.710 (notice by newspaper); § 17.40.720 (notice by mail); § 17.40.730 (notice by posted signs).

[56] The web site is www.nashville.gov/codes/bza.

These notice provisions are important and not just to the staff of the zoning board. Counsel for both sides should be aware of the requirements locally and, in the case of the applicant's attorney, some thought should be given at least to making sure that if the notice required is given by the city that it be given at the correct time and to the correct neighbors. These ordinance requirements, if neglected, can be waived[57] (by appearing at the hearing) but suppose that the notice is not given properly and a neighboring property owner who did not attend the meeting files suit alleging that the failure to give notice renders the decision of the board void. This can be a serious problem and most courts in Tennessee would likely invalidate the proceedings or remand for another hearing.

In a 2009 case from New York,[58] the published notice only referred to the tax map location of the subject property which the Court held to be insufficient and fatal to the proceedings. Further, the court held that the personal notice required was not given properly either. The town required notice to the address listed on the tax rolls; notice to the plaintiff was given to an old address, not the one listed on the tax records. Finally, the court found that the plaintiff's appearance at the hearing did not waive the defects because he found out about the hearing only 2 hours before it began and had no opportunity to prepare. He did raise the lack of notice however before the board. The Court concluded:

> in light of the defective public notice and the failure to provide petitioners with personal notice of the hearing as required under the Town Code, we find that Supreme Court erred in failing to grant the petition and annul the Board's determination.

I believe a Tennessee court would hold similarly.

---

[57] *Armour v. Meuller*, 36 Ill. App. 3d 23, 343 N.E. 2d 251 (1976).

[58] *Jones v. Zoning Board of Appeals of the Town of Oneonta*, 2009 WL 1149504 (N.Y.A.D. 3 Dept. April 30, 2009)

The applicant's attorney therefore wants to make sure that the basic notice provisions are complied with. But there is a limit as to how far that can go: if certified mail is required, let's say 21 days before the hearing date, to all surrounding property owners, and one of the properties is missed, or if the city usually relies upon the tax rolls, and there has recently been a change which is not reflected as of yet, it would be almost impossible for the applicant's attorney to catch that. Assuming that the applicant cannot show that the neighboring property owner did not receive notice by some other form, the decision may well be overturned. Similarly, the attorney for the neighboring property owners may find this an easy way to get the case back to the board.

In an interesting case from Wilson County,[59] neighboring property owners challenged a "use permitted on appeal"[60] for a concrete plant where although the board's rules only required newspaper notice, evidently some of the surrounding property owners also got mailed notice. The other neighbors argued that they should have also received mailed notice. The court concluded otherwise.[61]

> As already stated, the Board had no duty in this case to mail notices to any adjoining landowners, including petitioners, thus there is no basis to find fraudulent concealment. It is unfortunate for the petitioners that they did not have actual notice of the Board of Zoning Appeals' meeting. However, the Board discharged its obligations under the statute. *The Constitution does not afford interested landowners a right to actual notice in zoning matters.*

However, it takes little imagination to conclude that if the newspaper notice required by the zoning ordinance had not been given, that the

---

[59] *Kielbasa v. Wilson County Bd. of Zoning Appeals*, 2000 WL 546367 (Tenn. Ct. App. 2000)

[60] Generally thought of as another name for a conditional use permit (also known as a special exception).

[61] At *2, emphasis added.

court would have overturned the board's decision. Hence, it is incumbent upon the zoning board to ensure that the notice provisions are fully complied with and the attorney for the applicant should also ensure, to the extent reasonable, those provisions are met. If not, the attorney for the opposition will certainly mention it later!

3. Quorum

Most zoning ordinances, to the extent that any provision is made at all, provide that a simple majority of the board constitutes a quorum. Ordinarily, the business of the board may not be conducted in the absence of quorum. Usually, the procedural rules of the board will require that a quorum be present in order to begin a meeting, but that a meeting may go on in the absence of a quorum unless the absence of a quorum is pointed out by a member. Since the zoning boards usually consist of five members under the terms of the TPZES[62], a quorum is usually the presence of three members. [63] This also means that the application may be granted with as few as two votes in favor if a bare quorum is present.

---

[62] See TENN. CODE ANN. §§ 13-7-106 and 205.

[63] See also the discussion of voting and the board's decision at page 56.

4. Rules of Evidence

(a) Generally

The rules of evidence generally do not apply to a proceeding before a zoning board.[64] This loosens up the atmosphere of the proceedings and eliminates any requirement that the attorney representing any party be aware of potential evidentiary problems. It also has several significant procedural ramifications.

---

[64] There is one Tennessee case on this point. In *Goodwin v Metropolitan Board of Health*, 656 SW 2d 383 (Tenn. Ct. App. 1983), the Court held that the rules generally don't apply in administrative proceedings, except to the extent that the administrative body adopts them. There is quite a bit of authority in other states however (see *Conetta v. Zoning Board of Appeals*, 42 Conn.App. 133, 137, 677 A.2d 987 (1996) and *In Re Elizabeth Township Board of Zoning Appeals*, (Ohio App.) 1994 WL 527579). The Tennessee Rules of Evidence specifically note that "administrative hearings are not governed exclusively" by those rules, citing the Uniform Administrative Procedures Act, particularly TENN. CODE ANN. § 4-5-313(1). That leaves open the question of applicability in the context of local administrative bodies except for the *Goodwin* case. Most zoning boards do not have the expertise to deal with these legal issues raised by the rules and as a result, the technical rules of evidence should not apply.

(b) Hearsay Permitted

Typically, hearsay evidence is permitted in administrative proceedings.[65] This offers several possibilities which attorneys generally do not see in ordinary adjudicative proceedings. First, the attorney may offer all the testimony himself. He can summarize the position of his client, summarize the testimony of the planning experts, summarize the testimony of the engineers, summarize the testimony of the architects, and so on. Whether this is a good strategy is another question. Typically it depends on the amount of time involved. Frequently, an initial presentation by an attorney covering briefly all the points by the client and the experts is desirable.[66] The experts themselves and the client may be called upon to talk after the opposing side has an opportunity to present its case. In representing neighbors, it is generally better to have the experts testify immediately.

If time constraints are not a problem, then a longer presentation with the attorney serving as a moderator is perhaps the best objective. Remember that neither the attorney nor the experts should dwell to any great extent upon the actual legal criteria. The letter brief to the board should have taken care of that and because hearsay is admissible, the letter brief should be admitted into evidence before the board. That way, as previously mentioned, it can function as the legal basis for the relief assuming it is granted. Then in order of importance or whatever other strategic method is appropriate, the other witnesses should be presented. Ordinarily, when using this approach, the client should be

---

[65] Again, there appears to be no Tennessee precedent, but most other states so hold and logically, without the rules of evidence, there would be no impediment to the introduction of hearsay. See *In Re Elizabeth Township Board of Zoning Appeals*, 1994 WL 527579 ("As a general rule, administrative agencies are not bound by the strict rules of evidence. Thus, the hearsay rule is relaxed in administrative proceedings and the admission and consideration of hearsay evidence is not necessarily improper.")

[66] The rules of some boards restrict rebuttal testimony to those who spoke in chief. Therefore, it may be necessary to have the experts speak initially to preserve their opportunity to speak in rebuttal.

either first or last. If the client is a particularly fine speaker and will make a good presentation, he may be the last witness. Otherwise, he may go first and be quite brief.

Another ramification of the hearsay rule in an administrative context is that virtually any document from any area of federal, state or local government will be admitted.[67] Ofttimes there are numerous planning, engineering, or traffic control documents in other areas of a local government or state government which may be helpful to the case. Introduction without regard to the hearsay rule and without any foundation enables the attorney to make the best use of these documents without having to worry about anyone challenging authenticity.[68]

On the other hand, the attorney must remember that he may get as good as he gives. The other side is, of course, also free to utilize these same techniques against the client's position. If you have a worthy adversary opposing you, a five or ten day rule requiring submission of all exhibits prior to that time before the hearing, enables you to check what the opponents will be putting in and mount whatever attack you may have on those exhibits.

Another often devastating use of hearsay by the opponent is the indiscriminate use of quotations from the planning staff at the local planning commission, the local traffic engineer, or the local civil engineer, to the effect that this project is a terrible one and should not be permitted. From the neighbor's standpoint, the developer may make the same type of statement concerning the desirability of the project. Obviously, the attorney must argue that such verbal hearsay is extremely unworthy and a letter at the least should have been acquired

---

[67] Generally, no evidentiary foundation is required because the rules of evidence do not apply. But some indication of the value of the document is necessary from a common sense standpoint, so that the board will know what importance to attach to the document.

[68] It is important to give the zoning board some reasonable indicia of reliability; otherwise it might choose not to give the document much weight.

by the side offering the testimony. Sometimes a continuance may be requested and granted. Finally, the best bet is to have spoken with all of these individuals yourself and obtain a letter stating that official's position with as much specificity as is warranted or dared, and present that to the board in chief or rebuttal.

In conclusion, hearsay can be an extremely helpful weapon to an attorney in the course of these informal administrative proceedings. At the same time, it can be a terrible sword against the client's position.

(c) Cross-Examination

Usually, cross-examination is not permitted before a board of zoning appeals.[69] To the extent that cross-examination is permitted, it is usually permitted only through the members or the chair of the board of zoning appeals itself.[70] This discourages cross-examination to a great extent. Many an attorney, wishing to cross-examine an opposing expert, has begun the questioning, only to be interrupted by the chair asking that the questions be directed to the witness through the chair. Asking a question, then having it repeated by the chair to the witness, frequently gets the question garbled in translation. The chair usually wants to limit or eliminate cross-examination anyway. This is a tedious, tiresome, and unfortunate practice. There is no reason why an attorney should not be permitted to cross-examine an opposing expert. The rules of evidence do not apply. The chair does not need to be able to distinguish questions which are relevant versus irrelevant except in a very common sense kind of way, and such cross-examination would very likely be helpful to a determination by the board.[71] However, in

---

[69] See Anderson at § 22-33; see Rathkopf at § 37.06[5]; and Rohan at 51.05[4].

[70] Although *Waddell v. Board of Zoning Appeals*, 136 Conn. 1, 68 A.2d 152 (1949) holds that the practice of asking cross-examination questions through the board is an unjustifiable restriction of that right.

[71] See *Somerset v. Montgomery County Board of Appeals*, 245 MD 52, 225 A.2d 294 (1966).

preparing a case, the attorney must be cognizant of this limitation, and if important, object to the procedure. It can probably be waived by not rasing it before the zoning board.[72] A number of courts have concluded that the fundamentals of procedural fairness require cross-examination.[73] Many board hearings are conducted in an adversary environment. Both parties may be represented by counsel. In order to get at the truth, the Anglo-American system of jurisprudence has long recognized the efficacy of cross-examination. It is no different in the setting of a board of zoning appeals than it is in front of a trial level court.

Many chairs express the opinion that they do not have the wherewithal to control the nature or extent of the cross-examination. They are not trained in the formal rules of evidence. But that frankly is not the point. The chair does not need to have a legal education in order to understand what questions are within the ballpark of relevancy. Everyone, even laymen, has an intuitive understanding of what is relevant to a particular issue. At heart it is a philosophical decision, not a legal one. Furthermore, the chair has ample power to restrict cross-examination when it thinks the cross has exceeded the boundaries of appropriate decorum. The antics that many lay persons associate with lawyers in a courtroom, need not be tolerated by the board's chair. Civil cross-examination may be required by the chair. Effective cross does not have to be rude.

The chair can prohibit a particular question, a particular line of questions, require the discontinuation of the entire cross-examination, or, in an extreme case adjourn the hearing for several minutes, hours,

---

[72] See *Gibson v. Talbot County Board of Zoning Appeals*, 250 MD 292, 242 A.2d 137 (1968).

[73] This conclusion may not be justified. It is unclear why cross-examination is important in this context. With regard to a variance, the inquiry is whether there is an exceptional physical condition of the property. Why is cross important in that decision? As to conditional uses, the issue is whether the developer will develop the property consistently with the conditions imposed by the ordinance. Again, cross does not seem important in disclosing the truth in these decisions.

or days. If the cross-examination gets out of control, that would seem entirely appropriate and well within the jurisdiction of the board. Ordinarily, however, this will not happen. The lawyers appearing before the board of zoning appeals are well aware that these are laymen ordinarily and that spirited cross-examination may be more harmful than helpful. On the few occasions when I have thought cross-examination to be worthwhile, I have limited my questions to a very few, very concise, hopefully very pointed issues.[74] As a practical matter, most of the time the witnesses are not cross-examined in the zoning board hearing.

Strategically, the attorney needs to be careful about that decision. Only if cross-examination appears to be extremely important should it be utilized in the opinion of the author.

(d) Sworn Testimony

From the foregoing, it should be clear that sworn testimony is not required,[75] although the ordinance or the board rules may so require.[76] The lack of sworn testimony has been criticized in one Tennessee case.[77] The court was evidently dismayed over the informal nature of the proceedings. Two comments are appropriate. First, as we have noted

---

[74] Indeed, that is the author's practice in trial court as well; lengthy cross-examination may not be as effective as is often thought in either administrative or legal proceedings and for good reason: all you are doing is giving your opponent a chance to speak more. The author prefers to put his own witnesses on to prove his case.

[75] Rohan at § 51.05[3]; Anderson at § 22.34; Rathkopf at § 37-06[2][a].

[76] See TENN. CODE ANN. §§ 13-7-107 and 205 ("The chief legislative body may provide and specify . . . general rules to govern . . . procedure . . . and the board of appeals may adopt supplemental rules of procedure. . . .")

[77] *Sexton v. Anderson County*, 587 S.W. 2d 663 (Tenn. App. 1979).

throughout, the board hearings are very informal and, as a result, a Court of Appeals reviewing the administrative record may be unhappy with the way the proceedings were conducted because they do not appear to be consistent with the types of civil proceedings ordinarily resolved in a court of law. That obviously is not a valid objection or criticism of the board of zoning appeals because they have ordinarily no access to legal counsel and the staff has little or no legal expertise.

However, just because the board is conducted in an informal way, does not relieve it of the requirement of fundamental fairness.[78] If the court feels that the proceeding was fundamentally unfair, then the court should invalidate the proceeding as violative of either or both the state and federal constitutions.[79]

In *Ragan v. Hall*,[80] the Tennessee Court of Appeals expressly met this issue head on, and concluded that placing the witnesses under oath was not necessary.[81]

> In addition, we find no authority . . . that would require the Board to put witnesses under oath at its hearings. Moreover, this Court is not impressed with Appellant's argument that he was prejudiced by the Board's failure to put witnesses, including Appellant himself, under oath, where Appellant did not earnestly object to the Board's procedure at the time of the hearing.

This conclusion is obviously correct: given the informal atmosphere of local zoning procedures, there is no need to place witnesses under oath. As mentioned above, if the process becomes so unruly that the court believes that justice was thwarted, then the court on that ground can

[78] Rathkopf at § 37.06[2][a].

[79] Both the doctrines of procedural and substantive due process may apply under such circumstances. Anderson at § 22-24.

[80] 1995 WL 769269 (Tenn. App.,1995)

[81] 1995 WL 769269, *3 (Tenn. App.,1995)

reverse the decision. But to base a reversal solely on the ground that the witnesses were not sworn is inappropriate at this level of administrative decision-making.

(e) Transcript

Another factor which must be considered by both sides to a zoning controversy is the matter of how the record will be put together. An important question in this regard is whether the zoning board either employs a stenographer or makes an audio or video recording of the presentations. Many zoning boards in Tennessee do not do either. They rely instead on a summary of the presentation by way of minute entries.

Minute entries are not sufficient to permit judicial review and a new hearing may be necessary in the event of an appeal. In the landmark case, *Lewis v Bedford County*,[82] the Tennessee Court of Appeals reviewed this issue and for the first time concluded that the board of zoning appeals was required to provide an accurate transcript of the proceedings before the board in the event of an appeal. Relying on the text of the statute under which an appeal may be filed, the Court found it clearly required:[83]

> Immediately upon the grant of a writ, the board or commission shall cause to be made, certified and forwarded to such court a complete transcript of the proceedings in the cause, containing also all the proof submitted before the board or commission.

Under *Lewis*, the burden now rests squarely on the board itself to provide a transcript of the evidence.

The decision in *Lewis* has not changed the recording habits of most zoning boards to any great extent, however. Although it is now clear that the board has the obligation to provide a transcript,

---

[82] 174 S.W.3d 241 (Tenn. Ct. App. 2004).

[83] TENN. CODE ANN. § 27-9-109(a).

frequently it does not. Either the recording device fails, or some human error renders the recording ineffective. This leaves the advocate in a tough position. On the one hand, a court will almost certainly remand for a new hearing.[84] But in that case, your opponent and the board now know your approach to the case, and may fill any holes that were present the first time around. A remand only gives them the opportunity to make a better record than the first hearing. On the other hand, even if the minutes are sufficient for judicial review, certainly a reviewing court will treat the absence of a transcript in the same way that an appellate court would treat the absence of a transcript in a trial court: it assumes that there was evidence upon which to base the judgment of the court below.[85] Without a transcript then, there will be a very high burden on the party which appeals. Sometimes that is worth the risk, but the odds must carefully be weighed.

In any event, from the standpoint of any advocate, minute entries are far less satisfactory than an audio recording or a verbatim transcript of the testimony from a stenographer. As a result, if the local board does not tape record or hire a stenographer itself, then the attorney should strongly consider either tape recording the hearing or retaining the services of a court stenographer. The difficulty with merely taping the proceedings before the board is the concern that the board might contend at a future date in litigation that the tape recording has been altered, or that the transcription was not made accurately.

These concerns are pretty well resolved when a third party court reporter is retained. It would certainly be an unusual situation where the attorney for the board would contend that a court reporter's transcript of the hearing before the board would be inaccurate. The

---

[84] That is in fact what the *Lewis* court did.

[85] It is the duty of the appellant, on appeal to the Tennessee Court of Appeals, to prepare a record which conveys a fair, accurate and complete account of what transpired in the Trial Court with respect to the issues which form the basis of appeal. Tenn.R.App.P. 24(b). In the absence of an adequate record on appeal the Court must presume the trial court's rulings were supported by sufficient evidence. *Sherrod v. Wix*, 849 S.W.2d 780, 783 (Tenn. Ct. App.1992).

board may still not accept it as the official transcript, but it seems likely that a court would be willing to consider it, particularly if there is any dispute as to any issue regarding what proof was offered at the hearing before the board. This is a critical point given the fact any judicial review of the zoning board's deliberations is upon the record created before the board. If that record is limited to only the minute entries written by the board, its staff, or its attorney, as you may guess, trying to reverse the board, even in a case where the board was certainly in error, is extremely difficult. Retention of a stenographer is therefore critical in those areas where no recording is made, particularly in those cases where you expect an appeal will be filed by either party.

5. Staff Introduction

(a) Generally

The normal procedure in Tennessee is for a staff member to initially present the case. Ordinarily this entails an explanation of what type of application is before the board, the location of the property involved, and a brief history of the problem as it exists.

The staff member also will ordinarily present photographs of surrounding properties, display the zoning map of the area, and finally, present a simple plan of the proposed construction. This serves a very valuable purpose in orienting the board. If a staff member does not do it, the attorney should be aware that no introduction will be given and give one during his presentation.

(b) Reports of Other Agencies

It is a routine matter for zoning boards to receive reports from other agencies in the course of considering an application. Most notably, planning commissions very frequently make recommendations to the zoning board concerning applications which are pending before them. As has already been pointed out, hearsay typically is permitted in administrative proceedings.[86] Since hearsay is permitted, and since a report by another administrative agency is nothing more than hearsay, it is generally thought to be admissible. The routine presentation of such reports and their admission into the record before a zoning board is common. This includes not only planning commissions, but also traffic and parking boards, storm water management commission, park boards, historic zoning boards, and virtually any municipal administrative body that has ever been created.

The real question concerning the admissibility of such reports is the force and effect to be given to them. Let us assume first that the administrative agency recommends in its report that the project be approved. Suppose there is an absence of proof on this issue in any other way. That is, the applicant is relying upon the administrative report to demonstrate that one of the conditions which must be met is, in fact, met. It seems that this is appropriate. In *Gregory v. Metropolitan Board of Zoning Appeals*,[87] several of the requirements for the conditional use permit (for a demolition landfill) were met almost exclusively in the form of a recommendation of the Metro Planning Commission and the Metro Traffic and Parking Commission. The Chancellor at the trial level affirmed the Zoning Board's decision to deny the application but, on appeal, the Tennessee Court of Appeals reversed finding that there was no other proof which was valid and that the applicant had met all of the requirements. While there was no specific discussion of the impact of the presentation of these administrative reports, one must assume that the Court of Appeals implicitly accepted the validity of the recommendation of the Metro Traffic and Parking Commission and the Metro Planning Commission.

This certainly seems reasonable: the approval of both the Planning Commission and the Traffic and Parking Commission would seem ample evidence upon which a reasonable mind could conclude that the traffic in the area would not be significantly affected. The law in Tennessee does not speak to the issue of the quantum of proof necessary to successfully establish a *prima facie* case when applying for relief

[86] See section C 4(b) at page 36.

[87] 16 TAM 12-16, Court of Appeals, MS, Judge Todd (1991).

before a zoning board. As a general matter, however, the applicant's proof must be logically sufficient to support a favorable administrative finding. Since the zoning board action's are reviewed under the common law writ of certiorari, there must be evidence that "a reasonable mind might accept as adequate to support a rational conclusion and such as to furnish a reasonably sound basis for the action under consideration."[88] Under the common law writ, there must be something more than a scintilla or a mere glimmer of evidence. The evidence must be of a substantial material nature, the type that would require submission of a case to a jury.[89] It is also clear that substantial administrative evidence is not limited to direct evidence, but may also include circumstantial evidence or inferences reasonably drawn from direct evidence.[90]

The question then is whether a reasonable mind might accept the expert opinions of the Metropolitan Traffic and Parking Commission and the Metropolitan Planning Commission as adequate to support a rational conclusion by the Zoning Board, and to furnish a reasonably sound basis for concluding that the traffic generated by the landfill would be safely accommodated among major streets in the area. Where there is no competent evidence submitted in opposition, the recommendations of the other administrative bodies must be deemed sufficient.[91]

---

[88] *Pace v. Garbage Disposal District*, 396 S.W.2d 461, 463 (Tenn. App. 1955).

[89] *Pace*, S.W.2d at 463.

[90] *Wayne County v. Tennessee Solid Waste Disposal Board*, 756 S.W.2d 274, 280 (Tenn. App. 1988).

[91] There is an interesting case out of Georgia, *Rogers v. Atlanta*, 110 Ga. App. 114, 137 S.E.2d 668 (1964), where a group of Jehvah's Witnesses applied for a special permit for a church in a residential district. The church presented proof concerning their membership and the number of cars which attended their regular services, and the court noted that the Traffic Department of the City of Atlanta and the City Planning Department had recommended approval. The Georgia Court

It would certainly seem clear, therefore, that in a hearing before a zoning board, where an administrative agency which has a great deal of expertise on a particular issue makes a recommendation regarding that issue, the zoning board is not free, in the absence of other directly conflicting proof, to reject it. The zoning board is thus different from a regular jury which is always free to reject any evidence if it disbelieves it. A zoning board, if it has no contrary evidence, is probably not in a position to reject proof submitted by one side or the other.

One would assume that if the agency recommendation was against the proposal, and there was a lack of evidence in support on the issue addressed by the recommending agency, that the board would also be required to accept that recommendation and deny the application.

Finally, if there is proof on both sides, the agency's recommendation would be entitled to no more, or no less, consideration than any other proof. The board must accept it for whatever it deems it to be worth and, if countervailing proof is more persuasive, accept the countervailing proof and base its conclusion thereupon. Generally speaking, in the large majority of the boards that I have practiced before, reports from other administrative agencies are not given all that much weight in any event. Most of the zoning boards seem to believe that it is their call to make and, while it may be interesting to see what another agency deems important, the zoning board will make whatever decision it deems appropriate in any event.

This all also suggests another important strategy for the applicant. If another administrative agency must make a recommendation on the approval by the zoning board, it is certainly important to find out who the person or group is that makes the recommendation, and to meet with them and discuss the proposal with them. It is at least important to have some input into that process even if you are going to lose it anyway. You may be able to get a somewhat better recommendation in terms of the language used even if the recommendation is against your position. You also certainly want to

---

concluded that the relatively small number of vehicles which would be generated by church activity was insufficient to show a traffic hazard.

know about an adverse recommendation before you even set foot in front of the zoning board.

Along these same lines, it is often important to know whether a representative of that agency will be present at the zoning board during the hearing. If one of your experts is going to attack their recommendation as being unfounded, you certainly must know whether the author of the recommendation is sitting in the audience or at the table reserved for staff. If no one will be there from the recommending agency, it gives your expert a great deal more freedom to comment on the report; in a like manner, if a representative of the recommending agency will be there, the expert's words might be chosen a little more carefully in order to avoid inflaming the staff. Furthermore, a zoning board might take it hard if there is extreme criticism leveled at a member of the staff, even if it is the member of a staff of a sister organization. It seems warranted to avoid an inflammatory confrontation if that is possible.

6. The Applicant's Case

(a) Generally

Because the attorney should have already filed a letter brief discussing each of the legal criteria involved in the application, it is best at the public hearing to entirely forget the legal criteria except to the extent that the board itself brings them up. The attorney and each of the witnesses should emphasize the public good that will come out of the grant of the requested relief. If it is aesthetically pleasing, if additional workers will be employed as a result, if the tax base will go up, if it blends in with the historical area, it if will increase and enhance the reputation of the city, and any other number of other possibilities, can be argued and presented to the board. The attorney should also emphasize the lack of harm to the surrounding properties. Many times the absence of neighborhood opposition will demonstrate that in a graphic way. It should be pointed out certainly if no opposition is present. The number of ways of presenting this information to the board and the number of public benefits that may be taken into account is limited only by the imagination. The main thing to remember is that the board does not ordinarily care about the legal criteria. That is generally the last thing that it has on its mind. What the attorney and the applicant must demonstrate is that this is a good project, worthy of the relief sought, and that it will not cause harm to the surrounding properties.

(b) The Record

Above all, the attorney at the hearing should protect the administrative record. The attorney must make sure that proof of each individual element gets into the record. Other important portions of the record must be included if essential to the applicant's case. For example, has the zoning ordinance itself been introduced or is there a standing rule that it will be introduced on appeal? Ordinarily, this is not critical inasmuch as generally it can be introduced before the trial court or even on appeal. However, to avoid any problem, the introduction of the zoning ordinance should be taken care of at the administrative level.[92] It may be, although there is no case law on this issue, that the zoning ordinance must be submitted by the zoning board as part of the record under the holding in the *Lewis* case. To hold against the appealing party based on his failure to introduce the zoning ordinance, would place a heavy burden on neighbors who usually have little legal expertise.

Sometimes, the general plan of the community is necessary or desirable.[93] If the community has a general plan,[94] the attorney should

---

[92] See Tennessee Rules of Evidence § 202 (b). A court may take notice of local ordinances upon notice to all other parties. There is however, no need to have to worry about that if it is introduced before the board in the first place. Usually, that fixes the local law applicable to the case; in some long cases, disputes may arise as to what law governs because of changes to the zoning ordinance made after the case was appealed to court.

[93] See TENN. CODE ANN. §§ 13-3-301 and 13-4-201.

[94] It is clear in Tennessee that no comprehensive plan is required before a zoning ordinance may be adopted. See *Barrett v. County of*

obtain a copy of it and place it into the record. Probably a better approach is to select those portions which are necessary and appropriate to your case (and which advance your client's position) and place those into the record.

Like any trial, the lawyer should want to win before the zoning board without the necessity of an appeal. However, because of the frequency of unlawful political influences which accompany a board hearing, the preservation of the record is crucial so that the decision may be successfully appealed.

7. The Opponent's Case

The same observations should be made by the opponent only in reverse. First, the opponent must emphasize the lack of the public good which this project may generate, unless it is patently obvious that the project is a good one. Secondly, the neighbors should point out any failure by the developer to cooperate with the neighbors or discuss the matter with the neighbors. Third and finally, the neighbors should always point out either by way of letter brief, or in the hearing itself and preferably both (albeit briefly), the failure of the developer to comply with all of the provisions of the local ordinance and state statute. The neighborhood attorney also wants to protect that record and in particular those portions which would establish the failure of the

---

Shelby, 619 S.W.2d 390 (Tenn. App. 1981) and *Family Golf v Metro Government*, 964 SW 2d 254 (Tenn. Ct. App. 1997); Tenn. Code Ann. §§ 13-7-102 and 202 only require the planning commission to "make and certify . . . a zoning plan, including both the full text of a zoning ordinance and the maps. . . ." This is decidedly different from the Standard State Zoning Enabling Act, which provided that the ordinance would be "in accord with the comprehensive plan." Of course, the term "zoning plan" may mean something more than the ordinance and maps; it must include them but may require more, and more could be the land use element of a general plan. The author of the Tennessee zoning enabling legislation, Alfred Bettman of Cincinnati, Ohio, was a strong proponent of comprehensive planning. It is hard to believe that he would have intended for zoning without planning.

developer to prove the entire case. If each essential element of the application is not met by the developer, and the neighborhood attorney has pointed that out to the board, the neighborhood should be successful on appeal. To that end, it is important that the neighbors get the ordinance into the record, and also that they get the city plan in if one exists. But it may not be important for the neighbors to get the general plan in. The plan might show, once in the evidence, that the applicant does comply.[95] However, if the applicant has not put the plan in, and the application requires consistency with that plan, the opponents should be able to argue on appeal that this is a decisive failure on the part of the developer. However, some proof must be introduced that there does exist a plan. Many municipalities and counties in Tennessee do not have a comprehensive general plan and, as a result, some letter or other proof from some city official demonstrating the existence of the plan must be introduced. Otherwise the court sitting in review will not know that the plan should have been submitted.

8. Other Parties

A large number of other people tend to arrive at zoning board hearings for one reason or another. Members of the local legislative body frequently appear and make presentations either for or against the proposal; members of state legislative bodies oft times show up in order to curry favor with constituents; neighbors, of course, are always interested. In representing either side of a controversy before a zoning board, about the best you can do is to try and anticipate who might be there and what they might say. Certainly, the appropriate member of the local legislative body should be contacted. Ordinarily, they have no official role to play before a zoning board and, frankly, experience seems to indicate that their comments are largely ignored. But it certainly doesn't hurt to try and get the local council person on your team, so to speak. The same is true for the neighbors and even perhaps the state representative. As to more esoteric parties who might also show up in opposition, the representative of the parties before the board must make a decision on each individual case. I have seen local clergymen come to

[95] Plans can be notoriously general and many times both sides will find support for their position in the plan.

zoning board meetings and testify about the good character of the applicant; it seems highly unlikely that this type of testimony is helpful in any way and, certainly, there is not much for the attorney for the opponents to do with that kind of testimony.

9. Personal Knowledge of Board Members

It is not very unusual for one or more of the board members to have some familiarity with the area which is under consideration by the board. This does not appear to be inappropriate in any way. The mere fact that the board member may have some knowledge of the area should not disqualify the board member from considering the matter.

On the other hand, if there is some aspect of that personal knowledge which the board member intends to rely upon in casting his vote, in order to be fair, the member of the board should reveal that personal knowledge to the parties so that they can comment on whatever the salient aspect of the personal knowledge might be. Perhaps the member has a pre-conceived opinion that traffic at a particular intersection is already so heavy that no additional development should take place in and about that area. That is certainly the kind of information that the attorney for the applicant would want to know so that special consideration could be given to attempting to persuade this member of the board that his personal observations might not conform to standard traffic analysis.[96] This opportunity to speak to any issue brought up by personal observation of a board member should be given to both parties. Neither one may choose to comment, but it is important, out of a sense of fairness, to make sure that it is revealed on the record.

---

[96] Whether you will get very far with that is certainly open to quite some doubt.

10. Open Public Meetings

While it is probably not necessary to mention this, the Tennessee Open Public Meetings Act[97] certainly applies to meetings before boards of zoning appeals. Prior to the enactment of the Open Public Meetings Act, it was the practice of many boards to conduct an executive session in private during which they made the decision on all the applications. Under the provisions of the Open Public Meetings Act, this is no longer allowed. Both the public hearings section of the meeting and any decision-making part of the meeting of the board must be open to public inspection. Several boards within the experience of this author will hold all the public hearings during an initial phase of the meeting, and then re-call the docket at the end after hearing all the public hearings and vote on each case at the tail end of the meeting. This is a little unusual, but it is probably done to discourage the applicant from staying for the entire meeting and watching the vote. It certainly does not discourage the news media from staying, but many applicants may not have four or five hours necessary to wait for the hearing to be concluded before the actual vote.

Other boards, of course, take the hearings in order, take the evidence and then vote immediately following the hearing and then take up the next case. It is certainly within the discretion of the board to do it either way, but the important part is that all of the meetings must be open to the public.

Remember, too, that if board members meet privately, or discuss the pending application by telephone, the entire decision-making process of the board on that application is void. Suit may be brought to enforce this provision.

---

[97] TENN. CODE ANN.§ 8-44-101 et seq.

Finally, the advice of counsel is also subject to the Act.[98] If the attorney believes that board counsel will give an opinion favorable to his client's position, some attempt (such as a direct question from counsel or as a suggestion to the board) to get that opinion in the record is mandatory. In that way, if the board votes the other way, the board's attorney is faced with his own words in defending the board. From experience, the author knows that this is not a good position to be in, and it encourages some rather pointed judicial inquiries.

In an interesting case decided by the Third Circuit, *Whiteland Woods v. Township of West Whiteland*,[99] and applicant seeking approval for the development of a 162 acre residential community attempted to videotape the decision of the planning commission. At that very meeting, the Township solicitor, probably in response to the request to use videotape, presented the planning commission with a resolution which barred the use of all video cameras at future planning commission meetings. The resolution provided in part: "the following rules shall govern the use of mechanical/electrical recording and/or stenographic devices during public meetings:... (5) no videotaping or video-recording and no additional lighting shall be employed."

The developer brought suit both in federal court (the case being discussed here) and also in state court. In federal court, the court concluded that neither the Fourteenth Amendment nor the First Amendment entitled the applicant, constitutionally, to videotape a meeting of a local governmental body. In effect, the federal court held that so long as other reasonable opportunities were permitted for the applicant to record or otherwise preserve a record of the proceedings, that there was no constitutional right to videotape.

---

[98] See *Smith County Education Association v Anderson*, 676 S.W. 2d 328 (Tenn. 1984)(attorney may only provide advice concerning pending litigation in a private meeting; any action to be taken based upon the advice must be voted upon in a public meeting).

[99] 193 F.3d 177 (3rd Cir. 1999).

Interestingly, in the state court decision, this city conceded that pursuant to the Pennsylvania Sunshine Act,[100] the planning commission could not prohibit videotaping commission meetings or decisions. In *Hain v. Board of School Directors*,[101] the court held that the state Sunshine Act required Pennsylvania government agencies to permit videotaping of their meetings.

There is no Tennessee case under the provisions of the Open Public Meetings Act, but one would suspect that a similar result would obtain. Pursuant to the rules of the Tennessee Supreme Court, television cameras and videotape are generally permitted now in a courtroom; it certainly would be hard to justify restricting access of similar equipment to other types of governmental agencies.

11. Burden of Proof

The burden of proof is on the applicant before the zoning board. It is the applicant's burden to convince the zoning board that the requested relief should be granted. Failing to carry the burden obviously results in a denial of the application.

It is important to carry the burden of proof on each and every issue that relates to the application and relief sought. This is another good reason to file a letter-brief with the board of zoning appeals which covers every issue imaginable so that in the heat of a battle before the zoning board, you do not forget an issue which might later prevent you from successfully defending a grant of the requested relief. It is a lot easier to figure out what requirements must be met in the quiet of the office, and much more difficult to remember all of them when you are being attacked by the neighbors before a hostile zoning board. Doing what it is in fact considering, the attorney may be in a very difficult position in front of a judge when the case is appealed. This certainly happens with some degree of frequency, and the attorneys for the parties in the controversy should keep a wary eye out for such questions. It is ofttimes a good idea to have spoken with the municipal attorney

---

[100] 65 Pa. Stat. Ann. § 271-86.

[101] 163 Pa. Commw. 479, 641 A.2d 661, 663-64 (1994).

ahead of time to make sure that he or she does not think that there is something fundamentally flawed in your approach to the hearing itself.

The law in Tennessee does not speak to the issue of the quantum of proof necessary to successfully establish a *prima facie* case when applying for relief before a zoning board. As a general matter, however, the applicant's proof must be logically sufficient to support a favorable administrative finding. Since the zoning board action's are reviewed under the common law writ of certiorari, there must be evidence that "a reasonable mind might accept as adequate to support a rational conclusion and such as to furnish a reasonably sound basis for the action under consideration."[102] Under the common law writ, there must be something more than a scintilla or a mere glimmer of evidence. The evidence must be of a substantial material nature, the type that would require submission of a case to a jury.[103] It is also clear that substantial administrative evidence is not limited to direct evidence, but may also include circumstantial evidence or inferences reasonably drawn from direct evidence.[104]

12. Voting and the Board's Decision

The decision of the board, as noted above, must be made in public. Typically, at the close of the public hearing, one member of the board makes a motion to grant or deny the requested relief. If the motion receives a second, then discussion ensues among the board members

---

[102] *Pace v. Garbage Disposal District*, 396 S.W.2d 461, 463 (Tenn. App. 1955).

[103] *Pace*, S.W.2d at 463.

[104] *Wayne County v. Tennessee Solid Waste Disposal Board*, 756 S.W.2d 274, 280 (Tenn. App. 1988).

about the case.[105] If the motion does not receive a second, the motion fails for lack of a second and another motion may be made.

After the motion is made and seconded, no additional proof should be taken by the board. The public hearing is closed. Furthermore, it is not appropriate to obtain additional information about the case from the staff or other public employees. If it is necessary to do so, then the hearing should be reopened to allow the parties to make any comment that might be appropriate in light of the new proof.

Typically, the motion should indicate whether the requested relief should be granted or denied, the factual basis for the motion especially if the motion is to grant relief,[106] and any conditions that the board member believes warranted. Because of the complicated grounds for the issuance of relief for variances, conditional use permits, and non-conforming uses, I recommend that the motion simply touch on the reason for the board action, and have a rule which permits the staff or the winning attorney to draft a more detailed order (or minute entry) to be presented to the board at the next meeting for final adoption.[107]

The attorney should know what the required majority is under the local ordinance,[108] particularly in light of the fact that many

---

[105] It is very common that the board simply begins discussions concerning the case at the close of the public hearing, without the benefit of a motion. Ordinarily, there is nothing inappropriate about simply discussing the case: remember, the hallmark of the hearing should be informality.

[106] In some circumstances, other legal rules may require findings especially when the result is a denial of the requested relief. For example, the Federal Telecommunications Act so requires. See page 194 for further discussion.

[107] See page 63 for additional discussion.

[108] The statutes do not specify any special majority needed for any vote on any type of relief available. Is it legally correct for the local ordinance to specify some type of super-majority (for example 4 out of 5

ordinances specify some minimum number of votes necessary to obtain the relief whether or not the entire membership of the board is present for the hearing and the decision.[109] In other words, if a variance requires a minimum of 3 votes on a five member board, and only 3 members are present, to obtain relief the applicant will need 100% of the vote. I am unaware of any reported cases contesting such a situation, but such a requirement may be unfair. Requiring a unanimous vote because several members of the board are absent seems inappropriate. If you are the attorney for an applicant requesting affirmative relief, and only a bare majority appears at the board meeting, maybe it is time to think about a request for a deferral in the hopes that more members will be at the next meeting.

Another interesting provision under some local rules allows a board member, even though he may not have been at the hearing to cast a vote on the ultimate decision.[110] Most of the reported cases are cases where the member gets a summary of the proof and then votes. However, many local boards record their hearings and some local provisions allow an absent member to listen or watch the recordings and then cast a vote. There is a question which arises under the Tennessee

---

votes) for variances for example? This issue has not been tested in the Tennessee courts. On the other hand, requiring 4 votes out of 7 even if only 4 members attend the meeting would seem to present little problem, and has in fact been reviewed although that issue was not raised.

[109] The Metro Nashville Zoning Ordinance (MetZo), for example, requires a quorum of four of the seven members. However, if only four members appear, by ordinance, all four must vote affirmatively in order to grant the requested relief. MetZo § 17.40.240; MBZA Rule 7(C).

[110] Anderson, § 22.46. Metro Nashville also adheres to this procedure. By allowing members who missed the board meeting to listen to or watch the recording and vote thereafter, seems to lessen the possible difficulties or requiring a specific number of affirmative votes. The applicant has a chance to get the required votes after the meeting has concluded by having other members review the recording and cast a vote.

Open Public Meetings Act, and its requirement that the vote be cast in an open meeting. If the member listens to a recording of the proceedings and decides to vote for or against a particular proposal, s/he cannot cast the vote by simply informing the staff of his decision. S/he must wait until it appears at the next meeting of the board of zoning appeals and cast it publicly at that meeting even though the case may not ostensibly be before the board. It should also be noted that if more then sixty days have elapsed from the original decision of the board, the decision is in all respects final,[111] and no further consideration or action may be taken by the board. Thus, the casting of a new vote which may affirmatively grant or deny the application, after sixty days is not appropriate and likely beyond the power of the board.

Many zoning ordinances provide that the affirmative votes of the majority present (or a majority of the entire board) are required for any application to be approved. The terminology used is critically important and the parties and attorneys should certainly be aware of what it takes to approve the application. Under Tennessee law,[112] in the absence of such language, the majority of votes lawfully cast determines the issue. So, for example, if an applicant for a variance got 3 votes in favor, 2 votes against, and 2 votes abstaining, what would the result be? In this situation, the applicant has obtained three affirmative votes, but he does not have a majority of the members present. Or does he? Under the Tennessee rule, the abstentions are viewed as votes in favor of the application (although not as affirmative votes) and therefore, the applicant prevails. However, because many ordinances specifically provide that the affirmative votes of the majority present are required, the old Tennessee common law rule is irrelevant and the applicant loses. He simply failed to obtain a majority of the members present. Three votes is not enough if all seven members of the board are present. Notice that if ordinance says that a majority of the members present and voting determines the outcome, the result would change. Under that circumstance, the two votes abstaining would not be counted and three votes in favor would be a majority of the total of five members present and voting.

---

[111] See Chapter V, Section B.1.(d) at page 351.

[112] *Collins v Janey*, 147 Tenn 477, 249 SW 801 (1923).

Let's change the fact situation just a bit. Suppose that under the circumstances presented by the hypothetical above, that instead of all seven members of the board being present, only five were present. Assume further that there were three votes in favor, one vote against, and one abstention: what result? It seems clear here that because three votes were cast in favor of the application, a majority of the five members of the board then present, the application is approved.

Finally, suppose the applicant gets three votes in favor, three votes against, and one abstention. Once again, under Tennessee common law, an applicant for a relief would not be entitled to the variance because the abstention is not an affirmative vote.

It is extremely important for the zoning administrator to keep a detailed record of the proceedings of the zoning board, including the vote of each member, the absence of a member and any failure of a member to vote. These records should be carefully preserved in a central location.

It may be even more critical for the parties to fully understand the requirements of the local ordinance: a careful review of those requirements before the hearing is well advised.[113]

D. Post Hearing Proceedings

1. The Board's Order:
Findings of Fact and Conclusions of Law

Traditionally, a minute entry is the means of recording the decision or action of an administrative body. As the Court of Appeals noted in a well-known planning commission case:[114]

---

[113] The Tennessee enabling statutes do not specify the manner in which voting is to take place so the local ordinance generally is the only guide. Often, the local ordinance does not address the issue either, in which case the common law of Tennessee governs.

[114] *B & B Enterprises v. City of Lebanon,* 2004 WL 2916141 (Tenn. Ct. App.,2004)

> The official record of a governmental board's or commission's actions is customarily its minutes. The courts have repeatedly observed that boards and commissions, like the planning commission in this case, speak or act officially only through their minutes and records made at duly called meetings.

Furthermore, those minutes are usually the only proof needed or allowed:[115]

> A board's or commission's minutes, once approved, are the only competent evidence of its official actions. There is a strong presumption that official minutes are correct. Thus, the courts will not consider parole evidence that contradicts a board's or commission's minutes and will decline to go behind these minutes in the absence of a showing of fraud or mistake.

Zoning boards, at least in the middle part of the state, have frequently entered final decisions either by way of a minute entry or by a separate order. A significant number of local boards actually enter orders as to each case heard. From the author's perspective, either method is legally appropriate.[116] The Open Public Meetings Act, TENN. CODE ANN. § 8-44-101, does require that:[117]

> The minutes of a meeting of any such governmental body shall be promptly and *fully* recorded, shall be open to public inspection, and shall include, but not be limited to,

---

[115] Id.

[116] The author began practicing law in 1979, and from at least that date, the Metro Board of Zoning Appeals has prepared a separate order for each case. The decision of the board has never been reversed based on a failure to have a minute entry as opposed to a separate order dealing with a particular case. Likely, it has never even been brought up on appeal.

[117] TENN. CODE ANN. § 8-44-104.

> a record of persons present, all motions, proposals and resolutions offered, the results of any votes taken, and a record of individual votes in the event of roll call.

It may be therefore that minutes of all meetings should be kept by all zoning boards, even if the official decision is made by a separate order. Perhaps the order should be referenced in the minutes, and a copy attached. In the age of the digital information, it would be fairly simple to describe the appeal (many boards maintain an agenda or docket sheet anyway), and reference the order concerning the case. Obviously, the secretary would sign the entry for each meeting. It is frankly not clear that this is necessary if there is a separate order for each case, signed by the chair and the secretary. But the Act may so require.

Also note that the "fully recorded" language in § 104 refers to the minutes and is not a separate requirement that the entire meeting be transcribed for the purposes of the Open Public Meetings Act. In *Hutsell v Jefferson County BZA*,[118]

> Plaintiffs seek to have this Court construe the language to mean "complete and exact." Significantly, the statute does not state that the proceedings must be recorded by audio, video, or otherwise. Appellants' proposed construction of TENN. CODE ANN. § 8-44-104 overlooks that it is the "minutes" that are to be "promptly and fully recorded," not the entire proceedings. "Minutes" is defined as "Memoranda or notes of a transaction or proceedings. Thus, the record of the proceedings at a meeting of directors or shareholders of a company is called the 'minutes.' "

Remember, however, that the certiorari statute does require a transcript (that is, word for word) if a lawsuit appealing the decision of the board is filed.[119] So, there must be a recording or a court reporter

---

[118] 2005 WL 954646 (Tenn. Ct. App.,2005)

[119] Tenn. Code Ann. § 27-9-109 ("the board or commission shall cause to be made, certified and forwarded to such court a complete

present at the time of the hearing so that all of the testimony can be preserved in the event of a suit. In the *Hutsell* case above, there evidently was no transcript but no one raised the issue of the certiorari statute; only the Open Public Meetings Act was discussed. The *Lewis* case was decided a year before *Hutsell* but perhaps it had not yet been generally appreciated for its importance. Obviously, a permanent record of each order as entered and all minutes should be maintained by the board's staff.

Attorneys in Tennessee routinely prepare orders for entry by our state trial courts. For one reason or another, when attorneys make an appearance before an administrative fact finding body such as a zoning board, they forget a that if you want something done right, do it yourself. The attorney should ask permission to draft the order (or minute entry) for the board. The zoning board is almost always glad to have the lawyer take on the obligation of drafting the proper document. Most local zoning boards are understaffed, and furthermore, even if they have sufficient staff, the staff may not fully understand what is necessary to state in a final zoning board order/minute entry to ensure that the board is affirmed on appeal. The staff frequently simply enters form orders with no particular findings of fact, or a very limited reference to a factual finding. An attorney working for the client, will no doubt draft a better order which will have a greater chance of being upheld on appeal.

And while specific findings of fact may not be required in a given case, they are very helpful and should be included if the attorney has the opportunity to prepare the order/minute entry:[120]

---

transcript of the proceedings"); *Lewis v Bedford County BZA*, 174 S.W.3d 241, 245-46 (Tenn. Ct. App.2004)("As the statute clearly states, the Board had the responsibility to prepare a transcript of its hearing on the [petitioners'] request that included the evidence presented to the Board," at 247.)

[120] *Moore v. Metro BZA*, 205 S.W.3d 429 (Tenn. Ct. App. 2006); see also *Weaver v. Knox County Bd. of Zoning Appeals*, 122 S.W.3d 781, 785 (Tenn. Ct. App. 2003).

> We agree with the residents' assertion that findings of fact are helpful and important. In both administrative and judicial proceedings, findings of fact promote an understanding of the basis for the decision. They also help to sharpen the focus of issues raised on appeal. But as helpful as findings of fact might be in an administrative proceeding, administrative bodies such as the Board are not required to make specific findings of fact unless a statute or ordinance requires them.

Frequently, the ordinance will specifically require findings of fact by the zoning board and a failure to make findings under those circumstances will be reversible.[121]

The attorney's client has a much greater stake in making sure that the order is prepared correctly in an effort to prevent or win any appeal that might be filed. Thus, one of the most important responsibilities of the land use planning attorney when practicing before an administrative body such as the zoning board, is to aks permission to prepare the order or resolution of the board granting the requested relief. This may be done in several ways.

The attorney may draft a proposed order or proposed findings of fact for presentation to the board at the time of the hearing. This cuts down on delay, and it may prompt discussion by the members of the

---

[121] Interestingly, an earlier opinion by the Court of Appeals held slightly differently: "It is the position of this court that a reviewing court can not determine whether the decision of an administrative body is supported by material evidence unless the administrative body makes findings of facts setting forth the reasons for its decision. We do not express an opinion as to whether the Western Section was correct in concluding that it was not necessary for the Board to set out findings of facts absent four concurring votes. Instead, it is our opinion that a reviewing court can not determine if there was material evidence to support a decision if the reviewing court is unaware of the basis for the decision." *Hoover v Metro Board of Zoning Appeals*, 924 SW 2d 900, 905 (Tenn. Ct. App. 1996). The reason for the difference here was the local requirement of factual findings.

board which would further augment the letter brief submitted by the attorney before the hearing. Such a discussion would also demonstrate to the court that the board was thinking of the legal criteria necessary to render a decision. However, there is also one negative to it. If the board begins to think in terms of the legal criteria, or sees something in the proposed order which it does not agree with, or if the parties in opposition see the order and have an opportunity to criticize it, it may destroy an otherwise effective presentation. In other words, the attorney may, with the submission of the proposed findings of fact, snatch defeat from the jaws of victory.

Therefore, the author usually seeks permission (from either the staff or the board itself) prior to the hearing permitting him to file the order if successful. In the area of Metropolitan Nashville, the board's order is routinely entered by the submission to the secretary of the board who then affixes a facsimile of the signature of the chair by rubber stamp. In other words, the board itself has never actually seen the order. This may be subject to some dispute. However, I suggest that if brought up before a court upon certiorari, that the courts would simply remand to the board for findings of fact and conclusions of law. The board would almost certainly at that point adopt the order which had been prepared and the protesting parties would be back in the same position.[122]

Also, by submitting the proposed order after the hearing before the board, the attorney knows what happened at the board and may be able to put into the order much more than the bare and legal bones of what is necessary. Some elaboration may be permitted in the order to take into account those features which the board did truly look at and discuss. However, even under those circumstances, the order will to a great extent mirror the letter brief submitted by counsel. Whichever party prevails, be it the developer or the neighbors, the letter brief

---

[122] This can be avoided by the simple expedient of having the board, at its next public meeting, adopt specifically affirm all of the orders previously entered from the last hearing. In that way, there's an official resolution adopting all the orders and there can be no doubt of the validity of the board's order as prepared by counsel for the developer or the neighborhood.

submitted for that position should form the basis of the order. This important responsibility of counsel cannot be overestimated. Although findings of fact are not required here in Tennessee,[123] more and more courts are requiring findings of fact and conclusions of law of local administrative bodies including zoning boards. In *Topanga Association for a Scenic Community v. County of Los Angeles*,[124] the California Supreme Court required that the board make factual findings sufficient to enable the judiciary to review their decision.

> Consistent with the reasoning underlying these cases, we hold that regardless of whether the local ordinance commands that the variance board set forth findings, that body must render findings sufficient both to enable the parties to determine whether and on what basis they should seek review and, in the event of review, to apprise a reviewing court of the basis for the board's action. We hold further that a reviewing court, before sustaining the grant of a variance, must scrutinize the record and determine whether substantial evidence supports the administrative agency's findings and whether these findings support the agency's decision. In making these determinations, the reviewing court must resolve reasonable doubts in favor of the administrative findings and decision.

Thus, the board must follow a three-step process. A body of proof must be introduced before it. From that proof, the board must glean those facts which it believes to be correct. Third, and finally, the board must reach legal conclusions based upon the actual findings. The letter brief figures prominently in all three steps. It is a part of the proof introduced before the board. When the attorney writes the order of the board, the facts tendered by the letter brief can be adopted as the

---

[123] *Moore v. Metro BZA*, 205 S.W.3d 429 (Tenn. Ct. App. 2006); see also *Weaver v. Knox County Bd. of Zoning Appeals*, 122 S.W.3d 781, 785 (Tenn. Ct. App. 2003).

[124] 113 Cal.Rptr. 836, 522 P.2d 12 (1974).

findings of the board,[125] and the legal conclusion, that the relief should be granted or denied, should flow from those facts in the letter brief that has been appropriately drafted.

From the perspective of the practicing lawyer, the more detailed the findings of fact and conclusions of law, generally, the better. Many a difficult case has been won on appeal by a solid order prepared to cement the board's and the prevailing parties' position.

The mechanics of the adoption of the decision are also important (at least to the lawyers). Let's assume that a motion is made to grant a variance. The member making the motion either specifies the grounds of the motion or, as is more likely, there is little or no specification of the grounds for the motion. All of the requirements of the zoning ordinance have not been met by the motion. Does that mean that the motion is inappropriate? I would suggest that the answer to this question is no. Most of the time it is difficult for a member of the board to find reasons for each of the specific requirements for a variance. Variances as we will see later, are very a complicated means of obtaining administrative relief. As a result, I suggest that as a matter of course, the board have a procedure, specified by its rules, which permit the staff (or the lawyer for the prevailing party), after a motion has been made and passed, to draft an order or resolution or minute entry, specifying the reasons for the action taken by the board. This document should be presented to the board at its next meeting, and the board should vote to approve the it either as drafted by the staff, or with modifications as deemed appropriate. I would suggest that while this technically delays the final action of the board until the following meeting, it makes it much easier for the board to draft an order which makes good sense and which is also legally supportable. Certainly, any changes the board wishes to make to the language contained in the minute entry, order, or resolution can be made. In addition, if the board wishes to change its mind entirely, it may also do that.[126]

---

[125] Not by reference; the findings should be explicitly set out in the board's order.

[126] Although changing its decision entirely at the next meeting may raise issues of notice and cause some dissatisfaction with the

Before this procedure is objected to as allowing the board to put the parties in a bad situation, please consider the fact that under Tennessee law, there is always a 60 day window within which an appeal may be taken to court.[127] As a result, if the applicant proceeds with the development prior to the expiration of that 60 day time frame, he does so at his own risk. That is because the court may review the decision of the board and entirely reverse it. Thus, the applicant is not losing anything by virtue of this small delay and may gain a lot by virtue of the fact that it will certainly be easier to uphold the decision of the zoning board if a proper order is drafted and officially entered on the minutes.

2. Rehearing and/or Reconsideration

An appeal from a decision of the board of zoning appeals is generally pursuant to the common law writ of certiorari and must be taken within sixty days.[128] While there is a conflict in the other states,[129] and the only case in Tennessee appears to support the better rule: the board of zoning appeals may reconsider simply upon the evidence submitted to it at the prior hearing, or may decide to entirely rehear an application provided that the sixty day time period has not run, and also provided that an appeal has not been filed under the common law writ of certiorari.[130] Once the appeal is filed of course, the court must then consider the matter and reach a determination, the zoning board should take no further action.[131] Further, if sixty days have

process.

[127] TENN. CODE ANN. § 27-9-102.

[128] Id.

[129] Anderson at § 22.51; Rohan at § 51.07[1]; Rathkopf at § 37.08[1].

[130] *DE Ryan v Metro Board of Zoning Appeals*, 2004 WL 1944131 (Tenn. Ct. App. 2004)

[131] *Stone Man v Rutherford County Regional Planning Commission*, 1985 Tenn. App. Lexis 2607

passed, the time for appeal has run and the board has no power to revise, reconsider, or rehear the matter. It is suggested that if the board has granted an application for reconsideration or rehearing even though it has not actually reconsidered or reheard the matter before the appeal is taken to court, that the matter is not final from the administrative standpoint and the common law writ of certiorari should not lie until a final administrative decision has been made. Perhaps a better way of saying that is that reconsideration is the speediest method of review, one of the factors in the common law writ.[132]

As a practical matter, the courts should allow the board to rehear or reconsider an appeals case because it may obviate the necessity of an appeal. The goal of judicial economy may be advanced by allowing the board to resolve the matter fully and finally administratively before any common law writ it issued.

Strategically, a request for reconsideration or rehearing should be made only if the lawyer thinks that there is some good reason to believe that the administrative decision maker might change its mind. If, for example, you have been able to reduce or eliminate the neighborhood opposition, or if some other significant development has taken place which would affect the decision of the board as evidenced by their considerations in the prior hearing, only then should a request be made. The author's experience is that most such requests are a waste of time absent such a change in a determinative circumstance.

DE Ryan v Metro Board of Zoning Appeals[133] was an unusual case in which the Board itself brought the matter back up for reconsideration, believing that the applicant and his lawyer had misrepresented the facts to the board. A new lawyer was hired for the court appeal after the board revoked its previously conferred designation of non-conforming property. The Tennessee Court of Appeals never reached the issue concerning whether reconsideration beyond the 60 days was permitted because it found that there was no misrepresentation. The Court however tacitly agreed with both parties

[132] See Chapter 5.

[133] 2004 WL 1944131 (Tenn. Ct. App. 2004).

that the board had the power to reconsider the case within 60 days of its original decision. Because the board attempted reconsideration beyond that time (based on the alleged misrepresentation), the Court reversed on that issue.

The board's rules should make clear that only a member of the original majority of the board may move to reconsider or rehear. In the absence of such a provision, a member who was on the losing side of the vote might be able to move to reconsider the same case for the next 63 (or whatever) meetings of the board.[134] The only way such a motion makes sense anyway is if a member of the original majority is considering changing his/her vote. Thus, only a member of the original majority should be permitted to make the motion. Presumably, someone who voted in the majority has no interest in delaying the proceedings.[135]

3. Res Judicata

Once the sixty day period for appeal passes, the board's decision is final and the doctrine of res judicata applies.[136] It is perfectly obvious in the case of variances: because the variance is based on some unique physical feature of the property, if the variance was denied initially, no new applications should be accepted and considered by the board because a unique physical feature cannot be created without violating

---

[134] This might have the effect that the decision never becomes final; the applicant would never be able to proceed with the project theoretically.

[135] Of course, a crafty opponent might vote with the majority simply to have the right to move for reconsideration; the Board can deal with that possibility on an ad hoc basis, or pass a rule that there can only be one or two post-hearing requests.

[136] That's the majority rule. Anderson at §22.51; Rohan at §51.07[1]; Rathkopf at §37.08[1]. The *DE Ryan* decision however leaves open the possibility that the board may reconsider beyond 60 days if one of the parties misrepresented the facts at the hearing.

the self-created hardship rule for variances.[137] And thus of the three major powers of the board, certainly as to variances there is no reason to ever reconsider an application. Conditional use permits fall within the same rule although the underlying policy justification is not as strong. However, there is the interest in having a final decision which cannot be reopened. The doctrine of res judicata is generally used by the courts then to hold that the board does not have the power to reconsider the same or similar relief as sought by an old application.

The only exception to this rule is where there are changed circumstances.[138] The changed circumstance rule is, however, not appropriate under most circumstances, and should only rarely be considered. Most changed circumstances would be created by the owner of the property and in the context of a variance application, that would be self-defeating. However, there are occasions where the government has by eminent domain taken parcels of property or portions of parcels of property and put the land owner in a difficult position by way of the narrowness or shallowness or shape of the property. Assuming a hardship is created by one of the factors, a variance might be appropriate. Proof of the changed circumstance by way of government condemnation should be permitted. There may be other examples. Many times, the change in circumstances is only a change in neighborhood opposition. While the change in objections in the request for a rehearing or reconsideration on the original application may be justifiable, and probably is, the consent of surrounding property owners at a later point simply should not be taken into account. Proof of the elimination of restrictive covenants is also irrelevant. Changed circumstances also would have absolutely no effect on an application for non-conforming use. No changed circumstances could possibly effect the board's decision on a non-conforming use. The applicant may have not submitted evidence to justify a finding of legal non-conformity by the board, but that is no ground for a new application. Furthermore, even if new evidence comes up, the discovery of new evidence, as in a court

[137] See Chapter Four.

[138] *United Cities Gas Co. v. Tenn. Public Service Commission*, 789 SW 2d 256, 259 (Tenn. 1990); *Morris v. Esmark Apparel*, 832 SW 2d 563 (Tenn. App. 1991).

proceeding, should not entitle the applicant to a new hearing. Once sixty days has elapsed since the initial decision of the board, the board no longer has jurisdiction, and unless an appeal has been taken to the courts, the matter is finally and forever foreclosed.

E. Conclusion

Practice before a zoning board is a very unusual aspect of the practice of law. It is, however, a very challenging and rewarding experience. Above all, the attorney must remember that he is dealing with a group of laymen, and that they are interested in a common sense approach to the development of their community. To the extent that the attorney can combine this common sense public good approach with a clear demonstration that the applicant meets all the legal criteria, he will not only be successful legally but gain the trust of the board and may also make a significant contribution to the community as well.

Timetable

	Initial meeting with clients; contact planner, engineer, and/or other witness quickly
Jan 1	Make sure to have copy of zoning ordinance and board rules; draft brief
Jan 6	Status update with clients (review brief and proof)
Jan 8	File brief with Zoning Board
Jan 14	Final Meeting with Client
Jan 15	Zoning Board Hearing Date

Chapter Two

Administrative Appeals and Nonconforming Properties

A. The Statute

This chapter generally discusses the powers of a zoning board to review the decisions of the local administrative officer with regard to zoning concerns including issues regarding the largest category of such appeals, those involving non-conforming properties. Usually, these cases would be presented to the board pursuant to the first of its three basic powers, expressed in TENN. CODE ANN. § 13-7-207(1). This statute deals with municipal zoning boards but the county equivalent is virtually identical (see TENN. CODE ANN. § 13-7-109(1)). The former provision reads:

> The board of appeals has the power to:
>
> (1) Hear and decide appeals where it is alleged by the appellant that there is error in any order, requirement, permit decision, or refusal made by the municipal building commissioner or any other administrative official in the carrying out or enforcement of any provision of any ordinance enacted pursuant to this part and part 3 of this chapter . . .

A brief review of the statute is in order here. First the appellant (developer, property owner, or neighbor) must allege that there was some error in a decision made by the building commissioner or other administrative officer. The error could be in denying a permit, which is the typical case, or it could be granting the permit where it should not have been granted at all, a case in which a neighbor appeals the decision of the building commissioner or other official.[1]

---

[1] *Harding Academy v Metro Nashville*, 207 SW 3d 279 (Tenn. Ct. App. 2006) is an example of such a case.

Second, note that the error must have been made "in the carrying out or enforcement of any provisions of any ordinance enacted pursuant to this part and part 3 of this chapter . . ."[2] The quoted language is in Part 2 relating to municipal zoning; the referenced Part 3 deals with extraterritorial zoning by municipalities. So, TENN. CODE ANN. § 13-7-207(1) applies only to appeals arising in the context of zoning decisions, whether within the municipal boundaries or extraterritorial. Arguments have sometimes been made that an appeal can be from virtually any official enforcing virtually any kind of code, not just the zoning ordinance, but this is clearly wrong. Let's take the most logical example first: the building code, since the statute actually names the "building commissioner."[3] Can a developer (or neighbor) appeal a decision to the zoning board under the building code pursuant to § 207(1)? The answer must clearly be: NO!!!

The building code has its own set of appeal procedures.[4] This zoning provision (§ 207(1)) has nothing whatever to do with the building code, even though it refers to "refusal[s] made by the municipal [or county] building commissioner." This section of the zoning enabling legislation only applies when the building commissioner is enforcing the zoning ordinance or regulations; it does not apply when s/he is

---

[2] It is worthwhile to note that this language is verbatim from Alfred Bettman; for example, see Bassett, Williams, Bettman & Whitten, *Model Planning Laws* at 102 (Harvard 1935) (hereinafter referred to as BWBW).

[3] In the county enabling legislation, there is express authority to create the position of building commissioner to enforce the provisions of the zoning regulations. This too is straight from the language proposed by Bettman. BWBW at 103.

[4] Take a look at the 2006 International Building Code § 112. 2, or 2009 IBC § 113.2. The IBC is very restrictive with regard to such appeals. There is no power to grant variances for example. If a local zoning board illegally granted a variance in sprinkler (building code) requirements, it is safe to say that the Construction Board of Appeals would be legally precluded from granting the same application.

administering or enforcing the building code, a totally separate set of regulations.[5]

How about the fire code? NO! Again, this section (207(1)) only applies to zoning. The same is true for planning issues: the zoning board does not get to interpret subdivision regulations or other planning regulations promulgated by the planning commission or adopted by the local legislative body.

The language of the statue is clear: this appeal process only applies to ordinances adopted pursuant to "this part and part 3 of this chapter." That's Chapter 7 of Title 13 of the Tennessee Code Annotated; Part 2 is municipal ***zoning*** and Part 3 is extraterritorial municipal zoning. The county statutory provision references Part 1, county zoning. It is easy to read the statute and misunderstand it, but it is fairly clear. A zoning board should not be dealing with the building code, the fire code, the planning regulations (except in the form of the zoning ordinance or regulations), or any of the other myriad of technical codes that cities and counties adopt. Those areas of code enforcement are beyond the expertise of zoning boards, and beyond their legal jurisdiction.

Zoning boards do have the power to render administrative interpretations of the zoning ordinance. Administrative appeals often involve interpretations of the zoning ordinance itself. For example, what is a church,[6] what street access must an asphalt plant have[7] or how

---

[5] Of course, if the zoning board is the building code board (or vice-versa), the difference is not that great. But, the powers of the two boards are different and when sitting as a building code board the powers of the zoning board do not apply.

[6] *Capps v Metro BZA*, 2008 WL 5427972 (Tenn. Ct. App. 2008)

[7] *Eatherly v. Metro Board of Zoning Appeals*, 1989 WL 136960 (Tenn. App. 1989).

many acres must a high school have?[8] In this area, the zoning board is rendering a legal interpretation, and it has a good deal of discretion in such cases. Non-conforming property decisions on the other hand, are a specific subset of administrative appeals and usually involve specific fact determinations. Did the use of the property begin before the effective date of the applicable zoning ordinance?[9] Has the use continued without significant interruption since that time? Did the property have the required permits for the activity? As a result, the board gets both kinds of cases to decide: interpretations of the law and intensely fact based decisions in the form of non-conforming property issues. We will address each separately.

B. Administrative Appeals

The zoning board clearly has the power and authority to review administrative decisions of the zoning (or building official if s/he administers the zoning ordinance) official relating to zoning issues. Although there are usually not a large number of these appeals over the course of any given year, they are nevertheless certainly not rare.[10] "The statute permits a board of zoning appeals to consider a zoning administrator's decision de novo and to disagree with the zoning administrator if it determines that his or her decision was wrong."[11] Usually, the appeal involves an issue of how to define a particular land use: if the use is defined as "x" then it may be permitted as it is currently zoned. If it is defined as "y" then maybe it is not permitted.

---

[8] *City of Oak Hill v. State ex rel. First Christian Church*, 492 S.W. 2d 915 (Tenn. 1973).

[9] *421 Corporation v. Metro Nashville*, 36 S.W. 3d 469 (Tenn. App. 2000).

[10] The Metro Zoning Board hears about 10 to 20 such cases a year, depending on how they are counted. Interpretations are often combined with other types of relief (such as a request for a conditional use or variance). Those cases are not included.

[11] *Robison v Metropolitan Government*, 1992 WL 205268, at *4.

An interesting example of these cases it is *Metro Nashville v. Martin,*[12] a case in which the city sued for injunctive relief because an adult entertainment establishment bought a building and began operations in an area in which it was prohibited.[13] The defense was that the principal activity on the site was a nightclub and that only a small amount of the time was involved with "adult entertainment;" the argument was that under the definitions in the ordinance, the small percentage of time that the club was engaged in "adult entertainment" was insufficient to reach a conclusion that the club was an adult entertainment establishment. In effect, the argument was that the adult use was accessory to the principal night club use, and thus not in violation of the zoning law. Neither the trial court nor the Court of Appeals had any trouble dispensing with this argument:

> Defendants operate a "night club" which offers live and video entertainment and beverages. Each activity on the premises is calculated to attract patronage of the establishment hence it is an activity which "fulfills a primary function of the establishment" which is patronage and profit.
>
> The mere fact that the objectionable activity was conducted by relatively few of the employees or for a relatively small fraction of the time would not prevent it from being a part of the principal activity of the business if it was calculated to attract patronage of the establishment.

The allegedly accessory nature of the use was unconvincing to the courts.

---

[12] 1994 WL 470418 (Tenn. App. 1994).

[13] The adult entertainment establishment was too close to a school (in fact, it was immediately adjacent to Hume Fogg High School in downtown Nashville).

1. Principal Uses

Perhaps the most traditional role for the board in this area is to interpret the ordinance to determine what is and is not permitted in a particular zoning district, or what a particular use of property may be. In *Askey v Maury County Board of Zoning Appeals,*[14] the issue was whether a private airstrip was a permitted use in an agricultural zoning district which expressly permitted "recreational uses." The zoning board did not deem the airstrip as a permitted use within the meaning of the ordinance, but was reversed on appeal, the Court of Appeals finding the non-commercial use of the airstrip to fit naturally within the term "recreational uses."[15]

In *Capps v Metro Board of Zoning Appeals,*[16] several issues were presented to the board, including whether the Nashville Union Mission was a "church" within the meaning of the ordinance, and whether a nearby adult entertainment use had legally established its operations before the Mission was a church. Perhaps not surprisingly, both the zoning board and Court of Appeals had no trouble ruling against the nightclub, although the issue of whether the mission was a church (it had a pulpit in a room designed for worship services) or habitation for a transient population presented a very interesting question.

In ruling on these kinds of cases, perhaps the board is best advised to consider the impact of the use on the surrounding land uses.

---

[14] 2009 WL 837890, Tenn. Ct. App., March 30, 2009

[15] Although the issue seems a bit closer to the author, if the airstrip was not permitted in an agricultural zoning district, where would it be permitted? Surely, the less dense agricultural area is a better fit than residential, commercial, or industrial.

[16] The case was actually decided in the form of three separate opinions: 2008 WL 5427972, Tenn. Ct. App., December 31, 2008 (pre-existing use); 2008 WL 5428059, Tenn. Ct. App., December 31, 2008 (is the mission a church?); and 2008 WL 5428070, Tenn. Ct. App., December 31, 2008 (reinstated the First Amendment and Equal Protection civil rights claims).

It is not generally the activities inside a building (although those may be important also), but rather how those activities effect the neighbors on the outside. Thus, looking at a dictionary definition of the use may often miss the real point: how does that use impact surrounding property owners. In *Capps*, the Board and the reviewing Courts seemed to focus on the items of less importance such as tax status, and the corporate structure. Perhaps more important was the fact that over 500 people were housed and fed each evening on the premises, which suggested a closer connection to semi-transient habitation than to religious worship.

2. Accessory Uses/Home Occupations

Another common question is whether a particular type of use can be permitted as accessory to a principal use. In *Red Acres Improvement Club v Burkhalter*,[17] the issue was whether a physician's office in a Memphis subdivision was accessory to a residential use under the terms of the zoning ordinance and thereby permitted. The court concluded that it was. The good doctor evidently maintained a commercial office where he received patients from 8 AM to 4 PM; he would then return to his home and received patients at his home between the hours of 4 PM and 8 PM, averaging, according to the court approximately 15 to 25 patients per day coming to his office at his home.[18] No other physician worked with Dr. Burkhalter but he did have a receptionist to greet patients as they arrived. The court pointed out that the ordinance expressly permitted "uses customarily incident to any of the above uses when located on the same lot and not involving the conduct of a business; including also home occupations engaged in by the occupants of the dwelling not involving the conduct of a business on the premises, and including also the office of a physician, surgeon, dentist, musician or artist when situated in the same dwelling used by

---

[17] 241 S.W. 2d 921 (Tenn. 1951). It should be noted that this case was taken directly to the courts and was not heard by the local zoning board.

[18] Id at 922-3.

such physician, surgeon, dentist, musician or artist as his or her private dwelling."[19]

Obviously, the concern was the number of patients the doctor saw at the residence but the court pointed out that there was nothing in the zoning ordinance justifying an inference that it was intended to limit the number of patients who might see the doctor on a given day. The Tennessee Supreme Court concluded that under the terms of the zoning ordinance, the doctor was not violating its home occupation provisions.

These days, of course, there are generally express limitations on the number of patients or clients who can be served on site as part of a home occupation. For example, Metro Nashville expressly provides that "no clients or patrons may be served on the property."[20]

Generally speaking, an accessory use must be customary, incidental and subordinate to the principal use.[21] At least at the time of the *Burkhalter* decision, a doctor's office in his home was not unusual[22] and the court allowed it in that case. This particular type of accessory use is known as a home occupation. Most zoning ordinances now have sections devoted to restrictions on home occupations and the zoning board may be called upon to interpret those regulations.

The regulations often limit the size of the home occupation, limit or eliminate signage, limit patrons or customers and employees, among other restrictions.

It is also important to recognize that the accessory use must be subordinate to the principal use. For example, if the doctor's office in

---

[19] Id at 924.

[20] MetZo § 17.16.250 (C) (1).

[21] Modern zoning ordinances usually define the term, and most any reasonable definition is acceptable.

[22] This most likely is not true today.

Burkhalter had been twice the size of the residence,[23] the argument would be that the principal use of the property was commercial; presumably this would not be permitted in the residential district.

The two uses (principal and accessory) must also have some connection binding them together. In *Burkhalter*, of course, the physician's office was in his own home. The common feature was the fact that the doctor lived and worked there. That is, of course, the connection in all home occupation uses. The office use is accessory to the residential use. A business accessory sign is another type of accessory use: it advertises goods and services available on the site. If the same sign advertised goods and/or services off-site (a mile up the highway for example) it would be an advertising sign and very likely not permitted. An advertising sign, standing alone, on a separate property is a principal use of its own and must comply with the zoning regulations. Advertising goods available on-site establishes the connection between the sign and the principal use rendering the sign accessory.

In an interesting case from Lebanon, *City of Lebanon v. Harris*[24], the manufacturer of small wooden sheds (designed to store tools and such in a backyard) began locating the sheds on commercial properties prominently displaying his name and address so that a passerby could contact him if he wanted to buy one. While the manufacturer had the permission of the commercial property owner to place the sheds on the property, there was no relationship between the shed and the commercial use. One of the locations, for example, was in the side yard of a bank. What does a tool shed with the maker's name and phone number on it have to do with banking activities? That certainly an excellent question: the answer was nothing, in fact. As a result, the sheds could not be accessory uses -- they were in fact another principal use on the same zone lot, but not permitted because they were advertising structures.

---

[23] Expressed let's say in terms of square footage. In fact, the *Burkhalter* case indicates that the doctor's offices were quite small compared to the remainder of the residence. 241 S.W. 2d at 922-3.

[24] 2001 WL 1191406 (Tenn. Ct. App.)

3. Permit Revocation

Another area that zoning boards are frequently called upon to referee is the revocation of a permit. Obviously, the basis of the revocation must be the zoning ordinance[25] otherwise the zoning board lacks jurisdiction. Furthermore, although this issue has not been raised directly, while the board certainly should have the first opportunity to interpret the zoning ordinance (just as in the situation where the permit has been refused and the developer appeals), the issue of vested rights and equitable estoppel[26] is not from my perspective something the zoning board should be deciding. These complicated common law issues are for the courts: not for a lay board with little or no legal training. This is especially true where the only appeal mechanism is the common law writ which assumes the correctness of the zoning board's decision. Under the common law writ, even if the reviewing court felt that the zoning board was in error, it could not reverse unless the error rose to the level of arbitrariness or capriciousness. So, while the board should have the opportunity to interpret the ordinance, and that interpretation should be given appropriate deference, the issues of vested rights and equitable estoppel should be the sole province of a court of law or equity.

4. Rules of Construction

Whenever the board of zoning appeals is called upon to review and interpret provisions of its zoning ordinance there are several

[25] If it is another code altogether, there is usually another codes related board to consider an appeal, such as for example, the Board of Building Code Appeals for building code issues.

[26] These doctrines are in any case difficult to assert successfully. Usually, the developer must show that a building permit was issued legally, and the substantial construction under the permit has taken place. *Howe Realty v. City of Nashville*, 114 SW 2d 904, 906 (Tenn. 1940), and this is usually not the case.

applicable rules of statutory construction. Some of the most important rules which might apply to land use planning issues include:[27]

> Local governments lack inherent power to control the use of private property within their boundaries. Their power derives from the State through specific delegation by the General Assembly.[28] While local governments have considerable discretion to act within the scope of their delegated power, they cannot effectively nullify state law on the same subject by enacting ordinances that ignore applicable state laws, that grant rights that state law denies, or that deny rights that state law grants. *See generally State ex rel. Beasley v. Mayor & Aldermen of Fayetteville*, 196 Tenn. 407, 415-16, 268 S.W.2d 330, 334 (1954). Thus, local governments must exercise their delegated power consistently with the delegation statutes from which they derive their power. *See Henry v. White*, 194 Tenn. 192, 196, 250 S.W.2d 70, 71 (1952).
>
> When the language of an ordinance is clear, the courts will enforce the ordinance as written. When, however, the language of an ordinance is ambiguous, the courts will resort to the customary principles of statutory construction. *See Whittemore v. Brentwood Planning Comm'n*, 835 S.W.2d at 15. Accordingly, the reviewing courts will construe a zoning ordinance as a whole and will give its words their natural and ordinary meaning. *See Lions Head Homeowners Assoc., Inc. v. Metropolitan Bd. of Zoning Appeals*, 968 S.W.2d 296, 301 (Tenn. Ct. App. 1997); *Boles v. City of Chattanooga*, 892 S.W.2d 416, 420 (Tenn. Ct. App. 1994). They will also seek the interpretation that is most consistent with the ordinance's

---

[27] *421 Corp. v. Metro Government*, 36 S.W. 3d 469 (Tenn. App. 2000).

[28] See *State ex rel. SCA Chem. Servs. v. Sanidas*, 681 S.W.2d 557, 562 (Tenn. 1984); *Family Golf of Nashville, Inc. v. Metropolitan Gov't*, 964 S.W.2d 254, 257 (Tenn. Ct. App. 1997).

general purposes, but they will resolve ambiguities in favor of the property owner's right to the unrestricted use of his or her property. *See State ex rel. Morris v. City of Nashville*, 207 Tenn. 672, 680, 343 S.W.2d 847, 850 (1961); *State ex rel. Wright v. City of Oak Hill*, 204 Tenn. 353, 356, 321 S.W.2d 557, 559 (1959).

The well-known in pari materia rules also apply to the construction of zoning ordinances. Thus, zoning ordinances dealing with the same subject should be construed together. *See Lions Head Homeowners Ass'n v. Metropolitan Bd. of Zoning Appeals*, 968 S.W.2d at 301. In addition, zoning ordinances must also be construed in light of the state statutes empowering local governments to enact them in order to avoid conflict and to enable related statutes and ordinances to operate concurrently. *See City of Louisville v. Thompson*, 339 S.W.2d 869, 873 (Ky. Ct. App. 1960); *City of Dallas v. Sullenger*, 826 P.2d 34, 36 (Or. Ct. App. 1992); *Carroll v. Hastings*, 402 N.Y.S.2d 279, 283 (Sup. Ct. 1977).

In construing any zoning regulation, the board must always bear in mind these rules, but perhaps the most important is that zoning ordinances, being in derogation of common law and operating to deprive the owner of property uses which would otherwise be lawful, are to be strictly construed in favor of the property owner.[29] It is important to understand that the zoning ordinance itself must be ambiguous before this rule applies: if the ordinance is clear in meaning, then these rules of statutory construction are unnecessary. The zoning board need do nothing except give the ordinance its clear and ordinary meaning. But if the ordinance is unclear as applied in specific circumstances, these guides may help resolve the dispute.

[29] *Burkhalter*, 241 S.W. 2d at 923.

5. Appeals Under State Provisions

It is also important to notice that the zoning board cannot interpret all zoning issues. For example, the board should not have the authority to review decisions based upon statutory (as opposed to local ordinances or regulations) provisions. There are many of these statutes, including: manufactured and modular homes,[30] group homes,[31] scenic highways,[32] agricultural uses,[33] and perhaps most importantly, the Non-Conforming Property Act,[34] which will be addressed in the next section of this chapter. Additionally, the zoning board has no or should have no authority to interpret any other provisions of the Tennessee Public Zoning Enabling Statutes.[35] Otherwise the board could "interpret" the law in such a way as to give itself powers broader than those set by the General Assembly. TENN. CODE ANN. § 13-7-207(1) only provides for board review of decisions made under the terms of an ordinance, not any statutory provision. The same is true of the administrative provisions of its own ordinance: the zoning board cannot

---

[30] TENN. CODE ANN. § 13-24-201 et seq.

[31] TENN. CODE ANN. § 13-24-101 et seq.

[32] TENN. CODE ANN. § 54-17-101 et seq.

[33] TENN. CODE ANN. § 13-7-114 et seq. However, the Court of Appeals has in effect sanctioned review by a zoning board in *Brunetti v Williamson County BZA*, 1999 WL 802725, Tenn. Ct. App., October 07, 1999.

[34] TENN. CODE ANN. § 13-7-208(b) through (l). Although the Court of Appeals has ruled that there is in some circumstances a requirement that the land owner appeal to the zoning board before going to court. See Chapter Two, Section C.8 at page 143.

[35] TENN. CODE ANN. §§ 13-7-101 (counties) and 13-7-201 (municipalities). While some administrative bodies do have the power and authority to interpret statutory provisions, enabling acts, such as the zoning statutes, only permit the local government to adopt ordinances and it is those ordinances (regulations for counties) which are subject to zoning board interpretation, not the state statutes.

and should not by interpretation be able broaden its own power to determine zoning controversies. In fact, there is a very strong argument that the zoning board has only those powers granted under the statute, no more, but no less. In other words, the local government may not restrict the power of the board to less than that given by the General Assembly. We have no cases here in Tennessee concerning this issue but this seems a reasonable conclusion and other state courts have so held.

Of the zoning board's major powers, its authority to interpret the zoning ordinance is the broadest and hardest to reverse on appeal. The board's judgment and discretion in interpreting the substantive provisions of its own ordinance is at its zenith. Most courts are loath to overturn it on appeal.[36]

Procedurally, the appeal to the zoning board comes up with no presumption of correctness; that is, the zoning board makes its own decision on the merits without giving any particular weight to the zoning administrator's (building commissioner or other administrative official) decision.[37] Practically, of course, the board usually wants to uphold the decision of the zoning administrator if possible, although there are certainly exceptions to that rule, particularly if there are perceived political issues involved. Ultimately, interpretations of local zoning ordinances are "best left to local officials, and therefore, the courts are reluctant to second-guess local decisions unless arbitrary, illegal, or capricious."[38]

---

[36] *421 Corp. v. Metro Government*, 36 S.W. 3d 469 (Tenn. App. 2000).

[37] *Robison v Metropolitan Government*, 1992 WL 205268, at *4.

[38] Id.

6. Zoning Board Review of Planning Commission Decisions

One other question which sometimes comes up is the ability of the zoning board to hear appeals from other sources, not just the building official or zoning administrator.[39] Can the board review a decision by the planning commission for example? The statute, TENN. CODE ANN. § 13-7-207 (1) refers to decisions made by the building commissioner or "other administrative official." Technically, the planning commission or other administrative tribunal likely falls outside the scope of that terminology: the planning commission is not an official but is rather a tribunal. On the other hand, let's assume that the planning commission has some conditional use review powers granted to it under the terms of a private statute.[40] If the commission grants the conditional use, the permit must be obtained from a zoning official. Why can't such an appeal then go to the zoning board? Well, mainly, because it does not make much sense. There is simply no reason to have two administrative bodies review that type of application. It makes much more sense to allow a direct appeal to the courts pursuant to the common law writ of certiorari.[41] Notice of course that this does not give the parties the maximum flexibility because on appeal to the courts, the facts as found by the planning commission must be accepted as a matter of law. On appeal to the zoning board, presumably the board would hear the proof all over again and make its own decision concerning the facts of the case and thus its deliberations would have the maximum discretion and flexibility. This simply makes little sense; raising the possibility that a zoning dispute would have to go through two levels of

---

[39] And remember, that just because the statute allows an appeal from the decision of the building commissioner, that it does not allow the zoning board to interpret the building code. See page 74.

[40] Under the Tennessee Public Enabling Legislation, the planning commission has no such powers. See TENN. CODE ANN. § 13-7-207(2) and compare with TENN. CODE ANN. § 13-4-103, or another other section giving power to the planning commission. At most, there is a general grant of power "as necessary" but the zoning board has the power specifically delegated to it.

[41] See Chapter 5.

administrator review before reaching the courts seems very silly indeed. One of the solutions to this problem may very well be to keep the planning commissions out of zoning issues as applied to specific parcels of property.

The Court of Appeals has addressed this issue in the context of the mandatory referral provision of the Tennessee Planning Enabling Statutes.[42] In *Whittemore v. Brentwood Planning Commission*, the project was approved by the Planning Commission and the neighbors appealed to the zoning board. The board concluded that it lacked

---

[42] TENN. CODE ANN. § 13-4-104. This action taken by the Brentwood Planning Commission is called "site plan review" by the Court (and presumably the parties). Understandably, the Court was looking for statutory authority for that type of review and references the mandatory referral provision in the Tennessee Code for lack of better authority. However, I would suggest that there is no authority for site plan review in Tennessee at present and that enactment of a statutory proviso would be of great benefit to land use law in general in Tennessee. Many planning commissions attempt to exercise site plan authority but without a statute to outline the powers of the commission, planning commissions have begun requiring all kinds of inappropriate requirements in order to gain approval. Further, the planning commission tend to wander beyond the scope of authority which is proper on site plan review.

If site plan review is to be engaged in here in Tennessee, without the benefit of specific enabling legislation, then I submit that the zoning board has greater authority in the area. Special exceptions, under TENN. CODE ANN. § 13-7-207 (2) [13-7-109(2)] are nothing more than site plan submissions with the question of use included; that is, the board gets to decide not only if the proposed site is laid out appropriately, but whether the use is appropriate at that location (not ever permitted in site plan review). If the zoning board is specifically delegated that authority with regard to special exceptions, then surely it also should hear site plan review issues as well, and not the planning commission. The recent case of *Roten v. Spring Hill*, 2009 WL 2632778 (Tenn. Ct. App., August 26, 2009) suggests that I am incorrect in my thinking here.

authority to consider the appeal and the Court of Appeals affirmed.[43] There is however, another case decided in 1985 which reaches the opposite conclusion.

In *Stone Man v Rutherford County Regional Planning Commission*,[44] the planning commission appeared to be considering a conditional use/special exception, although the process was referred to as site plan review. Part of the difficulty is the very unusual nature of the Rutherford County ordinance.[45] For example, the Court in the second sentence of the opinion, indicates that the "Planning Commission declined to give its *preliminary approval* to Stone Man's site plan." Preliminary approval? Why should there be preliminary approval on a site plan, or for that matter, a conditional use permit? I suggest that the drafters of the local ordinance have confused site plan with subdivision approval. In fact, at a later point in the opinion, a staff recommendation is quoted as indicating that the plans "met the bare minimum requirements as set forth in the Subdivision Regulations for a site plan for a rock quarry operation." How can the subdivision regulations set such requirements? Subdivision regulations regulate subdivisions, not site plans. Site plan requirements should be set in the zoning ordinance (if such regulations are authorized by Tennessee statute at all, which is

---

[43] 835 S.W. 2d 11, 14 (Tenn. App. 1992). The Court reaches undoubtedly the right conclusion on this issue as it relates to mandatory referral, but does not discuss the conundrum: after the planning commission approves a project, the building official has to issue a building permit or a zoning permit (usually both). Cannot these permits be appealed to the zoning board? Furthermore, what is the interplay of site plan review and the zoning board? Again, without statutory guidance, it is hard to know the answer. Many states will allow the planning commission to issue a variance in site plan review but the planning commission in Tennessee has no authority to issue a variance at all.

[44] *Stone Man v Rutherford County Regional Planning Commission*, 1985 Tenn. App. Lexis 2607.

[45] For a more detailed discussion of its eccentricities, see *Crockett v Rutherford County*, 2002 WL 1677725 (Tenn. Ct. App. July 25, 2002).

questionable). It is surely not clear why multiple submissions should be required for site plan review.[46] Finally, the ordinance specifically allowed the administrative body to decide whether the use would be "detrimental to the district in which it is proposed to be located." This is characteristic special exception/conditional use language, not site plan review. In fact, the matter of whether the location is appropriate should never come up in site plan review. That should already have been decided. This matter should never have been before the planning commission in the first place. The delegation of this power to the planning commission was clearly ultra vires the state enabling legislation. It is doubtful this argument that this application was in reality a conditional use permit was raised.[47] Judge Koch, writing for the Court, did however note that the ordinance was "not written with the clarity one would expect . . ."[48]

In any event, without contrasting the authority of the zoning board to grant conditional use permits, the Court held:

> . . . it appears that the Rutherford County Commission has determined that it would be desirable to use a board to

---

[46] From the author's perspective, it is easy to distinguish site plan review from a special exception/conditional use: if the use is absolutely permitted in the zoning district, then it is a site plan; if the use is conditionally permitted, then it is a special exception/conditional use. It's not that tricky. Both forms of review I submit should be considered by the zoning board until some real enabling legislation is passed authorizing the planning commission to consider site plan review. But site plan review should not involve discretionary consideration of whether the use is permitted at that location. Site plan review is nothing more than a fancy way of granting a building permit and the discretion involved should be just as limited.

[47] There can be many reasons for such a strategic decision. For example, the developer may have felt that it was easier to get approval from the Planning Commission than from the Zoning Board.

[48] *Stone Man v Rutherford County Regional Planning Commission*, 1985 Tenn. App. Lexis 2607.

> review the requests for approval to operate rock quarries and other similar businesses. To the extent that this board is applying and administering local land use restrictions enacted pursuant to TENN. CODE ANN. § 13-7-101 et seq.,[49] its actions are reviewable by the Rutherford County Board of Zoning Appeals.

The Court specifically held that the fact that the board happened to be the planning commission was not important. The commission was simply serving as a county decision-maker.[50] But that misses the real issue: isn't the zoning board expressly given jurisdiction over that power by the Tennessee General Assembly under § 13-7-207(2)? If so, how can the local government violate state law with impunity?

Nevertheless, if the planning commission is acting under the zoning law, then its decision can be appealed to the zoning board, according to *Stone Man*. If the decision is under mandatory referral or presumably some other *planning* statutory provision, then there is no appeal to the zoning board, according to *Whittemore*. If we step back for a second, does this make any real sense? Again, I submit that the confusion comes about as a result of the use of site plan review which is not authorized under Tennessee law. If it is going to be employed, either there should be new enabling legislation or it should be delegated solely to the zoning board, which at least has a statutory basis for such review and a long history of reviewing similar applications by way of conditional use/special exceptions.[51]

---

[49] It is not clear that the planning commission was applying regulations adopted pursuant to this provision; if the regulations were found in the subdivision regulations, then those were adopted under an entirely different set of statutory authority.

[50] Id.

[51] Personally, I believe site plan review is a needed planning tool, but the confusion and lack of clear guidelines suggest that enabling legislation is necessary for that tool to function properly.

C. Non-Conforming Properties

1. Generally

Nonconforming properties constitute an area of Tennessee zoning law where one might say that a property owner's rights have truly vested.[52] A non-conforming property may be nonconforming for many different reasons. Possibly the most well-known type of nonconforming property involves a nonconforming use. Nonconforming uses are, however, not the only type of nonconforming property. In fact, properties may be nonconforming by virtue of violations of the bulk regulations, parking regulations, or any other type of regulation expressed in a zoning ordinance.[53] It is customary at least in some

---

[52] Under certain very limited circumstances, equitable estoppel might be available to prevent a local government from enforcing its zoning regulations against a property owner where the owner has changed his position based upon the issuance of a building permit. For example, if the zoning district was changed after substantial work on the development had begun. See *Howe Realty v City of Nashville*, 114 SW 2d 904, 906 (Tenn. 1940).

[53] In *Jacks v. City of Millington Bd. of Zoning Appeals,* 2009 WL 37599 (Tenn. Ct. App. 2009), the Court commented on exactly this issue and quoted E. C. "Bud" Yokley's treatise:

> Few sources, however, disclose what these self-evident differences [between nonconforming and noncomplying properties] are. One treatise explains that
>
> > [w]hile the term "nonconforming use" is universally and generically used, it should be noted that while the use itself – residential, commercial, industrial – may conform to the zoning district, an existing structure or even a parcel of raw land may not conform to development regulations, for example, setbacks, minimum lot size or frontage requirements and therefore be

Tennessee communities, to consider these other types of nonconforming properties to be what is called "noncomplying."

Furthermore, although many zoning ordinances distinguish between nonconforming uses and noncomplying structures or lots, the Tennessee Non-Conforming Property Act, TENN. CODE ANN. § 13-7-208 makes no such distinction. As a result, to the extent that the Non-Conforming Property Act applies to a particular parcel of property,[54] any treatment by a zoning ordinance which makes it more difficult for a property which has a nonconforming aspect may very well be unlawful.[55] Let's begin however with a few general observations concerning the most well-known type of nonconformity, nonconforming uses.

The "generally accepted significance of the word is pre-existing lawful uses which become unlawful only by the enactment of a zoning law and are therefore permitted to continue."[56] Another simple definition of the term is a use which lawfully pre-exists the enactment

---

"nonconforming."

E.C. Yokley, Zoning Law and Practice, 22-1 n. 1 (Lexis Nexis 2003).

[54] Naturally, in order to qualify, the property must have some nonconforming aspect. In addition, there is the pesky question, covered later in this chapter, concerning whether the Tennessee Non-Conforming Property Act applies to properties outside of municipalities. As I will discuss a little later, current treatment by the courts appears to conclude now that the Non-Conforming Property Act does apply to County zoning even though given the placement of the Act in the Tennessee code, it would appear to apply solely to municipal forms of government. The issue does not even get argued anymore.

[55] Local regulation of this type may be viewed as ultra vires the enabling legislation.

[56] *Smith v. City of Forest Hills*, Slip Opinion (Tenn. Ct. App. 1985).

of the applicable zoning ordinance.[57] Typically, when a zoning ordinance is passed, especially a new comprehensive zoning ordinance, there are a significant number of properties which are zoned in a manner inconsistent with the current use. For example, there may be a gasoline service station in an area which is predominantly residential and, as a result, the city zones it as residential. The gasoline service station would not be permitted to build in the residential district if it were to apply for a permit after the effective date of the ordinance. However, since it already pre-exists the enactment of the ordinance, such uses are generally permitted to continue.

The Standard State Zoning Enabling Act [58] did not even mention non-conforming uses. This was not because the blue ribbon committee who put the act together failed to think about it. The area was thought to be controversial and difficult to deal with. They preferred, instead, to allow the various states to address these difficulties on their own.

---

[57] And recently the Court of Appeals borrowed from Anderson's treatise:

> A nonconforming use is '[a] use which lawfully existed prior to the enactment of a zoning ordinance, and which is maintained after the effective date of the ordinance, although it does not comply with the zoning restrictions applicable to the district in which it is situated' citing 1 Kenneth H. Young, Anderson's American Law of Zoning § 6.01, 481-482 (4h ed. 1996 & Supp.2008)

Smith County Regional Planning Comm'n v. Hiwassee Village Mobile Home Park, LLC 2008 WL 3343001, 5 (Tenn.Ct.App.,2008)

[58] The Tennessee Public Zoning Enabling Statutes did not address non-conforming properties as originally adopted. Up until the amendments in 2004, TENN. CODE ANN. § 13-7-208 did not specifically refer to "non-conforming" uses or properties, although the 1973 amendments put in place the non-conforming property provisions.

Most states permitted nonconforming uses to continue. The general thought was there was a constitutional right to continue the nonconforming use and that to immediately declare the use invalid and unlawful would have worked a taking of the property such that the courts would not have upheld those zoning provisions. Certainly, *Euclid v Ambler Realty*,[59] and the early state court cases would probably have been much less anxious to sustain a zoning provision which immediately required a property owner who had been using his property for commercial purposes to immediately change it to residential as a result of the enactment of the zoning ordinance. In fact, such a provision might have tipped the scales, which were fairly close to begin with, against the constitutionality of the entirety of the zoning system. As a result, the cities generally did not opt for that route.

Over the years, however, it became clear that conforming uses do not gradually disappear as the leading authorities originally thought.[60] Ed Bassett,[61] for example, felt that there would be a natural winnowing away of the properties made nonconforming by the enactment of the zoning ordinance.[62] This proved to be incorrect.[63]

In fact, the system seemed to work the opposite way. Nonconforming properties became mini-monopolies. If you operated the only gasoline service station in an otherwise totally residential area, most of the residents would probably use your gasoline station. Your gasoline service station probably became more valuable as a result of

---

[59] 272 U.S. 365 (1926).

[60] Mandelker, *Land Use Law* (5th ed. 2003) § 5.68.

[61] Mr. Bassett is considered the "father of modern zoning" in the United States thanks to his pioneering work in New York City in the early part of the 20th Century. See Mandelker, Payne, Salsich and Stroud, *Planning and Control of Land Development: Cases and Materials*, 6th ed., 2005 at 209.

[62] E. Bassett, Zoning (rev.ed. 1940) at 113.

[63] Mandelker, *Land Use Law* (5th ed. 2003) § 5.68.

the zoning ordinance and its nonconforming status than it ever was before. After all, no new gasoline service stations could move into that general vicinity. The zoning ordinance in effect made the value of the property increase, possibly significantly. As a result, the incentives were to keep the gasoline service station in business rather than to allow it to gradually die out.

Today, local zoning ordinances allow the nonconforming property to remain, but limit expansion, often prohibiting any expansion at all, in an effort to discourage the continue use of the property. Reconstruction of buildings on the property, whether damaged by natural causes (storm damage) or by fire, is also generally impermissible. Certainly, planned demolition and reconstruction is ordinarily not permitted. We will discuss these factors further below.

But zoning ordinances themselves are not the only source of complexity in this area of the law. Because in Tennessee, while the local zoning ordinance may offer some protection, at the state level, there is a level of super protection for commercial and industrial nonconforming properties.

2. The Tennessee Non-Conforming Property Act

Here, in Tennessee, things were even more desperate than in many other states. The General Assembly amended the zoning enabling legislation[64] in 1973 to specifically provide that a non-conforming property might continue if it is a business, commercial, or industrial use.[65] Not only that, but the legislation specifically provides that the

---

[64] TENN. CODE ANN. § 13-7-208 was amended by adding several additional sections. As originally passed in 1935, § 208 only provided for suits to enforce the zoning ordinance; with the 1973 changes, the statute became a defense against the enforcement of zoning provisions for non-conforming properties.

[65] TENN. CODE ANN. § 13-7-208(b) - (l); see *Rives v City of Clarksville*, 618 S.W.2d 502 (Tenn. App. 1981). Remember that with any other use, residential most appreciably, the local zoning ordinance

non-conforming use may legally increase in size so long as additional property is not added.[66] This leaves cities with very little protection from non-conforming uses. There is little that can be done to terminate a non-conforming use after the adoption of a zoning ordinance, except possibly to make it conforming and regulate it in that fashion. Even more significantly and unlike most local zoning ordinances, the statute allows the nonconforming business to entirely destroy its current facilities and rebuild entirely new facilities, expanding if need be, virtually right up to the very boundaries of the property.[67] This effectively removes any incentive for the business owner to move to a conforming property. The one limitation is that it only applies to commercial and industrial properties.

Let's take a detailed look at one of the sections of the statute. Possibly the most significant section is TENN. CODE .ANN. § 13-7-208 (d) which applies to the destruction and reconstruction of buildings on non-conforming properties.[68] That section provides:

> Industrial, commercial, or other business establishments in operation and permitted to operate under zoning regulations or exceptions thereto immediately preceding a change in zoning shall be allowed to destroy present facilities and reconstruct new facilities necessary to the conduct of such industry or business subsequent to the zoning change; provided, that no destruction and re-building shall occur which shall act to change the use classification of the land as classified under any zoning

---

controls. Typically, the non-conforming house can remain but cannot expand. If damaged, usually the property must be brought into compliance with the current zoning regulations.

[66] See TENN. CODE ANN. § 13-7-208(c).

[67] See TENN. CODE ANN. § 13-7-208(d).

[68] TENN. CODE ANN. § 13-7-208 (b) allows the continuation of nonconforming properties while § 208 (c) allows the expansion of nonconforming properties.

> regulations or exceptions thereto in effect immediately prior to or subsequent to a change in the zoning of the land area on which such industry or business is located. No building permit or like permission for demolition, construction or landscaping shall be denied to an industry or business seeking to destroy and reconstruct facilities necessary to the continued conduct of the activities of that industry or business, where such conduct was permitted prior to a change in zoning; provided, that there is a reasonable amount of space for such expansion on the property owned by such as situated within the area which is affected by the change in zoning so as to avoid nuisances to adjoining landowners. No building permit or like permission for demolition, construction or landscaping shall be denied to an industry or business seeking to destroy and reconstruct facilities necessary to the continued conduct of the activities of that industry or business, where such conduct was permitted prior to a change in zoning; provided, that there is a reasonable amount of space for such expansion on the property owned by such industry or business situated within the area which is affected by the change in zoning, so as to avoid nuisances to adjoining landowners.

Subsection (e) adds the requirement that "the provisions of subsections (b)-(d) apply only to land owned and in use by such affected business, and do not operate to permit expansion of an existing industry or business through the acquisition of additional land." We will explore most of the other sections as we proceed with our overview of subsection (d).

It is, perhaps best to review this statutory provision piece by piece. The first sentence, broken down into its component parts, says:

(1) Industrial, commercial, or other business establishments

(2) in operation and permitted to operate under zoning regulations or exceptions thereto immediately preceding a change in zoning

(3) shall be allowed to destroy present facilities and reconstruct new facilities

(4) necessary to the conduct of such industry or business subsequent to the zoning change;

(5) provided, that no destruction and re-building shall occur which shall act to change the use classification of the land as classified under any zoning regulations or exceptions thereto in effect immediately prior to or subsequent to a change in the zoning of the land area on which such industry or business is located.

(6) No building permit or like permission for demolition, construction or landscaping shall be denied to an industry or business seeking to destroy and reconstruct facilities necessary to the continued conduct of the activities of that industry or business, where such conduct was permitted prior to a change in zoning;

(7) provided, that there is a reasonable amount of space for such expansion on the property owned by such industry or business situated within the area which is affected by the change in zoning, so as to avoid nuisances to adjoining landowners.

(8) apply only to land owned and in use and do not permit expansion of an existing business through the acquisition of additional land.

(a) Analysis of subsection (d)

Let's take the statute section by section to review its meaning and effect. We will confine our analysis to subsection (d) although subsection (c), which applies only to expansion of the nonconforming aspect of the property, is similar. The most important difference is the requirement under subsection (d) that the new facilities to be reconstructed be necessary to the conduct of the business. This business necessity requirement under (d) is sometimes overlooked by the owner of the nonconforming property but it is important to prove.

(1) Industrial, commercial or other business establishments

Obviously, the first requirement is that the nonconforming property must be utilized for industrial, commercial, or some other business operation. This appears to rule out residential uses, but it is not clear how to interpret the phrase "commercial or other business establishments." There are however several interesting cases discussing whether TENN. CODE ANN. § 13-7-208 applies to certain types of residential uses under certain types of circumstances, usually where the owner is leasing to a number of residential users. Apartments and mobile home parks can be subject to this interpretation.

In, 1987, the Middle Section Court of Appeals ruled that a mobile home park was a residential use and thus not subject to the protection of the statute. The Franklin Zoning Ordinance prohibited the operation of a "trailer court" except for non-conforming uses which were allowed to continue for 25 years. In 1985, the owners destroyed two of seventy units, added to the foundation of one and constructed a new unit on that foundation. It was about twice the size of the original demolished unit. They could not get a permit from the City; they appealed to the Board of Zoning Appeals which denied the permit; the Chancery Court of Williamson and the Court of Appeals for the Middle Section[69] (over the dissent of Ben Cantrell) affirmed the decision of the Board of Zoning Appeals.

The owners argued that the "trailer court" was a business establishment within the meaning of the statute and protected. The majority of the Court held:[70]

---

[69] *Clouse v Cook*, 1987 WL 9727 (Tenn. Ct. App. April 24, 1987)(perm app granted Nov 23, 1987).

[70] At *2.

> The test for classifying property under zoning ordinances is not the purpose for which the property is owned; it is the use made by the persons actually occupying the property. The occupiers, or tenants, of the plaintiffs' property use the property as residences. The owners (plaintiffs) rent the property for residential use.

The Court wryly noted that another construction of the statute would mean that a single family residence leased out would become a commercial use and that in fact the permit application by the plaintiffs was for a residential use.

In dissent, Judge Ben Cantrell argued that given the nature of the business, it would be more appropriate to consider it a commercial operation or a business establishment such that it would be protected by the provisions of the Non-Conforming Property Act. Judge Cantrell took an expansive view of the use of the property and mentions that the property would be taxed as commercial. At least in part, Judge Cantrell relied on fairness: taxing the use at commercial rates but not permitting expansion seemed unfair. [71]

Somewhat unusually, the case was accepted for review [72] by the Tennessee Supreme Court. The Supreme Court reversed, ruling that Judge Cantrell below had been correct; the Non-Conforming Property Act did protect the mobile home park. The Supreme Court felt that the occupants of the mobile home park were more realistically classified as customers of the trailer court, rather than occupants of residences. That

---

[71] At *3.

[72] Few zoning cases are accepted for review by the Tennessee Supreme Court. Ultimately, the Tennessee Court of Appeals hears a significant number of land use cases and has a very important impact on the way the law is applied. The compositions of the Supreme Court has changed since 2004 and the new Justices may be more willing to hear zoning and land use issues.

is, they saw the operation of the trailer court as more a commercial enterprise, than residential.[73]

> The bottom line is that the 'occupants' of the units are more realistically classified as customers of a trailer court operation than occupants of 'residences.' Defendants admit, and it is beyond question, that plaintiffs are engaged in a 'business' in the operation of the trailer park. In addition, plaintiffs have been permitted to operate the trailer court from the date of annexation to July 1985 as a nonconforming use, entitled to the benefit of Franklin Ordinance 11-205. If the 'use' was residential at the date of annexation, the City could have and should have, under its ordinances, terminated the operation immediately. We find from the undisputed facts in this record that the demolition of two units and the construction of a new single unit in their place, of the same type, except for size, did not change the use classification of the land, within the meaning of TENN. CODE ANN. § 13-7- 208(d) and plaintiffs are entitled to the benefits of Franklin Ordinance 11-205 and TENN. CODE ANN. § 13-7-208.

Given the difficulty of dealing with non-conforming uses at the local government level, this Supreme Court decision is unfortunate. Cities and counties should be given a fairly broad brush with which to paint nonconforming uses; the courts should interpret the nonconforming statute reasonably narrowly so as to avoid tying up the ability of the city to deal with nonconforming uses in reasonable ways.

In 2008, the Tennessee Court of Appeals revisited this issue. In *Smith County Reg. Planning Commission v Hiwassee Village Mobile Home Park*,[74] an unkempt mobile home park argued, based at least in part on *Clouse*, that is was protected by the statute. Notwithstanding

---

[73] 1988 WL 34834 at *2.

[74] 2008 WL 3343001 (Tenn. Ct. App. Aug. 11, 2008; perm. app. granted May 4, 2009).

the Supreme Court decision in *Clouse*, the Court of Appeals found that the mobile home park was not covered by the state statute. [75]

> The Supreme Court designated its opinion in *Clouse* as not for publication and not for citation . . . Based upon this designation, we do not consider that opinion to have precedential value beyond its application to the parties in that case.

Ordinarily, this might seem a bit unusual: the Court of Appeals essentially ignoring a Supreme Court decision which is pretty close to being right on point. In fact, the Court of Appeals relies on several of its own opinions, also unpublished (but not designated as not for publication), to reach its conclusion. However, the decision may not be that unusual after all: the attorney for the city in *Clouse* was Connie Clark, now Justice Clark on the Tennessee Supreme Court. It seems a safe bet that Justice Clark views this particular issue from the perspective of the local government. Not just because of her former representation, but because it is the best analysis of the statute. As Judge Bennett said for the Court of Appeals:[76]

> Because the mobile home park is or was used for human habitation, the logical conclusion based upon the cases cited above is that it should be considered a residential use. This conclusion comports with the general inclination of courts in other jurisdictions to classify mobile home parks as residential . . .

But then, what about other multi-family residential uses (apartments, condominiums, and others)? Not surprisingly, those get the same analysis and properly so. We have a couple of cases in Tennessee: *Bramblett v Coffee County Planning Commission*, [77] and *City*

---

[75] At *6.

[76] At * 6.

[77] 2007 WL 187894 (Tenn.Ct.App. Jan. 24, 2007).

of Red Bank v Phillips.[78] Then Judge Koch wrote the *Bramblett* opinion and held:[79]

> The Brambletts' reliance on TENN.CODE ANN. § 13-7-208, which the trial court apparently accepted, is misplaced. By its plain language, the statute protects only "industrial, commercial or business establishment[s]. In zoning parlance, use of real property for human habitation is generally classified as "residential," regardless of whether someone profits from it. Zoning laws typically employ terms such as "commercial," "industrial," and "business" in contradistinction to the term "residential."

Judge Koch concluded:[80]

> Although the Brambletts are not themselves living on the second tract, their use of it is indisputably residential in character. The Brambletts are not running a factory there, nor are they operating a grocery store or shipping facility. Instead, they are leasing out the two sides of the duplex to individuals and families for human habitation. The record on appeal confirms that much time has elapsed since this tract was used as the location of an "industrial, commercial or business establishment" within the meaning of the statute, except possibly when there was a small tractor repair shop on the property. TENN. CODE ANN. § 13-7-208(b)(1). Accordingly, TENN. CODE ANN. § 13-7-208 confers no grandfathering protection on the Brambletts with respect to the second tract.

---

[78] 2007 WL 4460223 (Tenn. Ct. App. Dec. 20, 2007).

[79] *Bramblett* at *9.

[80] Id.

This case may further explain *Hiwassee*: Judge Koch is of course now also on the Tennessee Supreme Court.[81] The *City of Red Bank* case follows the *Bramblett* analysis.

There are a number of other interesting uses which do not easily fit within the description of protected properties under the statute. It would seem that a church would not be an industrial, commercial, or other business establishment, yet, if it operates an elementary or high school, for which it charges a fee, is that a business establishment? A private school might be considered a business; a day care facility might fit the same description. It is sometimes tempting to ask if the "business" is for-profit, but even if it is not, does that change its land use characteristics? Suppose a church ran a grocery store, but at a loss, as a community service: is that any less a business entity? One would think not.[82] Assuming that the church is a legitimate religious institution, truly interested in distributing food but using a super market (commercial) distribution model, the impact on the surrounding land uses would be the same as or very similar to a regular supermarket. These types of community services often cause difficulty in interpretation but likely are protected by the statute.

Finally, assume that the nonconforming aspect of the property is a bulk regulation, not a use regulation. For example, a sign is too high, or a building bigger than permitted by the floor area ratio. Does the statute apply under those circumstances? The answer is clearly yes. In

---

[81] By the way, the fact that the state statute does not apply does not mean that the property is not legally non-conforming; in both *Bramblett* and *Hiwassee*, the courts reviewed the local ordinance to make a final decision. The use can certainly be legally non-conforming under the local ordinance (but not the state statute) and entitled to protection thereby. However, most local ordinances do not allow expansion of the non-conforming use and do not allow demolition and reconstruction.

[82] *City of Chattanooga v. Muse*, Slip Opinion, Tenn. App. 1985 (owner of grocery store after conviction of violation of zoning regulations, attempts to posture as a non-profit activity, including "donations" for goods in the store).

National Auto/Truck Stops v. Williamson County[83] the Court of Appeals held subsection (d) applicable to a sign under those circumstances.[84]

(2) in operation and permitted to operate

The next interesting phrase, section 2 above, is the language "in operation and permitted to operate." This applies in two ways: first, was the property ever nonconforming: did it actually operate as a nonconforming property? Second, was it still in operation at the time of the zoning change?[85]

In *Dickson County v Jennette,*[86] the issue was whether the nonconforming use of the property had ever begun.

> The evidence simply does not support a finding that there was such an industrial, commercial or business establishment in operation. Certainly, Appellants intended such an operation for the future and were working toward the same. However, courts uniformly agree that "[m]ere preparation for use of property before adoption of a zoning ordinance is not enough to show a devotion of the property to that use" in order to show a pre-existing nonconforming use.

Before the zoning change,[87]

---

[83] 2001 WL 434860 (Tenn. Ct. App. 2001).

[84] See additional discussion of this case at page 124.

[85] This issue however usually comes up in the context of abandonment or discontinuation.

[86] 2000 WL 1121550, at *7 (Tenn. Ct. App. Aug. 9, 2000).

[87] Id.

> Appellants had only blasted from the property on two occasions, and they had only made one sale of rock, seven truck loads, from the property. While there is some ambiguity, the overwhelming sense from the testimony of Clyde, Andy and Owen Jennette is that the two blasts were done to obtain rock to build a road and bridge on the property in order to prepare it for future commercial use. Indeed, until March of 1989, Appellants were under an agreement with Rogers Group which provided that they would not themselves operate or allow any other person to operate "any mining or quarrying business" including the exploration, examination, mining, quarrying, excavating, preparing for market, storing, marketing and removing from the property all the rock, stone, soil, sand and gravel existing upon or under the surface of the property.

Furthermore, the only equipment onsite was blasting rock and constructing the road. The owners themselves said they were "planning to start operations."[88]

> One of the more understandable and easily applied tests for determining whether there is enough of a use to merit continuation as a nonconforming use is articulated as follows: "an existing use should mean the utilization of the premises so that they may be known in the neighborhood as being employed for a given purpose." From the evidence, not even Appellants themselves considered that there was a quarry business in operation on their property as of October 1988.

The Court noted that others in the area also did not consider the operation a quarry and concluded that the operation was not protected by the statute because it was not "in operation" at the time of the adoption of the zoning ordinance.

Capps v Metro Nashville is similar: the operator of an adult entertainment establishment attempted to open but before the building

[88] Id at *8.

could be redesigned and opened, a local charity contended successfully that it was a church and that the building was too close under the Metro ordinance. Since the adult entertainment establishment was never operational, the statute did not apply.[89]

(3) destroy present facilities and reconstruct new

This is the key part of this subsection of the statute. The owner can tear down the current operating facilities and rebuild new facilities. Most local ordinances would not permit this or any expansion of the nonconforming use (under this subsection (d) or under subsection (c)). This statute works a total change in the way that nonconforming properties are eliminated. Discouraging the continued operation by preventing expansion and reconstruction is no longer a viable approach. That type of disincentive only works in light of the statute if the owner needs more property; the statute does not allow expansion onto property not owned at the time the zoning ordinance was established or amended.[90]

But how does this section relate to subsection (c) which allows the nonconforming property to expand. If the nonconforming property is made up of several structures, is the addition of a new structure an expansion under subsection (c) or is it rebuilding under subsection (d)? Does it matter if there was already a building on site that performed the function of the new building? For example, if American Widgets Company stored its widgets in Building A, had an office in Building B, and a manufacturing facility in Building C, is the construction of a new Building D an expansion or reconstruction if Building D serves as a new and bigger storage facility? Does it matter if the original storage facility, Building A, is converted to use as a recycling center for the property, a

---

[89] Id.

[90] TENN. CODE ANN. § 13-7-208 (e) provides: "The[se] provisions . . . apply only to land owned and in use by such affected business, and do not operate to permit expansion of an existing industry or business through the acquisition of additional land."

new but related use entirely? Has the storage facility been rebuilt under subsection (d), or has the nonconforming property simply been expanded under subsection (c)?

Further, does subsection (i) apply? That section reads:

> Notwithstanding the provisions of subsection (d), any structure rebuilt on the site must conform to the provisions of the existing zoning regulations as to setbacks, height, bulk, or requirements as to the physical location of a structure upon the site, provided that this subsection (i) shall not apply to off-site signs.

The reference to subsection (d) in the first clause suggests that if the new construction is part of an expansion under subsection (c) that (i) does not apply, but that if the facilities are entirely replaced under section (d) that (i) requires compliance with the bulk regulations of the zoning ordinance. Suppose the only aspect of the property which was nonconforming was the size of location of a building: does the statute not allow destruction and reconstruction? The only suggestion I can make here is that to the extent that there is no destruction of "present facilities" that the new construction is an expansion under (c), and not reconstruction under (d). However, if American Widgets takes down two buildings and builds three, then it seems that two of the new buildings could be considered reconstruction and would have to comply with the bulk regulations. The third building would be an expansion, and could be placed anywhere. I'm not sure that this interpretation makes much sense however; perhaps the trouble is with the statute, not with the interpretation.

Yet another problem: what are "bulk, or requirements as to the physical location of a structure?" Are floor area ratios, green space requirements, and impervious surface ratios covered by section (i)? If so, that presents new problems. Suppose the ISR is rather high, 85% for example. Suppose further that impervious surfaces already cover 50% of the property. Once again, American Widgets wants to build 3 new buildings, but tear down two old ones. If my suggestion in the previous paragraph was adopted, and two of the building had to comply with the ISR, then they could not be built because American Widgets already is above the permitted ratio. In effect, American Widgets under that interpretation would not be able to reconstruct the two building torn down. This would put a premium on rehabilitation of older structures.

Perhaps none of this is the correct interpretation of the statute: take look at subsection (g)(4) of the statute. Subsection (g) allows for a 30 month discontinuation period; but subsection (4)[91] states in part:

> the restrictions of subsections (g) and (i) shall only apply if the property owner intentionally and voluntarily abandons the nonconforming use of the property. In any contested matter on the use of such property, the government has the burden of proving an overt act of abandonment in such matter.

Subsection (i) is quoted on the previous page. Does this section (g)(4) mean that the bulk regulations (however broadly that term should be construed) are applicable only if the owner has voluntarily abandoned the use? Otherwise, even under § (d) the bulk regulations don't apply? If so, why have § (i) in the first place? The statute is difficult to understand in its current form; I must emphasize that no one knows the answers to these questions right now. They can be thorny problems.[92]

Perhaps another way of looking at the statute as amended is to think of it now as only effecting nonconforming uses, and that other aspects of nonconforming properties (the bulk regulations) are no longer protected by the statute. Without a conscious decision by the General

---

[91] As I have explained previously, this subsection (g)(4) appears to be miscodified; the last two sentences as passed appear to stand on their own and not as a part of subsection (g)(4).

[92] Judge Koch mentions subsection (i) in the *Bramblett* decision but only in passing. Its not clear that he considered the impact of § (g)(4) on § (i). The quote from *Bramblett* is: "Any new or rebuilt structure must, however, comply with the restrictions of the later enacted zoning law regarding setbacks, height, bulk, and other requirements relating to the physical location of structures on the site." *Bramblett* at *8.

Assembly to forego such protection, perhaps that is to broad a construction of the current statute.

(4) necessary to the conduct of such industry or business

Under section (d), in order to tear down the present facilities and reconstruct new ones, the owner must show that the new facilities are"necessary to the conduct of the business."[93] Often this issue is not contested; the necessity is often readily apparent. In cases where it is not apparent, the question remains what is a business necessity for the purposes of the statute and how does the owner/occupier go about proving it?

In *Outdoor West of Tennessee, Inc. v. City of Johnson City*,[94] a sign company argued that the size of most billboards was uniform and that 11 of its signs in the city were of insufficient size to accommodate prevailing industry standards. The company also demonstrated that it could not find new sites and was losing old ones by virtue of property sales and that finally, a significant portion of its business would soon be lost for unrelated reasons but reinforced the need for upgrades to remain competitive. The Court accepted these reasons as sufficient.

In *Alexander Ford-Mercury, Inc. v. City of Franklin*,[95] the car dealership asked to replace a sign with a new sign which was necessary because the parent company (Ford Motor) had adopted a new logo and required its franchisees to conform their signs with the national logo. The dealership was denied a permit because the new proposed sign, while smaller than the existing sign, was larger than the sign

---

[93] Notice that the business necessity requirement does not appear in section (c) of the ordinance. If the owner is expanding, but not tearing down and rebuilding, then there is no need to demonstrate business necessity.

[94] 39 S.W.3d 131 (Tenn. Ct. App. 2000).

[95] 2005 WL 549163 (Tenn. Ct. App. 2005).

regulations permitted (50 square feet). The dealership went to the zoning board which denied relief and then to court.

There is little discussion in this of several interesting issues: first, as I argue elsewhere in this book,[96] the zoning board should not be making these decisions about a state statute; there should be original jurisdiction in the state trial courts. Second, even if the case must go to the zoning board first, the appeal should be by the statutory law writ of certiorari: the trial judge should hear these cases de novo. These nonconforming properties are in the nature of property rights and the judiciary is constitutionally required to make decisions concerning issues which impact such rights.[97] The final paragraph of the decision makes clear how important this is:

> The plaintiff had the burden of proving that the reconstruction of the sign was necessary to the continued conduct of its business. This is a heavy burden to show that the administrative action was arbitrary or illegal. *McCallen v. City of Memphis*, 786 S.W.2d 633 (Tenn. 1990). Just how heavy the burden is may be found in the statement 'if there is any possible means' to uphold a zoning decision, whether it be legislative or administrative, the court is bound to do so.
>
> The judgment is affirmed at the costs of the appellant.

Clearly, the Court of Appeals deferred to the zoning board's decision: that seems inappropriate. The courts should protect the property right if there is a reasonable grounds to do so. This is one area where deference to the administrative body seems ill advised.[98]

---

[96] See page 85.

[97] See page 389.

[98] On the other hand, the trial court did indicate that the testimony of the owner's expert was "not meaningful," and perhaps the trial judge would have ruled the same way even if considered de novo.

My question concerning this case is more basic: why wasn't the fact that the parent company required the change a "business necessity." Could the company have continued its association with Ford without the changing the logo? I don't know the answer, but if not, doesn't that render the logo change "necessary for the conduct of the business?" There is no discussion of this issue in the case.

This is all the more remarkable because the proposed sign was to be smaller than the existing sign. If the sign was to be bigger, then some additional proof of business necessity may be appropriate, but if the sign is only being changed out for a different logo, or because the sign has become older and is structurally suspect or for any number of other reasons, then proof of business necessity doesn't seem that important. Think about it this way: the sign (or other structure) wouldn't be replaced at all if the business didn't think it worthwhile. Logo changes occur frequently; aren't those within the ambit of the statute without any other proof?

In addition, the differing treatment of on-site and off-site signs deserves some consideration. From a land use standpoint, that is, the impact of the signs on the surrounding land uses, the two are the same. If you have a 50 foot tall standard with a 200 square foot sign face, what difference does it make to the next door neighbor. Both signs advertising on site business and off-site business have an equal impact. Why does an off-site sign get an advantage under the terms of the statue? Is there any reason for the different treatment? [99] Can the different treatment be justified? It would seems somewhat difficult to me.

In *Alexander*, the city demonstrated that fourteen other dealerships in Franklin had smaller signs advertising their businesses, implying I suppose that the smaller signs were sufficient. Several points are relevant here: first, the implication is of course not accurate. We don't know what the other businesses think about the smaller signs. They may well have wanted larger signs but couldn't get them under the terms of the zoning ordinance. Second, because the proof came in at the zoning board level, there was no discovery and likely this was trial by

---

[99] I mean, other than the fact that the billboard lobby is very effective.

ambush. The business probably had no notice of the proof: this is the antithesis of modern litigation: it is also another reason why these cases should be heard de novo before the trial judge.

The *Alexander* case seems somewhat unsatisfactory. What does the business need to show? We still don't know although the required logo change is evidently no enough. But we can certainly surmise that the biggest problem for these nonconforming businesses is the deterioration of the business facilities and that the General Assembly was aware of those problems. I would suggest that "business necessity" need not be a stringent standard. For one thing, subsection (c) allows an expansion without any such showing. To the extent that "business necessity" is an arduous standard, businesses are simply encouraged to "expand" rather than destroy and rebuild. For example, suppose the sign fact in *Alexander* changed to advertise specials on new cars and another sign was built to put up the new logo required by Ford. That is clearly under subsection (c) and no business necessity need by shown. Now we have more signage.

I would suggest that so long as the reconstructed facilities are an important component of the business activities, then the test has been met. The business does not need to show that it will go out of business unless the new facilities are permitted. I suggest that this simple test is appropriate because of the practical effect of subsection (c). So long as the business can simply expand, the prudent business will simply add on without taking the existing facilities down. The statute should be construed to minimize the unnecessary continuation of facilities which may now be obsolete or antiquated.

Furthermore, contrast this with adding an entirely new although certainly related business activity on the site under subsection (c). In *BMC Enterprises v City of Lebanon*,[100] the a funeral home wanted to add a crematory but was in the wrong zoning district. The business was nonconforming under the state statute however and ultimately, the Court of Appeals held that this was a permitted expansion. Surely, the standard for "business necessity" under subsection (d) should keep in mind what the business may be able to do without a similar showing

[100] 273 SW 3d 619 (Tenn. Ct. App. 2008).

under the subsection (c). Business necessity can be and should be defined to allow a business to develop facilities to effectively increase the business and its profits; it does not need to be defined in terms of only keeping current customers and preventing a decrease in its business.

(5) provided there is no change in the use

The use of the property may not change. This is perhaps the one constant in all of nonconforming property concepts: the use must remain basically the same and a change of any significance will forfeit the nonconforming status. The statute itself is a little imprecise in its language, but that certainly seems to be the intent.[101]

There are several cases decided under the statutory terms. In *Lafferty v Winchester*, [102] a bed and breakfast applied to expand the use of the property but was denied by the zoning board. The Court of Appeals affirmed, finding that the business had illegally expanded well beyond the original use. [103]

> Property owners whose property qualifies as a nonconforming use under TENN. CODE ANN. § 13-7-208(b) may expand their business operations or may even reconstruct their business premises, as long as they continue to be engaged in the same business that they were engaged in when the zoning ordinance was passed. However, these provisions do not permit an established nonconforming use to be changed to some other nonconforming use.

---

[101] The statute provides in part: "no destruction and rebuilding shall occur which shall act to change the use classification of the land as classified under any zoning regulations or exceptions thereto in effect immediately prior to or subsequent to a change in the zoning of the land area on which such industry or business is located."

[102] 46 S .W.3d 752 (Tenn. Ct. App. 2000).

[103] Id at 758.

The Court summarized the evidence at the board hearing, saying the board

> knew that the Laffertys' property was in an area zoned residential and that the commercial use of their property as a bed and breakfast had been grandfathered in as a nonconforming use. The Board also knew about the first addition to the inn and that the Laffertys had misrepresented that the addition was nothing more than added storage space when, in fact, it was intended to be used for a bar called the Green Door Pub. At the hearing, the Board learned that the Laffertys regularly held dances at the Green Door Pub for which they imposed a cover charge. The Board also learned that the Laffertys had actually started to build another large addition to expand their bar without first obtaining the city's approval and that they had continued to erect the addition even after the stop-work order was issued.

And finally:[104]

> the Board heard complaints from their neighbors that the live music at the Green Door Pub created a noise problem in the neighborhood. The Laffertys' neighbors told the Board that they objected to what one woman described as "the drinking and dancing happening nightly." They also expressed their concern that the operation of the Green Door Pub was harming the value of their property.

---

[104] Id at 759. The Court expressed some concern about relying on the neighbors' testimony (citing *Sexton v Anderson County*), but that concern is misplaced. In *Lafferty*, the business was operating: the neighbors had first hand knowledge about the method of operation. In the Sexton case, and other conditional use permit cases, the business is not yet operational and thus the neighbors are testifying without first hand knowledge. An expert is needed under that circumstance.

The Court also found the board's skepticism based on past actions by the applicant to be reasonable.[105]

> The most telling material evidence supporting the Board's action are the undisputed circumstances surrounding the construction and subsequent use of the first addition to the inn. The Laffertys portrayed this addition one way in order to obtain approval for it, and then, after obtaining approval, they used the addition for something completely different. Accordingly, the Laffertys were able to transform a one-story 20' x 20' storage addition into a two-story public bar with a separate outside entrance. The Laffertys high-handedness no doubt weighed on the Board's mind in considering their request for another addition and undermined the credibility of their explanation about their plans for the 38' x 40' addition to the Green Door Pub.

Clearly, although the findings were easier to make by virtue of the misconduct on the part of the applicants, the use of the property had significantly expanded and did not fit within the strictures of the Nonconforming Property Act.

(6) No building permit shall be denied

If the applicant can demonstrate that s/he complies with the statutory requirements, the permit must be issued. In my experience, this is easier said than done. Many local governments are not pleased with the provisions of the act and as a result, interpret it strictly against the property owner, and unfortunately, refuse to issue the permit even when it should be issued. Usually, this means going to the zoning board or to a court of law to establish the right to continue, expand, or to clear and rebuild.

[105] Id at 760.

(7) provided there is a reasonable amount of space to avoid nuisances

The statute provides that there must be "reasonable amount of space for such expansion on the property owned by such industry or business situated within the area which is affected by the change in zoning, so as to avoid nuisances to adjoining landowners." Presumably this "reasonable amount of space" would be less than that provided for by the bulk regulations. But remember subsection (i) which, on its fact requires rebuilt structures to comply with the bulk regulations. If that is meant to apply in that way, why have this nuisance avoidance section at all? If the owner must comply with the bulk regulations, there will always be sufficient space and almost never any semblance of a nuisance. Perhaps this is some evidence that the qualifier in subsection (g)(4) (the last two sentences) renders subsection (i) inapplicable except in cases where the nonconforming use has been "intentionally and voluntarily abandoned." Perhaps the meaning is that if the owner gives up the nonconforming ***use*** (and notice the use of that word; it is not used often in this statute), then he also loses the other nonconforming aspects of the property, and must comply with the required setbacks and other bulk regulations.

Suppose there was no nonconforming use and the only aspect of the property which was nonconforming was with regard to the bulk regulations. I suppose if the owner had no nonconforming use to give up, then subsection (i) does not apply and he keeps his nonconforming property even if only related to bulk regulations.

Ultimately, there simply appears to be a critical conflict between subsection (i) and the last proviso of subsection (g). It is very difficult to interpret the two provisions so as to have both make some sense.

Within the meaning of the statute, what is a nuisance?[106] The Tennessee Supreme Court has defined the tort known in common law as a nuisance to mean:[107]

> anything which annoys or disturbs the free use of one's property, or which renders its ordinary use or physical occupation uncomfortable . . . [and] extends to everything that endangers life or health, gives offense to the senses, violates the laws of decency, or obstructs the reasonable and comfortable use of property.

The Court continued:[108]

> Depending on the surroundings, activities that constitute a nuisance in one context may not constitute a nuisance in another. Whether a particular activity or use of property amounts to an unreasonable invasion of another's legally protectable interests depends on the circumstances of each case, such as the character of the surroundings, the nature, utility, and social value of the use, and the nature and extent of the harm involved.

So "long as the interference is substantial and unreasonable, such as would be offensive or inconvenient to the normal person, virtually any disturbance of the enjoyment of the property may amount to a nuisance." [109]

---

[106] The nuisance analysis also applies under subsection (c) of the statute: "the nonconforming property may expand operations provided there is a reasonable amount of space so as to avoid nuisances to adjoining landowners."

[107] *Lane v WJ Curry & Sons*, 92 SW 3d 355, 364 (Tenn. 2002).

[108] Id at 364-5.

[109] Id at 365.

While certainly the circumstances of each case are different, two cases are of particular interest in this regard. In *Johnson v Malone,*[110] the alleged nuisance was the construction of additional "chicken houses" in an agricultural area, but in "close proximity" to plaintiff's home. The trial court's decision that the "chicken houses" were not a nuisance was affirmed by the Court of Appeals.

In a similar way, *Anderson v American Limestone Company*[111] involved allegations that a rock quarry and accessory asphalt plant was a nuisance in a rural area. The jury found no nuisance and the Court of Appeals affirmed. Again, the particular facts of the case are of decisive importance, but one cannot help but fear that a lay board will have difficulties applying the legal definition of nuisance in land use cases. Indeed, it is not easy for the courts to determine what a nuisance is; a zoning board will have just that much more difficulty.

Should this be a decision by a zoning board? It seems to me that this should be an issue for a court, chancery or circuit. The zoning board has no expertise in the area of nuisance law. Someone will have to provide a definition, and the common law of nuisance is pretty slippery under the best of circumstances. That's one of the reasons why we have zoning in the first place: to make objective the old common law of nuisance. With zoning, there is no guessing about what is or what is not a nuisance. Except in this area of nonconforming properties.

In my opinion, the zoning boards, to the extent they are permitted to resolve these issues (and I think the courts would do a better job), the term nuisance should be guardedly interpreted. Is there an unreasonable imposition on the neighbors? If not, the expansion should be permitted. The Tennessee Pattern Jury Instruction, § 9.13 concerning nuisance reads in part:

> A nuisance is an unreasonable or unlawful use of property that results in material or substantial annoyance, inconvenience, discomfort, harm, or injury to the plaintiff,

---

[110] 2002 WL 1063936 (Tenn. Ct. App. 2002).

[111] 168 SW 3d 757 (Tenn. Ct. App. 2004).

to plaintiff's personal comfort or to the plaintiff's free use, possession or occupation of the plaintiff's own property.

One of the criticisms of nuisance doctrine is its subjective criteria: what is substantial annoyance? That could be almost anything. In the context of a jury trial, the court is there to supervise: the verdict can be set aside if the court deems that the plaintiff's proof was insufficient. There is no judge at the proceedings before the zoning board.

(8) do not permit expansion through the acquisition of additional land

This requirement (actually § 208(e)) seems pretty clear, but there is at least one case on point. In *421 Corp. v. Metropolitan Gov't of Nashville,* [112] a business known as the Purple Onion attempted to expand onto an adjacent property which was purchased after the original store obtained its nonconforming status.[113] The zoning administrator in Metro Nashville refused to issue a permit, and the zoning board upheld his decision. The trial court and the Court of Appeals also agreed. The Purple Onion made several interesting arguments, but in the end the court simply didn't buy any of them. Expanding from one property onto another simply is a violation of the state statue, and although the owner argued that the local ordinance permitted the expansion, the Court disagreed.

Be aware however that subsection (b)(2) does allow off-site signs to expand onto adjacent properties under the same ownership. The signage provisions of the statute are distinctly different by the way from the provisions relating to other types of "industrial, commercial or other business establishments."

---

[112] 36 S.W.3d 469 (Tenn. Ct. App. 2000)

[113] Id at 473-4.

(b) Some Case Law under § 208

As discussed above, the statute clearly permits not only the continuation of a non-conforming property,[114] but also permits expansion and reconstruction of the property if necessary, under § 208(c) & (d). There are several interesting cases which illustrate these points.

In *Outdoor West v. City of Johnson City*,[115] an advertising sign company applied to the city seeking to enlarge the size of the 11 non-conforming signs which it owned within the city. The city denied the applications and the sign company sued based upon the provisions of TENN. CODE ANN. § 13-7-208(c). The sign company argued that the increase in the size of the signs was necessary in order to remain competitive with respect to other advertising sign companies. Furthermore, the company argued that the size of signs is relatively standardized so that the smaller signs which they had built within the city needed to be enlarged to fit the larger standard size prevalent at the time of the application. In some cases, the company wanted to expand the size of a single-based sign so that it would have two sides such that two advertisers could lease the boards. Again, the testimony was that this was a fairly standardized practice in the industry and that these modifications were necessary in order to remain competitive within that industry.

The city argued that the company had not successfully demonstrated the necessity of the expansion of the signs. The Court of Appeals held that they did.

> The City argues that subsection (d) applies, that Lamar has failed to prove that the destruction and reconstruction is "necessary to the conduct of such industry or business," and, therefore, the judgment of the Trial Court must be reversed. We agree with the City that subsection (d) appears to require a higher standard of proof by Lamar,

---

[114] This is usually permitted by the local zoning ordinances anyway.

[115] 39 S.W. 3d 131 (Tenn. App. 2000).

since under that section, Lamar must show that the reconstruction is "necessary to the conduct of [the] industry or business." The record in this case is not clear as to whether Lamar plans for all of the existing signs to be demolished and new signs installed, thus implicating subsection (d), or whether, in some cases, the existing sign is to be retained but enlarged, thus implicating subsection (c). The sign permit applications indicate that eight 300 sq. ft. double-face signs are to be enlarged to 672 sq. ft. double-face signs. Three 672 sq. ft. single-face signs are to be converted to double-face signs. Mr. Richard Drummond testified for Lamar that the company plans to "modernize" the billboards to standardize the sizes, to "upgrade" for safety reasons and to "maximize our existing inventory to accept clients that request coverage in Johnson City." He testified that, depending on the location, and whether the traffic count would justify the decision, some signs would be taken down and changed from multiple wooden pole to unipole steel construction, which creates a larger and safer billboard, generates greater revenue, and is very expensive to install. Since at least *some* of the billboards are intended for demolition and replacement, we agree with the City that Lamar must show that the proposed action is "necessary to the conduct of the business."

Among the reasons justifying the destruction and reconstruction, Mr. Drummond testified that the company loses revenue when property is sold and a sign taken down by new owners, because the zoning in Johnson City will not permit the sign being moved to another location. In such cases, all of Lamar's revenue is permanently lost. Also, the company will soon begin losing revenue due to the State tobacco settlement, which will prevent tobacco companies, representing 10 to 19% of Lamar's billboard clients, from advertising on billboards. Furthermore, advertisements for billboards are no longer painted individually. Instead, they are sent to the billboard company, i.e., Lamar, from the client in the form of plastic sheets, of uniform size and construction, and the billboards

> on which they are to be installed must be uniform to accept the ads. Lamar owns most of the billboards in Johnson City, and they must upgrade and maintain them according to prevailing industry standards in order to keep their advertising clients. We find the preponderance of this evidence shows that upgrading and/or replacing its billboards is necessary to the conduct of Lamar's business and reject the City's argument to the contrary.
>
> We hold that Lamar has satisfied the requirements of both subsection (d) and subsection (c) of TENN. CODE ANN. § 13-7-208. This being so, a determination of whether subsection (c) or subsection (d) is the controlling subsection is unnecessary under the facts of this case.

In another interesting case, *National Auto/Truck Stops v. Williamson County*,[116] the county had passed an amortization schedule with respect to all signs in the county. The plaintiff had an 86 foot tall sign which was immediately adjacent to the interstate and located on its property which was used as an auto/truck stop. The county denied a permit seeking to replace the old sign with a new one and also denied the applicability of the Tennessee Non-Conforming Property Act. After suit was initiated, the county defended on the basis that the sign amortization schedule had nothing whatsoever to do with the underlying use of the property which was commercial and which was permitted in the district in which was located. In other words, the auto/truck stop could continue because it was permitted by the zoning ordinance; there was no nonconforming use with respect to the principal activity on the lot. The County also argued that since the principal use was unaffected by the sign amortization schedule, the sign itself was not afforded any protection by virtue of the statute.

Of course, the plaintiff argued that the sign was necessary to the conduct of the auto/truck stop at a location adjacent to the interstate highway. As a matter of fact, the new county regulations prohibited a sign any taller than 12 feet tall. The company argued that a sign of that height at that location would be totally out of sight for motorists

---

[116] 2001 WL 434860 (Tenn. App. 2001).

on the interstate highway. Furthermore, the company argued that the sign was absolutely necessary to draw patrons to the site and that as a result, it was entitled to protection under the terms of the statute, § 208(d).

The Court of Appeals held in favor of the auto/truck stop. The court found that the fact that the sign itself was merely accessory to the principal use on the property did not prevent the application of the statute to that accessory use. The court pointed out that the statute did not distinguish between principal and accessory uses. Under the circumstances presented to the court, it was clear that the sign was an integral part of the business activity and given that fact, the county could not amortize the sign in such a way so as to deprive the auto/truck stop of the sign.

This case is significant in that it makes clear that even if the principal use of the property is permitted by the application of the district zoning regulations, if the local government has enacted legislation which might hamper the business activity by regulating an accessory use or structure necessary to that business, the provisions of the Tennessee Non-Conforming Property Act will apply and protect the business as against the new zoning regulations. Furthermore, this holding also prevents a local government from regulating differing aspects of a business activity with the objective of eliminating the business activity although appearing to permit it under the guise of the use provisions of its zoning regulations. In other words, although a local government may maintain that the zoning regulations allow a particular use to continue, it may be that the manner in which it has regulated the accessory uses or bulk regulations makes it difficult or impossible for the business to continue. This case would seem to make it clear that such conduct on the part of the local government is illegal.

On the other hand, with the 2004 amendments to the act, it is not clear how this case might come out today. With the adoption of subsection (i), which, as we discussed above, appears to require conformity with the bulk regulations when rebuilding, the business accessory sign might have to comply with the 12 foot height limitation.[117]

Section 208 (i) provides:

> any structure rebuilt on the site must conform to the provisions of the existing zoning regulations as to setbacks, height, bulk, or requirements as to the physical location of a structure upon the site, provided that this subsection (i) shall not apply to off-site signs.

This appears to require that any new building or structure (except an off-site sign) must conform to the existing bulk regulations. Suppose the owner simply builds a new sign (for example) and leaves the old one where it is. This would appear to fall under subsection (c) and the bulk regulations would not apply. What happens five years later if the owner then decides to tear down the old sign? Can the new sign be forced to comply since it looks, at that point, to be a rebuilt sign? We don't have answers to these questions yet.

And what about subsection (g)(4) which provides:

> The reactivation of the non-conforming use any time prior to the end of the thirty (30) month period; provided, however, that the restrictions of subsections (g) and (i) shall only apply if the property owner intentionally and voluntarily abandons the nonconforming use of the property. In any contested matter on the use of such property, the government has the burden of proving an overt act of abandonment in such matter.

Does this mean that could discontinue operations for a short time and that subsection (i) would not apply unless the owner had voluntarily abandoned the use? This statute will continue to generate significant

---

[117]. An off-site sign clearly does not have to so comply; what difference there is between the two from a land use or zoning standpoint is hard to fathom.

litigation because it is very complex and the legislative intent is not very clear in many of the sections of the law.

3. Abandonment and Discontinuation

The abandonment of a non-conforming use both under common law principles and under the terms of the statute, the Tennessee Non-Conforming Property Act, is complicated, and we may not yet know the real answer to the issue. Let's begin with a brief historical overview.

The Standard State Zoning Enabling Act was the basis upon which many state zoning acts were constructed; Tennessee was one of those with several significant exceptions not relevant here. The Standard Act and the Tennessee Acts (both municipal and county) did not when originally adopted mention nonconforming properties. Local governments dealt with that issue when they adopted zoning ordinances. As we have mentioned, usually the nonconforming property was permitted to remain, but if the facilities were damaged (by fire for example) or if the owner wanted to rebuild because the structures were becoming decrepit, the property usually had to come into compliance.

Suppose that a property owner has stopped using the property for a period of a year or two (or more). The ordinances in the early days of zoning usually said that if the owner abandoned the use of the property, that it could thereafter only be used for a conforming use. As the cases began to wind through the courts however, the Judges ruled that the local governments had to show an intent to abandon. In a zoning case, that is very difficult. The owner certainly wouldn't admit it, even if true. Other types of proof, that the property hadn't been used, that the structures weren't kept up, and so forth, don't really hit the mark as far as the owner's intent. As a result, the local governments frequently lost those cases.

In response to those court rulings, the language of the zoning ordinances changed. Instead of using the word "abandon," the ordinances contained a discontinuation clause. In Nashville, for example, beginning in 1974, if the owner discontinued the use of the property for two years or more, then the property had to be brought into compliance. The intent of the owner became irrelevant under the terms of the ordinances.

It seems clearer now that this strategy may work. The Tennessee courts seemed initially to nevertheless require an intentional abandonment by the owner but more recent cases head in the opposite direction. In *Boles v. City of Chattanooga*,[118] the owner of an adult entertainment establishment sued the city to prevent enforcement of zoning ordinance where the use of the property had been discontinued for over 22 months. The adult entertainment use had started in the early '70's but a 1977 ordinance had rendered the use non-conforming. In November of 1987, the local district attorney had sued the property owner for public nuisance, and a temporary injunction had closed it for 22 months. After the nuisance case ended, allowing the property to again operate, the city said that the 22 month discontinuation precluded the use as adult entertainment.

The Court of Appeals rules against the city holding that the term "discontinued" requires a voluntary cessation of activities. The ordinance reads:

> If such non-conforming building is removed or the non-conforming use of such building is discontinued for 100 consecutive days, every future use of such premises shall be in conformity with the provisions of this Ordinance.

The court noted the old rule of construction that zoning ordinances are in derogation of the common law and operate to deprive an owner of a use which would otherwise be legal. The ordinance must be interpreted strictly in favor of the property owner as a result. The court also looked to the laws of other states:

---

[118] 892 SW 2d 416 (Tenn. Ct. App. 1994). The case was decided before the 2004 amendment to TENN. CODE ANN. § 13-7-208 adding the 30 month discontinuation clause. Presumably, if the 2004 amendment had applied, the voluntariness of the discontinuation would not have been important because the lapse in the use was only 22 months.

> The various states are split over the meaning of "discontinued" (or derivatives) in zoning ordinances, but a clear majority of jurisdictions read in a requirement that the cessation of use be voluntary.
>
> The parties to this dispute each cite a plethora of cases to support their respective positions on the issue of whether "discontinued" includes an element of voluntariness.

The court reviewed the cases from other jurisdictions and concluded that the states were divided evenly on this issue, with some states having cases on both sides of the issue.

But the Court of Appeals seemed to think it should include element of intent:

> We believe that the term "discontinued" or words of similar import, as utilized in zoning ordinances with specific time limitations, should be construed to include an element of intent, combined with some act -- or failure to act -- indicative of abandonment. Landowners who have enjoyed a non-conforming use on their properties, often for many years, no doubt come to rely economically on those non-conforming uses.
>
> Moreover, discontinuances of non-conforming uses can occur for a wide variety of involuntary reasons, not all of which stem from alleged violations of the law and some of which may be laudable.

To hold that a non-conforming use can be cut off automatically by time limits on discontinuance, regardless of the reason for that discontinuance, struck the court as unfair. But that left the question of whether the discontinuation was voluntary?

> Clearly they could not have legally used their property for an adult-oriented establishment while the temporary restraining order was in effect between November 10, 1987, and May 3, 1988. During this period of time the

premises were padlocked by the injunctive order of the Hamilton County Criminal Court.

The City of Chattanooga argues that the failure to operate the adult-oriented establishment was voluntary from May 3, 1988, onward, because, according to the City, the court order of that date did not further enjoin the operation of an adult oriented establishment.

While this issue is not without some doubt, we conclude that the permanent injunction, in force from May 3, 1988, until August 30, 1989, could fairly be read to enjoin the operation of an adult-oriented establishment on the Boles' property.

The order of May 3, 1988, defined the nuisance to include "the business known as Brenda's Book and Video World" and the Boles were faced with a broad injunction enjoining them from operating a bookstore. We believe that they acted reasonably in obeying the May 3, 1988, order, and waiting an additional 16 months during the pendency of their appeal until the August 30, 1989, final and agreed order narrowed the injunction to forbid only illegal conduct such as prostitution or sexual battery before reopening an adult-oriented establishment on the site.

The fact that the parties to the Criminal Court litigation felt that it was necessary to clarify this point in their agreed order, is a strong indication that the District Attorney General, as well as the Plaintiffs Boles, believed that the injunction of May 3, 1988, was broad enough to prohibit the reopening of an adult-oriented establishment.

An individual must obey an injunction until it has been modified, set aside or otherwise declared to be illegal.

The Boles have never evinced any intention to abandon their non-conforming use, and their filing of an appeal after the May 3, 1988, order was an overt act on their part

> clearly indicating their continued interest in maintaining their non conforming use. We do not believe the legally-compelled closing of the adult bookstore for 22 months can fairly be held against them, despite the Chattanooga Zoning Ordinance's time limitation.

Boles seems to say that no matter what the ordinance says, the city (or county) must prove an intent to abandon the use.

After *Boles*, the issue was whether this same interpretation would be extended to cases where there was no court order. The next major case was *Toles v. City of Dyersburg*,[119] which reached the contrary result! *Toles* involved a tavern which had been operating since 1960 but the zoning was changed in 1998 to residential and the property became legally non-conforming. Before the zoning changed, the owners liquor and beer licenses had lapsed. After the zoning change, the operator applied for a new beer license but was denied because there was no business in operation at the time of the zoning change. The operator sued under the statutory writ of certiorari and argued that the intent to continue operating a business is sufficient to allow the property to be grandfathered (relying on *Boles*), while the respondent argued that the business must be in operation, which would include all applicable licenses and permits.

The Court agreed, and found Boles unavailing to the petitioner.

> Unlike the injunction in Boles, nothing prevented the operation of the Avalon Club as a tavern prior to the zoning change. After Linda Ward stopped operating the club, there was no extrinsic force which prevented the club from continuing its operations. The owner of the property had to find someone else to operate the club. That process apparently took some time. This is certainly not the concern of the Defendant. The Defendant did not prevent the club's operation during this time. After Ida Mae Toles

[119] 39 S.W.3d 138 (Tenn. Ct. App. 2000). Toles was also decided before the 2004 amendment to TENN. CODE ANN. § 13-7-208 adding the 30 month discontinuation provision.

> agreed to operate the club, the structural deficiencies which were found in the club did stall the approval of the application for a beer permit. However, there has been no assertion that these deficiencies were unfounded or that the inspections were undertaken as a stall technique. The building did not conform to the applicable codes, and the application for the beer permit could not be approved until the necessary repairs were made. The timing of the repairs was totally in control of the Plaintiffs. Had the repairs been made more quickly, then, presumably, the application could have been approved prior to the re-zoning.

In short, the Court found nothing "involuntary"about the cessation of the operation of the tavern, distinguishing it from the court ordered injunction in *Boles.* [120]

> We read *Boles* to support the proposition that "intent" is only important where some force outside the control of the property owner prevents the continued use of the land in a particular manner. Since no such force prevented the Plaintiffs from operating the Avalon Club as a tavern, their intent is not important and the Boles decision is thus distinguishable from the present case. Therefore, since the building was not being operated as a business at the time of the re-zoning, there is nothing to grandfather into the new zoning classification.

At the time of the *Toles* decision, it was unclear as to what direction future courts might take on this issue. It seems now that *Toles*

---

[120] Keep in mind that the statute, TENN. CODE ANN. § 13-7-208 (g) clearly lists litigation concerning the use of the property as a grounds of involuntary discontinuation ("The period in which an industrial, commercial, or other business establishment is party to any action in a court of competent jurisdiction regarding the use of the property until such time that a final settlement, order, decree, or judgment has been rendered . . .")

and not *Boles* is the predominant approach. Later cases seem to follow *Toles*. For example, in *City of Red Bank v Philips*,[121] the city sued to prevent the use of a property zoned for single family use as multi-family. A home which had previously been used for three families, lost two of the tenants and it took a considerable time to find new tenants. The owner, relying again on *Boles*[122], argued that there was no voluntary act evidencing abandonment. The court was not impressed with that argument.

> Unlike the injunction in Boles, nothing prevented the prior owners of this property from renting out the units. As found by the trial court, there was no extrinsic force which prevented the leasing of the property. There was nothing involuntary about the cessation of the nonconforming use.
>
> The trial court properly determined that "the protection of the grandfather clause had been lost long before Owner bought the property on July 21, 2005" and "the lack of any tenant for approximately twenty (20) months resulted in the loss of the grandfather clause's protection for . . ." The failure . . . to lease the property as a triplex, or rent to at least two tenants, was a discontinuance of the non-conforming use.

In a similar way, the failure to begin new landfill operations after previous litigation prevented the owner from successfully asserting a non-conforming use in *Custom Land Development, Inc. v. Town of*

---

[121] 2007 WL 4460223 (Tenn. Ct. App., December 20, 2007).

[122] Note that the statute would not apply here because the use was residential, not commercial or industrial. TENN. CODE ANN. § 13-7-208(b).

Coopertown[123]. *Smith County Regional Planning Commission v. Hiwassee Village Mobile Home Park* is also similar.[124]

Let us suppose that a commercial operation closes its doors with the idea of reconstructing its facilities and to open as a somewhat bigger and better version of the same commercial enterprise. Let us further assume that after the buildings have been removed but before any reconstruction begins, the municipality changes the zoning so that commercial uses are no longer permitted on this particular property. There is one final assumption: that is, that under the provisions of the local zoning ordinance, there is a one-year discontinuation clause. That is, the zoning ordinance provides that you may discontinue a land use, but if the discontinuation continues for more than one year, you may not begin again. May the property owner obtain a permit to reconstruct facilities, let's say within two months of the demolition of the original facilities, if the new zoning ordinance took effect in between the two events?

Technically, the statute requires that the business be "in operation;" does this hypothetical meet that requirement? Does the intent to continue the commercial operation satisfy the requirement that the business be "in operation." From a practical perspective it seems to me that there would be very little reason to construe the statute strictly against the property owner.

In 2004, the statute was amended to provide a 30 month discontinuation clause to industrial, commercial or other business establishments. Subsection (g) was added and now provides that the statute "shall not apply if an industrial, commercial, or other business establishment *ceases to operate* for a period of thirty (30) continuous months . . ." There are a number of tolling provisions which extend the 30 month period: litigation is one, and the reconstruction hypothetical above is another. Notice that the phrase "ceases to operate" implies discontinuation, not abandonment.

---

[123] 168 SW 3d 764 (Tenn. Ct. App. 2004).

[124] 2008 WL 3343001 (Tenn. Ct. App. 2008). See the previous discussion of this case at page 102, 221.

Let's try another hypothetical. This time assume that the use of the property is discontinued, but there is no present intent to begin anew at any particular time, but that there is also no intent to abandon the use. The owner has simply tired of the business and stops operations. Five years later, the same or a new owner applies for a permit to begin again. Is the property still nonconforming? The text of the final sentences of subsection (g) are worth reviewing here:[125]

> Provided, however, that the restrictions of subsections (g) and (I) shall only apply if the property owner intentionally and voluntarily abandons the nonconforming use of the property. In any contested matter on the use of such property, the government has the burden of proving an overt act of abandonment in such matter.

These last two sentences of subsection (g) make it clear that the discontinuation clause "shall only apply if the property owner intentionally and voluntarily abandons the nonconforming use of the property. In any contested matter on the use of such property, the government has the burden of proving an overt act of abandonment in such matter."

What does this mean? If the property has not been used for over 30 months, does the local government have to prove intentional abandonment of the nonconforming property? Probably not. But the last sentence requires an "overt act of abandonment?" What is an overt act of abandonment? Mere discontinuation? I wouldn't think so, because that is equally consistent with discontinuation: simply not operating the business for a period of time with the intent to return at some point in the future. It is certainly difficult to tell based on the statute. The courts will have to resolve this issue. We are back to same problem: does the municipality have to prove intent, something beyond discontinuation? If so, the 30 month tolling period may never expire because of lack of

---

[125] This quote is from Chapter 775 of the Public Acts of 2004; the version codified in the Tennessee Code Annotated inserts a semicolon instead of a period before the word provided and does not capitalize that word. This makes the last two sentences seem a part of subsection (g) but the original act does not format it in that way.

proof of an overt act of abandonment. My assumption based on the language is that is what the General Assembly intended. But we will need a decision from the courts before we know for certain how to construe these provisions.

Another difficult type of use under the statute are those which are inherently temporary, such as festivals, street fairs, and so forth. For example, in Nashville, for 25 or 30 years, the symphony sponsored an Italian Street Fair,[126] as a means of raising money. It was usually held in the late summer or early fall, for a period of two weeks or so. Assuming that the temporary use began before the zoning ordinance precluded it, the use is likely legally non-conforming. Unless the owner ceases the temporary use for several years, the 30 month discontinuation clause will likely never kick in. And of course, to the extent that the statute actually requires proof of an intent to abandon, the requirement is just that much more difficult. Temporary uses therefore would likely be protected by the statute although there have not been any decided cases as of yet.

4. Amortization

In response to the continuing vitality of nonconforming uses, local governments began to look for alternative means of dealing with them. Amortization quickly became a favorite technique. While amortization suggests that the value of the use is analyzed, and then some period of years which would roughly approximate the value of that use is given to the property owner so that s/he has that long period of time to continue operations, and thereafter shut down, amortization, in effect, became simply a short order means of ordering the discontinuation of nonconforming uses. For example, many municipalities would simply impose a five-year amortization period. That is, at the end of five years, the use had to be discontinued. Little if any study was done; there was simply a new regulation adopted with no means around it.

---

[126] *Steele v Metro Board of Zoning Appeals*, 1986 WL 3985 (Tenn. Ct. App. April 2, 1986) involved the fair's application for a conditional use permit; the fair was never legally non-conforming.

The leading case in Tennessee, *Rives v. City of Clarksville*,[127] involved an auto salvage business in Clarksville. The owner sued the City seeking an injunction against the enforcement of the ordinance. This case addresses several important issues. First, the Clarksville amortization period (at least as concerning auto salvage businesses) was for five years. The amortization clause was passed in 1967. Thus, some time in 1972, the nonconforming use should have been extinguished or discontinued by virtue of the amortization provision. The owner here, however, argued that the amortization provision itself was unconstitutional. Noting the propensity of nonconforming uses to continue given their mini-monopoly status, the Court of Appeals concluded that a zoning ordinance that requires existing uses to cease after a reasonable time is not different in kind from a zoning ordinance that restricts a future use, but only in degree. The Court found that the elimination of non-conforming uses was constitutional if reasonably effected. The Court notes that the public benefit must outweigh the private injury, that is, it must not only be reasonable in and of itself, but it also must be reasonable as it applies to the particular owner. The Court remanded the case to the Chancellor to consider (1) the structure located on the property; (2) the use of the property; (3) the location of the property; (4) the cost of the property; (5) the benefit to be derived by the public; (6) the period of the use; and (7) the amortization period. "In determining whether the amortization period is reasonable, consideration should be given to the length of the amortization period in relation to the property owner's investment and the length of the amortization period in relation to the use of the property."[128]

Thus, while the Court generally found the idea of amortization to be constitutional, it was quite concerned about its application to any particular property owner and insisted that the trial court measure the impact on the property owner. It may frankly be that five years is a very short period of time, especially when considered in relation to a well-established use of the property.

---

[127] 618 S.W.2d 502 (Tenn. App. 1981).

[128] 618 S.W.2d at 510.

The *Rives* court also addressed another extremely significant issue in this case, and that is the manner in which to construe the statute as it was amended in 1973, and effective on May 17, 1973. Notice that in *Rives*, the zoning ordinance which restricted the use of the property to five years was adopted in 1967. Assuming that the five-year amortization period was reasonable, the use of the property would have been fully amortized by 1972, about a year prior to the effective date of the amended statute. As a result, the nonconforming use should have been discontinued and was illegal at the time that the statutory provision took effect. As a result, TENN. CODE ANN. § 13-7-208 was of no protection to Mr. Rives in this case. In reaching its holding the Court noted that the statute has two requirements: "(1) There must be zoning where there previously was none, or there must be a change in zoning restrictions, and (2) there must be permissive operation of a business prior to the change."[129]

However, that means that all amortization provisions under Tennessee state law as adopted by municipalities (and counties too at this point), are most probably illegal and unenforceable. There is no way for a city, given the provision of §13-7-208 to validly amortize a use.

The nonconforming use statute has been applied in variety of contexts. In *Smith v. City of Forest Hills*,[130] the owner of a small commercial convenience store in an otherwise almost totally residential city adjacent to Metro Nashville, sought to expand the use of the convenience store by essentially tearing it down and starting again. They made various proposals to the City, all of which were rejected. In 1975, the developer began to make changes on the property amounting to a substantial development of the lot for the commercial convenience store. The Court of Appeals held that the nonconforming use statute expressly permitted this expansion of the nonconformity. In a subsequent case between the same parties, a request to build an office building on the same site was rejected because no office uses had been

---

[129] Id at 505.

[130] *Smith v. City of Forest Hills* Slip op. February 13, 1985 (Tennessee Appeals, Middle Section by Todd).

nonconforming as of the effective date of the Forest Hills zoning ordinance.[131]

5. Making a Non-conforming Property Conforming

It may be that the best way now to protect municipal interests in the area of non-conforming properties is to make them conforming. That is, simply recognize that discontinuation of the use by legislative fiat is not now possible, and concentrate on the regulation of the activity. If the use is made conforming, then the expansion of the use can be regulated by the city so as to disallow expansion which would, from the city's standpoint be counterproductive. Instead, then of the "reasonable" expansion allowed by virtue of the statute, the city could specify how much expansion would be permitted subject only to the very broad limits of substantive due process.

The city loses the power to prohibit the use, but gains back the power to regulate the manner in which the activity will be conducted. Since cities have very little choice about this, it would seem that this is a good way of making the best of a bad situation.

The city of Forest Hills did just that after losing the Granny White market case. It zoned the property as historic commercial and imposed regulations on the way it could develop in the future. This gave the city the best control it could have under the circumstances.

6. Applicability to Counties

This is a controversial issue, but it now appears resolved. In *Chadwell v. Knox County*,[132] the Tennessee Court of Appeals considered this issue and ruled that even though the Non-Conforming Property Act was located in the municipal zoning enabling legislation, there was

---

[131] Id.

[132] 980 S.W. 2d 378 (Tenn. App. 1998).

nothing to suggest in the language of the statute that the General Assembly intended to limit its application solely to municipalities.[133]

> Since TENN. CODE ANN. § 13-7-208 is found under the title, chapter and part dealing with municipalities, it would appear, on the surface, at least, that TENN. CODE ANN. § 13-7-208 has no application to counties. A closer scrutiny, however, reveals otherwise. We are not at liberty to overlook the clear, unambiguous language of any statute and must interpret it in accordance with well-established rules of construction.

The Court then quoted TENN. CODE ANN. § 13-7-208(b) and concluded:

> As can be seen, the above section applies not only to municipalities but to any governmental agency of the state or its political subdivisions. Clearly a county is a political subdivision of the state of Tennessee and falls within the contemplation of the legislation.

This is not the only decision which has reached the same conclusion. In *Lane v. Barr and Cheatham County*,[134] the Tennessee Court of Appeals was once again asked to review a case involving a non-conforming use within a County zoning scheme. Once again, the Court of Appeals concluded that based on the provisions of TENN. CODE ANN. § 13-7-208 (b), the use of the property was legally non-conforming. In *Lane*, the issue involved whether a tire disposal business had started before the effective date of Cheatham County's comprehensive zoning ordinance. That ordinance was initially passed in June of 1973. The trial court concluded that not only was the main parcel of property used for the business legally nonconforming, but that so also were several other parcels which were after acquired. The testimony before the zoning

---

[133] In *Fields v. White*, 1989 WL 5456 (Tenn. App. 1989), the Middle Section Court of Appeals ruled on this same issue, only with the opposite result. The *Chadwell* court seems not to have been cited this case by the parties and in subsequent cases, it has not been mentioned.

[134] 1998 WL 289341 (Tenn. App. 1998).

board and before the court tended to indicate that all the parcels of land had been utilized as a "tire landfill" prior to the effective date of the first comprehensive zoning ordinance in the County. In fact, the testimony was that those properties were in use at least two years before the adoption of that first zoning ordinance.

The Court of Appeals held:

> After a careful review of the record before us, we find that there is sufficient proof in the record to support the trial court's finding that the Barrs were using parcels other than 102.04 in their tire disposal business. Barr testified that he was using property other than parcel 102.04 in 1971, at least two years before Cheatham County's first comprehensive zoning ordinance came into being. Consequently, the use of a tire landfill on this land comes within the scope of TENN.CODE ANN. § 13-7-208 (b) as a prior non-conforming use.

The important point here is the conclusion of the Court of Appeals applying the provisions of TENN. CODE ANN. § 13-7-208 to a County comprehensive zoning ordinance. Although this court did not discuss its rationale for applying this provision to the County, it was decided approximately two months after the decision in *Chadwell.* One cannot help but conclude that the *Chadwell* decision, without reference to the opinion, was the basis upon which the court applied the Non-Conforming Property Act to the County.

There have been other cases in which the NCFP Act has been applied to county governments. In one of those, *National Auto/Truck Stops v. Williamson County,*[135] the County conceded the point and did not argue that the statute did not apply to it. At this point, the *Chadwell* seems well established, most counties do not argue the point; it seems too late to resurrect the argument that the statute does not apply to counties.

---

[135] 2001 WL 434860 (Tenn. App. 2001).

7. Legal Effect: NCFP runs with the land

The statute does not address this particular issue and it has not come up in the case law here in Tennessee either. Does the nonconforming nature of the property run with the land so that a subsequent purchaser acquires the rights to the NCFP at the time of purchase? Clearly, the answer must be yes. This is a species of property right which vests by statute, ordinance, or possibly under common law doctrine. Sale of the property does not divest the nonconforming status. It runs with the land and inures to the benefit of subsequent purchasers.

This does bring up some interesting issues. Suppose the property is held by tenants in common but only one of the tenants has operated a business on the property and that business is non-conforming under the statute. Can the business operator tenant in common sell his interest in the land and business and does the non-conforming use go with the sale? The answer here would seem to be an obvious yes. Is there any change in outcome if the business is incorporated and the corporation has no interest in the land except that the one of the stockholders is a tenant in common? Again, although it would be better if the corporation had a property interest so that the non-conforming right attached to the land, if the stockholder was a tenant in common, there seems little harm done.

Can the business be leased to a third-party and must the lease specifically include the right to continue the non-conforming use? If the lease doesn't mention the non-conforming use, is it nevertheless part of the transaction by implication? It seems to me, either way, that the non-conforming use should be recognized.

Let's turn to the other tenant in common. Can the other tenant set up a business identical in use to the original while the original is still in operation? Does the fact that s/he has an undivided interest in the property mean that s/he also has a right to begin a new business and claim non-conforming status based solely on that property interest? The answer would seem to be no. The second business would need to be operating before a change in the zoning as required by the statute, the same as any other. Just because the other tenant has a common property interest does not mean that s/he has the right to begin a business in violation of the zoning ordinance.

Let's approach that from a slightly different perspective. Suppose the original business fails and now the other tenant in common wants to begin an identical business. Does his ownership right give him the right to do so? Assuming that less than 30 months have gone by (the statutory discontinuation period), there would seem to be no reason why the other tenant could not start a new business that mimicked the old one. To be safer, the original business should be bought out. That would make it much cleaner and clearer.

8. Exhaustion of Administrative Remedies

Whether the owner of a purported non-conforming property must appeal to the local zoning board before going to court is another very interesting issue. To the extent that there is some factual issue which must be decided, an appeal to the board is likely necessary. However, if the facts concerning the non-conforming use are reasonably well established, as they often are in these cases, and the only function of the board is to apply the law, my feeling is that the case should go directly to court. The board has no business interpreting a statute: its only authority is to construe its zoning ordinance. It cannot and should not be permitted to interpret state law.

The statute granting power to the board limits its jurisdiction to hearing appeals where an error has allegedly been made enforcing "any provision of any ordinance enacted pursuant to" the public municipal zoning enabling statutes, Part 2, Chapter Seven, Title 13.[136] The board has the power to consider errors in applying an ordinance, not the statute. Nowhere is the board given any such power.[137]

---

[136] TENN. CODE ANN. § 13-7-207(1).

[137] There are 3 well-known exceptions to the requirement:

One such exception is where a party is challenging the validity of an ordinance or a statute that would be applied

The Tennessee Court of Appeals recognized the difficulty here but grants the board a bit broader scope of authority than I believe is given by the zoning enabling statutes. In *B.F. Nashville, Inc. v. City of Franklin,*[138] the Court confronted a typical case. The plaintiff filed a declaratory judgement action against the city arising out of storm damage of its on-site advertising sign. After the sign was damaged, the city ruled that the sign could not be rebuilt except in conformity with applicable zoning regulations, notwithstanding that the sign was legally non-conforming. The city moved to dismiss because the owner failed to exhaust its administrative remedies. The plaintiff contended that:[139]

> because it has a vested right to reconstruct the sign, it is not required to seek a permit or appeal to the board. It also contends that it should be allowed to avail itself of the exception to the general rule for those situations where "resort to the administrative route is futile or the remedy inadequate." Plaintiff also argued that while the Board of Zoning Appeals is authorized to grant conditional use permits and variances, it does not possess the authority to construe the non-conforming use statute, and thus resort to the Board would be futile.

The Court disagreed:

> Thus, to the extent B.F. seeks to challenge an administrative determination that the sign it now

---

> by the administrative agency making the decision. Another is where the party seeking judicial review raises only questions of law rather than questions of fact. In such a circumstance, there is no obligation to exhaust administrative remedies. A third exception is where the pursuit of administrative relief would be futile or useless.

Colonial Pipeline v Morgan, Tenn. Ct App. July 2, 2007.

[138] 2005 WL 127082 (Tenn. Ct. App. 2005)

[139] BF Nashville v City of Franklin at *5.

> proposes to erect is prohibited, or an administrative determination denying permission to build such a sign, the proper avenue for judicial review is common law writ of certiorari. Consequently, as to those issues involving application of the ordinance or statute to a particular situation or a local official's exercise of discretion in applying them, B.F. is required to appeal the determinations of the sign administrator to the board of zoning appeals and obtain a decision based upon an evidentiary record that the court can review in a common law writ of certiorari action.
>
> However, to the extent that B.F. seeks a declaratory judgment regarding the validity of Franklin's sign ordinance, in view of the state statute grandfathering noncomforming uses, that issue was subject to determination by the court in a direct action for declaratory judgment, without the requirement of the exhaustion of administrative remedies. B.F. argues the ordinance cannot be applied to its sign because of the statute. Thus, its challenge can be viewed as one of validity or applicability.

The court concluded that the "questions of the validity of the ordinance and whether it can be applied in this situation predominate because the answers to those questions determine the course of any future administrative action that may be required." The court then considered the statute as applied to the sign at issue.[140]

But consider the Court's conclusion here. The zoning board, by statute, is only allowed to consider the ordinance, not zoning statutes.[141] The courts of this state should construe statutory law, not some zoning

---

[140] The Court concluded that the statute did protect on-site advertising signs but that the property owner had abandoned the sign by not applying for a permit for 3 years after the damage was done.

[141] TENN. CODE ANN. § 13-7-207(1) only gives the board authority over ordinances.

board which has little or no expertise in interpreting state law. Why should the Maryville zoning board determine how the entire state of Tennessee should construe some state statute? The simple answer is that it shouldn't.

In addition, the Court mentions the common law writ; but if the allegation is that there is a vested right, then the statutory writ may apply, not the very restrictive common law writ. It may be that the Court of Appeals has already foreclosed these issues, but certainly it is worth vigorously presenting them again as key issues.

In *National Auto/Truck Stops of America v Williamson County*,[142] a similar argument was made by the county. The trial court however found that there was no need to exhaust administrative remedies. The trial court ruling was not appealed and is not a part of the Court of Appeals decision, but the lower court felt that only questions of law were to be decided and that there was nothing for the zoning board to determine. The sign at issue was still standing so there was no abandonment; the sign admittedly predated the zoning ordinance; there was no issue of nuisance;[143] and finally, the county did not contest business necessity. The remaining issue was the applicability of the statute to a on-site advertising sign, which the court decided in favor of the owner. But for our purposes here, the trial court found no reason to require that the owner go to the zoning board first.

---

[142] 2001 WL 434860 (Tenn. Ct. App. 2001).

[143] As described elsewhere, the nuisance issue should be decided in a court of law, not a zoning board. See page 120.

Chapter Three

Conditional Use Permits or Special Exceptions: A Special Permit By Any Other Name?

A. Use Conditioned On Criteria

A conditional use permit is just that: a zoning permit for a use of land which is conditioned on meeting certain requirements set forth in the ordinance. Conditional uses go by many names, and the appropriate technical name under the Tennessee Public Zoning Enabling Legislation is "special exception."[1] This phrase, though, is thought of now as archaic.[2]

---

[1] TENN. CODE ANN. § 13-7-107, 13-7-109(2) (relating to county zoning), 13-7-206 and 13-7-207(2) (relating to municipal zoning) are essentially the same. Section 13-7-107 states in relevant part:

> The zoning ordinance may provide that the board of appeals may, in appropriate cases and subject to appropriate principles, standards, rules, conditions and safeguards set forth in the ordinance, make special exceptions to the terms of the zoning regulations in harmony with their general purpose and intent.

Section 13-7-109(2) provides in relevant part:

> The board of appeals shall have the following powers:
>
> (2) To hear and decide, in accordance with the provisions of any such ordinance, requests for special exceptions . . .

[2] Norman Williams, 5 American Planning Law (2006) § 148.07. See also Mandelker: *Land Use Law*, (5th Ed. 2003) § 6.53; Rohan: Zoning and Land Use Control, § 44.01[1]; ALI: Model Land Development Code (1975) § 2-207. One Tennessee Court, *Nance v. City of Memphis*, 672 S.W.2d 208, 212 (Tenn. App. 1983), quoting Corpus Juris Secondum with approval, has indicated that the terms "special

> The unfortunate phrase "special exception" used in the early enabling statutes and ordinances, caused a good deal of confusion, and has been criticized as a misnomer. This phrase has now been widely superseded by a variety of other terms -- "special permits," "special uses," "use permits," etc. All have the same meaning and the name used has generally (and wisely) been treated by the courts as irrelevant.

The basic idea behind the conditional use permit[3] is that the local legislative body, county or municipal, has already examined those areas where the use might be acceptable and conditionally permitted the particular use in that area.[4] Normally, conditional use permits involve such things as landfills,[5] schools,[6] mobile home parks,[7] apartment

---

exception" and "conditional use permit" are the equivalent one of the other. Interestingly, Metro Nashville adopted a new comprehensive zoning ordinance in 1998, and reverted to the use of the older term "special exception," evidently based on a feeling that the ordinance should be consistent with the terminology in the Tennessee Public Zoning Enabling Statutes.

[3] The statutes (TENN. CODE ANN. §§ 13-7-109(2) and 13-7-207(2)) also provide that the board may "hear and decide . . . other special questions upon which such board is authorized by any such ordinance to pass . . ." If there are issues which can be identified, and a guide for the board to follow established, this "other question" provision can be helpful. One example might be side yard violations on new construction.

[4] See, e.g., *South Woodbury Taxpayer's Association v. American Institute of Physics*, 428 N.Y.S. 2d 158 (S.Ct. 1980); *Tullo v. Township of Milburn*, 54 N.J.Super. 483, 149 A.2d 620, 624-25 (App.Div. 1959).

[5] *Sexton v. Anderson County*, 587 S.W.2d 63 (Tenn. App. 1979).

[6] *Father Ryan v. City of Oak Hill*, 774 S.W.2d 184 (Tenn. App. 1988).

[7] *Harrell v. Hamblen County*, 526 S.W.2d 505 (Tenn. App. 1975). This case probably involved a planned unit development, rather than

complexes,[8] daycare centers,[9] theaters,[10] mental health clinics[11] and the

---

a conditional use permit. The planning commission was clearly involved in the deliberations and it appears that the ultimate denial was by the local legislative body "sitting as a zoning board of appeals." 526 S.W.2d at 507. The local entities evidently were acting under private enabling legislation which is different from the public enabling legislation discussed here. However, because the legal standards employed by the court to review a planned unit development and a conditional use appear to very similar, see *Mullins v. City of Knoxville*, 665 S.W.2d 393 (Tenn. App. 1983), and *McCallen v. City of Memphis*, 786 S.W.2d 633 (Tenn.1990), the consideration of it in this context is not inappropriate.

[8] *Meritt v. Wilson County*, 656 S.W.2d 846 (Tenn. App. 1983). This case is an instance where the author was called to testify as an expert by the petitioners. It is not clear that an attorney can be called as an expert witness in a zoning case and likely is practice that should be frowned upon. Sam Edwards, on the other hand, is a planner (and a lawyer) and his testimony was appropriate, if not procedurally correct because of the limitations on oral proof under the common law writ of certiorari. One of the issues in the case at the Court of Appeals was

> whether the testimony of George Dean, attorney, and Samuel Edwards, Planner, [was] proper and admissible when it consisted of their opinions concerning the interpretation of the zoning law in Tennessee, the Wilson County zoning ordinance, and their opinion as to whether or not the Appeals Board exceeded their jurisdiction.
>
> In other words, Woodlake's insistence is that both Dean and Edwards testified as to the "ultimate issue of law" of the case and that the Chancellor erred in relying on their testimony in arriving at his decision. Woodlake concedes that Dean and Edwards were qualified experts and could testify as to the ultimate issue of fact, but that it was error for the Chancellor to admit and rely on their testimony as to the "ultimate issue of law."
>
> We deem it unnecessary to address this issue. This case is

like. Generally, they are used by urban planners to place uses which are not totally incompatible with the surrounding area, but which may be incompatible if not controlled under the circumstances. Thus, a set of specific conditions (requirements) are usually mandated by the zoning ordinance for each separate type of use and if the applicant demonstrates compliance with each of the specific criteria, the issuance

---

> before us for a de novo hearing. Tenn.R.App.P. 13(d). Our de novo review of the record, without relying upon Dean and Edwards' interpretation of the law, supports the judgment of the Chancellor. Even if the Chancellor were in error in allowing Dean and Edwards to testify regarding their opinions, the error was harmless(Citations omitted).

[9] Under Metro Nashville's current zoning ordinance, these are allowed without zoning board action if it meets all requirements. MetZo § 17.16.035.

[10] Under Metro Nashville's current zoning ordinance, these are allowed without zoning board action if it meets all requirements. MetZo §17.16.120.

[11] *Nance v. City of Memphis*, 672 S.W.2d 208 (Tenn. App. 1983). This case apparently arose under the Memphis private legislation, see, e.g., Private Acts of 1921, Chapter 424 as amended by Private Acts of 1925, Chapter 428 (although note the change to the public act standards in Chapter 142 of the Private Acts of 1955), the Court does not discuss it and that is evidently quite different from the public enabling legislation, allowing the local planning commission and local legislative body to issue conditional use permits (unless of course the case is a planned unit development masquerading as a conditional use; it is often difficult to tell). Land use planning counsel and the reviewing courts have frequently in Tennessee case law not explicitly considered the statutory authority at issue in the case. Because the enabling legislation is often crucial to proper analysis, any discussion of land use planning law should begin there. Furthermore, it is sometimes difficult to follow precedent from other states because of differences in the enabling legislation (this is especially true of variances).

of a permit is presumed. Failure to satisfy all of the requirements results in denial by the Board of Zoning Appeals.

B. Distinguished from Other Land Use Planning Techniques

A conditional use permit should therefore be carefully distinguished from a variance, the other major power of a local zoning board.[12] The essential difference is that a conditional use is ***legislatively permitted*** in a specific zone subject to conditions specified by the ordinance and a variance is ***legislatively prohibited*** but may be granted by the board under certain tightly controlled circumstances amounting to a hardship.[13] Consequently, while variances should be granted only sparingly, conditional use permits should presumptively be granted.[14] The technique allows flexibility in the placement of uses with special land use difficulties, yet balances this flexibility against the right of the applicant to know the limits of the zoning restrictions on the subject property by imposing reasonably specific criteria for each use. It is this tension between flexible placement and specific criteria that leads to many of the legal disputes

---

[12] TENN.CODE ANN. § 13-7-109(3) (county) and § 13-7-207(3) (municipal); *see, e.g., McClurkan v. Metropolitan Board of Zoning Appeals*, 565 S.W. 2d 495 (Tenn.App. 1977).

[13] See *102 Glenstone v. Board of Adjustment of Springfield*, 572 S.W.2d 891 (Mo.App. 1978); *Verona, Inc. v. Mayor and Council of East Caldwell*, 49 N.J. 274, 229 A.2d 61, 65 (1967); *Tullo v. Township of Milburn*, 54 N.J.Super. 483, 490-1, 149 A.2d 620, 624-5 (App.Div. 1959); Rathkopf Law of Zoning and Planning, § 41.05 (4th Ed. 2005); N. Williams, 5 American Planning Law, (2006) § 148.01 et seq.; 82 Am.Jur.2d Zoning and Planning, § § 255 and 281.

[14] Mandelker at § 6.39 (variance is harder to obtain than a special exception) and § 6.56 (burden in CUP case shifts to neighbors); *Metropolitan Historical Commission v. Colony Associates*, 13 TAM 46-17 (Tenn.App. 1988) (variances should be sparingly granted.)

involving such permits. One of the most respected American jurists in land planning law further articulates this distinction:[15]

> The theory is that certain uses, considered by the local legislative body to be essential or desirable for the welfare of the community and its citizenry or substantial segments of it, are entirely appropriate and not essentially incompatible with the basic uses in any zone (or in certain particular zones), but not at every or any location therein or without restrictions or conditions being imposed by reason of special problems the use or its particular location in relation to neighboring property presents from a zoning standpoint, such as traffic congestion, safety, health, noise and the like. The enabling act therefore permits the local ordinance to require approval of the local administrative agency as to the location of such use within the zone. If the board finds compliance with the standards and requisites set forth in the ordinance, the right to the exception exists subject to such specific safeguarding conditions as the agency may impose by reason of the nature, location and incidence of the particular use. Without intending here to be inclusive or to prescribe limits, the uses so treated are generally those serving considerable numbers of people, such as private schools, clubs, hospitals, and even churches, as distinguished from governmental structures or activities on the one hand and strictly individual residences and businesses on the other. This method of zoning treatment is also frequently extended to certain unusual kinds of strictly private business or activity which, though desirable and compatible, may by their nature present peculiar zoning problems or have unduly unfavorable effect on their neighbors if not specially regulated. Gasoline stations . . . are an example of this second category. The point is that such special uses are permissive in the particular zone

---

[15] *Tullo v. Township of Milburn*, 54 N.J.Super. 483, 490-1, 149 A.2d 620, 624-5 (App.Div. 1959).

under the ordinance and neither non-conforming nor akin to a variance.

Conditional use permits are therefore the antithesis of variances.[16]

Procedurally, conditional uses are also different from variances. Usually, the applicant for a variance has applied to the zoning administrator or the building code official for a permit which is denied because the proposal violates some provision of the zoning ordinance. The applicant then appeals the decision of the zoning administrator or building code official and requests a variance of the board of zoning appeals.[17] The zoning administrator has no right, however, to issue a conditional use permit. It is not within the ambit of his powers. Thus, he merely accepts an application (without ruling on it in any way) on behalf of the zoning board and presents the application to the zoning board at a public hearing. The applicant for a conditional use permit is therefore before the zoning board upon an initial application; the board has original jurisdiction, it is not hearing an appeal of any decision of the administrative offices below.[18] It is therefore inappropriate for the board to presume that the local administrative official was correct in his dealings with the applicant and there is no requirement that he meet the exceptional requirements required by a zoning variance.[19]

---

[16] This is especially true when the variances involve changes in the use of the land. These "use" variances, which the author believes are not permitted under Tennessee Zoning Enabling Legislation, but which are nevertheless granted by many boards of zoning appeals, effectively allow a use which is absolutely prohibited in a particular area into that area usually with no conditions attached and frequently, with very little thought as to the impact on the surrounding land uses.

[17] Rohan at § 44.01[3].

[18] Id.

[19] Id.

Furthermore, conditional uses should not be confused with either planned unit developments[20] or site plan review. While both of those zoning techniques are beyond the scope of this article, suffice it to say that planned unit developments and site plan review are generally thought of as committed to the regional or municipal planning commission rather than the board of zoning appeals (as in the case of conditional use permit) and both are omitted from express grants of authority under the Tennessee Public Zoning Enabling Statutes (TPZES).[21]

Planned unit development (PUD) is a technique which grew up in opposition to traditional subdivisions. In a traditional subdivision, houses are placed on lots which are typically of uniform size throughout the subdivision.[22] This can lead to a great deal of wasted space and a lack of exciting visual opportunities. A planned unit development, in contrast to this, is designed to accommodate the same or possibly more dwelling units or other types of uses[23] but the uses are placed on one or several areas of the lot and not spread uniformly over the entire parcel of property. In this way, open spaces may be retained for other kinds of

[20] See, e.g., *Mullins v. City of Knoxville*, 665 S.W.2d 393 (Tenn.App. 1983); *McCallen v. Memphis*, 786 S.W.2d 633 (Tenn.1990).

[21] Thus, both are still suspect to question as being *ultra vires* the enabling legislation under Tennessee law. Most land use planning attorneys in Tennessee believe that both planned unit developments and site plan review are allowable under Tennessee law as an implied power but this theory has never been tested. The Supreme Court's decision in *McAllen*, supra, note 19, did not address the issue of enabling legislation. Shelby County, however, does have specific enabling legislation for PUDs. See Chapters 71 and 72 of the Private Acts of 1973. See also Mandelker at § 9.26.

[22] Mandelker at § 9.24.

[23] Frequently, zoning ordinances give a bonus for planned unit development over subdivision usage ratios. Theoretically, highly specific site plan recommendations off-set any adverse impact and justify the more intense use.

uses on the same property. For example, a park (swimming facilities or other such public amenities) may be placed in a planned unit development. The dwelling units may be concentrated in one area with the open space being reserved for the use of the residents or other occupiers. However, generally, these types of approvals are done by the legislative body with the recommendation of the planning commission. It is not a function of the board of zoning appeals as in the case of a conditional use permit, and in effect, it is a zone change subject to pre-set administrative guidelines.

When first started in Nashville, for example, the base zoning district was overlaid with a planned unit development district and this planned unit development district specifies exactly the use to which the property may be put.[24] Frequently, in this process, the planning commission gives highly specific recommendations and requirements as to how the site must be laid out in order to gain legislative approval. This bears some resemblance to a conditional use permit,[25] but is significantly different inasmuch as the conditional use permit is merely the administrative application of a set of pre-set conditions to a particular proposed use whereas a planned unit development involves a proposed zone change with planning recommendations as to how to lay out the site.[26]

Site plan review, on the other hand, is a minute review of the lay-out of a particular site (there is usually no discretion concerning the use

---

[24] Nashville has not employed the PUD style development for the last several years. Recently, however, the city has begun experimenting with SP [Specific Plan] zoning, which from legal standpoint, appears quite similar.

[25] As noted earlier, see footnote 7, the legal analysis is reasonably similar: If the applicant meets all the requirements, the permit must be issued. *Mullins v. City of Knoxville*, 665 S.W.2d 393 (Tenn. App. 1983).

[26] Site plan review in conjunction with a conditional use permit application is certainly possible and is in fact generally considered part of the process. This will be discussed later in the chapter, beginning at page 158.

of the property inasmuch as it is permitted). The emphasis is upon the subject parcel and how to best arrange development on the site, not the use to which the site is put.[27]

> Many modern zoning ordinances contain provisions for site plan review, and this is one of the most useful techniques involved in modern zoning. In many communities, especially largely built-up ones, most new development takes place by the assembly of several lots and their redevelopment by private investment, usually without public assistance. In regulating such redevelopment, site plan review performs a function analogous to subdivision control (on vacant land) and urban renewal (for worn-out areas). Like most administrative arrangements, such provisions may, of course, be misconceived or misused, to deal with matters far beyond their appropriate function. Properly conceived, such regulations are concerned primarily with (a) the layout of buildings and open space, including parking areas, and (b) the provisions for access to and from the public street system.

Thus, site plan review is extremely narrow and it does not under any circumstances deal with the proposed use of the lot. By contrast, that is exactly what conditional use approval by a zoning board is. The zoning board is considering whether this particular use at this particular location is appropriate under the requirements set out in the zoning ordinance. Site plan review, properly conceived, should not ever reach the question of whether the particular use at that location is appropriate. It should only be concerned with the layout of the actual site and the way that layout interconnects with other off-site facilities such as the street pattern.[28] While the site plan review function is

---

[27] Williams at § 152.01.

[28] For example, should a street ramp be placed within 10 feet of the property line if there is another ramp 10 feet on the other side of it? These kinds of site planning problems, having nothing to do with whether or not the particular use is appropriate at that location, are appropriate. They should not, however, be confused with the issue of

normally delegated to the planning commission, there would appear to be no reason that the zoning board could not perform this function. In fact, special exceptions/conditional uses are usually accompanied by a site plan to be considered by the zoning board.[29]

It is extremely important, therefore, that the applicant, administrative tribunal, or reviewing court, clearly understand what zoning technique is being considered or employed. Different rules attach to the use of different techniques and different local agencies make the final decisions. Without a clear understanding of the technique which is being employed in any particular application or case, the applicable legal rules will not be clearly understandable.

C. Conditional Uses Are a Function of the Board of Zoning Appeals

Under the Tennessee Public Zoning Enabling Statutes,[30] the power to grant a special exception or conditional use permit is vested exclusively in the Board of Zoning Appeals. It would appear to be *ultra vires* the enabling legislation for the local legislative body to delegate this responsibility to any other tribunal, such as the local planning commission or even retain it itself.[31] There have evidently been no cases in Tennessee to consider this point.

The local legislative body itself is an inappropriate group to hear an application for a conditional use permit. The function of the local

---

whether the actual use is desirable in that locale.

[29] In fact, here in Tennessee, where there is no specific site plan authority, it would seem more reasonably to delegate the authority to the zoning board. It is very close to the issues raised in a special exception/conditional use, and there is specific authority for that function given to the board. There is also a long history concerning how such cases should be heard by the board.

[30] TENN. CODE ANN. §§ 13-7-107, 13-7-109, 13-7-206 and 207.

[31] *Depue v. City of Clinton*, 160 N.W.2d 860 (Iowa 1968).

legislative body, although it may arguably in some instances when considering a zone change, be quasi-judicial, is usually legislative.[32] For the most part, local legislative bodies are not set up to make quasi-judicial determinations on a record which would be required to sustain the decision on appeal. Frankly, although it is certainly open to some doubt,[33] a local legislative body is assuredly somewhat more political than the local board of zoning appeals. Thus, both because of the inherent political nature of the deliberations before the local legislative body and the form that those deliberations normally proceed, the local legislative body itself is particularly inappropriate to consider an application for a conditional use permit.

Alternatively, the planning commission is sometimes thought of as an appropriate administrative tribunal to exercise the power of granting conditional use permits. The difficulty with this approach is that if the conditional use permit process is linked to site plan approval, the same body that exercises site plan approval would be involved in the conditional use approval process. Site plan review, as indicated in the previous section, should most properly be considered to involve only a review of the site design. The matter of the use to which the location is to be put should be decided separately by another decision maker. As one commentator has said:[34]

---

[32] The Tennessee Supreme Court has expressly rejected this approach the quasi-judicial functional analysis in the context of a straight zoning change. See *Fallin v. Knox County*, 656 S.W.2d 338 (Tenn. 1983). The action of the Knox County legislative body in *Mullins* though was explicitly administrative and quasi-judicial. Query whether *Fallin* requires a declaratory judgment on the "fairly debatable" standard under those circumstances. Apparently it would. In the wake of *McAllen v. Memphis*, 786 S.W.2d 633 (Tenn. 1990), it appears that a conditional use permit application would be reviewed under the common law writ even if addressed to the local legislative body, although *McAllen* itself involved a planned unit development.

[33] In the experience of the author, local zoning boards tend to be highly political even though that should certainly <u>not</u> be the case.

[34] Williams: 5 *American Land Planning Law*, 2006 § 152.01.

> While the distinction in function between special permit and site plan review is perfectly clear, it is important that the distinction be maintained -- particularly in those states where the planning board is not permitted to take over the special-permit function. If in the course of site plan review, the planning board takes over the power to decide whether the proposed use is appropriate at that spot, in terms of its adverse impact on the neighborhood, the traffic it generates, etc., then site plan review becomes assimilated to the special permit function, and there is no difference between them. In order to avoid this, it is therefore important in drawing up a site plan review ordinance to spell out the grounds of review in detail – and so to avoid making everything a special permit use by the planning board.

Therefore, to the extent that site plan review is going to be involved in the conditional use permit process, the planning commission consultation is extremely desirable. The local urban planners ought to have a chance to give their input on the arrangement of the use of the site. But the final decision as to whether or not the use should be permitted in that area should be left to the board of zoning appeals.[35] Several courts outside of the state of Tennessee have reviewed this issue. In New Jersey where the enabling legislation was at the time similar to that in Tennessee, the New Jersey Superior Court, Appellate Division,[36] has held clearly that a planning commission has no right to

---

[35] Ordinarily, local boards of zoning appeals have somewhat less access to professional planning services than do planning commissions. Thus, a planning commission could rely on its staff to help with a site plan review. A zoning board ordinarily has a little more difficulty in doing that. Many times, zoning boards are staffed by codes enforcement personnel who may or may not have any training in the area of urban planning.

[36] *Saddle River Country Day School v. Saddle River*, 51 N.J. Super. 589, 144 A.2d 425, 433 (App. Div. 1958). This opinion was written by Judge Hall. See also *Swimming River Golf & Country Club v. Borough of New Shrewsbury*, 30 N.J. 132, 152 A.2d 135, 137 (1959).

issue a conditional use permit, or, as it was known under their legislation[37] (and is under ours), a special exception.

> Such special uses, denominated "special exceptions" in New Jersey, are specifically provided for in our zoning law . . . under which the board of adjustment is the only agency empowered to hear and decide requests for same "in accordance with the provisions of any such ordinance," i.e., on the basis of standards specified therein . . . Under the scheme laid down by our enabling act, zoning must be accomplished by the creation of appropriate districts in which permitted uses are specified in the ordinance, with regulations respecting the same uniform throughout the district and similarly spelled out in the legislation . . . The only variations from such a pattern permitted by the statute are "special exceptions" and "variances" provided for by [the legislation]. Treating the Saddle River Amendment as an attempt to treat non-public school uses as "special exceptions," it must likewise fall since the board of adjustment is left out of the procedural scheme contrary to the statute . . . The matters committed to the board by the statute and the exercise of its powers may not in any way be circumscribed, altered or extended by the municipal governing body.

A similar result has obtained in Kentucky.[38]

> We conclude that so much of [the city ordinance] as attempts to empower the [planning] commission to entertain appeals from orders of the building inspector or to grant special permits is void.

---

[37] New Jersey enacted the Municipal Land Use Law of 1975 and the rules in New Jersey have changed as a result. Planning commissions in that state may now issue conditional use permits. See N.J.S.A. § 40:55 D-67.

[38] *Franklin County v. Webster*, 400 S.W. 2d 693, 696 (Ky.App. 1966).

The Kentucky Court indicated that the statutory authority for the exercise of this power was committed solely to the board of zoning appeals under Kentucky law, not given to the planning commission.[39] In conclusion, it is inappropriate under the Tennessee Public Enabling Legislation for any body other than the local board of zoning appeals to have the jurisdiction to hear conditional use permit cases. Further, not only would it be *ultra vires* the enabling legislation, but in addition, from a policy standpoint, it makes no sense to have the local legislative body review conditional use permit applications because of the inherent political nature of such a body, and finally, the planning commission should not because of the possibility of confusing its normal site plan review orientation with a determination as to whether a particular use is permitted on the property. The better reasoned decisions hold that in the absence of specific enabling authority, no other administrative or legislative tribunal should hear conditional use permit cases other than a board of zoning appeals.

D. Specific Standards

Many Tennessee ordinances speak in extremely broad or general terms when setting the criteria by which to judge whether a conditional use permit should issue.[40] This process is entirely inappropriate.[41] The

---

[39] Id.

[40] Many writers have indicated that broad and general standards are many times upheld by the courts. See N. Williams: 5 *American Land Planning Law*, § 150.01; Rohan: 6 *Land Use Planning Control*, § 44.03[1]. While this may be true, it does not make it desirable either from an urban planning standpoint or from a legal standpoint.

[41] One Court, instead of invalidating the ordinance, went so far as to issue a mandamus requiring the issuance of a conditional use permit where the zoning regulation stated only broad legislative purposes and did not provide any standard for approval or denial of the application. *Kosinski v. Lawlor*, 177 Conn. 420, 418 A.2d 66, 68 (1979). See also *Kiser v. Parish of Jefferson*, 498 So.2d 115 (La.App. 1985), cert. den. 500 S.2d 423 (La. 1986); *Lithonia Asphalt v. Hall County*, 258 Ga. 8, 364

standards should be carefully crafted for each type of conditional use, describing in detail what the applicant must show in order to prevail. Specific standards are the only way that the applicant can know what is expected of him in the first place, and furthermore, are the only way in which reasonable judicial review of the decision can be made. If, for example, the criteria is that the proposed use be "compatible with all surrounding uses," the applicant has no idea of what he must show, and the reviewing court has even less. The zoning ordinance, when drafted by the local legislative body, should set out specific criteria dealing with the ways in which the proposed use must be compatible with the surrounding land uses. Otherwise, the legislative body has improperly delegated legislative power to an administrative board.

Of course, as noted earlier, because by definition the uses conditionally permitted in a given area indicate that a legislative judgment that those uses are reasonably compatible with the surrounding land uses, a broad "compatibility" standard is particularly inappropriate. The local legislative body would never have made it a conditional use in that area of the county or municipality in the first place if it was not reasonably compatible. Thus, to rely on a restriction which says that the use must be "compatible" with the surrounding land uses, invites the administrative body to do nothing other than second guess the legislative determination.[42] An administrative body should never have the power and clearly lacks the authority to review the action of a local legislative body in delegating the original authority to them in the first place. To put it another way, a zoning board should not be called upon under the terms of the zoning ordinance to determine whether a school, for example, is compatible with the surrounding land uses. The local legislative body should have already, in the specific standards applicable to schools, set out what kind of school it is talking about, how it should be designed and placed on the lot, what kind of

---

S.E.2d 860 (1988); *Davidson Mineral v. Monroe County*, 257 Ga. 215, 357 S.E.2d 95 (1987); *Sherman v. Colorado Springs*, 763 P.2d 292 (Colo. 1988); *Wakelin v. Yarmouth*, 523 A.2d 575 (Me. 1987); *Erigan Co., Inc. v. Town of Grantwood Village*, 632 S.W.2d 495, 498 (Mo.App. 1982).

[42] *Father Ryan*, 774 S.W.2d at 186.

access is required and other such particular land use planning standards. Broadly delegated standards fail miserably in this respect.

Furthermore, many ordinances will set out reasonably specific criteria for each individual conditional use, but will add a catchall category of general conditions with which the proposed use must also comply. Such catchalls may include the requirement that the use be conducive to the public health, welfare and safety, or compatible with surrounding land uses, or not increase traffic congestion, or decrease the property values, or other such general requirements. All such requirements are too vague to be meaningful. The first one noted above, the public health, safety and welfare, has been held by the Middle Section Tennessee Court of Appeals to be *ultra vires* the enabling legislation.[43] Lack of compatibility with the surrounding land uses is the legislative issue here. The local zoning ordinance should have set out specific requirements which would guarantee, upon compliance by the applicant with the requirements, that it is compatible. To enact a broad, vague standard such as "compatibility" tells the applicant, the zoning board and the reviewing court nothing.

In addition to the lack of meaning, such broad and vague standards invite other evils to which local zoning boards are already prone.[44]

---

[43] *Father Ryan High School v. City of Oak Hill*, 774 S.W.2d 184 (Tenn.App. 1988). The author believes that based on the reasoning by Judge Franks in this Court of Appeals decision, all of the general criteria usually relied upon by counties or municipalities are inherently suspect as being *ultra vires* the enabling legislation. The enabling legislation in Tennessee does not allow inquiry into any of these general criteria. These are the kinds of factors that the local legislative body should be considering when they adopt the zoning ordinance in the first place; they are not the factors that a local administrative body such as a board of zoning appeals should be considering in granting a specific application.

[44] *Osius v. City of St. Clair Shores*, 344 Mich. 693, 700, 75 N.W.2d 25, 28 (1956).

> Without definite standards, an ordinance provides an open door to favoritism and discrimination, a ready tool for the suppression of competition through the granting of authority to one and the withholding from the other.

Even without intentional discrimination, does not the local board's susceptibility to community pressures make it a particularly inappropriate agency to delegate such broad unbridled power? Requirements prohibiting increases in traffic congestion and decreases in property value are also virtually meaningless. ***All developments*** increase traffic congestion.[45] The question is not whether traffic congestion is increased but whether the project unreasonably increases traffic congestion. Specific criteria should be set out by the local legislative body as to what degree of increase in traffic congestion is warranted and what is not. Such values can be expressed either in absolute terms[46] or in relative terms.[47]

Finally, decreases in property values are nothing more than a public opinion poll.[48] That is, the value of any property is a function of the subjective evaluation of what a willing buyer will pay a willing seller. However, assuming that this criteria is one which is justifiable, the local legislative body should prescribe some reasonably objective criteria, again expressed either in absolute or relative terms, which would give the administrative board a guide by which to determine

---

[45] *Toohey v. Kilday*, 415 A.2d 732 (R.I. 1980); *Flowers Baking Co. v. Melbourne*, 537 So.2d 1046 (Fla.App. 1989); *C.R. Invs. v. Shoreview*, 304 N.W.2d 320 (Minn. 1981). The construction of a single family residence increases the traffic congestion to some extent, even if it is only two trips per day.

[46] Such as how many additional trips per day would be justified under the circumstances, or restricting additional traffic to preserving the current level of service.

[47] That is, expressed as a percentage of the number of trips already existing in the area.

[48] *Williams* at § 15.04.

whether the decrease is so severe as to warrant a denial of the application. For example, if the standard required that the surrounding property values not be decreased by over 25 percent, proof could be taken on whether or not the surrounding properties would be decreased by the presence of a particular use in the area by that amount. This is at least a reasonably objective criteria on which the board may hear proof, possibly conflicting, and reach a deliberate decision. A reviewing Court would then be able to review the evidence presented to the board, determine whether in fact there was proof in the record from which the board could determine that the value would be decreased by the requisite amount, and then determine whether the legal conclusion (that the permit be denied) clearly flowed from the evidence adduced at the board hearing.

Specific criteria enumerated in the local zoning ordinance is therefore indispensable concerning what the applicant must prove to the local board of zoning appeals in order to have a conditional use permit granted, indispensable so that the local board of zoning appeals can apply the law to the facts of the case and not employ its own unbridled discretion, and indispensable to a reviewing Court to make a judgment about whether the board of zoning appeals had proof in front of it allowing it to reach a decision justifying the legal conclusion.

E. Burden of Proof

It seems clear that the burden of proving compliance with each of the individual requirements for a conditional use permit is on the applicant. The Tennessee cases seem to assume this[49] and other authorities make it perfectly clear.[50] Professor Williams has noted that

---

[49] *Harrell* at 508, "We think it is abundantly clear (. . . that the [applicant] had fully complied) with the requirements of the ordinance . . .; *Father Ryan* at 187, "Since the [applicants] have satisfied all of the requirements or conditions of the zoning ordinance, the zoning board must issue the requested use permit."

[50] Rohan: 6 *Zoning and Land Use Control* § 44.02[2][b]; *Berman v. Manchester Township*, 540 A.2d 8 (Pa.Commwth. 1988).

there are two general approaches to the issuance of conditional use permits: on the one hand, some states indicate that the board of zoning appeals has "a good deal of discretion" to decide whether a conditional use permit shall issue.[51] On the other hand, Professor Williams points out that a presumption exists in some states that a special permit should normally be granted in the absence of some strong reason to the contrary. "Under the usual formulation of this theory, a developer has a right to a special permit if he has satisfied all of the standards."[52] Professor Williams is somewhat critical of this presumptive entitlement theory, but the Tennessee Courts appear to have adopted it in *Harrell*, *Sexton*, *Merritt*, and *Father Ryan*.[53] Furthermore, Williams' criticism that the presumptive entitlement theory does not work with an ordinance that only specifies vague standards is easily rebutted by requiring reasonably specific standards. If a local legislative body cannot specify reasonably the criteria by which an administrative body is to judge whether the proposed use should be allowed in this particular area, then either the use should not be permitted in the area, or some different zoning technique should be employed to facilitate its placement. The Tennessee Courts have appropriately adopted the presumptive entitlement approach without calling it such.

---

[51] N. Williams 5 *American Land Planning Law* § 148.04.

[52] Williams at § 148.05. Other case examples include *Fulton County v. Bartenfield*, 257 Ga. 766, 363 S.E.2d 555 (1988); *LaFame v. Atlanta*, 258 Ga. 631, 373 S.E.2d 212 (1988). There is little discussion in the cases concerning the possibility that the board might find the applicant's proof incredible. This, however, shouldn't be much of a concern. First, the codes enforcement staff should be knowledgeable of any outright fabrications; second, the staff often makes a preliminary finding of compliance before the board hearing is set. Conversely, to permit the board to make a finding of no credibility in the absence of contrary proof gives the board absolute authority to deny the permit in any case. The possible abuse and discrimination inherent in such a system is self-evident.

[53] In each of these cases, the board's decision denying the permit was reversed by the Court.

Secondly, Professor Williams indicates that even with more specific standards, the conditional use permit is to some extent discretionary.[54] That is of course true to the extent there is a factual conflict between the proponents and opponents. Under Tennessee law, it is clear that if there is conflicting proof about the applicant's compliance with the conditions, the board of zoning appeals makes a decision which is final on the facts. That is to say, if the requirement for a day care center in Nashville, Tennessee is that the day care center be no closer than 250 feet to any other day care center on the same residential street, if the applicant puts on proof tending to show that he is 256 feet away from the nearest daycare center, but the neighbors, in opposition, put on proof to show that in fact he is 246 feet from the nearest daycare center, a question of fact is presented to the board of zoning appeals which then has the discretion to rule one way or the other. The Board makes this determination based upon the credibility of the witnesses and other information which it may have available.[55]

This is a world apart from the situation where the City of Oak Hill rules that a private high school cannot come in because it is against the public interest.[56] How any applicant can contest this determination is utterly impossible to know. It is possible conceptually that the

---

[54] *Williams* at § 148.05.

[55] Under the Tennessee Common Law Writ of Certiorari, TENN. CODE ANN. § 27-8-101 et seq., the Board's determination of the facts is final and binding upon a court of law. Only if there is no evidence in the record on which the board could make that finding of fact, would a court be entitled to reverse the board's decision. Thus, if the board found for the neighbors in the example, that the proposed daycare center was within 246 feet of another daycare center, and if even one of the neighbors had testified that he had measured the distance, that would be a sufficient factual basis upon which the board could deny the application. The whole point here, though, is that absent such specific factual findings, the board should not deny applicants a conditional use permit.

[56] *Father Ryan v. City of Oak Hill*, 774 S.W.2d 184 (Tenn.App. 1988).

original burden of production and persuasion should be upon the applicant to meet the specific criteria set up under the ordinance. However, upon satisfying those criteria, the burden might be shifted so that the neighbors would have the burden of production and persuasion to show that the use would violate the health, safety and welfare of the community or whatever other general language might be contained within the ordinance.[57] The opponents then have the opportunity to raise specific factual grounds concerning the requirements contained in the ordinance as well as any alleged adverse impact on the health, safety, welfare or other general conditions, and then the burden would once again shift to the applicant to prove that those specific concerns were unfounded.[58] One other conceptual way of approaching this problem is to hold that the compliance with the specific criteria of a zoning ordinance relating to conditional use permits establishes a presumption that the general requirements have been met and that the objectors must then come back with proof to show that the general conditions have in fact not been met.[59] The best approach is, however, to prescribe specific standards for each use, and omit any general standards at all. *Father Ryan* appears to endorse this approach.[60]

The nature of the proof which must be adduced by the neighboring property owners in opposition has been minutely discussed in the Tennessee cases. Typically, the applicant puts on proof of compliance with the specific criteria, only to have a vast number of irate neighboring property owners who would not be in support of the proposal under the best of circumstances, parade to the podium and

---

[57] *Mandelker* at § 6.56.

[58] *Mulligan v. Zoning Board of Adjustment*, 495 A.2d 647 (Pa.Commw.Ct. 1985); *Robinson Township v. Westinghouse Broadcasting Company*, 440 A.2d 642 (Pa. Commw. Ct. 1981); *Value Oil Company v. Town of Irvington*, 156 N.J. Super. 354, 377 A.2d 1224 (L.Div. 1977), aff'd 164 N.J. Super. 419, 396 A.2d 1149 (App. Div. 1978).

[59] *Value Oil Co. v. Town of Irvington*, 152 N.J. Super, 354, 377 A.2d 1225, 1232, (1977).

[60] 774 S.W.2d at 186.

denounce the project because of the increase in traffic, the decrease in property values, noise considerations, and the like. Essentially these amount to a feeling that the public health, safety and welfare is not met by allowing this use into the surrounding vicinity. In *Harrell v. Hamblen County*,[61] the Court was presented with an application for a mobile home park. The Court reversed a denial and held that:[62]

> It is obvious that the planning commission and the quarterly court denied the permit to the petitioners because of the objection of the adjacent property owners, which they were without authority to do. Although these adjacent property owners may be justifiably concerned as to the adverse effect that may be had on the value of their property, this does not permit an administrative agency to deny an adjoining property owner the right to use his property for lawful purposes and not in violation of zoning or restrictions.

Again, in *Sexton v. Anderson County*,[63] the Court was presented with a board of zoning appeals decision denying a conditional use permit, this time for a landfill. As one might suspect, a large segment of the community appeared and voiced opposition. The Court reversed:[64]

> Various members of the community expressed beliefs and opinions that the presence of the landfill would create noxious odors and result in falling property values. They also thought that trucks delivering refuse to the site of the fill would cause additional damage to the local roads. These statements were offered on the issue of whether the intended use is "potentially dangerous, noxious or offensive." None rises to the dignity of being material

---

[61] 526 S.W.2d 505 (Tenn.App. 1975).

[62] *Harrell*, 526 S.W.2d at 508-9.

[63] 587 S.W.2d 663 (Tenn.App. 1979).

[64] *Sexton*, 587 S.W.2d at 666.

> evidence on the issue. In each instance, the statements amount to an expression of opinion on the ultimate issue, unsubstantiated by factual premises. Speculations, expressions of fears, and considerations of an aesthetic or political nature do not form a basis to support a decision made by an administrative body charged with adjudicatory responsibility.

The problem that the neighbors were having in these cases is not that they did not have a right to speak out against the proposed use. The technical problem was that their proof was not competent. None of the neighbors qualified as an expert. And while it is of course true that the owner of a piece of property may testify as to the value of the property,[65] there is no reported case in Tennessee which indicates that a property owner may testify about the future value of his property if a school, landfill, or other use is located adjacent to it. It would seem that this calls for the testimony of an expert witness either in the area of land use planning (that is, an urban planner), or in real estate appraisals.[66] Testimony concerning the supposed increase in traffic generation is also another problem with which the ordinary lay person has little experience. It would appear that a traffic engineer is probably the most appropriate expert to testify on these kinds of issues.

Thus, if the neighboring property owners, rather than appearing and just voicing their own, albeit sincerely held, but nevertheless lay

---

[65] *State ex rel. Smith v. Livingston Limestone Co.*, 547 S.W.2d 942 (Tenn. 1977).

[66] One caveat worth noting here is that sometimes the use applied for is repeated across the municipality or county. If the neighbors were to call a neighbor of an already existing daycare, operated by the same management, the testimony of the second neighbor as to property value, traffic, and so forth might be admissible because the second neighbor has first-hand information. He can testify about the conditions before the daycare located in his area, and after the daycare located in his area.

beliefs, hired an expert[67] or perhaps found an expert witness within the municipal government itself,[68] and if such pertinent proof is put on by a competent witness, the board of zoning appeals may then properly consider the evidence and make a decision as to which submission is the most credible. If the applicant's proof appears to be the most credible in the eyes of the board, then the applicant should be granted the conditional use permit and an appropriate order entered. If, on the other hand, the neighbors' proof is thought to be the most credible, then the conditional use permit should be denied on evidence by a competent

---

[67] In an interesting variation on the theme expressed in the preceding note, in *Joseph Company v. Bailey*, 14 TAM 5-19 (Tenn.App. 1988), the Court reversed a trial court's reversal of the denial of a "use permitted on review." The application was to permit the operation of a metal shredder but the neighbors introduced the testimony of a former operator of a slightly different and smaller type of metal shredder who had operated on this same property over 15 years before. This "neighbor/expert" testified about the kinds of problems she had faced in her shredder operation and testified that the applicant would have similar problems. The trial court reversed because this was not "material evidence" but was rather "speculation" and "unfounded opinion." The appellate court properly reversed because this testimony was obviously competent. The administrative decision-maker (the Knoxville City Council) had competent proof on both sides of the issue and found the proof more credible on the neighbors' side of the case. The applicant challenged the neighbors' expert as being a disgruntled former employee but ". . . the determination of a witness' credibility lies in the first instance with . . . the Knoxville City Council, and will be given great weight by the reviewing court, as it had the opportunity to see the manner and demeanor of [the witness] as she testified." Sl.Op. at 6. See page 167.

[68] Local governments are replete with various kinds of "free" experts. Urban planners usually staff the local planning commission; traffic engineers are usually available at the public works department or other areas; other engineers are usually available from the highway department. Neighbors may also find "free" experts at state levels of government asking for opinions concerning the impact of the proposed use on traffic patterns on state highways and other such information.

witness that goes directly to one or more of the specific standards enumerated in the ordinance and an appropriate order entered. Under those circumstances, the applicant has had a fair hearing: he has had an opportunity to put on proof going directly to the merits of the case and his proof has been found not as credible as other proof submitted to the administrative body.

There are several troublesome cases which appear to hold to the contrary with regard to lay testimony. In the first, *Cone Oil v Williamson County Regional Planning Commission*, [69] a conditional use permit for the expansion of an existing refueling station was denied by the regional planning commission. [70] The planning staff recommended approval; the traffic engineers for both the planning commission and the applicant agreed that "the traffic impact would not create a safety problem and would be manageable." [71]

As against these expert witnesses, [72]

> Local residents were again allowed to air their views, the first of whom was a county commissioner and former truck driver who feared that too many trucks would be backed up at the station . . .

---

[69] 1996 WL 465222 (Tenn. Ct. App. August 16, 1996).

[70] As we have previously discussed, a planning commission has no authority to consider conditional use permits under Tennessee law. The local ordinance in Williamson County is flawed in this regard; this case should have been heard by the zoning board but the ordinance is not set up that way and the developer is usually not in a position to argue with that point. See page 157. This conclusion may be called into question by the recent case *Roten v. Spring Hill*,2009 WL 2632778 (Tenn. Ct. App., August 26, 2009).

[71] At *1.

[72] Id.

If the truck driver was familiar with this operator at this or another location, perhaps that would be reasonable. But that was not indicated. He ***feared*** that too many trucks would be backed up. That should not be sufficient, especially in the face of expert testimony. This is all the more true since he was also a county commissioner, and one can bet that there was more than a small hint of politics in his opposition. Why couldn't these folks hire an expert to contest the other testimony? The applicant has spent a considerable amount of money to get approved and on the "fears" on one man, the project is denied. This is simply inappropriate.

The Court of Appeals at the end of the opinion says:[73]

> It is true that most of the ten residents who spoke in opposition to the granting of the permit merely expressed their opinions, but we know of no reason why the views of concerned residents whose experiences are relevant, i.e., the former truck driver, cannot be considered concomitantly with those of experts.

The reason that concerned residents cannot testify is because they lack the qualifications. A witness must have knowledge relevant to the inquiry. The court seems to believe that just by virtue of driving a truck that the driver is qualified to give opinion on roadway design safety. If this were true, our courts would have a very different approach to making decisions. The answer is to require experts to testify. Lay opinion testimony, even in the informal setting of a zoning board should not be permitted.

Gibralter Taft Highway Ltd Partnership v Town of Walden is similar.[74] In that case, the application was for a planned unit development of residential town homes. The legal standards for CUPs and PUDs are very similar. In this case, the planning commission approved the application but PUDs are usually considered by the local legislative body as well and the application was disapproved. The Court

---

[73] Id at *3.

[74] 2004 WL 2715280, Tenn.Ct.App., November 30, 2004.

of Appeals focused on sewer and traffic issues in upholding the denial but again, based on testimony of the neighbors. With regard to sewage disposal plans, it is unclear why the town needed more information other than that the Hamilton County Wastewater Treatment Authority was willing and able to service the development.

With regard to traffic, the entrance to the site was thought by the neighbors to be dangerous:

> While the plaintiff presented testimony that the entrance to the PUD was well within the sight distance required by the Tennessee Department of Transportation, several citizens expressed their concerns about the entrance, including the dangers presented by fog, slick roads, and a blind curve near the entrance. As pointed out by the Board, these citizens were familiar with the road off of which the entrance would be located and the weather conditions that would adversely affect driving in that area. This court has previously stated that "we know of no reason why the views of the concerned residents whose experiences are relevant . . . cannot be considered concomitantly with those of experts." [citing *Cone Oil*]

Fog, slick roads and blind curves? Most areas have fog and many have slick roads: these do not seem to be a reason to deny the application. A blind curve could be, but how does that reconcile with the testimony that the development complied with TDOT regs? Most lay testimony should not be permitted to address future conditions. That is the role of an expert witness.

It is difficult frankly to reconcile the four earlier cases (*Sexton, Harrell, Father Ryan* and *Merritt*)[75] with *Cone Oil* and *Gibraltar*. In *Sexton*, the conditions of the road and the impact of heavy trucks was the subject of lay testimony; if permitted in *Cone Oil*, why not in *Sexton*.

---

[75] Not to mention several other cases that do not directly involve CUPs, such as *Cost v City of Lebanon*, 2009 WL 856643, (Tenn.Ct.App. March 31, 2009) and *Davis (MC) Group v Metro Nashville*, 912 SW 2d 178 (Tenn. Ct. App. 1995).

It is far preferable to require expertise in these cases. Lay testimony should not be accepted accept on issues where the lay witness would have first hand knowledge, such as how far away the development is from other similar developments and so forth. Where, as in the four Tennessee cases cited above, neighbors put on no competent proof at all (only unsubstantiated expressions of fear), and the only proof before the administrative body is that of the applicant demonstrating compliance with all of the specific standards, the conditional use permit must and should issue.

F. Conditions on Issuance

It is clear that a zoning board, in issuing a conditional use permit, may impose whatever restrictions[76] it deems appropriate subject only to a few rules of limitation. The Tennessee Public Zoning Enabling Legislation specifically provides that special exceptions may be granted, "in appropriate cases and subject to appropriate principles, standards, rules, conditions, and safeguards set forth in the ordinance."[77] While the language of that statutory provision appears to require that the "conditions" be set forth in the ordinance, most courts have held that a board may impose conditions other than those set forth in the ordinance.[78] Generally, of course, "a valid condition must be designed

[76] The terminology here can get confusing. Typically, in Tennessee, once the conditions (requirements) of the ordinance are met, the applicant is presumptively entitled to the conditional use permit. The board may, however, impose conditions (restrictions) of its own which are separate and distinct from the specific conditions (requirements) contained in the ordinance. This confusion may augur in favor of a different term, such as special permit.

[77] TENN. CODE ANN. § 13-7-107, and § 13-7-206.

[78] *Nance v. City of Memphis*, 672 S.W.2d 208 (Tenn.App. 1983); *Borough of North Plainfield v. Perone*, 50 N.J.Super. 1, 148 A.2d 50 (App.Div. 1959); *Nassau Children's Home v. Board of Zoning Appeals*, 430 N.Y.S.2d 683 (App.Div. 1980); *Williams*, § 151; *Rohan* at § 44.04; *Mandelker* at § 6.57.

to promote some of the statutory purposes of zoning."[79] The board certainly may not waive any of the conditions, restrictions, safeguards, or requirements set out under the local zoning ordinance.[80] Further, it appears clear that the types of conditions must actually relate to the use of the property. For example, a school use could not have a condition imposed as to the types of course taught. It is generally believed that a condition on the non-transferability of the use is invalid as well.[81] Tennessee Courts have specifically condoned a time limit,[82] but these types of time limits have been severely criticized by many of the commentators.[83]

In Tennessee, before imposing some such condition, there must be proof before the zoning board that such a restriction is justified. Without such proof, the condition is beyond the power of the board and is illegal.[84]

---

[79] Williams, at § 51.01.

[80] Rohan at § 44.04[1].

[81] See *McClurkan v. Metropolitan Board of Zoning Appeals*, 565 S.W.2d 495, 497 (Tenn.App. 1977); this case involves a zoning variance, but the author submits that the analysis is the same for conditional use permits.

[82] *Nance v. City of Memphis*, 672 S.W.2d 208 (Tenn.App. 1983). The "special use permit" at issue in this case was issued by the local legislative body, and that may provide extra protection in an administrative appeal, even if it is not supposed to. The case involved a mental health "day care and treatment center;" originally, the permit was granted for only a year, and then was extended to 3 years.

[83] 3 Anderson: *American Law of Zoning 3d* § 21.33 (1987).

[84] *Demonbreun v. Metro Board of Zoning Appeals*, 206 S.W.3d 42, (Tenn.Ct.App., December 7, 2005).

Appropriate conditions, including types of hours of operation,[85] buffers, setbacks (to the extent not already controlled by the ordinance), traffic patterns, and other similar types of land use considerations are obviously within the power of the board to impose conditions.

Furthermore, to the extent that the board grants a permit with a condition, if the landowner begins construction under the permit without contesting the condition, he is estopped from later contesting the condition. In *Stevenson v. Palmer*,[86] the Plaintiff owned a parcel of property zoned for multiple dwelling use. The Memphis Zoning Ordinance provided that multiple dwellings had to be constructed all within the same building and the Plaintiff, wishing to construct an apartment complex consisting of nine units of eight apartments each, applied for a building permit which was denied. An appeal was taken to the Board of Adjustments which granted an "exception" subject to certain specified conditions, one of which was that the Plaintiff construct a brick wall around three sides of the development. Based on the Board's decision, the Plaintiff obtained a building permit and constructed the apartments.

About a year and a half later, the Plaintiff returned to the Board of Adjustments requesting a "variation" in order to be relieved of the requirement of building the brick wall imposed by the Board in its original order. On appeal, the developer argued that the Board of Adjustments had no power or jurisdiction to grant an exception to the zoning ordinance requiring the construction of the brick wall and the decision of the Board insofar as it required the construction of the brick wall was void.

This case evidently arises under the Private Zoning Enabling legislation concerning the City of Memphis.[87] The Court held that as a

---

[85] Id.

[86] 223 Tenn. 485, 448 S.W.2d 67, 69 (1969).

[87] 448 S.W.2d at 69: The Supreme Court cites the Private Act of 1925, Chapter 428, which amended the original Memphis Zoning Enabling legislation. Note the possible applicability of Chapter 142 of

general rule the Board of Adjustments in granting the exception could not impose a condition or requirement more strict than the requirements of the ordinance under which it acted. At the same time, the Court held that "the grant of broad power to a Board of Adjustments in zoning matters is necessary in order for the Board to have the needed flexibility to properly function." The Court concluded that the Board of Adjustments had the power to require the brick wall as a condition for the granting of the exception. It further held that inasmuch as the original order of the Board was not appealed but that the developer obtained a building permit and constructed the apartments, it was now estopped to complain of that decision of the board.

It seems clear that as to both holdings, the Supreme Court was correct. First, the construction of the brick wall around the apartment was surely designed to buffer the surrounding land uses from the apartment complex. Presumably, the land uses in the surrounding vicinity would have had some adverse impact from both the noise and aesthetic standpoints. Hence, the condition imposed was obviously related to the use of the land on the proposed site and was valid.

The failure of the developer to appeal the original order of the Board with the imposed condition should certainly preclude a challenge later on. The developer's failure to appeal the decision and his choice to begin the construction under a permit obtained solely because the Board granted the order is not justifiable. If the Courts were to allow a developer to appeal a decision like that at a later point in time, developers would be seeking to change imposed conditions on most projects.

Furthermore, while it is not blatantly apparent on the face of the opinion, it seems clear that the developer was actually asking for a variance from the Board of Adjustments to eliminate the required former condition. It would seem clear that the variance power of the Board should not be used in that way under any circumstances.

On the other hand, the Supreme Court's broad language vesting great discretion in the Board of Zoning Appeals appears to be

---

the Private Acts of 1955.

unnecessarily strong. The Board is merely an administrative body and should act under the powers delegated to it. In this case, the City of Memphis had evidently not supplied any conditions in their zoning ordinance. It is arguable that the private nature of the Memphis zoning enabling legislation gives the city more power than what would have been ordinarily the case under the public zoning enabling legislation,[88] but even under that enabling legislation, specific standards should be required before a Board of Zoning Appeals may grant special exceptions.[89] Certainly under the public enabling legislation, which would appear to be much less broad, specific conditions must be laid down by the local legislative body before the Board can be given the power to issue special exceptions, and their authority should not be considered as broad as the Memphis Board considered in *Stevenson.* Thus, while the condition actually imposed in the *Stevenson* case seems easily justifiable, the broad language utilized by the Court in its analysis should generally be rejected under Tennessee law.

By the time of the decision in *Nance v. City of Memphis,*[90] the Memphis legislation authorizing the exception was evidently changed. Because the legislative body, in granting the special exceptions, had always imposed a time limitation, the applicant reappeared at the conclusion of the preceding time limitation seeking an extension. The Court approved a time limitation of three years.[91]

> . . . the ordinance authorizing special use permits to be issued on such conditions as prescribed by the granting

---

[88] Memphis also may have greater authority by virtue of its home-rule status, Section 9, Article 11, Tennessee Constitution; Nashville does in fact make such claims under its Metropolitan home-rule form of government.

[89] It is unclear whether *Stevenson* is actually a special exception case or not. The Court used that language but it is nevertheless less than obvious given the text of the opinion.

[90] 672 S.W.2d 208, 212 (Tenn. App. 1984).

[91] Id.

> authority is broad enough to include, where appropriate, time limitations. Such provision is suitable to allow for the continuing supervision of a special use under the conditions and standards as required. It appears to this Court that time limitations calling for renewal are beneficial to those who might oppose the special use permit rather than a benefit to the holder of the special use permit.

Thus, the Western Section Court of Appeals approved a time limitation. While there is certainly a split of authority on whether time limitations are appropriate,[92] it would appear clear, however, that a change in the ownership should not affect the grant of the permit.[93]

So long as the conditions relate to the actual use of the property, the Court should uphold the condition imposed by the Board. Conditions which affect the development of the site, such as landscaping, paving, and access to the highway system, would appear to be clearly acceptable. Conditions limiting the hours of operation or the manner in which the use is operated, such as in the example above, limiting the use of teaching style or materials in a school, would clearly be unacceptable.

---

[92] Compare *Room & Board Homes v. Gribbs*, 67 Mich.App. 381, 241 N.W.2d 216 (1976) with *Nance.* See also *Scott v. Town of Salina*, 88 A.D.2d 767, 451 N.Y.S.2d 499 (1982).

[93] *Anza Park Corporation v. City of Burlingame*, 241 Cal.Rptr. 175 (Cal.App. 1987); *Mechem v. City of Santa Fe*, 634 P.2d 690 (N.M. 1981); *McClurkan v. Metropolitan Board of Zoning Appeals*, 565 S.W.2d 495 (Tenn.App. 1977) involves a variance, but its reasoning, invalidating such ownership restrictions, applies equally well to conditional use permits.

G. Application of Federal Law

1. Generally

While it does not come up very often in Tennessee because it is unusual for Tennessee zoning boards to impose mandatory exactions[94] upon an applicant, *Nolan v. California Coastal Commission*,[95] is also important in the context of conditions placed upon an applicant. In that case, the Court held unconstitutional a condition which imposed an easement requirement upon the issuance of a coastal development permit. The condition required the landowner to grant an easement permitting public access to a portion of their beachfront property in return for the permit. Justice Scalia, writing for the majority of the Court, focused on the purpose of the regulation and refused to defer to the California Coastal Commission's stated purpose for the regulation. The condition must substantially advance a legitimate state interest and not deny the owner an economically viable use of his property. In *Nolan*, the condition did not substantially advance any legitimate state interest.

The application of other areas of federal law to local zoning administration is also important to evaluate. While a thorough analysis of the many important areas of applicability is beyond the scope of this book, several important developments are worthy of comment. In *City of Cleburne v. Cleburne Living Center*,[96] the Supreme Court invalidated the denial by a local zoning board in Texas of an application to operate a residential home for the mentally handicapped.[97] The Court, without using any heightened degree of scrutiny, found that the decision of the

---

[94] A condition that requires the developer to donate land to the city ostensibly to offset some perceived negative impact of the development.

[95] 483 U.S. 825, 107 S.Ct. 3141, 97 L.Ed.2d 677 (1987)

[96] 469 U.S. 1016, 105 S.Ct. 427, 87 L.Ed.2d 313 (1985).

[97] Tennessee protects small homes for the mentally handicapped by statute, see TENN. CODE ANN. § 13-24-101 et seq.

zoning board simply did not have any rational basis and must therefore fall. The reasons proffered by the city as legitimate for the denial of the permit were carefully considered by the Court and rejected as being pretextual. There are two important lessons in *Cleburne*: first, while the mentally retarded are not either a suspect class or a quasi-suspect class for the purposes of the equal protection clause of the Fourteenth Amendment, one cannot help but suspect that some heightened degree of scrutiny was imposed by the Court in order to render the municipal action invalid; second, to the extent that there was really no heightened scrutiny by the Court because of the status of the proposed residents in the home, *Cleburne* is a marked movement away from the traditional deference shown by the United States Supreme Court in equal protection and substantive due process analyses.[98]

The result in *Cleburne* suggests the more active federal role in many types of zoning disputes, not just those relating to housing for the mentally retarded. For example, in *Marks v. City of Chesapeake*,[99] the City denied a conditional use permit to permit the use of a commercial property for the operation of a palmistry and fortune telling business. Notwithstanding the fact that the Director of the City Planning Commission testified that the operation of the palmistry was expressly permitted, the local council denied the application apparently based on public comments which demonstrated religious objections to palmistry and fortune telling.[100] The City articulated an ostensibly legitimate reason for the denial in that the proposed use would generate "too

---

[98] In *Euclid v. Amber Realty Company*, 272 U.S. 365, 47 S.Ct. 114, 71 L.Ed. 303 (1926), the Court upheld zoning using the rational relationship standard: "If the validity of the legislative classification for zoning purposes be fairly debatable, the legislative judgment must be allowed to control." 272 U.S. at 388. Arguably, *Cleburne* and *Nolan*, see note 88, both mark a departure from traditional federal constitutional analysis. The Court appears to be digging more deeply into the state and local motivations before allowing state and local legislative judgment to prevail.

[99] 883 F.2d 308 (4th Cir. 1989).

[100] 883 F.2d at 309.

limited a benefit"[101] to justify the grant of the permit. The Court ruled that the:[102]

> dispositive question is whether "local officials have . . . singled out a permit applicant for adverse treatment due to illegitimate, political, or, at least, personal motive. Such purposeful discrimination against a particular individual . . . violates the Constitution even where no recognized class based or invidious discrimination was involved.

Because the opponents to the application all (save one) offered religious reasons for their opposition to the permit,[103]

> The necessary and obvious inference -- given the council members' explicit concessions at trial that they were in fact influenced by the public's expressions of concern -- is that their deliberations were impermissively tainted by irrational neighborhood pressure manifestly founded in religious prejudice.

The Court upheld the District Court's ultimate conclusion that the City had acted both arbitrarily and capriciously.[104]

Thus, under *Cleburne* and *Marks*, it would appear that any decision which is not rationally related to a legitimate governmental objective may be subject to challenge in the Federal Courts and

---

[101] 883 F.2d at 312.

[102] 883 F.2d 311.

[103] 883 F.2d at 313.

[104] See also *J.W. v. City of Tacoma*, 720 F.2d 1126 (9th Cir. 1983); (the Court reversed a denial of a special use permit for a group home housing former mental patients as being inappropriate for the denial was not based on criteria in the ordinance but on the opposition of neighbors at a public hearing).

notwithstanding the traditionally narrow grounds for review,[105] the Federal Court may overturn the decision as being irrational, arbitrary or capricious.[106]

Another means by which the application of federal law might be sought is illustrated by *East-Bibb Twigs Neighborhood Association v. Macon Bibb Planning and Zoning Commission*,[107] where a group of adjoining property owners brought a civil rights action alleging a denial of the equal protection clause when the commission granted a conditional use permit allowing an applicant to build a sanitary landfill. The Court held against the neighbors finding that they had not presented sufficient evidence to demonstrate that "the commission acted with a discriminatory intent when it approved [the landfill], or that the commission engaged in a historical pattern of discriminatory conduct."[108] Certainly to the extent that the local board is granting a conditional use

---

[105] Id. at 1130-31.

[106] The Fair Housing Amendments Act of 1988, which amended Title VIII of the Civil Rights Act of 1968, also provides further protection to handicapped citizens. The Fair Housing Act, as amended, makes it unlawful: "To discriminate in the sale or rental, or to otherwise make unavailable or deny, a dwelling to any buyer or renter because of a handicap of (A) that buyer or renter, (B) a person residing in or intending to reside in that dwelling after it is sold, rented, or made available, or (C) any person associated with the buyer or renter." 42 U.S.C. § 3604(f)(1) and (3). See also *Familystyle of St. Paul v. City of St. Paul*, 728 F.Supp. 1396 (D.Minn. 1990). Furthermore, this Act may also offer protection to AIDS victims (or those who would attempt to provide housing for them). One Court has already issued injunctive relief where a "special use permit" was denied a person who intended to offer housing to AIDS victims where the evidence tended to demonstrate that the denial was based on irrational fears concerning the consequences of AIDS. See *Baxter v. Belleville*, 720 F.Supp. 720 (S.D.Ill. 1989).

[107] 896 F.2d 1264 (11th Cir. 1990) superceding 888 F.2d 1573 (11th Cir. 1989), and affirming 662 F.Supp. 1465 (M.D.Ga. 1987).

[108] 896 F.2d at 1267.

permit to allow the location of a use of property commonly thought of as undesirable, the board must have specific legitimate reasons for the placement. Here again, reliance by the board on vague and general criteria do not insulate it against charges of racism or other invidious discrimination. Specific criteria, however, would tend to offset such allegations[109] and make such actions more easily defensible.

Three other particular uses offer special problems. In *Haskell v. Washington Township*,[110] the Sixth Circuit (and the trial court below) concluded that a local zoning ordinance requiring that a conditional use permit be obtained for an abortion clinic was unconstitutional. Procedurally, the case is difficult to summarize, but suffice it to say that in 1982, the township enacted a zoning resolution which placed abortion clinics in a different classification from other medical facilities. A doctor had to choose between providing only abortion services or providing medical services other than abortion. Under the resolution, abortion clinics were required to file for a conditional use permit. At the time of the original enactment, there were only 3.317 acres zoned in the appropriate manner, and all of that was fully occupied by a cement company.[111]

The township insisted on adopting the resolution notwithstanding the advice of numerous attorneys opining it unconstitutional.[112] Finally, in 1986, the township acted to expand the classes of businesses allowed in those areas but did not define the term "abortion clinic." The District Court concluded that both of the zoning resolutions were unconstitutional. The first because it unconstitutionally infringed upon the effectuation of women's abortion decision rights, and the second

---

[109] Which is not to say that the same discriminatory intent may not be present.

[110] 864 F.2d 1266 (6th Cir. 1988).

[111] 864 F.2d at 1270.

[112] Id.

resolution because it was unconstitutionally vague.[113] The result here is that if the zoning ordinance bears on a fundamental right, the Court is going to look with strict scrutiny upon the enactment.[114]

2. Religious Uses and RLUIPA

Another area where similar considerations would seem to apply is in the area of religious uses. In *Islamic Center of Mississippi v. Starkville*,[115] the city zoning ordinance required a special exception to be granted. The board refused to grant a permit to the Islamic Center even though nine churches had previously been granted permission. In fact, the Islamic Center was the only church ever denied a conditional use permit.[116]

The Court did not have to labor hard over this opinion. "The record makes it clear that the city did not act in a religiously neutral manner when it rejected an exception for the Islamic Center."[117] The City insisted that it based its denial on traffic congestion and public safety. However, immediately next door was a pentecostal christian

---

[113] *Haskell v. Washington Township*, 635 F.Supp. 550, 551 (S.E.Ohio 1986). (The Court concluded that the township had to justify the zoning ordinance by the demonstration of a compelling state interest, an almost impossible task).

[114] *Deerfield Medical Center v. City of Deerfield Beach*, 661 F.2d 328 (5th Cir. 1981); *Mahoning Women's Center v. Hunter*, 610 F.2d 456 (6th Cir. 1979), vacated and remanded on other grounds 447 U.S. 918 (1980); *Framingham Clinic v. Zoning Board of Appeals*, 415 N.E.2d 840 (Mass. 1981).

[115] 840 F.2d 293 (5th Cir. 1988); see also *Love Church v. City of Evanston*, 671 F.Supp. 508 (N.D. Ill. 1987).

[116] 840 F.2d at 294 (the Court speaks in terms of "exception" and the author believes it to be a conditional use permit as discussed in this chapter).

[117] 840 F.2d 302.

worship center which the City did not concern itself with in any way other than to grant the required permit.[118]

It should be clear that a zoning ordinance requiring a conditional use permit for the use of property as either an abortion clinic or a church should contain specific religiously neutral or medically neutral standards to reduce the likelihood of discrimination and to require uniformity in the issuance of the permit.[119]

---

[118] Two other cases, not involving conditional use permits, reflect the balancing approach currently favored by the Federal Courts. In less aggravated conditions, *Grosz v. City of Miami Beach*, 721 F.2d 729 (11th Cir. 1983) involved an elderly orthodox Jewish rabbi who converted a garage at his residence to accommodate religious worship. The Court, in a sophisticated analysis, first asked two threshold questions: Did the regulation affect religious belief or opinion or did it affect conduct; second, the law must have both a secular purpose and a secular effect. The Court found that the zoning ordinance at issue passed both of these threshold inquiries. 721 F.2d at 733. The Court then balanced the City's legitimate interests in zoning objectives against the burden on the plaintiff's right to free exercise of religion and concluded that because the City did make available more than half of the city for religious services, including a location very close to the plaintiff's property, the regulation was a valid time, place and manner restriction. The Sixth Circuit ruled similarly in *Congregation of Jehovah's Witnesses v. City of Lakewood*, 699 F.2d 303 (6th Cir. 1983). The Court in this case determined that because the zoning ordinance only restricted the choice of location for the construction of a sanctuary, this was a minor burden, which when balanced against the important zoning objective at stake, did not outweigh the public's planning purposes.

[119] See Reynolds, *Zoning the Church: The Police Power vs. the First Amendment*, 64 B.U.L. Rev. 767, 769, 786-89 (1985). See also *Christian Gospel Church v. San Francisco*, 896 F.2d 1221 (9th Cir. 1990) (there is a rational basis for requiring all places of public assembly to obtain conditional use permit before establishment in residential neighborhood to minimize noise and traffic problems).

The *Islamic Center* case is decided purely on constitutional issues. With the advent of the Religious Land Use and Institutionalized Persons Act[120] cities are forced to be very careful in making decisions concerning religious activities. The act shifts the burden of persuasion from the plaintiff challenging the regulation or decision to the city if religious exercise is "substantially burdened."[121] That decision is the key part of the process; if the religious activity is substantially burdened then the court must apply the "compelling governmental interest test" and least restrictive means analysis.[122] The government is for the most part going to lose every case in which that high standard is required.

The federal Religious Land Use and Institutionalized Persons Act of 2000 (RLUIP)[123] basically reenacts the Religious Freedom Restoration Act of 1993 (RFRA).[124] The older act was declared unconstitutional in *City of Boerne v. Flores.*[125] The new RLUIP act seeks to avoid the constitutional infirmities and yet accomplish the same result: in effect, granting religious land uses some type of preferential treatment in the form of immunity from local zoning and land use planning regulations.

The Act is fairly simple in language:[126]

> No government shall impose or implement a land use regulation in a manner that imposes a substantial burden on the religious exercise of a person, including a religious assembly or institution, unless the government

[120] 42 USC § 2000cc.

[121] 42 USC § 2000cc(a).

[122] Id.

[123] 42 USC § 2000cc.

[124] 42 USC § 2000bb

[125] 521 U.S. 507, 117 S.Ct. 2157, 138 L.Ed.2d 624 (1997).

[126] 42 USC § 2000cc-1.

> demonstrates that imposition of the burden on that person, assembly, or institution--
>
> (1) is in furtherance of a compelling governmental interest; and
>
> (2) is the least restrictive means of furthering that compelling governmental interest

The Act therefore requires that if the local government is going to "impose a substantial burden" such as, by requiring special conditions for the location of a place of worship, or to add on another accessory use to an existing place of worship,[127] the government must have a "compelling state interest" and choose the "least restrictive means" of accomplishing the objective.

It is important to note that in most constitutional litigation over the last 75 years or so, the "compelling state interest test" generally has forced the government to prove a very high need for the regulation. In fact, when the test is applied, usually the government cannot sustain its burden and frequently loses.

The key question then becomes whether the actions of the local government impose a substantial burden on religious exercise. The Sixth Circuit has recently addressed the "substantial burden" language in an effort to guide the lower courts within its jurisdiction. And it applied a sensible test to the facts. In *Living Water Church of God v Charter Township,*[128] a small congregation in Meridian, Michigan applied for and received a "special use permit" for daycare facilities (limited to 72 children) and an elementary school (K-8, 280 children). However, the Township informed Living Water that the permit would expire if not used by May of 2001. Although the Township had previously granted extensions, that changed shortly before May of 2001

---

[127] The definition of land use regulation under the act seems to exclude its application to building codes. Under the old law there was a possibility that even extremely important building code objectives might be ruled in violation of the act; the RLUIP act seems to avoid that problem.

[128] 2007 WL 4322157 (December 10, 2007).

and at least one extension was denied another applicant. Living Water was unable to obtain an extension.

Living Water ultimately reapplied in 2003, increasing the size of the building sought (about 35,000 square feet) but decreasing the number of students (280 to 125). The Township board (the legislative body) approved the school enrollment size, but denied the building size. Living Water filed suit.

The central issue in the case was whether the denial by the Township imposed a substantial burden on Living Water's religious exercise. The Court found that it did not (and reversed the lower court). The test formulated by the 6th Circuit was whether:

> the government action placed substantial pressure on Living Water to violate its religious beliefs or effectively bar the church from using its property in the exercise of its religion?

The Court noted that the municipality might make religious exercise more expensive or difficult, but that was insufficient. Here, the Township granted the school with up to 125 students but denied the building size requested. However, since the zoning ordinance permitted construction of a facility of up to 25,000 square feet by right, the church had the option of proceeding accordingly, and needing no additional governmental approvals. Thus, the action of the township did not substantially burden the religious exercise of the church.

This area of the law will continue to evolve. It is certainly a challenging area, not the least because of the tension between the free exercise and establishment clauses of the federal constitution. The court noted:[129]

> On one hand, RLUIPA's definition of religious exercise covers most any activity that is tied to a religious group's mission, and "RLUIPA bars inquiry into whether a particular belief or practice is 'central' to [an individual's]

[129] Id at *6.

> religion." On the other hand, and in tension with this broader definition of religious exercise, Congress has cautioned that we are to interpret "substantial burden" in line with the Supreme Court's "Free Exercise" jurisprudence, which suggests that a "substantial burden" is a difficult threshold to cross. If the term "substantial burden" is not to be read out of the statute, RLUIPA cannot stand for the proposition that a construction plan is immune from a town's zoning ordinance simply because the institution undertaking the construction pursues a religious mission.

The federal courts will continue to struggle with this statute.

Perhaps a thornier questions is whether the churches need federal protection. Some authors [130] have asked for empirical evidence of widespread religious discrimination and conclude that in the absence of such proof, that the act does more harm than good. Ultimately, the religious institution seems to get an advantage that other land uses do not get, a type of special preference, or super priority, for religious uses.[131]

The city may be best advised in these controversies to allow at least some religious use of the property at issue. Denying totally the ability to practice religious beliefs seems a dangerous course. On the other hand, from the church's viewpoint, if the city can grant only partial relief constitutionally, the church winds up in a difficult situation. Likely, the Living Water property is not more than a stopgap after the 6th Circuit decision. There are big risks on both sides of any lawsuit in this area.

---

[130] Salkin and Lavine, *The Genesis of RLUIPA,* 40 Urban Lawyer 195, 256 (2008)

[131] Is there an Establishment Clause violation here? Probably not on its face, but as applied there might be.

3. Adult Entertainment

Jumping from churches to adult entertainment may not be the best segue, but both are frequently conditional uses and hence the discussion of both in this chapter. Specific criteria may be desirable but appear not to be mandatory when dealing with adult entertainment uses. In *11126 Baltimore Blvd. v. Prince George's County*,[132] the operator of an adult bookstore brought suit challenging a zoning ordinance which required a conditional use permit[133] for the operation of the bookstore. Notwithstanding the vague standards, including that the applicant demonstrate that his proposal would be in harmony with the zoning plan and not substantially impair the integrity of the master plan or adversely affect the health and welfare of the residents in the area or be detrimental to the use and development of adjacent properties, the Court reversed a lower Court decision[134] which held the ordinance invalid. It is far beyond our purpose to engage in an analysis of adult entertainment zoning here. The Supreme Court has spoken forcefully on these issues,[135] and has generally upheld zoning regulations restricting adult entertainment uses as valid time, place and manner restrictions on First Amendment freedom of speech. The Court concluded first that the ordinance here was a content neutral time, place and manner regulation. Second, the Court analyzed the impact of the ordinance under the four prong standard of *United States*

---

[132] 886 F.2d 1415 (4th Cir. 1989).

[133] The terminology used in *Prince George's County* was "special exception."

[134] 684 F.Supp. 884 (D.Md. 1988).

[135] *Young v. American Mini Theatres*, 427 U.S. 50, 96 S.Ct. 2440, 49 L.Ed.2d 310 (1975); *City of Renton v. Playtime Theatres*, 475 U.S. 41, 106 S.Ct. 925, 89 L.Ed.2d 29 (1986). In Tennessee, see *Entertainer 118 v. Metropolitan Sexually Oriented Business Licensing Board*, 2009 WL 2486195 (Tenn.Ct.App. August 14, 2009).

v. O'Brien.[136] The Court found that the ordinance complied with all four elements of the constitutional requirement.

The Trial Court had also held the ordinance unconstitutional because of the vague standards applicable to this conditional use permit. Frankly, the Appellate Court's analysis on the land use planning implications is specious. The Court analyzed the applicant's position assuming a zoning board would accept the applicant's side of the case. For example, the Court noted that the general requirements could be satisfied by witnesses for the applicant explaining the proposed use and addressing specifically any problem, such as traffic and noise, which were apparent from the application.[137] The Court did not note that obviously opponents to this kind of a use will show up at the hearing, and it would be quite a simple matter for the zoning board to accept the opponents' version on general and vague criteria as opposed to the position of the proponents. Furthermore, somewhat humorously, the Court looked to Maryland case law and concluded that:[138]

> Under Maryland case law, a county's decision pertaining to a special exception application is to be supported by competent material and substantial evidence in the record. Such a standard, well understood by Maryland Courts and zoning administrators, act as a clear check on the manipulation and arbitrary application of the terms of a special exception provision.

---

[136] 391 U.S. 367, 377, 88 S.Ct. 1673, 1679, 20 L.Ed.2d 672 (1968). A governmental regulation is sufficiently justified, despite an incidental impact upon First Amendment interests, (1) if it is within the constitutional power of the government; (2) if it furthers an important or substantial governmental interest; (3) if the governmental interest is unrelated to the suppression of free expression; and (4) if the incidental restriction on the First Amendment freedom is no greater than is essential to the furtherance of that interest.

[137] 886 F.2d at 1427

[138] Id. at 1427-8.

One might well ask why the substantial evidence test would act as a check on manipulation and arbitrary application of the ordinance. If neighbors appear in opposition, in the absence of specific criteria for guidance, the board may well deny the application by hiding behind broad general criteria. The neighbors may introduce any proof tending to show that the general criteria are not met, and the board, predisposed against the use, will accept that proof and rule against the use. A reviewing court will have great difficulty in overturning the board's finding. Anyone who believes that the neighborhood could not easily put substantial evidence of the detrimental impact of adult entertainment into a zoning record has never attended a zoning board meeting.[139] The result in *American Mini Theatres*, *Renton*, and *11126 Baltimore Blvd.* may all be best explained by the adult use which is being considered. Certainly, material bordering on the obscene is not viewed by anyone as having much intrinsic value, and the Supreme Court has itself noted that sexually explicit forms of expression merit less First Amendment protection than other kinds of speech.[140] Because of the undesirable type of land use under consideration, the Fourth Circuit may have been content to allow rather vague criteria to mask a discriminatory animus on the part of zoning boards in Maryland.

4. Telecommunications Act of 1996

The Federal Telecommunications Act of 1996 (FTCA) has come more and more into play on local zoning board agendas. It was designed to protect telecommunications providers in many different ways, but one of the principal concerns was the difficulty frequently met by telecommunications companies in attempting to locate towers for wireless phone service. The FTCA was enacted "to provide a pro-competitive, de-regulatory national policy framework designed to

[139] See also *F.W/PBS, Inc. v. City of Dallas*,493 U.S. 215 (1990); *Genusa v. City of Peoria*, 619 F.2d 1203 (7th Cir. 1980) (invalidating ordinance that denied license for adult bookstore to applicant who was not of good moral character in the community in which he or she resides).

[140] *Renton*, 475 U.S. at 49, note 2, 106 S.Ct. at 929, note 2.

accelerate rapidly private sector deployment of advanced telecommunications and information technologies and services ... by opening all telecommunications markets to competition ...."[141]

As a result, the Act imposed several requirements on local zoning authorities. Congress found "siting and zoning decisions by non-federal units of government have created an inconsistent and, at times, conflicting patchwork of requirements which will inhibit the deployment of Personal Communications Services as well as the rebuilding of a digital technology-based cellular telecommunications network."[142]

In enacting § 332, Congress sought to strike a balance between encouraging the growth of telecommunications systems and the right of local governments to make land use decisions. Encouragement of the growth of the telecommunications industry is fostered by the FTCA's requirement that local authorities act on any request for authorization to construct personal wireless service facilities within a "reasonable period of time."[143] Further, in regulating the "placement, construction, and modification" of wireless services facilities local governments are expressly prohibited from: (1) unreasonably discriminating among providers of functionally equivalent services, and (2) prohibiting or having the effect of prohibiting the provision of personal wireless services.[144]

After the Act was first passed, the general perception was that these requirements tilted the field in favor of telecommunications companies and made it more difficult to deny an application to locate a cell phone tower in any given jurisdiction. (This perception existed even

---

[141] *Cellular Tel. Co. v. Town of Oyster Bay*, 166 F.3d 490, 492-93 (2d Cir.1999) (quoting H.R. Conf. Rep. No. 104-458, at 206 (1996)).

[142] *Omnipoint Corp. v. Zoning Hearing Bd. of Pine Grove Township*, 181 F.3d 403, 407 (3d Cir.1999) (quoting H.R. Rep. 104-204, at 94 (1995), reprinted in 1996 U.S.C.C.A.N. 10, 61).

[143] 47 USC § 332(c)(7)(B)(ii).

[144] 47 USC § 332(c)(7)(B)(i)(I) and (II).

in the face of the Act itself which states: "nothing... shall limit the authority of a State or local government or instrumentality thereof over decisions regarding the placement, construction, and modification of personal wireless service facilities.")[145] Indeed, the early cases decided under the Act seemed to reinforce this point of view. However, as more cases have been decided by the federal courts, it appears now that the Act provides generally a procedural scheme which insures that there is a fair hearing and a written reason for the denial of any tower application. So long, however, as the reasons given are based upon evidence at the hearing and make some sense, the board will be upheld.

There still remains the very interesting question as to whether a tower application may be denied based upon subjective determinations made by a local zoning board, such as, for example, a finding that the tower is not compatible with the surrounding land uses from an aesthetic standpoint. While those issues have yet to be entirely sorted out, we do have strong indications now from the federal courts. We will look at some 6th Circuit Court of Appeals opinions, the federal appeals court which hears cases from Tennessee.

The provisions of the Telecommunications Act of 1996 relating to land use planning law are really very simple. First, the local authorities may not entirely exclude telecommunications towers so as to create a gap in coverage; second the local authorities may not discriminate against a new provider who is attempting to locate new service within the area; and finally, in any decision regarding the construction of telecommunications towers (or other facilities) the local authorities (often the local board of zoning appeals) must give a reason in writing for denial of the application it denied, and that reason must be based on substantial evidence contained in a written record. The FTCA also requires that the written findings be separate from the transcript of the evidence.[146]

---

[145] 47 USC § 332 (c) (7) (A). See also *Tenn. ex rel. Wireless Income Prop., LLC v. City of Chattanooga*, 403 F.3d 392, 398 (6th Cir.2005).

[146] *Southwestern Bell Mobile v. Todd*, 244 F. 3d 51 (1st Cir. 2001) (Leicester, Mass)

Generally speaking, the requirements are not hard to meet. For example, the standard of review is not onerous:[147]

> A court reviewing denial of request to place, construct, or modify personal wireless service facilities under the substantial evidence standard of the Telecommunications Act of 1996 (FTCA) is not to weigh the evidence contained in the record or substitute its own conclusions for those of the fact finder, but rather is to determine whether there is substantial evidence in the record as a whole to support the challenged decision. Upon judicial review of a local board's denial of a wireless service facility siting permit application, courts must uphold the board's action if it has substantial support in the record as a whole; courts are not free to substitute their own judgment for that of the board, even if they would decide the matter differently as an original matter.

Notice the similarity between this standard and the standard which is employed by the Tennessee courts under the common law writ of certiorari discussed in Chapter 5. The term "substantial evidence" as used in the FTCA, means "such relevant evidence as a reasonable mind might accept as adequate to support a conclusion; it requires more than a scintilla but less than a preponderance."[148] This definition seems consistent with the Tennessee procedure under the writ of certiorari.

Perhaps the easiest way to summarize the holding of the 6th Circuit in this area is to review the recent decision in *Cellco Partnership v Franklin County, KY,*[149] an appeal from a denial of an application for a cell tower. The first issue had to do with the time within which to file the suit challenging the decision. The statute requires that it be filed within 30 days of the decision (the statute expressly includes the failure

---

147 *360 Degrees v. Board of Supervisors of Albemarle County*, 211 F. 3d 79 (4th Cir. 2000).

148 Id.

149 553 F. Supp. 2d 838 (E. D. Ky. 2008).

to act).[150] In this case, the parties had agreed that the Planning Commission would issue a decision by April 26, 2007. The Commission failed to make a decision and the suit was filed on May 25, 2007. The commission argued that the suit should not have been filed until after the minutes of the meeting were approved on June 14, 2005. Suit was filed too early under that approach. The court easily concluded that the failure to act on April 26 was actionable without waiting for the entry of the minutes. The Court distinguished *Omnipoint Holdings, Inc. v. City of Southfield,*[151] which had held that a city council's vote to deny an application became final when the minutes were approved and is perhaps closer to the Tennessee rule under the writ of certiorari.

Next the Court turned to the substantive issues. In *New Par v. City of Saginaw,*[152] the Sixth Circuit held:

> [F]or a decision by a State or local government or instrumentality thereof denying a request to place, construct, or modify personal wireless service facilities to be "in writing" for the purposes of 47 U.S.C. § 332(c)(7)(B)(iii), it must (1) be separate from the written record; (2) describe the reasons for the denial; and (3) contain a sufficient explanation of the reasons for the denial to allow a reviewing court to evaluate the evidence in the record that supports those reasons.

In the *Cellco* case, the minutes were offered as the "written" decision denying the application. The court found that the minutes were insufficient because they were not separate from the meeting's written record concerning other matters. Frankly, this seems a very strange application of the law: as long as the minutes contain a reasonable basis for the conclusion, why does it matter that other matters may be within the same document? The 6th Circuit has expressly noted that total separation may not be necessary, but it is unclear as to when that might

---

150 47 U.S.C. § 332(c)(7)(B)(v).

151 355 F.3d 601, 603, 605 (6th Cir.2004).

152 301 F.3d 390 (6th Cir.2002).

apply.[153] As a result, if you are representing a zoning board considering a cell tower request, remember that the board's decision should best be written in the form of an order for that one case. Minutes can be typed up for the entire meeting, but the order should represent the decision of the board for that particular application.

As the *New Par* court pointed out, the decision must give reasons for the denial, and explain the decision sufficiently so that a court can review the decision and the evidence that supports it. The *Cellco* Court concluded that the Planning Commission had not done either of those things sufficiently well.

The FTCA requires that the decision be supported by substantial evidence in a written record.[154] Substantial evidence is more than a mere scintilla. It means such relevant evidence as a reasonable mind might accept as adequate to support a conclusion.[155] The district court summarized the evidence:

> Thus, the evidence in the record before the Planning Commission consisted of the testimony and report of a radio-frequency engineer demonstrating the need for the proposed tower and that there was no other suitable location. Likewise, the record included the testimony and report of a structural engineer attesting to the structural soundness and safety of the proposed tower. Finally, the record included the report and testimony of a real estate appraiser concluding that the proposed tower would not decrease property values in the area.
>
> Area residents questioned the safety of the proposed tower, the need for it, whether there were other suitable locations for it, and whether it would affect property

[153] *City of Southfield* at 606.

[154] 47 U.S.C. § 332(c)(7)(B)(iii).

[155] *Richardson v. Perales*, 402 U.S. 389, 401, 91 S.Ct. 1420, 28 L.Ed.2d 842 (1971).

> values. There is no evidence, however, that any of these residents had any personal knowledge regarding these issues. Nor did any of these residents offer any evidence in support of their concerns. Thus, this testimony is "unsupported opinion," and does not constitute evidence supporting the Planning Commission's denial of the application. Telespectrum, 227 F.3d at 424; see also New Par, 301 F.3d at 399 n. 4 (community concerns based upon conjecture or speculation lack probative value and will not amount to substantial evidence).

The Planning Commission however, did not base its decision on any of these objections. Instead,

> it denied the application on the grounds that the local zoning ordinance requires it to consider the visual impact of the proposed tower and that several of the persons who spoke before it objected to the visual impact of the tower. The Planning Commission also denied the application on the grounds that the zoning ordinance provides that a residential area is the least preferred place to locate a communications tower, that the proposed site was zoned [residential].

The court found both reasons specious:

> . . . the ordinance does not prohibit the construction of a communications tower in areas zoned Rural Residential. Thus, without some evidence demonstrating that the proposed tower would be incompatible with the rural residential character of the proposed site, the simple fact that the proposed site is zoned Rural Residential is not a sufficient basis to deny the application.

And with regard to the visual impact basis for the decision:

> In this case, only five residents explicitly objected to the visual impact of the tower. They objected primarily because they would see the objections represent

> "generalized expressions of concern with aesthetics." The same objection could be made by any resident in any area where a tower was proposed. The Sixth Circuit has never found that lay opinion evidence alone constitutes substantial evidence supporting the denial of an application [citations omitted].
>
> Even if the objections of some of these residents should be considered as specific objections to the placement of the tower in this particular area because it is rural and residential, the objections of a few residents is not substantial evidence warranting the denial of an application where there is uncontradicted evidence that the tower is necessary and there is no other suitable location.[156]

By the way, after finding a violation of the act, the Court concluded that the remedy was a court order requiring the issuance of the permit.

A brief summary is perhaps in order. It is critical for the zoning board (or planning commission) to issue a written decision, separate from the other matters it may have considered, with an explanation of its decision, and based on substantial evidence in the record to justify the conclusion. There is nothing hard about this: in fact, although the Tennessee courts do not require it for all decisions, I strongly believe that the zoning board should always act in this manner. Ultimately, the decision-making process will be better.

Some courts have been fairly lenient with regard to the issue of visual impact. In *Southwestern Bell Mobile v. Todd*,[157] Court upheld the board's denial based upon the board's finding that the tower would

---

[156] There were other towers already located in the area, one of which was 265-feet tall. There was no evidence as to why the Planning Commission believed the subject tower was incompatible with the rural character of the area when other towers are located in the same vicinity.

[157] 244 F. 3d 51 (1st Cir. 2001) (Leicester, Mass).

minimally impact the visual environment. The zoning regulation required:

> [t]he applicant shall successfully demonstrate to the satisfaction of the Board that the proposed facility will have minimal visual impact and constructed so it is reasonably capable of accommodating other users including other wireless communication companies and local police, fire and ambulance companies unless it is determined to be technically infeasible based on the Board's evaluation of information submitted.

The court found that there was enough evidence, (although it was in short supply) to uphold the decision.[158]

The limitations upon local authority in the FTCA do not state or imply that the FTCA prevents municipalities from exercising their traditional prerogative to restrict and control development based upon aesthetic considerations, so long as those judgments do not mask, for example, a de facto prohibition of personal wireless services.[159] In assessing the visual impact of the proposed tower, a zoning board is entitled to make an aesthetic judgment about whether that impact was minimal, without justifying that judgment by reference to an economic or other quantifiable impact.

> Nonetheless, that aesthetic judgment must be grounded in the specifics of the case. Few people would argue that telecommunication towers are aesthetically pleasing. Some of the disapproving comments in the cases about generalized aesthetic concerns refer to negative comments that are applicable to any tower, regardless of location. See *Oyster Bay*, 166 F.3d at 495 (resident comments suggested

---

[158] Id.

[159] See *Aegerter v. City of Delafield*, 174 F.3d 886, 891 (7th Cir.1999) (holding that the FTCA does not prohibit local authorities "from applying general and nondiscriminatory standards derived from their zoning codes").

misunderstanding of "what the proposed cell sites would actually look like," where residents objected to "a mass of spaghetti wires" and suggested that "antennae would project from the top of the water tank like 'a small birthday cake with candles' "). In other cases, the aesthetic objections were demonstrably without substance because of evidence that the towers and transmitters were either difficult to see or were aesthetically compatible with the character of the area.

Although some of the evidence before the Board did consist of general statements that the tower was an eyesore, these statements did not dominate the debate. The majority of the objections to the visual impact of the tower specifically addressed whether this 150-foot tower was appropriate for this particular location, on the top of a fifty-foot hill in the middle of a cleared field. The location has no trees, was in the geographic center of town, would be visible at all seasons of the year, and would be seen daily by approximately 25% of the Town's population. It was also located in close proximity to three schools and two residential subdivisions. The closest of these two subdivisions, the Carey Hill Estates, had houses that were located only 200 feet away. Indeed, this subdivision was in such close proximity to the tower that Southwestern Bell used Carey Hill Estates construction plans as a reference map when drawing up the proposed plans for the tower. Purchasers who had placed deposits on houses that were to be built in this subdivision indicated that the tower would be plainly visible from their land. One of those purchasers had placed his deposit unaware that a tower was proposed in such close proximity. Concerned about this situation, two members of the Board visited other towers that had been described as comparable by Southwestern Bell's real estate appraiser. The members concluded that these towers were not in a location as exposed as Southwestern Bell's tower and the houses were not as close. The School Committee, though voicing no formal opposition, was "concerned about the aesthetics of

> placing a cell tower with its associated dishes and arrays in proximity to school buildings." Several witnesses, pointing to the Bylaw's requirement that the "tower shall be of monopole or similarly unimposing design," argued that the lattice design of the tower was not an "unimposing design."

The lesson here would seem to be then that so long as the opponents and the Board couch the opposition in terms of the specific location of the tower, that a denial based upon aesthetic concerns may be appropriate under the FTCA. Remember that the 6th Circuit may be less willing to consider such arguments.

In another important case, reaching contrary results, *SBA Communications v. Zoning Commission of Franklin,*[160] the Zoning Commission denied SBA's application to erect a monopole for use as a telecommunications tower.

> While requiring review of local zoning determinations regarding the placement of wireless facilities, the FTCA and the courts interpreting this statute acknowledge the legitimate local interest in such determinations. As the Second Circuit recently noted in *Sprint Spectrum,*[161] the goals of increasing competition and rapid deployment of new technology do not "trump all other important considerations, including the preservation of the autonomy of states and municipalities. Rather, in the context of constructing a national wireless telecommunications infrastructure, Congress chose to preserve all local zoning authority over decisions regarding the placement, construction, and modification of personal wireless service facilities. The legislative history of the FTCA illustrates the importance of preserving local land use authority. As stated in the Senate Report, § 332 "preserves the authority of State and local governments

---

[160] 164 F. Supp. 2d 280 (D. Conn. 2001).

[161] L.P. v. Willoth, 176 F.3d 630 (2d Cir.1999).

over zoning and land use matters except in the limited circumstances" specified in that section.[162]

The Second Circuit has also held that a local government may reject an application for construction of a wireless service facility in an under-served area without thereby prohibiting personal wireless services if the service gap can be closed by less intrusive means.[163] There are numerous ways to limit the aesthetic impact of a cell site. It may be possible to select a less sensitive site, see *Gearon & Co. v. Fulton County*, 5 F.Supp.2d 1351, 1355 (N.D.Ga.1998), to reduce the tower height, see *Town of Amherst*, 173 F.3d at 14-15, to use a preexisting structure or to camouflage the tower and/or antennae, see, e.g., *Cellco*, 3 F.Supp.2d at 185, 186 (D.Conn.1998) (describing antennae placed on water tower, and permitting applicant to reconstruct church steeple with six antennae placed inside); *Smart*, 995 F.Supp. at 59 (D.Conn.1998) (describing an antenna placed on a billboard and current applicant seeking to conceal tower with seven evergreen trees). A local government may also reject an application that seeks permission to construct more towers than the minimum required to provide wireless telephone services in a given area. A denial of such a request is not a prohibition of personal wireless services as long as fewer towers would provide users in the given area with some ability to reach a cell site.

In this case, in denying SBA's application, the Commission relies on: (1) the aesthetic effect of the proposed monopole; and (2) the decline in property values due to the construction of the proposed monopole.

---

[162] See Sen. Rep. No. 104-230, at 458 (1996).

[163] See *Town of Amherst*, 173 F.3d at 14 (explaining that "individual denial is not automatically a forbidden prohibition," but disallowing "the only feasible plan ... might amount to prohibiting personal wireless service.").

Courts have split as to the weight to be afforded to constituent testimony on aesthetics.[164] Nonetheless, because the court concluded that there were only a few generalized expressions of concern with "aesthetics" the court does not need to address this issue.

Neither the Commission nor the residents offered expert evidence that the proposed monopole would cause a decrease in property values. SBA in return presented an expert report stating that the proposed monopole would have no impact on the property values of nearby homes.

As the Second Circuit has recognized, the evaluation of property value evidence under the FTCA raises some difficult questions. In addition to the uncertain weight to be afforded to citizens' views, this argument raises the issue of how to weigh residents' unsupported expressions of concern against a proffer of expert testimony. See *PrimeCo*, 26 F.Supp.2d at 1063 (holding that, in the face of expert testimony evidence, unsupported constituent testimony in opposition to a cellular tower permit will not satisfy the substantial evidence test); *Cellular Telephone Co.*, 24 F.Supp.2d at 372 (holding that "essentially non-expert testimony presented by local residents with possible biases ... is not enough to discredit the testimony of qualified experts"). Further, since property values can be objectively proven, it is not clear if the Commission must receive traditional evidence that would tend to demonstrate that cell sites have a negative impact on property values in order to satisfy the substantial evidence test. See *Sprint Spectrum L.P. v.*

---

[164] Compare *Omnipoint Corp. v. Zoning Hearing Bd.*, 20 F.Supp.2d 875, 880 (E.D.Pa.1998) (holding that "unsubstantiated personal opinions" expressing "generalized concerns ... about aesthetic and visual impacts on the neighborhood do not amount to substantial evidence") with *AT & T Wireless PCS*, 155 F.3d at 430 (holding that constituent aesthetic concerns could constitute "compelling" evidence for City Council).

Town of North Stonington, 12 F.Supp.2d 247, 254 (D.Conn.1998) (holding that in order for the Town Planning & Zoning Commission to deny a permit application based on property values, the Town bore the burden of putting evidence into the record tending to show such a negative impact).

Nonetheless, the court must determine whether the volume and specificity of the comments were adequate to satisfy the requirement of the substantial evidence standard.[165] There must be more than a few generalized concerns about a potential decrease in property values, especially in light of SBA's contradictory expert testimony.

Once again the Commission does not provide the court with any citations to the record to support its assertion that substantial comments were made regarding concerns about property values. Instead, in summary fashion, the Commission argues that statements made by property owners regarding the decline in property values, without any apparent factual basis, were sufficient to deny SBA's application. This is so despite the fact that Commissioner Fisher stated on the record that the issue regarding property values was unresolved. Consequently, the conclusory assertions of residents do not constitute substantial evidence upon which a denial could be based, particularly in light of the expert report presented by SBA. Moreover, even if the resident comments had a factual basis, the volume and specificity of those comments were not adequate to satisfy the requirement of the substantial evidence standard.

---

[165] See *Cellular*, 166 F.3d at 496; see also *Iowa Wireless*, 29 F.Supp.2d at 922 (finding that "concerns of citizens regarding potential aesthetic and economic effects may amount to substantial evidence in some circumstances" but holding that in that case public concern was too limited to satisfy the substantial evidence standard).

The court also allowed the Civil Rights Act claim, meaning that the plaintiff might get damages and attorneys' fees.[166]

Finally, one more case giving liberal discretion to the board, *360 Degrees v. Board of Supervisors of Albemarle County,*[167] the court allowed what appears to have been very subjective evidence of visual impact and other factors which sometimes can be employed to mask an underlying reason for the decision.

It is perhaps important to note that in Virginia, the grant or denial of a conditional use permit is a legislative act, as is the adoption of a zoning regulation.[168] This of course contrasts with the rule here in Tennessee where the decision to grant or deny a conditional use permit is acute has an administrative decision. As a result, the decisions in *ATT v. City of Virginia Beach*[169] and *360 Degrees* may be distinguishable on that basis.

In *Virginia Beach,* the court concluded that the substantial opposition from local residents to an application for two cellular towers based on their rational fears that the towers would damage the character of their residentially zoned neighborhood, which contained no significant commercial development, no commercial antenna towers, and no above-ground power lines, amounted to "substantial evidence" and was therefore a lawful basis for the city council's decision to deny a permit for the towers. Similarly, in *AT & T Wireless PCS, Inc. v.*

---

[166] 42 USC §§ 1983 and 1988.

[167] 211 F. 3d 79 (4th Cir. 2000).

[168] See *County Bd. of Arlington County v. Bratic,* 237 Va. 221, 377 S.E.2d 368, 370 (Va.1989); *City Council of City of Virginia Beach v. Harrell,* 236 Va. 99, 372 S.E.2d 139, 141 (Va.1988).

[169] *AT & T Wireless PCS, Inc. v. City Council of the City of Virginia Beach,* 155 F.3d 423, 430 (4th Cir.1998) (quoting *Universal Camera Corp. v. NLRB,* 340 U.S. 474, 477, 71 S.Ct. 456, 95 L.Ed. 456 (1951))

Winston-Salem Zoning Board of Adjustment,[170] the same court held that the Winston-Salem Zoning Board had "substantial evidence" to deny a special use permit for the construction of a 148 foot antenna tower near a historical house that was surrounded by low density, single home, residential property with no commercial property nearby. In Winston-Salem, approximately 150 local residents objected to the tower, either in person or by petition, because it would change the character of the neighborhood.[171]

> In the record made before the Board of Supervisors, it is undisputed that the proposed tower would rise from the ridgeline of Dudley Mountain and extend 40 to 50 feet above the tree canopy. Except for the property owner who had intended to lease the property to 360 Degrees Communications to build the tower, the citizens of Albemarle County spoke unanimously in opposition to the tower siting. Thirteen spoke in opposition at the public hearing before the Planning Commission on June 2, 1998, giving varying reasons. Similarly, at the meeting of the Board of Supervisors on August 12, 1998, ten citizens spoke in opposition, objecting to the tower's visibility, its inconsistency with environmental preservation goals, and its impact on the character of the area. Also, 40 citizens signed a petition opposing the proposed siting of the tower.
>
> In addition to this virtually unanimous citizen opposition, the Board of Supervisors had evidence before it that the proposed tower would be inconsistent with the Comprehensive Plan, the Open Space Plan, and the County's Zoning Ordinance. The Comprehensive Plan and Open Space Plan note that "any serious modification of the

---

[170] 172 F.3d 307, 315 (4th Cir.1999).

[171] Id at 315-6. The Court contrasted its ruling in *Petersburg Cellular Partnership v. Board of Supervisors of Nottoway County*, 205 F.3d 688, 696 (4th Cir.2000), where it held that a county board decision, which was based upon "the irrational concerns of a few constituents," was not supported by "substantial evidence."

> natural ridge lines in the County will modify the visual character of an entire area," that "activities which alter the continuity of the ridge line ... should be discouraged," and that "issues related to soil erosion [and] surface water runoff " are amplified in mountainous areas. The Zoning Ordinance provides that the Board must find that the proposed use will not be of substantial detriment to adjacent property, that the character of the district will not be changed thereby, and that such use will be in harmony with the purpose and intent of [the zoning] ordinance, with the uses permitted by right in the district, with additional regulations provided in [the] ordinance, and with the public health, safety and general welfare.[172]

The court ultimately held that "at bottom, these issues, as to which conflicting evidence was presented, are of the type that zoning boards are typically qualified to resolve" and upheld the decision of the local authorities denying the application.

It is important to realize that the *Cellco* case discussed at the beginning of this section however, is illustrative of the more restrictive 6th Circuit approach to these cases. In order to deny an application, the zoning board must ensure that it has good cause to turn it down, and that those reasons are based on evidence in the record before the court and that the order explains how the decision was reached, that is, what evidence persuaded it to rule as it did. In the absence of these procedural requirements, the decision may well be overturned.

---

[172] Albemarle County Zoning Ordinance § 31.2.4.1. This is certainly a very common type of provision; generally I recommend that more specific controls be placed in any kind of conditional use regulation, designed for the specific type of land use activity involved.

5. Fair Housing Amendments Act of 1988

A final area that is of some importance in administering land use regulations is the Fair Housing Amendments Act (FHAA) of 1988.[173] In general, the FHAA prohibits discrimination in the sale, rental or use of a dwelling based upon a handicap.[174] It also imposes an obligation to reasonably accommodate a handicapped person in order to afford that person an equal opportunity to use and enjoy a dwelling.[175]

Originally, a separate provision of the FHAA seemed to protect local governments from concern in this area. Reasonable local restrictions on the maximum number of occupants permitted in a dwelling are beyond the reach of the FHAA.[176] Therefore, to the extent that a local ordinance specified a maximum number of occupants, the FHAA seemingly did not apply.

Then the United States Supreme Court got involved and issued its opinion in *City of Edmonds v. Oxford House, Inc.*[177] The Court held that the exemption described above does not apply except to numerical ceilings that serve to prevent overcrowding in living quarters. This interpretation of the statute means that for the most part, the types of

---

[173] 42 USC §§ 3601 et seq. The Fair Housing Act, as originally enacted in 1968, prohibited discrimination based on race, color, religion, or national origin. See 82 Stat. 83. Proscription of discrimination based on sex was added in 1974. See Housing and Community Development Act of 1974, § 808(b), 88 Stat. 729. In 1988, Congress extended coverage to persons with handicaps and also prohibited "familial status" discrimination, i.e., discrimination against parents or other custodial persons domiciled with children under the age of 18. 42 U.S.C. § 3602(k).

[174] 42 USC § 3604(f)(1) and (2).

[175] 42 USC § 3604(f)(3)(B).

[176] 42 USC § 3607(b)(1).

[177] 514 US 725, 115 S. Ct. 1776, 131 L. Ed. 2d 801 (1995).

zoning restrictions limiting the number of occupants must be considered by local zoning authorities as a starting point in determining how many occupants might live at a given facility.

For example, in *Oxford House*, a group home for 12 recovering alcoholics opened in a single-family residential district in the city. The city's definition of family restricted to five the number of people who could live together unrelated by blood or marriage.[178] Recovering alcoholics are clearly covered by the definition of "handicapped" in the FHAA[179] and so the Court had to decide whether the 5 person limit in the family definition was protected by the exemption.

Analyzing the zoning and building code provisions, the Court concluded that the Congress had intended only to exempt building code type maximum occupancy regulations.[180] The court felt that those regulations apply uniformly to all residents of all dwelling units and prevented overcrowding.[181] The zoning regulations on the other hand, were used to protect the composition of a family and not therefore subject to the exemption. The city in fact, also had a maximum

---

[178] Family "means an individual or two or more persons related by genetics, adoption, or marriage, or a group of five or fewer persons who are not related by genetics, adoption, or marriage." Edmonton Community Development Code § 21.30.010.

[179] 24 CFR § 100.201(a)(2).

[180] Maximum occupancy restrictions cap the number of occupants per dwelling, typically in relation to available floor space or the number and type of rooms. See, e.g., International Conference of Building Officials, Uniform Housing Code § 503(b) (1988); Building Officials and Code Administrators International, Inc., BOCA National Property Maintenance Code §§ PM-405.3, PM-405.5 (1993) (hereinafter BOCA Code); Southern Building Code Congress, International, Inc., Standard Housing Code §§ 306.1, 306.2 (1991); E. Mood, APHA-CDC Recommended Minimum Housing Standards § 9.02, p. 37 (1986)

[181] 115 S. Ct. at 1780.

occupancy provision, requiring only 120 feet for the first two occupants and 50 feet per occupant after that.[182]

The upshot of all of this is that if a group home which might house alleged handicapped individuals under the FHAA, the zoning board must be careful to evaluate the application and probably without regard to the maximum number of occupants under the ordinance.

The court did not address what was a reasonable accommodation, or how it can be accomplished in a zoning context. As a result of the decision, it is reasonable to expect that local zoning boards could be called upon to determine issues relating to "reasonable accommodation." The best way of doing this is to require all group homes to get conditional use permits and require minimum buffering in the yards, or other means of reducing potential impact. The local government must be aware that it cannot treat homes with handicapped individuals differently from other group homes and care should be taken to craft the requirements accordingly. The ordinance could also require that as the size increases, that the buffering and other conditions also increase.

Another small problem is the authority of the board to review cases of "reasonable accommodation." TENN. CODE ANN. § 13-7-206[183] allows the board to pass on particular questions assigned in the ordinance.[184] The local legislative body could (and likely should) assign this issue to the board. On the other hand, if the boards were only given objective criteria by which to judge, neutral to the occupants, the legal question most often would simply be whether the application met the legal requirements.

---

[182] 115 S. Ct. at 1782.

[183] TENN. CODE ANN. § 13-7-107 is the county zoning statute which reads essentially the sam way.

[184] The statute does say that the board can pass on lot lines, district boundary line or similar questions; this may not be a similar enough question but I believe most Tennessee courts would not find that objection convincing.

Finally, the board should keep in mind that the question of who is handicapped under the FHAA is also an important one. Related to this is the fact that other kinds of groups homes may be entitled therefore to protection. For example, in *Cohen v. City of Cheltenham*[185], the court concluded that the board did not violate the FHAA because the residents (abused, neglected or abandoned children) of the proposed group home were not "handicapped" within the meaning of the Act. These residents did not necessarily have any physical or mental impairment.[186] Therefore, the board's decision was upheld. In *Keys Youth Services, Inc., v. City of Olathe,*[187] the court reached the opposite conclusion with regard to a similar group home for neglected and abused children. This type of decision would have to be made in consultation with counsel; certainly the board would have no expertise in addressing whether the residents of the proposed project were handicapped under the terms of the FHAA.

H. Revocation

Suppose the permit is granted and the permittee does not live up to the letter of the law or the conditions which might have been imposed by the Board of Zoning Appeals. What remedies are available to deal with such a problem? Generally, once the 60 day time frame for an appeal has expired, the case is final.[188]

There may be two remedies nonetheless. First, and probably least satisfactory, is the filing of suit, either in city court or a court of record,

---

[185] 2001 WL 1450619 (ED Pa).

[186] At *19.

[187] 52 F. Supp. 2d 1284, 1297-1300 (D. Kan. 1999) rev'd on other grounds, 248 F. 3d 1267 (10th Cir. 2001). Another case going the other way is *Sunderland Family Treatment Services v. City of Pasco*, 127 Wash. 2d 782, 903 P. 2d 986, 989 (Wash. 1995).

[188] *DE Ryan v Metro Board of Zoning Appeals,* 2004 WL 1944131 (Tenn. Ct. App. 2004).

to enforce the conditional use permit. The provisions of TENN. CODE ANN. § 13-7-208(a)[189] are broad enough to encompass such a suit.

> In case . . . any building, structure or land is . . . proposed to be used in violation of any ordinance enacted under this part [municipal zoning], the building commissioner, municipal counsel or other appropriate authority of the municipality, or any adjacent or neighboring property owner who would be specially damaged by such violation, may, in addition to other remedies, institute injunction, mandamus or other appropriate action or proceeding to prevent such unlawful erection, construction, reconstruction, alteration, conversion, maintenance or use . . .

The problem is that at the city court level, the fine which may be imposed is capped at $50 per day. Many land use activities can pay that much out of operating expenses as though it was a cost of doing business. In courts of record, where the cap does not apply, and where a court order halting operations entirely might be obtained, it is still a long process and expensive: hiring a lawyer will undoubtedly be necessary. In appropriate cases, this may be needed, but our second option makes this easier, if it is permitted under Tennessee law.

The zoning board may be able to revoke a conditional use permit previously granted. This is not clear under Tennessee law. However, given that revocation of demolition permits by a building code board was tacitly approved in the Harding Academy case,[190] revocation of a zoning permit by a zoning board also seems appropriate. However, the city or county could elect to simply prosecute in municipal court or circuit court as well.[191]

---

[189] TENN. CODE ANN. § 13-7-111 is similar on the county side.

[190] Harding Academy v Metro Government, 222 SW 3d 359 (Tenn. 2007).

[191] TENN. CODE ANN. § 13-7-208 (b).

I. Conclusion

Conditional use permits are an important part of comprehensive land use planning today. Its application is a form of controlled flexibility: The local legislative body has chosen the general area for the particular use, but given specific criteria for the ultimate particularized location of the use. It is graphically different from a variance in that it is presumptively permitted whereas a variance should only sparingly be granted. Usually in Tennessee it is granted by the Board of Zoning Appeals, although in some instances, local legislative bodies have retained the power themselves to grant the permit, an approach which is possibly inconsistent with the public enabling legislation here in Tennessee, and definitely not desirable from a policy standpoint. The burden of proof to demonstrate compliance with the conditions is on the applicant, but once the burden has been surmounted, the applicant is entitled to the permit. Reasonable conditions may of course be imposed on the issuance of the permit but those conditions must actually relate to the use of the property and not to some secondary consideration in an attempt to control the use located thereupon.

Finally, and most importantly, the more specific the criteria by which the board makes its judgment, the easier it is for the board to restrict itself to justifiable grounds for its decision, whether it be to grant or to deny. On the other hand, broad discretionary requirements such as those which require the applicant to demonstrate compliance with the comprehensive plan of the local governmental entity, to demonstrate that the application is for the public welfare, or to benefit the health, safety and welfare of the community, or that it will not reduce property values or that it will not increase traffic congestion, all allow misunderstandings even on the part of the most sensitive of board members and may, in the worst cases, prompt outright discrimination. Specific criteria by which to render a decision enables the applicant to know exactly what he must present to the board in order to succeed on the merits of his case, enables the board members to admit relevant evidence into the record and make a judgment thereupon, and finally enables the judiciary to review the board's decision meaningfully, without having to guess at the meaning ascribed by the board to such general terms as the public's health, safety, and welfare. In the absence of such specific criteria, the board may simply not know how to apply the vague generalizations to a specific application, and worse yet, may intentionally discriminate against applicants entitled to a permit.

Chapter Four

Variances in Tennessee: Muddle Reigns Supreme

A. The Typical Situation

The situation is typical: a landowner wants to attach a carport to his home but in such a manner as to place it within two feet of his property line. The local zoning ordinance requires that all side yards measure a minimum of five feet. Undaunted, the landowner appears before the local board of zoning appeals to request relief. He asks for a variance. The board must decide whether under the circumstances of the case the landowner may lawfully develop his property inconsistently with the literal terms of the ordinance.

This situation, or others which are substantially similar, arises innumerable times each day. In Tennessee alone, thousands[1] of landowners appear each year to plead for a variance from the local Board. But, despite the numerosity of the requests, the grounds upon which a variance from the strict application of a zoning ordinance may be granted in this or most any other state is, to say the least, unclear.

Should the landowner in the example cited above be granted a variance solely for the sake of convenience? If not, under what

---

[1] While, to the author's knowledge, there is no record kept of the number of variances sought on a state-wide basis, the Metropolitan Board of Zoning Appeals for the Metropolitan Government of Nashville and Davidson County processed approximately 500 cases each year at the time of the original publication of this book in 2002. Of those, approximately 200 involved at least one variance and ofttimes more. Assuming that the other major metropolitan areas in Tennessee experienced the same rate of requests, the number of variance applications in the state must have, at that time, approached 2,000 per year and may have numbered higher than that. There is no reason to believe that number has decreased since the original publication of this book.

circumstances should such a variance be granted? What policies are furthered by a variance? Is a variance a means of modifying, or worse, circumventing, the law without resorting to the legislative process? These are, without exaggeration, some of the most perplexing questions in all of land use planning law.[2] And the answers to the questions as given by the American Courts have reflected this confusion:[3]

> . . . the law on special permits has been fairly clearly defined, both as a concept and as a series of rules to carry out that concept. No one familiar with the case law would ever make the same statement on the subject of variances. Considered purely as a coherent body of law to deal with certain types of problems . . . the law of variances is in great confusion . . . [A]nyone who attempts to organize and set forth a clear picture of the American law on variances either (a) has not read the case law, or (b) has simply not understood it. Here, far more than elsewhere in American planning law, muddle reigns supreme.

Unfortunately, the situation in Tennessee is not any better.

The object of this chapter is to review and discuss the law of zoning variances in Tennessee. Its thesis is that because of early dissatisfaction with broad and vague standards for variances, the Tennessee public enabling legislation was drafted to restrict the discretion of boards of zoning appeals in granting variances.[4] However,

---

[2] 5 Williams at Section 129.01; Rathkopf at Section 38.01[2]. Williams gives three reasons for these difficulties. First, the criteria for variances are not well defined [in most enabling statutes]; second, the judicial decisions do not always follow the established criteria; and finally, the boards themselves pay little attention even when the criteria are absolutely clear. As to the latter point, see also Rathkopf at 38.01[2]. As we shall see, the lack of attention to clearly established criteria certainly has applied in Tennessee, or at least in Nashville.

[3] Williams at § 129.01.

[4] BWBW at 64.

because the powers of the board in granting variances were misconstrued in three early cases arising out of Memphis and Shelby County, a false impression of a board of great discretion and great latitude in power was created. This impression continues at least in the members of the individual boards of zoning appeals; on many occasions, I've heard more than one board member say that "This is a board of common sense. Don't tell me about the law. We're gonna do what's right, even if the law doesn't permit it."[5] Even though there are now several reported cases which clearly indicate the more restrictive true scope of the board's power, this attitude remains.[6]

Three important cases from Memphis and Shelby County will be examined in detail, suggesting that the cases gave an unduly broad scope to zoning discretion as exercised by boards of zoning appeals and in fact outright missed the appropriate limitations existing at the time of the decision on zoning discretion. The chapter will then address in detail the provisions of the Tennessee public enabling legislation, reviewing cases within Tennessee and those from without Tennessee which may suggest the means by which Tennessee Courts may more critically review the actions of local boards and indeed, to suggest how the boards themselves should judge an application for a variance. The chapter finally examines the propriety of attaching conditions upon the grant of a variance and the circumstances under which such conditions may legally be attached. The effect of granting a variance, its possible revocation and subsequent changes in the zoning ordinance will conclude the overview of variances in Tennessee.

Overall, entirely too much discretion has been accorded local boards of zoning appeals and the courts, to the greatest extent possible, should review more critically the actions of those boards.

---

[5] Perhaps I've spent too much of my professional time before zoning boards.

[6] See *McClurkan v. Board of Zoning Appeals*, 565 S.W.2d 495 (Tenn.App. 1977).

B. Variance Defined

Essentially, a variance is a relaxation of the zoning ordinance as it applies to a particular piece of property because of exceptional physical or topographic conditions of the property. One well-known explanation of the difference maintained:[7]

> In order that our subsequent discussion of the issues in this case may be viewed in their proper legal perspective, we interrupt the factual narrative to comment on the true nature of a special exception under our statute. The term might well be said to be a misnomer. Special use or special use permits would be more accurate. The theory is that certain uses, considered by the local legislative body to be essential or desirable for the welfare of the community and its citizenry or substantial segments of it, are entirely appropriate and not essentially incompatible with the basic uses in any zone (or in any certain particular zones), but not at every or any location therein and without restrictions or conditions being imposed by reason of special problems the use or its particular location in relation to neighboring properties presents from a zoning standpoint, such as traffic congestion, safety, health, noise, and the like. The enabling act therefore permits the local ordinance to require approval of the local administrative agency as to the location of such use within the zone. If the board finds compliance with the standards or requisites set forth in the ordinance, the right to the exception exists, subject to such specific safeguarding conditions as the agency may impose by reason of the nature, location, and incidence of the particular use.

---

[7] *Tullo v. Township of Millburn*, 54 N.J.Super. 483, 490-91, 149 A.2d 620 (1959) (this opinion was written by the eminently well-respected and later Supreme Court Justice Frederick Hall of New Jersey; Justice Hall's opinions are frequently cited for a number of propositions in the area of land use planning law). For a further explanation of conditional use permits, see Chapter Three, Conditional Use Permits.

> The point is that such special uses are permissive in the particular zone under the ordinance and neither non-conforming nor akin to a variance. The latter must be especially clearly distinguished.

Thus, the conditional use permit (special exception) allows the board to consider particular uses at specific locations under the guidance of the zoning ordinance; variances are special privileges granted because of the physical conditions of the property and are in no way anticipated as in the case of special exceptions.

The variance should also be distinguished from a zone change, a rezoning of the property by the local legislative body. While a zone change may appear to be much akin to a use variance, and it is somewhat similar, under the provisions of the Tennessee Public Zoning Enabling Act, a variance can only be granted by a board of zoning appeals, and a zone change or rezoning can only be granted by the local legislative body.[8]

Planned unit developments bear a marked resemblance to conditional use permits but are generally granted by the local legislative body in Tennessee. PUDs ordinarily cannot be granted by a board of zoning appeals.

Finally, the other main power (in addition to variances and conditional use permits) of the board of zoning appeals is to hear any appeal from an order of the zoning administrator alleged to be wrongful, illegal or in error. Frequently, under this provision, non-conforming properties are brought to the board. Non-conforming properties are uses of property which legally predate the enactment of the applicable zoning ordinance as we discussed in Chapter Two. While the ultimate result may appear to be the same, a non-conforming use is not required to show any exceptional physical or topographic condition or any exceptional hardship or practical difficulty in order to obtain the relief sought. A non-conforming use is a matter of the right of a property owner who utilized his property in a certain way prior to the enactment

---

[8] Compare TENN. CODE ANN. § 13-7-207 (3) with TENN. CODE ANN §13-7-204.

of the zoning ordinance to continue the use of that property legally after the adoption of the zoning ordinance.

C. Zoning Variances: A Little History

1. Edward Bassett and Unlimited Variance Discretion

The earliest zoning ordinances delegated almost unlimited discretion to the members of boards of zoning appeals.[9] Led by Edward Bassett,[10] and New York City, ultimately most states gave extremely broad powers to local zoning boards. The first comprehensive zoning ordinance was adopted by the City of New York,[11] but contained no authority for the creation of a board of zoning appeals.[12] However, after the original comprehensive zoning ordinance was adopted, the City Zoning Commission determined that:[13]

> No commission, however wise, could draft detailed regulations to fit all cases that might arise: for these rules intimately affect extensive land areas of very diverse character, location, and value, of many sizes and shapes,

---

[9] S.I. Toll: Zoned American (1969) at 23.

[10] Bassett has been called the "father of zoning" and his contribution and impact cannot be overestimated. Mandelker, Payne, Salsich and Stroud, *Planning and Control of Land Development: Cases and Materials*, 6th ed., 2005 at 209.; S.I. Toll: Zoned American (1969) at 143.

[11] E.M. Bassett: Zoning at 23 (2nd Edition, 1940); Bassett, Williams, Bettman & Whitten: Model Planning Laws, Harvard City Planning Studies, Volume 7 (1935) at 10.

[12] Id. at 134. Bassett, Williams, Bettman & Whitten: Model Planning Laws, Harvard City Planning Studies, Volume 7 (1935) at 10.

[13] Bassett, Williams, Bettman & Whitten at 10. One early Tennessee decision echoed this sentiment.

> and in varying stages of improvement and building development. They saw that from time to time exceptional instances of practical difficulty or necessary hardship to landowners (and therefore of disadvantage, on the whole, to the community) would inevitably occur. For both practical and legal reasons, therefore, they recognized the necessity of machinery for constant adjustments of permits to special cases as they arose.

The original enabling legislation provided that: "Said regulations . . . may provide that the board of appeals may determine and vary their application in harmony with their general purpose and intent and accordance with general or specific rules therein contained."[14] Within a short time, and certainly by 1919, the New York Building Zone Resolution provided in part:[15]

> Where there are practical difficulties or unnecessary hardships in the way of carrying out the strict letter of the provisions of this resolution, the board of appeals shall have the power in a specific case to vary any such provision in harmony with its general purpose and intent, so that the public health, safety and general welfare may be secured and substantial justice done.

Evidently, this zoning variance provision was taken from a New York law of 1862, which created the Department of Buildings in the City of New York.[16] The building code variance provision was extremely

---

[14] Chapter 601, Laws of New York (1917); Bassett at 136.

[15] Bassett at 141. For a brief, but interesting discussion of this historical development as applied in a modern decision, see *Matthew v. Smith*, 707 S.W.2d 411, 414 (Mo. 1986).

[16] Bassett, Williams, Bettman & Whitten at 12.

broad[17] and that explains in part why the provision as it related to zoning was also extremely broad.

This rule of practical difficulty and unnecessary hardship was copied into the zoning enabling acts of a large number of states. In 1924, Herbert Hoover, the then-Secretary of Commerce, called together a number of influential zoning authorities from across the country and this blue ribbon commission promulgated what is now known as the Standard State Zoning Enabling Act.[18] The phraseology in that Act

---

[17] This was generally true of building code variance provisions. The Standard Building Code variance provisions had been very broad until about 1990. The 1988 Standard Building Code, Section 105.3.1, allowed the Board to vary any provision of the code when in its opinion, enforcement would do "manifest injustice." The 1991 Standard Code was much more restrictive and the 1994 Standard Building Code, §108.4.2, carries forward those changes. Special findings peculiar to the building site were required. The interesting question is why the building code provisions have never been subjected to any significant attack. See SBCCI, Legal Aspects of Code Administration and Enforcement (1983) at 67. The newer International Building Code has provisions for administrative relief, but there is no variance provision. 2009 IBC § 113.2; see GA Dean, *Legal Handbook for Tennessee Codes Officials* at p. 97. Waiver of code provisions is expressly prohibited under the 2006 & 2009 IBC. Id.

[18] The revised standard state zoning enabling act was promulgated in 1926. This was, of course, only a guide to help the states develop their own legislation, but it became very influential and was ultimately adopted by a great many of the states in one form or another. Variance law in New York at 758, n. 19. The variance language, very similar to that of the 1925 Memphis Act, is certainly not any more helpful than that act. The terminology is never defined and the circumstances under which a variance should issue are thereby obscured. It is important, however, when comparing case law from other jurisdictions, to take care to examine the legislation under which the authority to issue the variance in the particular state and in the particular case arises. Since so many of the other states still retain the SSZEA, its terminology should be kept in mind; while it is often useful

concerning variances differs somewhat from the Bassett-New York model, but "the intention of the framers was that the meaning should be the same."[19] The standard act provided:[20]

> To authorize upon appeal in specific cases such variance from the terms of the ordinance as will not be contrary to the public interest, where, owing to special conditions, a literal enforcement of the provisions of the ordinance will result in unnecessary hardship, and so that the spirit of the ordinance will be observed and substantial justice done.

Bassett saw this variance power as "the comprehensive safety valve of the zoning plan, . . . always provided in the State Enabling Act, and . . . often referred to as the appellate jurisdiction of the Board of Appeals."[21]

But it was not long before this broad power was criticized both by reviewing courts and by commentators. The boards were granting variances where no justification existed. The power was being abused. In August of 1927, *The American City* published an article entitled, "Zoning's Greatest Danger -- Lawless Acts by Boards of Appeals."[22] The article not only cited several cases[23] but also quotes Bassett himself in

---

to compare across state boundaries, in the area of variance law, the SSZEA is not as specific as Tennessee and generally is useless for purposes of comparison.

[19] Bassett at 142.

[20] Standard State Zoning Enabling Act, Section 7.

[21] Bassett, Williams, Bettman & Whitten, at 11.

[22] At p. 231.

[23] See esp. *People ex rel. Fordham Manor Reformed Church v. Walsh*, 244 N.Y. 280, 155 N.E. 575 (1927).

condemnation of a specific action by the New York City Board.[24] Furthermore, in the early 1930's, a New York State Legislative Committee conducted an intense investigation, revealing a pattern of corrupt practices before the New York City Board.[25] But even without the corruption, too many variances were granted.[26]

As early as 1935, Bassett referred to criticism of the scope of this power.[27]

> As we have just seen, the Standard Zoning Act . . . grants in broad terms to boards of appeals the power of variance for practical difficulty and unnecessary hardship. Of this breadth there has been considerable criticism. We believe that in any narrowing of this power there is the risk that cases of hardship and injustice will arise for which no practicable remedy is provided, with the result that the community will be injured, as it is in all cases of injustice, and the constitutionality of the law imperiled.

Thus, by as early as 1935, there was an ongoing debate concerning the breadth of the enabling legislation. Further, Bassett referred to the two important policies which variances were supposed to advance: to prevent inequality amongst landowners by virtue of the failure of the ordinance itself to take into account some difference in property; and further, to help guarantee the constitutionality of the ordinance.[28] The thought at that time was without this kind of safety value[29], the Courts

---

[24] *The American City*, August 1927 at 233-4.

[25] Toll at 208-210.

[26] Question whether this has changed; see my estimates of the current levels here in Tennessee in footnote 1 to this chapter.

[27] Bassett, Williams, Bettman & Whitten at 13.

[28] Bassett at 122 and 165.

[29] This language, perhaps a little over-worked, is certainly descriptive of the function originally foreseen for local zoning boards.

would be more willing to strike down the ordinance as an unconstitutional confiscation of private property.[30] Bassett did recognize the possibility of error.[31] He felt that complaints will always be made against boards of appeals, and probably such boards will abuse their discretion once in a while. If, however, a city administration is not able to establish a competent board of appeals, it probably is not able to administer a zoning ordinance fairly. To Bassett, an occasional wrong decision by such a board was of less importance to the community than the unrelieved arbitrariness of an ironclad ordinance which first in one particular application and then in another may be criticized by the courts. A board of appeals should be able to ameliorate the exceptional instances wherein alone lies the danger to the entire zoning plan. These cases demand the most careful attention, for the integrity of a zoning plan under the police power, as the courts have repeatedly pointed out, depends on its reasonableness, and a zoning regulation is not reasonable if it is arbitrary. In justifying fairly broad powers of judicial review, Bassett went further and said:[32]

> Usually these boards are honest, but often, left wholly to themselves, they do not fully know the nature and extent of their powers, and are inclined to grant relief in the interest of the applicant which is contrary to the public interest. The possibility of a court review tends to keep the actions of these boards within reasonable limits, and so restrained, the local board, intimately acquainted with local conditions, is a most efficient instrument in the administration of the zoning law, appeals to the court being infrequent.

Bassett concluded that "not only technically, therefore, but fundamentally, we believe the critics of the board of zoning appeals as

---

Variances have also disparagingly been referred to as steady leaks.

[30] Bassett at 122.

[31] Bassett at 166-7.

[32] Bassett, Williams, Bettman & Whitten at 14-15.

such to be wrong." [33] Thus, even before 1935, criticism of the broad powers given a board of zoning appeals under the variance provision was already forthcoming. This is especially interesting inasmuch as the Standard State Zoning Enabling Act was promulgated only in 1926. Less than 10 years later, there were already problems.

2. Alfred Bettman and Limited Variance Powers

One of the Bassett critics was Alfred Bettman.[34] Mr. Bettman, in addition to filing the amicus curiae brief for the National Conference on City Planning (and others) in *Euclid v. Ambler Realty*,[35] was also ***the*** drafter of all of the Tennessee zoning and planning enabling legislation[36]. Of particular importance for our object, he drafted the Tennessee public zoning enabling legislation, in particular, both of the

[33] Bassett, Williams, Bettman & Whitten at 14.

[34] Mr. Bettman collaborated in the book *Model Planning Laws* published in 1935. In the preface, the editor of research and chairman of the School of City Planning at Harvard University, indicated that, "We believe that it is natural and desirable that the four experienced collaborators in this report have in some instances agreed to disagree. On the whole, Mr. Bassett and Mr. Williams of New York represent one point of view, and Mr. Bettman of Ohio and Mr. Whitten represent another. They are all in close agreement as to the results which they believe to be desirable, but they differ, sometimes widely, as to the methods which they consider best adapted in the long run to produce these results." Bassett, Williams, Bettman & Whitten at v.

[35] 272 U.S. 365, 71 L. Ed. 303, 47 S.Ct. 114 (1926). This brief is generally credited with winning the case. See, for example, Mandelker and Cunningham, *Planning and Control of Land Development* (Sixth Edition, 2006) at 88. Indeed, Bettman was instrumental in the entire process; he and Bassett disagreed on whether to support Euclid in this matter; both felt the Euclid ordinance was a bad piece of legislation. Id. at 96.

[36] See page 257.

provisions relating to variances.[37] Mr. Bettman was definitely a critic of the powers of the boards of zoning appeals.[38]

> The statute books of almost all the American states now contain zoning enabling legislation in forms which have not as yet disclosed any such defects or produced any such dissatisfaction as to demonstrate the need of radical changes in principles or procedures. In two rather basic respects, however, lessons from experience under existing measures should receive recognition and reflection in new or amended forms of zoning legislation.
>
> . . . Experience under existing zoning laws and ordinances has disclosed an important problem which is of more difficult solution [than the preceding one]. Boards of appeals had long been used in the administration of building codes as a mode of preventing or minimizing illegal, arbitrary, or mistaken rulings of building commissioners. Mr. Bassett, in drafting the first model for zoning acts, wisely saw the need of a similar tribunal for making adjustments of the general standards prescribed by the zoning ordinance to the special or exceptional situations of individual pieces of property. The ordinary building code, dealing as it does with structural requirements, could easily supply definite standards, leaving a very limited field to the discretion of the board of appeals. On account, however, of the different nature of zoning regulations, and the relative paucity of experience, it was impossible to supply boards of zoning appeals with definite rules, and it was necessary and appropriate to grant them an extensive field of discretion. *The test adopted to govern that discretion was the rather vague, elusive, and elastic clause known as the practical difficulty and unnecessary hardship clause, which provides, in a*

---

[37] TENN. CODE ANN. §§ 13-7-109 and 207.

[38] Bassett, Williams, Bettman & Whitten at 63-65, (emphasis added).

most generous way, that the board may vary the requirements of the zoning regulations where strict application would produce practical difficulty or unnecessary hardship.

By and large, the board of zoning appeals device has worked with a considerable degree of success and satisfaction; but we ought to face the problems raised by experience under this hardship clause. One result of its vagueness is that now and then a Court declares it to be unconstitutional, on the ground that it transfers a rule making or law making power to an administrative board, thus violating the constitutional prohibition of the delegation of legislative power. Fortunately such decisions have not been numerous; nevertheless, this constitutional point presents a certain lurking danger. A more serious consequence of the indefiniteness of the hardship clause is the advantage taken of it by many boards of appeals, so that, in practice in many places, the cumulative effect of the allowances of variances and exceptions represents a more serious impairment of the integrity of the zone plan than results from Court decisions or councilmanic spot zoning.

For these reasons, it would be wise to attempt to specify some greater degree of definiteness in the description of the situations in which the board of zoning appeals may act by way of variances or exceptions, or in the rules to be applied in such actions; and experience ought sooner or later to disclose typical and recurrent situations for which more definite rules could be formulated to govern the board's necessary, though dangerous, power of allowing variances from the standards set forth in the zoning ordinance. In order that each community may develop these rules through its own experience and thus make the rules which are to govern the allowance of variances and exceptions a product of this actual experience, the form I propose leaves it to each municipal council to specify the scope and degree of the powers of its own board of appeals and the conditions of the exercise of these powers. This method seems to have worked satisfactorily in those states in which it has been used.

For those state legislatures which prefer to define and limit in detail the jurisdiction of boards of zoning appeals, rather than leave this definition and limitation to the discretion of municipal councils, useful models for developing the phraseology of provisions on this subject already exist, as, for instance, . . . Section 6 of my form for County and Regional Enabling Act . . ..

Remember that this discussion is taking place shortly before 1935. That is the same year when the Tennessee public zoning enabling legislation was adopted. Mr. Bettman's suggested form (in Section 6 of the book) is virtually identical to the Tennessee public zoning enabling legislation and, of course, is so for the very reason that he drafted the Tennessee public zoning enabling legislation.[39]

---

[39]As Bettman noted in the text quoted above, his form for municipal zoning enabling legislation was very broad. See Bassett, Williams, Bettman & Whitten at 82. The form specified by Mr. Bettman for a county and regional zoning enabling act was exceedingly narrow, Bassett, Williams, Bettman & Whitten at 99, 103, providing: "Where, by reason of exception of narrowness, shallowness, or shape of a specific piece of property at the time of the enactment of the regulation or by reason of exceptional topographic conditions or other extraordinary and exceptional situation or condition of such piece of property, the strict application of any regulation enacted under this Act would result in peculiar and exceptional practical difficulties to or exceptional and undue hardship upon the owner of such property, to authorize, upon an appeal relating to said property, a variance from such strict application so as to relieve such difficulties or hardships, provided such relief may be granted without substantial detriment to the public good and without substantially impairing the intent and purpose of the zone plan and zoning ordinances." Notice the similarity to the Tennessee provisions.

In 1938, Bettman again raised his voice in condemnation of the broad powers given to boards of zoning appeals.[40]

> As there may be individual pieces of land here and there in which, owing to exceptional characteristics, conformance to the district regulations might impose extraordinarily unjust hardships upon the owners, our statutes or ordinances have customarily entrusted to the zoning board of adjustment or appeals the power to ease up on the literal enforcement of the district regulations in such cases. This rather general language opens up to the board of zoning appeals the opportunity or temptation to substitute gradually a system of regulations by individual lots or small groups of lots as distinguished from regulation by districts; thus producing a system in which a facade of regulation by districts is retained but the remainder of the actual structure makes that facade somewhat of an illusion.
>
> For these reasons, which inhere in human nature and are therefore not completely escapable, it becomes of the greatest importance that zoning legislation carefully reflects not only the essential principle of regulation by districts but also the essential difference between exceptions and variances. The problem of a variance clause is more difficult to solve. In general, the direction of its solution is to define the conditions which justify a variance *in terms of the physical size, shape, topography, and conditions of the individual lot, thereby reducing the influence of a merely financial test and reducing the zoning board's discretion to a point at which it will not have statutory justification for decisions which are in essence zoning amendments or departures from the principle of zoning by districts.* Some of the later statutes carefully state the differentiation between exceptions and variances,

---

[40] Bettman, Planners' Journal, November-December, 1938, Volume 4, Number 6, Pages 135-137, reprinted in A. Bettman, City and Regional Planning Papers, Harvard University Press (1946) at 59-60.

and contain forms of the variance clause which experiment in the said direction.

Thus, the two great champions of early zoning had distinctly dissimilar ideas about how broad the powers of a board of zoning appeals should be in regard to variances.[41] Bassett expected that the boards themselves would gradually develop rules which would give more meaning to practical difficulty and unnecessary hardship.[42] Furthermore, he felt that the judiciary would step in and correct problems by further defining the terms "unnecessary hardship and

---

[41]This is not the only area in which they disagreed. It is obvious that Bettman placed a much higher priority on planning in general and fitting the zoning within the sphere of planning than did Bassett. In the *Bassett, Williams, Bettman & Whitten* book, the order of appearance of the forms is interesting. Bassett and Williams have their zoning enabling act placed first; Bettman places his planning enabling act first. See *Bassett, Williams, Bettman & Whitten* at 31 and 59. Bassett and Bettman also disagreed on the necessity of providing for judicial review of the administrative decision making process within the enabling legislation itself. Bettman concluded that "there is no need whatever for any express provision for court adjudication on any question of law which can arise on or under zoning ordinances and administration" because "under the American system of jurisprudence, the regular Courts of law may always be resorted to by any landowner or other person who wishes to attack the validity of any zoning regulation or the legality of any administrative act . . ." Id. at 63. Bassett on the other hand felt that the superior position was to include an express provision for judicial review in the enabling legislation itself. "One great advantage of the statutory [provision of judicial review] as part of the Zoning Enabling Act is that it provides an aggrieved neighbor the means to obtain relief in Court. If it is omitted, he is without remedy because he was not a party to the proceedings before the board of appeals." *Bassett, Williams, Bettman & Whitten* at 14. In 1940, Bassett's opinion remained the same. *Bassett* at 154.

[42]*Bassett* at 123 and 168; see Bettman's reference to experience in *Bassett, Williams, Bettman & Whitten* at 64-5.

practical difficulty."[43] The expertise of the local boards of zoning appeals[44] never materialized. Training before appointment to the board has not been required[45] and there is no institutional link between the local government planning staff and the zoning board.[46] "The Board, . . . not only lacks expertise itself, but also lacks any institutionalized ties to the city or county planning staff. Local planning experts may present evidence and make recommendations to the board, but the board is not required to adopt them. Similarly, the board is required to deal with such legal questions as the difference between an unconstitutional taking and unnecessary hardship, often without any formal legal advice."[47] In short, the boards never had an opportunity to develop any common thread of experience because they lacked the expertise to do so.

Judicial review of board decisions has also proven ineffective under the Bassett formulation.[48]

> Initially, the statutory language gives broad discretion to the board. Therefore, many board actions which may be undesirable in practice are nevertheless legal within the statutes [which grant only a narrow avenue of judicial oversight].[49] Secondly, courts reviewing board decisions

---

[43] *Bassett* at 167-169.

[44] *Bassett* at 156-7.

[45] Such as requiring board members to be architects, engineers, or urban planners. Note: Variance Administration in Indiana -- Problems and Remedies, 48 Ind. L.J. 240, 245 (1973) (hereinafter cited at "Indiana").

[46] See generally, *Indiana* at 245, Note: Administrative Discretion in Zoning, 82 Harv.L.Rev. 668, 673 (1969).

[47] *Indiana* at 245.

[48] *Indiana* at 246-7.

[49] Tennessee is no exception to this. Appeal is only by virtue of the Tennessee Common Law Writ of Certiorari as a decision of the board

which grant variances use the substantial evidence of probative value standard. Even though a great deal of evidence may indicate that a variance should not have been granted, the Court is powerless to review that evidence; it can only determine whether there was sufficient evidence to support the board's finding. Thus, the board has great latitude without effective control. Finally, judicial review is necessarily ineffective since it is seldom exercised, and because Courts, like boards of zoning appeals, lack the technical expertise required to solve land use problems.

Finally, it has come to be recognized that Bassett's fear of the judiciary holding comprehensive zoning ordinances unconstitutional in the absence of a broad variance provision was not well founded.[50] The constitutionality of a zoning ordinance is now recognized to be independent of its variance provisions.[51]

In the early days of zoning, variances were provided for and granted due to apprehension that otherwise a "taking" of property without due process might be found to have occurred through enforcement of the zoning law. As the general validity of zoning as an exercise of police power has come to be judicially established, such concern is lessened. Variances had been retained as a means of correcting occasional inequities created by general zoning ordinances -- as a kind of "escape hatch" or "safety valve" that removes not only possible constitutional claims of improper confiscation but, more importantly, politically

---

may be overturned only if it is arbitrary, capricious, fraudulent, illegal, or beyond the jurisdiction of the board. See *Hoover Motor Express v. Public Service Commission*, 195 Tenn. 593, 261 S.W.2d 233 (1953).

[50] See, e.g., *Bassett* at 122.

[51] O. M. Reynolds, *Self-Induced Hardship and Zoning Variances: Does a Purchaser Have No One but Himself to Blame?*, 20 The Urban Lawyer at 1, 3 (1988).

> unpopular situations of injustice to individual landowners. As thus viewed, variances have come to be regarded as special dispensations to which there is, in any particular case, no legal right.

Especially in light of the *First England Lutheran Church* case[52], it is absolutely clear that a challenge to the confiscatory aspect of a zoning ordinance may be made and it makes little difference that any provision for a variance may exist.[53]

Thus, the only remaining policy for the presence of a variance in a land use planning scheme at all is to adjust unanticipated[54] inequities in the ordinance itself as applied to particular pieces of property.[55] This limited purpose behind variances would also seem to

---

[52] 482 U.S. 304 (1987).

[53] In *Williamson County Regional Planning Commission v. Hamilton Bank*, 473 US 172 (1985) the US Supreme Court held that if a variance procedure is allowed, it must be used before going to Federal Court for invalidation of the ordinance itself. Presumably, if the variance procedure is not available under local law, the owner may proceed directly to federal court (after exhausting whatever administrative avenues are open).

[54] Many types of variances are seen over and over again. For example, new construction which misses the side setback is a frequent subject of variance requests. But those can be anticipated and the local government could specifically provide for those (perhaps allowing some arbitrary adjustment based on certain criteria – something like 10% permitted upon a showing of unintentional violation) under TENN. CODE ANN. 13-7-207(2) which provides the power to "hear and decide . . . other special questions upon which such board is authorized by any such ordinance to pass . . ." The local government must just not call it a variance.

[55] The continued policy basis for variances is somewhat slim it would seem at this point. Functionally, it might be better that they did not exist at all. Because most state enabling legislation mandates the

augur for a limited power to grant variances. The tremendous discretion argued for by Bassett and codified by most state enabling legislation is important only to the extent that it is necessary to combat the possibility of a finding of confiscatory impact by the Courts.

The Bassett versus Bettman confrontation continues today because of the adoption of these different models of zoning variance powers for the local boards of zoning appeals. Tennessee suffered from the same problem and it has affected our variance law ever since.

3. The Memphis and Shelby County Private Legislation

The logical starting place in any analysis of state variance law is the state enabling legislation.[56] Already the confusion begins. For not only are there two sets of public enabling acts in Tennessee,[57] one for

---

variance power from boards of zoning appeals, that state of affairs could only take place with considerable modification of existing enabling legislation.

[56] Dillon's Rule is alive and well in Tennessee, and the local governments have only those powers given to them by the Tennessee General Assembly. *Southern Constructors v Loudon County*, 58 S. W.3d 706 (Tenn. 2001). If the power is not authorized (expressly or implicitly) by the statute, then presumably it is not available at the local level.

[57] It is not unusual for the several states to have different forms of enabling legislation. For example, see note, *Variances and Parcel Rezoning: Relief from Restrictive Zoning in Nebraska*, 60 Neb.L.Rev. 81, 89, 90, and 93 (1981) (hereinafter cited as Nebraska) (note also the reference to Neb.Rev.Stat. § 19-910 (Cum.Supp. 1980), which bears a striking resemblance to the Tennessee Public Zoning Enabling Legislation, except for the deletion of the grounds of exceptional topographic conditions; note, *Variance Administration in Indiana*, 48 Ind.L.J. 240, 241 (1973).

counties,[58] and the other for municipalities,[59] there is also a multiplicity of private acts granting authority to individual local governments.[60] And while it may fairly be said that the public acts are roughly similar,[61] the private acts are often dissimilar not only from one another, but also from the public acts.[62] The best means of imposing order on this chaotic situation is to discuss the enactments chronologically. Because of the primacy of three variance cases from Memphis and Shelby County, the Memphis Triumvirate, and because zoning in Tennessee began in Memphis,[63] the private acts from that West Tennessee city and county will be briefly reviewed.

The first piece of zoning legislation in the State of Tennessee was adopted in 1921.[64] It applied only to the city of Memphis and authorized the enactment of a zoning ordinance.[65] No mention was made of the

---

[58] TENN. CODE ANN. § 13-7-109.

[59] TENN. CODE ANN § 13-7-207.

[60] See, e.g., 1921 Tennessee Private Acts, Chapter 165 (Memphis); 1925 Tennessee Private Acts, Chapter 209 (Nashville); and 1925 Tennessee Private Acts, Chapter 428 (Knoxville).

[61] Regarding the circumstances under which variances may be granted, the Public Acts are nearly identical. Compare T.C.A. §§ 13-7-109 and 207.

[62] Many states suffer this same confusion. *Indiana* at 241-2; *Nebraska* at 89-96.

[63] *Spencer-Sturla v. City of Memphis*, 155 Tenn. 70, 81, 290 S.W. 608 (Tenn. 1926).

[64] 1921 Tennessee Private Acts, Chapter 165.

[65] More precisely, the Act applied to all municipalities "having a population in excess of over 160,000 inhabitants by the Federal Census of 1920, or by any subsequent Federal Census . . ." 1921 Tennessee Private Acts, Chapter 165, § 1. In 1921, Memphis was the only municipality with a population of that size at that time.

power to issue variances,[66] but extremely broad powers were given to an administrative tribunal.[67]

> . . . the legislative body may create an administrative board to administer the details of the application of the ordinances and regulations and may delegate such board, in accordance with the provisions set forth in the regulations, the power to hear and determine appeals from the refusal of building permits by building commissioners or other officers to exercise jurisdictional powers with respect to the administration of the regulations as specified herein . . .

The failure of this piece of legislation and others like it throughout the United States to specify the circumstances under which the board could act created a void which has not yet been filled.[68] The boards, both then and now, had no way of knowing or understanding the limits of their power.[69]

---

[66] On the national scene at this time, the debate over how to structure zoning ordinances was taking place. As we have seen, the New York City model was still evolving and one might guess that Memphis based its zoning effort principally upon the New York City example. See *Bassett* at 133-141. The lack of a provision for variances as such is therefore not surprising.

[67] Chapter 165 of the Tennessee Private Acts of 1921, Section 5.

[68] Again, the Bassett model provision gives vast power and no standard by which to exercise it.

[69] In 1925, the City of Nashville was authorized to establish zoning within its confines. The language employed in this act is quite similar to the 1921 Memphis Private Act. It suffers from the same disability: The board was given no guidance as to when any of its powers may justifiably be exercised. *Bubis v. Nashville,* 174 Tenn. 134, 124 S.W.2d 238 (1939) is an example of the problem; see footnote 79.

The Legislature amended the Memphis Private Act in 1925.[70] The amendment attempts to more specifically set out the powers and duties of the administrative board. It provides that:

> The Board of Adjustment shall have the following powers:
>
> . . .
>
> 3. In passing upon appeals, where there are practical difficulties or unnecessary hardship in the way of carrying out strict letter of such ordinance, to vary or modify the application of any of the regulations or provisions of such ordinance relating to the use, construction or alteration of buildings or structures or the use of land so that the spirit of the ordinance shall be observed, public safety and welfare secured and substantial justice done.

This legislation certainly did clarify the powers of the board, but unfortunately, it did not go far enough. It essentially is the Bassett model variance provision: the terms "practical difficulties" and "unnecessary hardship" are nowhere defined. The type or degree of hardship or difficulty is not identified. The ambiguity of the terms "spirit of the ordinance," "public safety and welfare," and "substantial justice" are self-evident.[71] The board was left to its own devices to determine what those terms meant and when the power should be exercised.[72] The amendatory effort was laudable but of no practical significance.

---

[70] 1925 Tennessee Private Acts, Chapter 428, § 1.

[71] Similar criticisms have been made of similar laws in other states. See, e.g., comment, *Variance Law in New York: The Examination and Proposal*, 44 Albany L.Rev. 781, 785 (1980).

[72] The leaders of the zoning movement in this country thought that the Courts would define the terms over time. See E. Bassett, *Zoning* at 113 (2d Ed. 1940). From a practical perspective, this has not occurred.

In 1931, the Tennessee General Assembly enacted legislation which permitted the City of Memphis to regulate via the zoning ordinance an area located outside of, but within five miles of this boundary to the City of Memphis.[73] The variance provision in this legislation is identical to the variance provisions in the 1925 Memphis Private Acts. Thus, the City of Memphis and the five-mile zone both had identical legislation.

In 1935, a private act was passed to comprehensively regulate land uses within Shelby County.[74] Interestingly, even though the Public Acts were adopted that same year, the language is nevertheless not as specific as that found in the Public Acts. The 1925 Memphis Act, the 1931 Shelby County Five-Mile Zone Act, and the 1935 Shelby County Act, are, for variance purposes, identical to one another but dissimilar to the public acts adopted in 1935.[75] After the 1935 county zoning enabling legislation, the legislation throughout the area of Shelby County was identical insofar as zoning variances were concerned.

In 1955, two new acts changed the complexion of the private enabling legislation. First, the Memphis legislation was changed to bring it into accord with the public legislation.[76] The language is identical. Furthermore, an act was passed to consolidate the functions

---

[73] 1931 Tenn. Private Acts, Chapter 613.

[74] 1935 Tenn. Private Acts, Chapter 625.

[75] The 1935 Tennessee Private Acts, Chapter 625, Section 6 provides: "[The] Board of Adjustment shall have the following powers: . . . (3) in passing upon appeals, where there are practical difficulties or unnecessary hardships in the way of carrying out the strict letter of such regulations, to vary or modify the application of any of the regulations passed pursuant to this Act, relating to the use, construction or alteration of building or structure or the use of land so that the spirit of the regulations and this Act shall be observed, the public health, safety, morals, convenience and welfare secured and substantial justice done."

[76] 1955 Tennessee Private Acts, Chapter 142.

of various boards in Memphis and Shelby County.[77] This consolidation will be discussed shortly. The net effect of this legislation should have been to strengthen and tighten the circumstances under which variances would have been issued. However, because the Courts originally failed to look at the enabling legislation at all, bad case law developed. Vast discretion was accorded the board even where the statutory standards were much more specific and were in fact not met.

D. The Memphis Triumvirate

1. *Reddoch v. Smith*

A triumvirate of cases out of Memphis and Shelby County reflect the very broad power given zoning boards under the terms of variance provisions contained in the very earliest of Tennessee zoning legislation and clearly illustrate the muddle created by the lack of reasonable governing standards in this[78] and other zoning legislation.[79] Since these

---

[77] 1955 Tennessee Private Acts, Chapter 353.

[78] 1921 Tennessee Private Acts, Chapter 165 (Memphis); 1925 Tennessee Private Acts, Chapter 209 (Nashville); and 1925 Tennessee Private Acts, Chapter 428 (Knoxville).

[79] Nashville initially adopted a zoning ordinance under the authority of a private act which gave the board similarly broad powers. 1925 Tennessee Private Acts, Chapter 209. Only one reported case apparently arose contesting the board's power under this ordinance. In *Bubis v. City of Nashville*, 174 Tenn. 134, 124 S.W.2d 238 (1939), neighboring landowners challenged an action of the board permitting the extension of an apartment building into a single family residential district. The Court relied upon the fact that the ordinance specifically provided for such extensions, and the broad language of the enabling act. No physical feature or unique condition of the property was noted at all which might justify the issuance of the variance.

were the first[80] of only a handful of reported cases[81] in Tennessee dealing explicitly with variance law,[82] the triumvirate from Memphis came to have, perhaps mistakenly, considerable importance.

---

[80] There is one earlier case out of Memphis. In *Arendale v. Rasch*, 196 Tenn. 374, 268 S.W.2d 102 (1954), the real issue was the time within which an appeal from the zoning board must be taken. In the course of ruling against the appellant, because he failed to file within 30 days of the board's decision, the Trial Court also held that the variance as granted was within the power of the board. The Supreme Court specifically refused to follow that holding, ruling instead only on the procedural issue.

[81] There are several other cases which may involve variances such as *Qualls v. Memphis*, 15 Tenn. App. 575 (1932), and *Memphis v. Qualls*, 16 Tenn. App. 387, 64 S.W. 2d 584 (1933). These cases more likely involve a straightforward interpretation of the Memphis zoning ordinance. Furthermore, *Arendale v. Rusch*, 196 Tenn. 374, 268 S.W.2d 102 (1954) clearly involves a variance application but was decided on procedural grounds, as noted above, eliminating the need for review of the substantive law.

[82] It is difficult to tell even in some of the later cases whether the issue involved a variance or some other zoning technique such as a conditional use permit (special exception) or a non-conforming use. See, e.g., *Hickerson v. Flannery*, 42 Tenn.App. 329, 302 S.W.2d 508 (1956) (conditional use permit); *State ex rel. Smith v. City of Nashville*, 51 Tenn.App. 23, 364 S.W.2d 106 (1962) (this appears to be a request for a use variance for the location of a mobile home park in the "Residence A District;" the board denied the request and was ultimately affirmed); *Stevenson v. Palmer*, 448 S.W.2d 67 (Tenn. 1969) (conditional use permit); and *Union Trust Company v. Williamson County Board of Zoning Appeals*, 500 S.W.2d 608 (Tenn. 1973) (this is a request for a variance where the hardship appears to have been self-created by reason of a subdivision).

When viewed against this background of private legislation, *Reddoch v. Smith*[83] may be placed in perspective. Zoning litigation (although the ordinances had been around for awhile) was relatively new and the concepts not well understood. The developer in that case applied for a "variation" in the use provisions of the Memphis zoning ordinance so as to use his property located in a residential (R-1) zone district[84] for the operation of a gasoline service station.

The Court refers to the application to the board as a "rezoning" at some points, and at others, as a "variation." In the first paragraph of the opinion, the Court says " This appeal involves the authority of the . . . Board of Adjustment to grant a zoning variation." In the next sentence, the Court seems to suggest otherwise: "The Board of Adjustment granted the application . . . for a re-zoning of the particular property from R-1 residential to commercial . . ." While it appears on the whole that the application must have been for a variance, the Court's lack of recognition of the intrinsic differences between variances and zoning changes is somewhat unnerving: the zoning change is legislative and the board has no power to grant such a request and no business even considering it. Under the provisions of the applicable private enabling legislation, only the local legislative body could have rezoned the property. The Court's inability to get the appropriate zoning technique described appropriately in the opinion makes it much less likely that the appropriate legal test is going to be employed. Furthermore, if the Court doesn't get it right, how can the board of zoning appeals?

---

[83] 214 Tenn. 213, 379 S.W.2d 641 (1964).

[84] The fact that a commercial gasoline station was proposed for a residential zoning district makes this application a use variance, something zoning boards should never be permitted to do under Tennessee law.

In any event, the Board granted the request. In upholding the Board's determination, the Supreme Court of Tennessee cited the private act[85] and held that:[86]

> . . . This board . . . is given the power to *change* certain properties "where there are practical difficulties or unnecessary hardships in the way of carrying out the strict letter of such regulations . . ." and in so doing the board is "vested with a wide discretion and courts will not interfere with that discretion unless it is abused."(emphasis added)[87]

---

[85] The Court cited 1935 Private Acts, Chapter 625, Section 6, Subsection 3, 379 S.W.2d at 645, but it relates to Shelby County; the appropriate enabling legislation was most likely 1931 Tennessee Private Acts, Chapter 613, Section 11, as amended by 1935 Tennessee Private Acts, Chapter 707. The language is the same, however, (both are broadly phrased with no objective standards) and so the result is the same anyway. The more restrictive language of the Tennessee 1955 Private Acts, Chapter 142 did not apply to either the five-mile zone or the remainder of Shelby County, only to the City of Memphis. To the extent that the board was a joint city and county board, county law governed outside the city's jurisdiction. 1955 Tennessee Private Acts, Chapter 353, Section 7.

[86] 214 Tenn. at 223, 379 S.W.2d at 645.

[87] The language quoted by the Court is from E.C. Yokley's treatise. Mr. Yokley lived and practiced in Nashville and his treatise was nationally prominent at this time. Yokley was an important figure both in the Nashville legal community and in political circles as well. He was actively involved in the government consolidation effort in Nashville in the late fifties and early sixties. See Don H. Doyle, *Nashville Since the 1920s* at 199-200 (UT Press 1985). Notice also that he was one of the counsel of record in *Bubis*, supra, footnote 79. His name is liberally sprinkled through the Tennessee cases involving zoning and land use.

Clearly, the Court equated the ambiguity of the terminology in the enabling act with a wide discretion invested in the Board.[88] The Board's discretion is not and should not be as wide as the Court allows in this case. These early variance provisions provided little or no guidance to the board concerning the execution of its duties and amounted to allowing the board to legislate on zoning matters. This in turn led to an extensive system of bribery concerning the New York City zoning board in the 1920's and 30's. [89]

---

[88] The use of the word "change" in the quoted language is especially troublesome. It implies that the board could usurp the legislative power of the local legislative body and change the zoning on the property. From the author's perspective, even with the broad language applicable in this case, no board of zoning appeals should have that power.

[89] For example, see Conrad Black, *Franklin Delano Roosevelt*, (2005) at p. 204, and Gregory F. Gilmartin, *Shaping the City: New York and the Municipal Art Society* (1995) at 202. As Gilmartin explained:

> ... zoning turned out to be useful to Tamany [Hall] itself, for the Board of Standards and Appeals had the power to review requests for zoning variances, a wide discretionary power that was ideally suited to the practice of "honest graft." Bribes, in the strictest sense of the word, never needed to change hands. All Tammany had to do was to make sure that certain lawyers, closely connected to the Democratic machine, enjoyed astonishing success when representing clients before the board.

The attorneys in turn would make large contributions to the party to ensure that the proper "party hacks" were appointed to the board.

After noting that the case was before the Court pursuant to common law certiorari[90] and emphasizing the limited nature of judicial review under such a writ, the Court phrased the issue as:[91]

> Whether the Board . . . acted illegally and arbitrarily in granting this variation. The gist of this [issue] is [whether] the Board had [any] competent evidence before it to authorize the variation granted.

This statement of the issue before the Court is quite satisfactory; the only problem is that the Court did not have any more of an idea of what kind of evidence was a necessary predicate to the issuance of a variance than did the Board.

Turning to a consideration of the evidence, the Court pointed out that the "variation" was sought because the owner could sell the property for fifty thousand ($50,000) dollars if it could properly be used as a service station.[92] The Court held that while financial or pecuniary loss alone was insufficient grounds on which to grant a variance, it was one factor that could be considered.[93] The Court examined the other evidence and found that the property was located on the southeast corner of an intersection. On the northwest corner, there was a vacant lot formerly occupied by the Tennessee Highway Patrol. The northeast corner was the location of the Memphis Memorial Park Cemetery. A new expressway interchange was one thousand (1,000) feet to the west. A restaurant was nearby; the street accommodated a large volume of traffic. In addition, the owner proved that he had offered the property for sale for eight years with no result, and offered expert testimony to

---

[90] For a detailed discussion of the common law writ of certiorari, see Chapter Five.

[91] 214 Tenn. at 224, 379 S.W.2d at 645.

[92] Id.

[93] 379 S.W. 2d at 646.

show that the property was of little or no value without the "variation."[94] The same experts testified that the "present zoning of the property was not correct" and that to refuse the variation was a denial of a property right.[95] The Court concluded from its review of the evidence that the variance was justified.[96]

Reddoch is clearly an unfortunate decision. The reviewing posture of the Court is standard in cases of administrative review; but the determination that the evidence presented justified the variance is not correct. Even given the lack of specificity in the private enabling legislation, the Court should have insisted that some peculiar physical feature of the subject property exist which caused the hardship. No such proof was adduced. All the developer did prove was that the zoning ordinance itself, without regard to any peculiarity of his property, made the property less usable, or perhaps unusable. This kind of evidence is appropriate in an application for a zone change,[97] and indeed, if the zoning ordinance as applied to this property rendered it worthless, the ordinance should have been modified or adjudged unconstitutional.[98] What distinguished the subject property from its neighbors? Why should limited administrative relief be granted? If the properties all suffered similarly, then relief should have been granted to all through a zone change. A zone change is an act of a legislative body; it is not a function of an administrative tribunal, such as a Board of Zoning Appeals. The broad discretion necessarily implied in the policy-making

---

[94] Id.

[95] Id.

[96] Id.

[97] In fact, the proof offered by the applicant sounded more like that presented in a zone change application than what is normally offered for a variance.

[98] See, e.g., *Nectow v. City of Cambridge*, 277 U.S. 183 (1928). Just because the property may not have much value as a result of the current zoning on a piece of property does not give the zoning board authority to grant a variance.

arena of a legislative body is inappropriate in an administrative form; instead, the latter's exercise of power should be confined to those subjects assigned by the legislature with precisely drawn standards and guidelines.[99]

The attorneys for the neighbors in *Reddoch* certainly recognized that the Board had transgressed the boundaries of its authority, as witness their argument in the petition to rehear. The argument was based upon *Grant v. McCullough*[100] and the concept of spot zoning. Strictly speaking, of course, *Reddoch* does not involve spot zoning. To that extent, the Court's denial of the petition was correct. However, it is a triumph of form over substance. For *Reddoch* is a perfect example of a use variance. The Board granted the developer the right to use the property in a way not otherwise permitted by the ordinance; a commercial use was permitted in a residential district.[101] In practical effect, there is little distinction between this use variance and a spot zone.[102] The developer absolutely got what he wanted. Spot zones and use variances are mirror images of one another; one is an unlawful

---

[99] In *Spencer-Sturla Company v. City of Memphis*, 155 Tenn. 70, 290 S.W. 608 (1927), the first important zoning case in Tennessee, the Court reviewed, in passing, the variance powers of the Memphis Board of Adjustment, and indicated approval of the delegation of broad powers to that body.

[100] 196 Tenn. 671, 270 S.W.2d 317 (1953).

[101] The opinion of the Court does not indicate what uses a residential district in Memphis might have permitted at the time, but generally residential zone districts do not permit any commercial uses. Obviously, given that assumption, a service station would not be permitted in a single-family residential district.

[102] There is one difference; with a zone change, the developer would be able to use his property for any use permitted in the new district. A use variance only permits the specific use which was the subject of the application.

legislative act,[103] the other, an undesirable (at the least) administrative act.[104] *Reddoch* apparently validates the practice of granting use variances in Tennessee, but the precedent should be limited to Memphis and Shelby County only, by virtue of this private enabling legislation and its ambiguous language.

2. *Glankler v. City of Memphis*

The second case[105] in the triumvirate is *Glankler v. City of Memphis.*[106] The developer wished to construct apartment buildings on a 13.7 acre tract of land in the city. After an unsuccessful attempt at

[103] A spot zone is an unlawful legislative act in that it bears no rational relationship to any legitimate governmental objective. *Euclid v. Ambler Realty*, 272 U.S. 365 (1926); *Spencer-Sturla Company v. City of Memphis*, 155 Tenn. 70, 290 S.W. 608 (1927). Some courts have also found that spot zones may be more in the nature of a judicial action and thus subject to stricter review. See *Fasano v. Board of County Commissioners of Washington County*, 264 Ore. 574, 567 P.2d 23, 29 (1973).

[104] Use variances clearly are *ultra vires* the Tennessee public zoning enabling legislation. For example how can a change in use be justified by some exceptional physical feature of the property? It simply cannot be.

[105] The intervening case of *Stevenson v. Palmer*, 448 S.W.2d 67 (Tenn. 1969) might involve a variance, but the Court refers to it as an "exception," a totally different zoning technique. See Chapter Three (the "exception" to which the court refers may be a special exception which is another name for a conditional use permit). In any event, there is no discussion of the evidence upon which a variance can be granted, although the Court knows that the board is vested with "broad powers."

[106] 481 S.W.2d 376 (Tenn. 1972).

rezoning the property,[107] the developer appealed to the Board for a variance on the grounds of hardship. The Board granted the variance. Both the Trial Court and the Court of Appeals affirmed the Board's action. So did the Supreme Court.

The main failure of the *Glankler* Court was to ignore the differences between the enabling legislation in *Reddoch* and itself. *Reddoch* involved property within the five-mile zone; Glankler's property was within the city limits of Memphis.[108] The enabling legislation was different. In *Reddoch*, the Bassett model applied,[109] in *Glankler*, the Bettman model was in force.[110] The extremely different criteria for variances was never recognized by the Court. It simply cited *Reddoch*, noting that the board was "administrative body which enjoys a wide latitude and great discretion in the granting of variances . . ."[111] The issue on appeal (as always under the common law writ of certiorari) was whether the Board exceeded its jurisdiction or acted illegally. The evidence proved that the property was in a flood plain and that because of the cost of filling the land, it was economically prohibitive to develop into single family structures. Multi-family structures were

---

[107] The tract was zoned R-IA which permitted only single-family dwellings. The developers wanted it changed to R-3A, permitting apartments. This case is an example of an interesting political phenomenon in zoning: when political pressure is too great for the legislative body to act, ofttimes the zoning board will accomplish the same objective via use variances.

[108] 481 S.W.2d at 376.

[109] The Bassett model gave the local government very broad discretion to decide when and where to grant a variance. The Bettman model limited that discretion to 4 very specific categories and 1 catch-all category. Bassett felt that the Bettman model was too restrictive to useful in practice; Bettman felt Bassett was too prone to abuse. BWBW at 12-15; 64-5.

[110] 1955 Tennessee Private Acts, Chapter 142.

[111] 481 S.W.2d at 378.

economically feasible and would not create a traffic hazard or impose an undue burden on transportation facilities.[112] No further discussion was deemed necessary by the Court; the variance was affirmed. Once again, the Courts sanctioned a variance in the use provisions of the zoning ordinance.

This was truly an unfortunate decision. The Court relied heavily on *Reddoch.* As we have seen, the statutory variance language in that case was vague and arguably broad enough to encompass the *Reddoch* decision.[113] But *Glankler* came up under another private act, the 1921 Memphis Private Act which by this time had been amended (in 1955) to contain the much more specific language of the Bettman modified variance provision and as we shall see, what became the Tennessee public enabling legislation provision as well.[114] The parties did not appear to notice this decisive distinction and did not even appear to notice that *Reddoch* involved Shelby County, not Memphis and entirely different enabling legislation. Neither difference was mentioned in the case at all. Arguably at least under the more restrictive standard, the board of zoning appeals does not enjoy "great latitude and discretion in the granting of variances."[115] The public acts and the 1955 Memphis Private Act sharply restrict the board's discretion as Alfred Bettman had intended. A variance clearly cannot be granted unless some exceptional physical feature of the land itself creates the hardship.

Did the flood plain in *Glankler* justify a variance? It certainly is a physical feature of the property, but is it exceptional? How many surrounding property owners suffered from the same handicap?[116] The opinion does not say; there was probably no proof on that issue before

---

[112] Id.

[113] This author, however, does believe it to have been improperly decided.

[114] See Section E of this chapter at page 257.

[115] *Glankler*, at 378.

[116] See Section F(1) of this chapter at page 262.

the zoning board. Surely, if the flood plain affected not just this one property owner, as is likely, but many others in the same vicinity, it is unfair to single out this owner and award a variance. The appropriate vehicle of change would have been a legislative zone change. The owner had tried that unsuccessfully before and possibly some litigation was in order.[117] But a variance was simply not proven. Unfortunately, the appropriate legislative criteria was not reviewed.

The parties and the court undoubtedly did not check and felt intuitively that the enabling legislation was all the same. But it was not so then, and it is frequently not so now. *Glankler* makes clear that in every zoning case, the parties (and the Court) must clearly identify the controlling enabling legislation. Simple references to cases thought to be controlling are insufficient.

3. *Houston v. Memphis and Shelby County*

The final case in the Memphis triumvirate is *Houston v. Memphis and Shelby County Board of Adjustment.*[118] Here, the developer again applied for a variance to allow the use of his property, zoned residential, as an automobile service station. The Board granted the variance, and the trial court affirmed the Board's decision.

The Appellate Court reversed. The primary thrust of the reasoning was that the property was already used in a way consistent with a zoning ordinance: an apartment building existed there. The Court pointed out that very few of the tenants had moved recently, thus contradicting the owner's assertion that desirable tenants were hard to find and keep. The Court further pointed out that many of the

[117] The owner could sue for a "taking" of his property. And although *First English Lutheran Church v. County of Los Angeles*, 482 US 304 (1987) was many years off, *Pennsylvania Coal v Mahon*, 260 US 393 (1922), had already been decided by the US Supreme Court ("if a regulation goes too far, it becomes a taking").

[118] 488 S.W.2d 387 (Tenn. App. 1972).

neighboring properties were apartments and they had no problem with leasing the premises. The Court concluded that:[119]

> There was no material evidence before the Board from which it could find the owner suffered practical difficulties or unnecessary hardships due to the zoning restrictions placed on the subject property . . . The Board in the instant case exceeded its jurisdiction and did attempt to zone the subject property, which is a legislative prerogative denied the Board.

Thus, a patent use variance was denied for the first time by a Tennessee appellate court in a reported case. However, there was still no guidance as to what constituted "practical difficulties" or "unnecessary hardship," unless it be that the applicant suffers a difficulty or hardship only when his property is vacant or unused, as in *Reddoch* and *Glankler*.[120] Furthermore, the appropriate statutory authority was not cited and likely the parties simply assumed it was the same as in *Reddoch* and *Glankler*.[121]

All three of the cases discussed so far arose out of the Memphis and Shelby County area, under ordinances enacted pursuant to private enabling legislation. As previously mentioned, the original private acts were very broad in granting the Board power to issue variances by virtue of their failure to define, in any way, the terms "practical difficulty" or "unnecessary hardship." And even when the statutory criteria was substantially restricted, the parties and the court evidently failed to note the change and operated under the assumption that the broad language was still applicable. The public acts do not suffer from this infirmity.

---

[119] Id. at 389.

[120] Perhaps the size of the property could be some explanation for the variances.

[121] It appears that the joint boards were authorized by yet another private act, chapter 353 of 1955, and section 7 is especially important as it pertains to variances.

E. The Public Acts: A Brief History and Overview

The original Memphis legislation was obviously heavily influenced by Edward Bassett's model based on his New York experience. The public acts, insofar as they address variances, are equally obviously based on Alfred Bettman's model. And, for good reason; he wrote them.

Alfred Bettman was an attorney from Cincinnati, Ohio, who had a special interest in land use planning law. His work in the field spanned several decades, up until the time of his death in 1945.[122] His connection with Tennessee probably began in the early 1930's as a consultant to the Tennessee Valley Authority's Division of Land Use Planning and Housing.[123] The Tennessee State Planning Board thereafter retained him to prepare comprehensive zoning legislation.[124] Bettman presented his proposals to representatives of the TVA and the TSPB on 11 June 1934.[125] Governor Bill McAlister sponsored the bills before the Tennessee General Assembly.[126] The bills were quickly enacted into law and thus in 1935, the two most important pieces of zoning legislation ever to be adopted by the Tennessee General

---

[122] See Introduction to Bettman, *City and Regional Planning Papers* (Harvard University Press, 1946).

[123] *The First Fifteen Years: A History of the Tennessee State Planning Commission* (University of Tennessee 1949) at 4. His task was "to make a complete investigation and report on the state constitution and all legislative acts in Tennessee relating to planning . . ." Id.

[124] Id.

[125] Id. at 8, citing a "Memorandum of Conference Held at Knoxville, Tennessee, Monday, June 11th, by Alfred Bettman, Chairman of District No. 5, . . . on the Subject of a Program for Planning Legislation for Tennessee."

[126] Id.

Assembly were put in place. Both were drafted almost entirely by Alfred Bettman.[127] One applied to counties,[128] and the other to municipalities.[129] These are of great importance because they serve as the foundation upon which most local governments in Tennessee base their zoning ordinances today.[130]

There is also, from the perspective of variances, a radical change from the extraordinarily broad language of the private acts. The relevant provision reads as follows:[131]

> The Board of Appeals shall have the following powers:
>
> . . .
>
> (3) Where, by reason of exceptional narrowness, shallowness or shape of a specific piece of property at the time of the enactment of the zoning regulation, or by reason of exceptional topographic conditions or other extraordinary and exceptional situation or condition of such piece of property, the strict application of any regulation

---

[127] Id. See also Foreword to Bettman, *City and Regional Planning Papers* (1946) at xvii. The State Legislature made some changes but not in the zoning variance provisions with which we are concerned here.

[128] TENN. CODE ANN. § 13-7-101 and following; the variance provision is at TENN. CODE ANN. § 13-7-109(3).

[129] TENN. CODE ANN. § 13-7-201 and following; the variance provision is at TENN. CODE ANN. § 13-7-207(3), and is virtually identical to its county cousin.

[130] Note should be taken of the fact that the public acts specifically provided for the continuing effect of the private acts. TENN. CODE ANN. §§ 13-7-115 and 210. If the local government still adopts the zoning regulations pursuant to a private act, there may be significant differences from an ordinance adopted under the public acts. It is therefore extremely important to know precisely the source of the authority for the zoning regulation.

[131] TENN. CODE ANN. §§ 13-7-109(3) and 207(3).

> enacted under this chapter would result in peculiar and exceptional practical difficulties to or exceptional and undue hardship upon the owner of such property, to authorize, upon an appeal relating to said property, a variance from such strict application so as to relieve such difficulties or hardship, provided such relief may be granted without substantial detriment to the public good and without substantially impairing the intent and purpose of the zone plan and zoning ordinance.

This language should be carefully studied.[132] In form it is similar to the private acts. It is obviously a cousin of the Standard State Zoning Enabling Act. But Bettman[133] substantially reduced the authority of the local boards to grant variances. Authority is granted only where a land owner, because of the strict application of the zoning ordinance, is confronted with:

> (1) a peculiar and exceptional practical difficulty, or
> (2) an exceptional and[134] undue hardship.

---

[132] It is certainly a rather complicated legislative scheme and its complexity explains the difficulty upholding any variance granted against attack.

[133] Bettman's papers, housed at the University of Cincinnati, appear to indicate that he originally recommended the broad form variance provision to the Tennessee authorities. It is not clear how or why this was changed but among his various drafts of the legislation, the change to the more specific language we now have is made.

[134] The "or" which appears here in the Tennessee public enabling legislation is a typographical error. The original public enabling act, chapters 43 and 44 of the Public Acts of 1935, both were properly worded with the word "and." In codification, however, a mistake was made and the word "or" was inserted instead of "and." It is doubtful that this error is of any significance. It is clear, however, that Alfred Bettman used the word "and" so that the hardship would have to be both exceptional and undue. BWBW at 103, and that the original enactment in Tennessee also is correct showing the word "and."

Standing alone, the terms "practical difficulty" and "undue hardship" do not describe with any greater degree of specificity than the private acts the grounds upon which a variance should issue. But the statue initially provides that the difficulty or hardship must be caused by one of five factors relating to the land itself in order to justify the issuance of the variance.

The difficulty or hardship must exist by reason of:

(1) exceptional narrowness;
(2) exceptional shallowness;
(3) exceptional shape;
(4) exceptional topographic conditions; or
(5) other extraordinary and exceptional situation or condition.

This is the key: the difficulty or hardship must be related in some way to a condition or feature of the land itself.[135] Nothing else will do. Unless some feature of the property itself creates the problem, no relief is available by means of a variance. This change is the most important and is indeed a crucial difference as between the original Memphis private act and the public acts. In fact, these restrictive grounds distinguish the Tennessee public zoning variance provision from the variance provisions in many other states.[136]

Further, it is obvious that Bettman, in his model, simply added the word exceptional to both the practical difficulty and the hardship clauses. It would have made little sense to use the conjunctive in the former and the disjunctive in the latter. Judicial interpretations of the provision should give it the original legislative intent, and construe the clause as though "and" appears instead of "or." Incidentally, the miscodification does not appear in the county public enabling legislation, TENN. CODE ANN. § 13-7-109(3).

[135] Osborne Reynolds, Jr., "*The 'Unique Circumstances' Rule in Zoning Variances – An Aid in Achieving Greater Prudence and Less Leniency*," 31 Urban Lawyer 127, 132 (1999).

[136] Compare TENN. CODE ANN. § 13-7-207(3) with N.H. RSA § 674:33 which, for example, provides in part that the zoning board may

As noted earlier,[137] comparisons across state lines in this area of land use planning law can be almost useless because of the tremendous difference between the Tennessee Act and many of the others.[138] In analyzing variance cases from other states, our attorneys, boards and courts must be cautious of the other states' enabling legislation. Very often, the other state will provide much greater latitude (using the Bassett model) to the local boards in granting variances. This reduces the precedential value of case law of our sister states except of course those few with similar provisions.

Under the Tennessee-Bettman provision, the exceptional physical characteristics of the land itself form the basis of the variance.[139]

> . . . the statute . . . make[s] characteristics of the land itself the overriding criterion by which the board is to decide the issue of hardship to an owner.

This "overriding criterion" is a jurisdictional threshold: if proof as to one of the five conditions listed above is not presented to the board (or found in the record by a reviewing court), no further analysis is needed: the

---

"authorize upon appeal in specific cases such variance from the terms of the zoning ordinance as will not be contrary to the public interest, if, owing to special conditions, a literal enforcement of the provisions of the ordinance will result in unnecessary hardship, and so that the spirit of the ordinance shall be observed and substantial justice done." P. Loughlin, New Hampshire Practice: Land Use Planning and Zoning, §§ 24.01 & 24.03 (Lexis 2006). This is word for word the language of the Standard State Zoning Enabling Act.

[137] See Section E of this chapter at page 257.

[138] With some notable exceptions; New Jersey, for example, has a variance provisions which is fairly similar to Tennessee; see NJSA § 40:55D-70.

[139] *McClurkan v. Metropolitan Board of Zoning Appeals*, 565 S.W.2d 495 (Tenn. App. 1977).

application should be, and must be denied.[140] Absent some exceptional feature of the property, no variance may be granted under the Bettman formulated Tennessee variance provision.

F. Detailed Analysis of the Variance Provision

It is useful to break down the statute, phrase by phrase, and word by word, in order to get a fuller understanding of its meaning. This analysis will go a long way to clearing up the muddle.

1. Exceptional

The condition or conditions of the property must be "exceptional" if a variance is to issue: "***Exceptional*** narrowness, shallowness, or shape . . . ***exceptional*** topographic conditions or other ***extraordinary*** and ***exceptional*** situation or condition." In all, the word "exceptional" is used five times in subsection (3) of the statute. This emphasis is important. The insertion and interpretation of this word helps to greatly restrict the circumstances under which a variance may issue.

A simple and accepted synonym for "exceptional" is "uncommon."[141] If the subject property must be "exceptional," the conditions causing the difficulty or hardship must ***not*** be common to other properties in the general vicinity. It is appropriate, then, even mandatory, to compare the features of the subject property with those

---

[140] While the terminology "jurisdictional threshold" may not be strictly accurate, it succinctly expresses the point that the first and most important factor concerning the issuance of a variance is the existence of some unique (exceptional) physical feature on the property. If one does not exist, the succeeding issues of hardship/difficulty, causation, and the negative criteria, as well as the sub-issues of pecuniary considerations and self-created hardship, to name only a few, should not even be considered.

[141] American Heritage Dictionary.

of the surrounding properties which are in the same zoning district.[142] If the surrounding properties all share the same or substantially similar features, then it may safely be said that the condition of the applicant's property is not exceptional, and no variance should be granted.

But even "uncommon" may be too expansive of a synonym for the term "exceptional" as used in this statute. Many Courts have held that variances should only rarely be granted.[143] These holdings have probably resulted from the instinctive judicial reaction that administrative adjustments such as variances must, by their very nature, be only occasionally employed.[144] But certainly the term "exceptional" implies the same. If circumstances justifying a variance must be exceptional, then only a small number of applicants will be capable of surmounting the burden of proof [145] required and only a small number of variances will be granted.[146] A synonym for

---

[142] *Otto v. Steinhilber*, 282 N.Y. 71, 24 N.E.2d 851 (1939) (the New York Court of Appeals held that as part of the criteria to be applied in the State of New York, the applicant must demonstrate that "the plight of the owner is due to unique circumstances and not to the general conditions of the neighborhood which may reflect the unreasonableness of the zoning ordinance itself"); *Williams* at § 142.01.

[143] *Metropolitan Historical Commission* at 20; *Beirn v. Morris*, 103 A.2d 361, 364 (1954), *Kohl v. Mayor and Council of Fairlawn*, 50 N.J. 268, 234 A.2d 385, 389 (1967); *Williams* at § 141.01.

[144] The Bettman modification was expressly designed to further restrict the board's powers.

[145] The burden of proof is on the applicant; see Chapter One, Section C(11) at page 55.

[146] Most commentators and courts at least cite the rule that variances be sparingly granted. For example, in *Rebound Inc. v Goodlettsville Board of Zoning Appeals*, 1989 WL 150670, Judge Cantrell, concurring with the majority, said that "The power to grant a variance, however, should be used sparingly, only in rare instances and under exceptional circumstances." At *5. The Bettman model variance

"exceptional" in this sense would be "unique."[147] The condition or feature of the property must be unique to itself; it cannot be shared by other properties in the immediate vicinity. If it is, then it is not truly unique, not truly exceptional, and therefore not a proper basis upon which to grant a variance. The policy underlying this requirement is that the board, an administrative body, should not intrude into legislative functions. Where more than one property in any community suffers under the same handicap, the remedy should be legislative, not administrative. The local legislative body should change the zoning on all the properties, treating everyone who is similarly situated the same. The board of zoning appeals has no such authority. In fact, if the board grants a variance in such a situation to one of the property owners, it has effectively granted a special privilege to one person where many others labor under the same handicap. This result is unfair and inequitable: either all should be suffering or all should enjoy the privilege. Our boards of zoning appeals must be especially careful not to grant such special privileges and the courts should be even more alert to this possibility when scrutinizing board decisions on appeal.

Of course, a further problem is the definition of the "general vicinity" or "neighborhood." No hard-and-fast rules can be laid down. Each case must be judged on its own facts. In some instances, the neighborhood will only be a block or two in size; in others, it may be twenty acres. The fundamental principle should be that similarly situated landowners should be treated similarly under the law. If the zoning district boundaries are nearby, that is one easy way to demarcate the boundaries of the neighborhood. If the subject property is zoned in "District A," and one block in each direction is another zoning district, the Board should confine itself to comparing the properties in "District A," within that two block area. Inasmuch as properties in other districts

---

provision, however, gives new meaning to the rule. Variances in Tennessee should almost never be granted.

[147] See *Otto v. Steinhilber*, 282 N.Y. 71, 24 N.E.2d 851, 853 (1939); Rathkopf at § 38.03[3]; Williams at § 142.01; Anderson at § § 20.38 and 20.60; *Elwyn v. Miami*, 113 So.2d 849, 851 (Fla. 1959); *Lumund v. Board of Adjustment of Rutherford*, 6 N.J.Super. 474, 480, 69 A.2d 361 (1949) (aff'd, 4 N.J. 577 (1950)).

are affected by different zoning restrictions, either more or less restrictive, comparisons across district boundaries are not at all helpful. Additionally, it should be noted that because the subject property is located two doors down from a less restrictive zone district, no basis for a variance is presented.[148] Legislative relief may be available, but not administrative. The fact that other properties are subject to different regulations has nothing whatsoever to do with any unique or "exceptional" physical characteristics on the subject property itself. Without such characteristics, a variance is simply not justified under the public enabling legislation.

While it would be helpful to have a more concrete notion of "general vicinity," none is available. The board must simply examine this on a case-by-case basis. In practice, this is not normally very difficult. Usually, the properties are homogeneous and the neighborhood can be defined without too much difficulty. And frankly, most boards never get to this level of analysis anyway.

An interesting case is *Topanga Association for a Scenic Community v. County of Los Angeles.*[149] In *Topanga*, the applicant wished to obtain a variance for a twenty-eight-acre tract of land so as to locate a 93-unit mobile home park.[150] The property was zoned for light agriculture and single family residences.[151] The application was granted.[152]

On appeal, the California Supreme Court reversed.[153] "The variance can be sustained only if ***all*** applicable legislative requirements

---

[148] See Section F 7(c)(6) of this chapter at page 305.

[149] 113 Cal.Rptr. 836, 522 P.2d 12 (1974).

[150] 522 P.2d at 14.

[151] Id.

[152] Id.

[153] Id.

have been satisfied."[154] This includes not only the state enabling legislation, but the local ordinance as well.[155] In this case, the state act was not satisfied. That act provided:[156]

> Variances from the terms of the zoning ordinance shall be granted only when, because of special circumstances applicable to the property, including size, shape, topography, location, or surroundings, the strict application of the zoning ordinance deprives such property of privileges enjoyed by other property in the vicinity and under identical zoning classification.

"This language emphasizes ***disparities*** between properties, not treatment of the subject property's characteristics in the abstract."[157] As even a quick reading of the California statute shows, it is significantly different from the Tennessee Act. However, it is submitted, that the California Act only makes explicit what is implicit in the Tennessee legislation. The term "exceptional" invites a comparison, and the only comparison which can be made is with other properties in the vicinity. Thus, implicitly, the Tennessee Enabling Act mandates the same comparison as does the California Act explicitly.

The California Court concluded that the record before it contained insufficient evidence comparing the properties.[158]

> The data contained in the Planning Commission's Report focuses almost exclusively on the qualities of the property for which the variance was sought. In the absence of comparative information about surrounding properties, these

---

[154] Id. at 19-20.

[155] Id. at 20, note 18.

[156] Id. at 14-15.

[157] Id. at 20.

[158] Id.

> data lack legal significance. Thus knowledge that the property has rugged features tells us nothing about whether the [applicant] faced difficulties different from those confronted on neighboring land. Its assurances that it would landscape and terrace parts of the property and leave others in their natural state are all very well and good, but they bear not at all on the critical issue of whether a variance was necessary to bring the [applicant] into substantial parity with other parties holding property interests in the zone.

This same factor must be considered by the Tennessee Boards and the Tennessee Courts.[159]

---

[159] Another important aspect of *Topanga* (in fact, the most well-known aspect of the case) was the court's requirement that the board make factual findings sufficient to enable review by the judiciary.

> Consistent with the reasoning underlying these cases, we hold that regardless of whether the local ordinance commands that the variance board set forth findings, that body must render findings sufficient both to enable the parties to determine whether and on what basis they should seek review, and, in the event of review, to apprise a reviewing court of the basis for the board's action. We hold further that a reviewing court, before sustaining the grant of a variance, must scrutinize the record and determine whether substantial evidence supports the administrative agency's findings and whether these findings support the agency's decision. In making these determinations, the reviewing court must resolve reasonable doubts in favor of the administrative findings and decisions.

522 P.2d at 16. Our Tennessee boards should follow this same directive even in the absence of any provision in the Tennessee public zoning enabling acts requiring detailed findings of fact. Courts should be aware that many local ordinances do require such findings of fact of the board as a prerequisite to the grant of administrative relief; this would

In another important case, *Beirn v. Morris*,[160] the New Jersey Supreme Court considered variances under its enabling legislation. New Jersey is particularly instructive in this regard since its enabling legislation is strikingly similar to that of Tennessee.[161]

> The Board of Adjustment shall have the power to:
>
> c. Where by reason of exceptional narrowness, shallowness or shape of a specific piece of property, or by reason of exceptional topographic conditions, or by reason of other extraordinary and exceptional situation or condition of such piece of property, the strict application of any regulation enacted under the Act would result in peculiar and exceptional practical difficulties to, or exceptional and undue hardship upon the owner of such property, to authorize, upon an appeal relating to such property, a variance from such strict application so as to relieve such difficulties or hardship; provided, however, that no variance shall be granted under this paragraph to allow a structure or use in a district restricted against such structure or use.

---

appear to be an appropriate topic of regulation for the local governmental entity's ordinance.

160 103 A.2d 361 (N.J. 1954).

161 N.J.S.A. § 40: 55-39(c); this provision has changed somewhat in the last several years because of the adoption of the New Jersey Municipal Land Use Law, N.J.S.A. § 40: 55D-70. It should also be pointed out that even in 1954, New Jersey had a separate variance provision for use variances, 40: 55-39(d), which was (and is) as liberal as subsection (c) is restrictive. Interestingly enough, subsection (c), originally adopted in 1948, was amended in 1953 to add the proviso that "no variance shall be granted under this paragraph to allow structure or use of a district restricted against such structure or use." This should be instructive to Tennessee Courts. New Jersey does not allow its zoning boards to consider use variances under precisely the same variance language and neither should Tennessee.

. . .

> No relief may be granted or action taken under the terms of this section unless such relief can be granted without substantial detriment to the public good and will not substantially impair the intent and purpose of the zone plan and zoning ordinance.

In *Beirn*, the plaintiff purchased a parcel of property intending to erect a garage thereon for the housing of 12 busses employed for the transportation of children to the township's schools.[162] At the time of the purchase and at the time of the decision of the lawsuit, the property was located within a residential district which prohibited such use of the property.[163] Furthermore, the purchasers of the lot were thoroughly acquainted with this restrictive zoning.[164] According to the Court, this zone district could be used only for single family detached dwellings, non-business clubs and lodges, educational and religious uses.[165]

The plaintiff pointed to the other uses in the vicinity. Next door to the property under consideration in the case was a fire station. There was a "combination" gasoline station and confectionary store near by and a "combination" garage and gasoline station in a block the other direction.[166] Both of these "combination" garages were non-conforming uses. There were some single family residences with staggered setbacks. The result of these circumstances was that if the plaintiffs built a residence maintaining the same setback they would be looking out of their dwelling at the middle or toward the rear of the firehouse and because of the peculiar angle of the intersection facing the gas station on either corner across the way. In addition "any house not built

---

[162] 103 A.2d at 362.

[163] Id.

[164] Id.

[165] Id.

[166] Id. at 363.

in line with the peculiar setback and pattern of the street would not only stand out like a sore thumb but would unfavorably affect the looks of the neighborhood."[167]

A number of witnesses testified in support of the applicant's petition. In fact, one was the Chairman of the Board of Zoning Adjustment for a nearby city. However, the Court was not moved.[168]

> These considerations are manifestly insufficient for the exertion of the statutory power to vary the terms of the general regulation. The land owners acquired the property fully cognizant of the use restrictions avowedly to make a more profitable use of the land than conformance to the use regulation would permit, if that could be accomplished -- such as would serve their own private business interest at the time; and the profit motive is not an adequate ground for a variance.

The Court went on.[169]

> It is basic in the statutory zoning process that the use restrictions be general and uniform in the particular district; an arbitrary deviation from the general rule is impermissible. It is of the very nature of the constitutional and statutory zoning principles that all property in like circumstances be treated alike. The zoning power may not be exerted in the service of private interest under the cloak of the public good. The variance provided by subdivision (c) affords the means of relief where a particular lot is so uniquely circumstanced as that the application of the general rule of the ordinance, according to the strict letter, would result in "peculiar and exceptional practical difficulties" or "exceptional and undue hardship," so as to

[167] Id.

[168] Id.

[169] Id at 364.

> accommodate fundamental common and individual rights in the service of the essential statutory policy, and thus to avoid an arbitrary and capricious interference with the right of private property. The inquiry is whether the use restriction, viewing the property in the setting of its environment, is so unreasonable as to be confiscatory. A variance for undue hardship is grounded in conditions peculiar to the particular lot as distinguished from other property in the use district. General hardship is relievable only by a revision of the general rule of the ordinance, a local legislative process, or by the judicial process.

The Court found that this property was reasonably usable for residential purposes. The Court found that the factors augured against the placing of a residence on this lot were plainly not peculiar to this particular parcel of property. The adjacent dwelling units were similarly affected. The Court concluded by saying:[170]

> A variance from the general regulation is permissible only in rare instances and under exceptional circumstances. This is of the very essence of the zoning process -- an attribute indispensable to its integrity. Relaxation of the general rule is to be had only for the relief of specific instances, peculiar in their nature. The community at large as well as individual land owners in the particular use district have an interest in the security of the zone plan that may not arbitrarily be set at naught.

The word "exceptional" in the public enabling legislation requires that the applicant prove (and the Board find) that the subject property is affected with some physical feature or condition which is not common to any of the properties in the general neighborhood.[171] If the feature or

---

[170] Id.

[171] In *Metropolitan Historical Commission v. Colony Associates*, 1988 WL 109234 (Tenn. Ct. App. November 1987) the Court implicitly recognized this:

condition is common in the neighborhood, then no variance may be granted by the Board. The underlying principle should be that no one property owner be treated differently from his similarly situated neighbors.

In *Elwin v. City of Miami*,[172] the Florida Supreme Court explained it this way:

> The authorities seem uniform on the proposition that the difficulties or hardships relied on must be unique to the parcel involved in the application for the variance. They must be peculiar to that particular property, and not general in character, since difficulties or hardships shared with others in the area go to the reasonableness of the zoning generally, and will not support a variance. If the hardship is one which is common to the area, the remedy is to seek a change of the zoning for the neighborhood rather than to seek a change through a variance for an individual owner. Thus, some exceptional and undue hardship to the individual landowner, unique to that parcel of property and not shared by property owners in

---

> The only condition of the property asserted by the owner is the fact that it is bounded on four sides by streets and is not as large as some city blocks. There is no evidence of the size of the subject property in relation to other tracts bounded by four streets. The evidence shows that property immediately south (across Church Street) and immediately north (across Bank Street) fronts on three streets.

Slip Opinion at 17. The lack of evidence of physical differences between the subject lot and other properties in the area was one factor considered by the Court. This is ***the*** crucial factor: It simply was not shown by the applicant. In passing, it should be noted that size is not an appropriate criteria upon which to base a variance. If the lot is too small for the building, no variance should be granted.

[172] 113 So.2d 849 (Fla. 1959).

the area, is an essential prerequisite to the granting of such a variance.

2. Narrowness, Shallowness, or Shape

These three exceptional features of a property are perhaps the easiest to understand. A property which is narrower, shallower, or odder in shape than its neighbors is a likely candidate for a variance. The underlying reasoning is perfectly clear: simply because an owner's property is narrow, shallow, or oddly-shaped, he should not be deprived of a function or benefit of his property that his neighbors ordinarily would have.[173] The unusual point is how rarely such cases actually turn up.[174] There are very few in the country,[175] and none at all in Tennessee.[176] Perhaps the best example comes in *Evans v. Augusta-*

---

[173] Note that just because the property is narrow, shallow or odd-shaped, does not mean that it is smaller than that required by the zoning regulations. For example, if the ordinance requires a 20,000 square foot lot, it might be 100 x 200 feet or 25 x 800 feet. If the lot bears the latter dimensions, and also requires a side yard 10 feet wide on each side, the building envelope can only be 5 feet wide. An obvious variance situation seems to be presented here provided it was not self-created.

[174] Osborne Reynolds, Jr., *The 'Unique Circumstances' Rule in Zoning Variances – An Aid in Achieving Greater Prudence and Less Leniency*, 31 Urban Lawyer 127, 129-130. (1999).

[175] As this chapter notes and the Reynolds article confirms, zoning boards tend to be very lenient in granting variances. Id. at 148.

[176] There is one case at the trial level in Nashville, which involved a shallow lot which met the requirements. *Jacksonian Foundation v. Walgreens and Metro Board of Zoning Appeals*, Docket 98C-1755, Davison County Circuit Court, decided on April 30, 1999. Actually, the evidence was so clear in this case, that the Court had very little difficulty in affirming the decision of the board. The hotly contested issue had to do with the standing of the applicant.

Richmond County Board of Zoning Appeals.[177] The owner of a triangular lot, bounded on all three sides by public highways, sought a variance from the applicable front and side yard requirements. The Board granted a variance of five feet in the front yard and ten feet in the side yards. Obviously, in this situation, the triangular shape of the property created a practical difficulty which was insurmountable in the absence of a variance from the Board.[178] The shape of the property created the hardship.[179]

Narrow lots also provide a justification for a variance. In *Griffin Construction Company v. Board of Adjustment of Township of Teaneck,*[180] the owner of a narrow lot was denied a variance and the Court reversed. In this case, the property had been subdivided prior to the enactment of the zoning ordinance.[181] The original subdivision called for twenty-foot lots. Two of those lots were owned by the current applicant giving him a lot with the forty feet.[182] However, unfortunately, the applicable zoning ordinance required seventy-five feet of frontage and therefore he did not comply with the requirement.[183] The Court noted that there were a total of fifty-seven buildings within the two block area and that eleven of them involved buildings on lots of

---

[177] 113 Ga.App. 113, 147 S.E.2d 455 (1966); one Tennessee Court has called this "an outstanding example of a situation justifying a variance." *Metropolitan Historical Commission* at 23.

[178] 147 S.E.2d 457.

[179] Id. The lot was created before the enactment of the zoning ordinance.

[180] 85 N.J. Super. 472, 205 A.2d 313 (1964).

[181] 205 A.2d at 314.

[182] Id.

[183] Id.

forty foot widths.[184] The Court found that this unusual narrowness, created by no fault of the current owner, was a sufficient hardship upon which to grant a variance.[185] The Zoning Board and the lower Court had denied the variance based on the fact that the new property owner purchased the property with knowledge of the zoning deficiency.[186] The Court here found that if a prior owner could have been entitled to relief, that the right to such relief was not lost to a purchaser simply because he bought the property with knowledge of the zoning regulation involved.[187] This situation is not within the realm of self-created hardship which generally bars relief.[188]

In a similar fashion, shallow lots should be permitted variances as well. Unfortunately, there appear to be no reported cases involving variances on a shallow lot, although the author was personally involved in one on West End Avenue in Nashville where the variance was issued based on the exceptional shallowness, and affirmed on appeal at the trial court.[189]

These lessons can be applied to the carport, discussed in the introduction to this chapter. The land owner asked for a variance to allow the construction of a carport within two feet of the property line. The zoning ordinance provides that all side yards must measure a

---

[184] Id. These would appear to be legally non-conforming and frankly should not serve as a basis for a variance, see Section F 7(c)(6) of this chapter at page 305. Obviously, the legislative decision to create a large number of non-conforming properties is a serious one.

[185] Id at 315.

[186] Id at 314.

[187] Id at 315.

[188] This is, however, a disputed area, with differences from state to state.

[189] *Jacksonian Foundation v. Walgreens and Metro Board of Zoning Appeals*, Docket 98C-1755, Davison County Circuit Court, decided on April 30, 1999.

minimum of five feet. Therefore, the property owner is requesting a variance of three feet. Assuming for a moment that the property is the same general width, shape, and depth of the other properties in the community, it would seem that this application must be denied. However, if the width, shape, or depth of the lot is markedly less than the other lots in the community, a condition not created by the present owner and the condition dates to the time before the enactment of zoning regarding the property,[190] then this may be a proper subject for a variance by the Board of Zoning Appeals.

The Board must consider carefully any variance application where the property is so substantially smaller than the other properties in the neighborhood that it does infringe on the zone plan for the community. How much smaller the property must be in order to be substantially different from the other properties in the community is a matter of judgment best left to the Board of Zoning Appeals. Once a unique physical feature in the property itself is found, the major hurdle to the grant of a variance has been overcome.

3. At the Time of the Enactment of the Zoning Regulation

Narrowness, shallowness, and shape all relate to dimensions of property which are essentially man-made. They certainly are not what may be called natural conditions, unlike topography, which will be discussed next. A narrow or shallow lot, or an odd-shaped lot, would primarily be caused by the pattern of land development in the vicinity, including the placement of roads and other public facilities, and subdivisions (either regulated or unregulated).[191] Interestingly enough, the statute requires, as to the first three dimensions, that the hardship exist "at the time of the enactment of the zoning regulation." This same restriction does not apply to topographic conditions or "other

---

[190] See the next section (F 3).

[191] See Tennessee public subdivision enabling legislation, TENN. CODE ANN. § 13-3-401 (regional subdivision regulations), and 13-4-301 (municipal subdivision regulations).

extraordinary situations or conditions."[192] This restriction prevents the issuance of a variance where these man-made attributes of the property, allegedly creating a difficulty or hardship on the owner, did not exist at the effective date of the ordinance.[193] This type of hardship (assuming it really is a hardship, meeting the "exceptional" standard, discussed above) is viewed as self-created,[194] and bars the relief sought.[195]

This provision was not in the original Memphis private acts at all. It appears first in the public enabling legislation. Similar language is also absent from the Standard State Zoning Enabling Act. The policy was, of course, to prevent manipulation of the man-made features of a lot so as to create the basis of a variance. For example, it is possible to plat a subdivision[196] in such a way as to create an unusual shape, or an

---

[192] Possibly, the drafters of the legislation felt that the topographic condition of a parcel of property existed naturally from time immemorial. Therefore, the restriction that the hardship exists at the time of the enactment of the zoning ordinance (and so not be self-created) would be clearly superfluous regarding natural features of the land. Those features had been there forever; there was no need of the restriction. The validity of this assumption is now open to considerable doubt since modern construction techniques are capable of almost totally altering the face of the land.

[193] *Williams*, §§ 142.02-3.

[194] See O.M. Reynolds, *Self-Induced Hardship in Zoning Variances*, 20 The Urban Lawyer 1 (1988).

[195] If a variance is a means of achieving equitable land use planning decisions, the self-created hardship doctrine roughly parallels that old equity maxim: "He who comes into equity, must come with clean hands." William H. Inman, *Gibson's Suits in Chancery*, 6th Ed., § 18; *Winters v. Allen*, 62 SW 2d 51, 166 Tenn. 281 (1933). A landowner who has created the basis of the variance himself brings "unclean hands" before the board and should not be granted relief.

[196] See TENN. CODE ANN. § 13-4-301 (municipal); 13-4-402 (regional).

exceptionally narrow or shallow lot. Assuming that this feature creates a hardship or difficulty for the developer, should a Board of Zoning Appeals exercise its power in favor of such an applicant? The statute says no, unless the lot "existed at the time of the enactment of the zoning regulation."[197] Inasmuch as the enabling legislation was adopted in 1935 and many of the local governments enacted zoning "regulations" shortly thereafter, very few lots are legally nonconforming. For example, in Nashville, the earliest zoning ordinance dates to 1933, even before the date of the public enabling legislation[198] and therefore in many instances the applicant must prove that his property had assumed the shape about which the complaint is lodged prior to 1933. This is needless to say a difficult task.

Please also note that the particular zoning regulation may increase in severity from the date of the first enactment to the most recent enactment. So, for example, in the *Griffin Construction Company* case,[199] the ordinance had originally required a minimum lot width of less than seventy-five feet but gradually worked its way up to seventy-five feet. Naturally, if the lot was seventy feet in width, the developer would not have to show that his lot was created prior to all zoning ordinances enacted in the community; he would only need to show that his lot was created prior to the time of the enactment of the ordinance which imposed the seventy-five foot lot width requirement.[200]

Therefore, any newly subdivided lot which suffers an unusual shape, or which is unusually shallow or narrow, is not qualified for a variance under the public enabling legislation in Tennessee.

---

[197] TENN. CODE ANN. § 13-7-207(3).

[198] Nashville had private enabling legislation at that time.

[199] 85 NJ Super. 472, 205 A. 2d 313 (1964).

[200] In fact, after the passage of the Nonconforming Property Act TENN. CODE ANN. 13-7-208) in 1973, perhaps the property would be nonconforming anyway and a variance would not be necessary. We have no case law on this issue.

It is clear that self-created hardships are intolerable where the creator applies for the variance. In most states, a more difficult question is presented when a subsequent purchaser makes the application. Should that applicant be punished for the transgressions of a predecessor in title? The Tennessee Public Enabling Legislation admits of no exception: If the particular narrowness, shallowness, or shape did not exist at the time the regulation was enacted, no variance is appropriate. In effect, the purchaser steps into his predecessor's shoes. If the exceptional features of the property were created by the owner after zoning was imposed, no variance may issue. This is a hard rule. Only one other state in the country definitely follows it.[201] Otherwise, a subsequent purchaser, if knowledgeable of the problem, and intent upon exploiting it, could reap a windfall by obtaining a variance. Further, a zoning board should not have to attempt to distinguish the intentional from the unintentional buyer. The job would become quite tedious.[202] The Tennessee enabling legislation entirely avoids this problem.

Another set of cases within the parameter of the self-created hardship rule develops out of the construction of an improvement designed for a use not allowed under the zoning laws. While in other jurisdictions, because of their heavy reliance upon the Bassett model variance provision, the owner could still argue that he had an undue hardship due to a unique situation.[203] It is not unfair to deny a variance where the conditions have been self-created by the property owner, or his predecessor in title.[204]

> The rule of self-created hardship is likely to be applied wherever a property owner makes improvements without the necessary legal permits and then seeks a variance to

---

[201] New Jersey.

[202] Any inquiry into the purchaser's state of mind is likely to be difficult at best.

[203] 20 Urban Lawyer at 7.

[204] 6 *Rohan* 43.02[6]; 20 Urban Lawyer at 8.

> allow use of such improvements. Thus, in an oft-cited Kentucky case, the owner of a non-conforming milk bottling plant was ordered by health authorities to put a new roof on the premises. He obtained the necessary building permit for the roof, but during the course of its construction discovered that the old wooden walls of the building were not structurally sound and quite possibly would not support the new roof. Without obtaining the legally required building permit, he proceeded to construct new brick walls; but due to the lack of a permit, the building inspector halted construction. The Board of Appeals refused to issue the variance to permit completion of the job, and the Court affirmed this refusal, stating that the property owner had created his dilemma by raising the frame walls and beginning replacement of them when his permit only allowed repair of the roof.

One of the most recurring examples of this situation comes into play where a builder has constructed the home too close to the lot lines in violation of the setback restrictions. Typically there is no exceptional physical feature of the property, and the variance could be denied on that basis alone. However, because the builder created his own hardship, (and presumably under the Tennessee Enabling Legislation, the creation took place after the adoption of the zoning regulation), he is not entitled to a variance anyway.[205] There are many similar instances.[206]

---

[205] See, e.g., *Deer Glen Estates v. Board of Adjustment*, 39 N.J.Super. 380, 121 A.2d 26 (1956).

[206] Id. at 10, quoting A.B.A. Commission on Planning and Zoning of Section of Local Government Law and Committee on Public Regulation of Land Use, Section of Real Property Law, Probate and Trust Law (Report), *Zoning Variance Criteria -- Viewpoints of Lawyers*, 8 Real Property Probate and Trust L.J. 33 (1973). In Tennessee, the local government can chose to give the board authority to grant relief under these circumstances as mentioned earlier in note 54.

> The same result has been reached even if such mistake appears to have been made, not by the owner himself, but by the surveyor or foundation contractor, and even though the encroaching structure will probably have to be demolished unless a variance is granted. The same is true where the offending builder has relied upon a contract of sale that turns out to have contained an erroneous description of the property. A variance has also been denied where the property owner constructed improvements under the mistaken assumption that a predecessor had obtained the necessary building permit. Though some of these results may appear harsh, it has been noted that relevant statutes offer no basis for discriminating 'between innocently self-created hardships and those which result from the scheming of clever lawyers and developers.'

While of course it is a little easier here in Tennessee to decide these cases because there is in fact no exceptional physical feature of the property to which a variance would apply anyway. Thus, not only is the variance application defeated because of the self-creation of the hardship by the owner, but it is also defeated because the statutory requirements are simply not met by the landowner.

In one such case, *J.D. Biggs v. Metropolitan Government of Nashville and Davidson County*,[207] the property owner requested a variance where he constructed a portion of his dwelling at an improper location on the lot. The Board of Zoning Appeals turned down the request for a variance, was affirmed by the Trial Court, and the Trial Court's decision was affirmed on appeal.

However, there is one aspect of these cases which poses some difficulty. Ofttimes the applicant for a building permit has been improperly advised by the zoning administrator or other local building code official. Given the complexity of zoning and building regulations these days, this probably happens more frequently than is thought. The

[207] 7 TAM 27-17 (Tenn. App. 1982).

case is most properly one adapted to equitable estoppel,[208] but it is generally considered that equitable estoppel does not apply against a local governmental entity.[209]

In other jurisdictions, a variance can be issued notwithstanding the fact that there is no unusual physical condition of the property because of the breadth of the Bassett model variance provision. For example, in *Jaynes Estates v. Raynor*,[210] the landowner relied on the local building code official who had ruled that a permit would issue and spent large sums of money in the construction of an apartment house. However, his permit was subsequently revoked and he applied for a variance which was denied. The Court of Appeals found extreme detrimental reliance justifying a finding of unnecessary hardship and the Court ordered the grant of the variance even though the uniqueness of the lot was not satisfied at all.

There is a similar case here in Tennessee. In *Rebound, Inc. v. The Goodlettsville Board of Zoning Appeals*,[211] the Plaintiffs obtained a contract for the purchase of real property subject to acceptable zoning. Rebound was to use the property to provide care for individuals who suffered traumatic head injuries and was to lease the property for a 10-year period. The Plaintiffs spoke with the codes administrator for the city describing the proposed use of the property. The codes administrator directed the Plaintiffs to a code provision entitled "Family Boarding Home" and a letter was sent to the Plaintiffs stating

---

[208] An estoppel may be set up where the local government says or does something which induces another party to change position to his or her detriment. It is usually difficult to prove such a case against a local government. *Howe Realty v City of Nashville*, 141 SW 2d 904, 906 (Tenn. 1940).

[209] *Park View Associates v City of New York*, 71 NY 2d 274, 525 NYS 2d 178 (1988).

[210] 22 N.Y.2d 417, 239 N.Y.S.2d 75, 293 N.E.2d 713 (1968).

[211] 15 T.A.M. 3-10 (Tenn. Ct App. 1989).

that the property was located so that it could be used as a "boarding home" assuming it met all of the applicable code provisions.

Based on the zoning administrator's letter, the Plaintiffs purchased the property, a building permit was obtained for the renovation of the structure which was subsequently revoked after the City learned that the home would be used for the treatment and care of adults rather than children. Between the date of purchase and the letter revoking the permit, the Plaintiffs had either completed or substantially completed the improvements. The total expenditures amounted to $678,299.92. As a result of the revocation of the permit, the Plaintiffs applied for a variance, but it was denied.[212]

The Trial Court reversed the Board and the Board appealed, contending first that there was no jurisdiction for the Board to grant a variance. On technical evidentiary grounds, which appeared not to have been appropriate, the Court of Appeals affirmed the decision of the Trial Court. The most important question in the case was whether or not the Board could grant this variance. But there was absolutely no evidence in the record, at least not as discussed by the Court of Appeals, which would have indicated that any exceptional physical feature existed on the property. The Court did not have to go so far as to consider whether or not this issue was raised in the answer in the Trial Court below. Based on *McClurkan's* holding, it would seem that this application for a variance was totally without foundation and proof, and certainly could not meet the Tennessee Public Zoning Enabling Legislation, which is a matter of judicial notice, not record proof. In dissent, Judge Ben Cantrell clearly indicates that there was no basis for a variance.[213] Judge Cantrell, however, would have allowed the project to continue based on equitable estoppel principles.

These equitable estoppel cases are extremely difficult. It must be submitted that the majority in the *Rebound* case felt it inequitable to prevent Rebound from using this property after the expenditure of such a large sum of money and substantial completion of the project. Two

[212] Slip Opinion at 4.

[213] Slip Opinion at 9-10.

points should be made here. The first is that Rebound or any representatives of the Plaintiffs could certainly have obtained a copy of the zoning ordinance and made a determination themselves as to whether or not they fit within the definition. Certainly, they could have asked legal counsel to do so and if legal counsel made a mistake, counsel could be liable in malpractice for the wrong opinion, assuming he deviated from the standard of care required. In other words, both parties had access to the facts in this case. Where both parties have equal knowledge, it may not be appropriate to apply an estoppel. One might argue that the codes administrator certainly knew the law better than the Plaintiffs in the *Rebound* case. But at the same time, the Plaintiffs knew the facts better. In the everyday rush of administering a codes administration, it is difficult to give ad hoc legal opinions about whether a particular use will comply with a specific definition of the zoning ordinance. That is why there is a legal profession; so that those kinds of opinions can be given by a professional trained in the law, capable of making particular decisions in this regard. The failure of the Plaintiffs to obtain such an opinion, or if they got one, to bring suit against the attorney, is suspect.

Secondly, most of these kinds of cases can be attributed to a mistake on the part of the codes official. A building built too close to the lot lines can be laid at the feet of the codes administration because there is an inspection done of the footings and one might argue that the failure of the building code official to pick up the fact that the footings are too close to the property lines is a violation of his duty. The building code plans examiner reviews the plans for compliance with the building code. He is also generally a member of the codes administration. If he fails to note a zoning violation, that too can be argued as a grounds upon which an estoppel may arise.

The public policy advanced in not granting an estoppel against a municipality generally refers to the defenselessness of the neighboring property owners. In the *Rebound* case, for example, there is now a residential unit in an area of Goodlettsville where, according to the Goodlettsville Zoning Ordinance, it should not be. The local code administrator does not suffer by virtue of this (unless he happens to live nearby). It is the neighbors who suffer. They are the ones whose rights have actually been impaired. In the *Rebound* case, the author believes that both parties could have known of the problem. Thus, Rebound has no cause to complain. Furthermore, in many cases, it seems a more appropriate remedy might be to award damages in favor of the aggrieved property owner and against the municipality. Of course, under our state law, TENN. CODE ANN., § 29-20-101 et seq., the Tennessee Governmental Tort Liability Act would not allow that from the issuance of a building permit. However, there is the danger that there may be liability on the part of the zoning or building officials. That is a certainly a less equitable remedy.[214]

Finally, remember, the Courts struggle with these cases because the perceived value of enforcing the zoning ordinance may well be less than the cost of reconstruction of the building. This is a powerful sentiment: is a 17 foot infringement on a rear yard worth destruction of a $300,000 home? Maybe not.

It is clear in the *Rebound* case that there was no justification for any variance. The technical reason for the decision was the failure of the Board to raise the issue in the Trial Court. But there was no need to raise this particular issue. All the Board should have been obligated to do is to demonstrate from the record before the Board of Zoning Appeals that no proof of unique physical feature of the property was shown. It clearly was not. Therefore, the Board's decision denying the variance was in all respects appropriate. Variances should not be used as a way of doing "good." The Boards have no way to define that, and frankly, neither have the Courts.[215]

However, if an applicant for a variance has created the hardship himself or one of his predecessors did after the enactment of the zoning regulation, even if there is a unique physical feature of the property, no variance should be issued because the hardship was self-created. That

---

[214] See also *J & B Development Company v King County*, 29 Wash. App. 942, 631 P.2d 1002 (1981), affirmed on different legal reasoning, 100 Wash.2d 299, 669 P.2d 468 (1983)

[215] The *Rebound* decision, of course, is eminently reasonable from a standpoint of equity. One cannot blame the Court for wanting to help Rebound.

applies whether the creation of the non-conformity was by virtue of inappropriate subdivision of lots, or by the construction of improvements in violation of zoning law. If it involved the construction of improvements, the self-created hardship rule should apply regardless of whether the builder knew that he was violating the law or not. Finally, in those situations where the variance is requested on the grounds that the zoning official led the applicant into his hardship, the conduct of the parties should be examined minutely and the proper remedy is not a variance, but rather some form of estoppel or damage remedy.

Applying these rules to the hypothetical carport yields different results. If the unique feature existed prior to the zoning regulation, a variance would be in order. Otherwise, no variance should be granted by the Board, even if the applicant is a subsequent purchaser, notwithstanding the fact that he may have acquired the property without any knowledge of the unique feature.

4. Exceptional Topographic Conditions

The fourth unique physical feature which can cause a hardship warranting a variance is an exceptional topographic condition. Naturally, there are many kinds of topographic conditions which might give rise to a variance. A stream, ravine, steep incline, or gully all might cause a hardship justifying a variance. Care must be taken to ensure that the same topographic condition does not exist on surrounding properties, else it is hardly exceptional.[216] But assuming that the topographic condition is not common in the neighborhood, the variance may be granted.

The same qualification, that the feature exist at the time of the enactment of the zoning regulation, does not apply to topographic conditions as it does to "man-made" features.[217] This probably

---

[216] The flood plain in *Glankler* is a good example. 481 S. W. 2d 376 (Tenn. 1972).

[217] Narrowness, shallowness, or shape.

represents the thought that while the man-made features could be manipulated, topographic conditions are unalterable. This thought now is open to considerable doubt. Thus, if a developer alters the physical conditions of the property in an attempt to acquire a variance, a Board or Court should hold that it is a self-created hardship and thus an inappropriate basis for a variance.

In *Menefree v. Board of Adjustment of Taylor Mill,*[218] the owner cited as an exceptional topographic condition the existence of a sinkhole over which he would be required, by virtue of the front and side yard restrictions in the applicable zoning ordinance to locate his home.[219] He accordingly applied for a variance which was granted by the Board and affirmed on appeal.[220] Clearly, the existence of the sinkhole was an ample basis upon which to rest the application, and the Court so held.[221]

In our carport hypothetical, the landowner will in all probability be unable to argue that topographic conditions on the property prevent the placement of the carport elsewhere. However, if a sharp topographic break just in the rear of the house occurs, perhaps an argument can be constructed that placement of the structure on the side of the house is the only feasible position. Assuming that the same topographic break does not exist on other properties and that the neighbors are able to enjoy this convenience, the zoning board may lawfully grant a variance. These circumstances may be expected to be quite rare.

---

[218] 494 S.W.2d 519 (Ky.App. 1973).

[219] Id. at 519-20.

[220] Id.

[221] Id.

5. Other Extraordinary and Exceptional Situation or Condition

(a) Generally

This fifth condition for which a variance may issue is obviously a catch-all. It is designed to cover those situations where the shape of the lot, its narrowness, shallowness, or topographic condition are not the source of the hardship. Notice, however, that the "situation or condition" must not only be "exceptional," but also "extraordinary."[222] Further, as with all the others, this fifth condition must relate to the property itself.[223] There are no cases which have been decided under this clause in Tennessee and there is doubt of the purpose for its inclusion. Given that, it is difficult to illustrate in the hypothetical.

This catch-all should not be used to circumvent the otherwise strict requirements of this provision. If some exceptional difficulty or hardship is created by virtue of a feature of the property other than its narrowness, shallowness, shape or topographic condition, both the local board and the reviewing Court should be certain that the proposed basis of the variance is something more than illusory.[224] The basis of the variance must be akin to the other four statutorily explicit bases of variances. If not, the application should be denied. Otherwise, this catch-all has the potential of swallowing whole the other reasons for a

---

[222] Notice that the other four factors must be "exceptional," while the fifth must be both "extraordinary and exceptional." It is doubtful that the additional adjective adds any meaning. The two words are often in fact used synonymously. Probably this catchall was added just in case a particular problem, although associated with and peculiar to a specific piece of property, did not fall within any of the other four categories. To protect against abuse, the additional requirement ("extraordinary") was added.

[223] *McClurkan*, 565 S. W. 2d 495.

[224] Applicants are entirely capable of making the most routine problems seem an insurmountable hurdle and grounds for a variance.

variance and expanding the legitimate basis of the variance power. This is an undesirable result.

(b) Size Not Grounds for Variance

Although the Courts have certainly made references to size as a grounds for a variance,[225] size, however, does not appear to be one of the grounds found in the Tennessee enabling legislation for the issuance of a variance. Essentially, the Tennessee Public Zoning Enabling Acts look to shape or topographic condition, not size.

To be sure, narrowness and shallowness to some extent are affected by size but only as it relates to a specific portion of the property. For example, the property could be three acres in size, but be so narrow as to only have a 20-foot frontage. The narrowness might be grounds for a variance. A triangular lot, by virtue of its unusual shape, might be grounds for a variance. However, if it was an extremely large triangular lot, the setback and side yard regulations probably would cause no problem and thus to some extent, the unusual shape must be accompanied by a smaller size in order to generate the hardship. So far, from planning theory, there would appear to be no difficulty.

However, when a property owner with no unique physical condition of the property attempts to obtain a variance merely because the size of the property is too small to permit the construction of the improvement which he is attempting to obtain approval for, the fact that the property is simply too small to accommodate the development is not grounds for a variance. Anyone with the same size property would have the same difficulty. The property owner might argue that his property was much smaller than all the surrounding properties and thus he was faced with a unique situation. But assuming that the property is not

---

[225] *Metropolitan Historical Commission v. Colony Associates*, Slip Opinion at 17 ("It is seen that the state statute and local ordinance, read together, require proof and finding that a particular hardship . . . is imposed upon the owner by (1) size (2) shape or (3) topographical conditions of the property.").

merely a remnant,[226] the zoning ordinance requirements are simply to prevent the overuse of any particular parcel of land. By granting a variance to one developer to allow a larger project on his property than the ordinance contemplates, is a disservice to those property owners who have larger properties but who would not be able to obtain the same relief. Thus, the size of the property is not an appropriate grounds for the issuance of a variance.

6. Of a specific piece of property

Any of the five conditions[227] must be rooted in the property itself. If the unique circumstances relate to something other than the property, say, for example, the personal medical problems of the applicant or his family,[228] no basis for a variance is stated. Thus, not only must the situation or condition creating the hardship be "exceptional," but it must also be intimately connected to the subject property.

This requirement is, in a sense, redundant. It goes without saying that narrowness, shallowness, shape, or topographic condition all relate to the property itself. This phrase may then be read as emphasis on the requirement of unique physical features. If one were to stop in and witness a meeting of any local board, one would quickly perceive that the board members are not aware of this requirement. Virtually any reason other than factors relating to the property are given as a justification for a variance. In our carport example, clearly if the applicant argued that the carport was needed because his mother-

---

[226] The efficacy of attempting development on a remnant is somewhat questionable in any case.

[227] Narrowness, shallowness, shape, topographic condition or other condition of the property.

[228] *McClurkan*, 565 S. W. 2d 495.

in-law was sick and needed to park at his house, no variance should issue.[229] We may be sympathetic, but a variance is not justified.

7. Peculiar and Exceptional Practical Difficulties to or Exceptional and Undue Hardship Upon

(a) Generally

This is the bottom line. The five conditions discussed previously have no effect on the Board's deliberations unless one or more of them cause[230] some practical difficulty or undue hardship. Here again, the word "exceptional" is employed quite emphatically. Its use here implies that the difficulty or hardship must be unusual or unique in the general vicinity of the subject property. It should be borne in mind that this does not involve the uniqueness of the physical feature or condition; rather, it is the hardship on the owner which here must be unique. The goal which the landowner seeks to accomplish must be one which other landowners in the neighborhood can accomplish, but which he cannot by virtue of the unique physical feature of his land. It is only when both these requirements are in conjunction that a variance may issue.[231]

The case law is not helpful as an illustration of this point because usually if the Court is of a mind to deny the variance, the decision is based upon a finding that there is no unique physical feature or that the feature is not unique or exceptional, but is rather, general to the entire neighborhood. Thus, no consideration of the second issue is necessary. A better means of illustration is by way of reference to other state enabling legislation. Kentucky's legislation is the most remarkable.[232]

---

[229] Id. The frequency of variance applications based on such hardship is surprising.

[230] See page 306.

[231] The exceptional physical feature must cause the difficulty.

[232] Ky. Rev. Stats. Section 100.241.

> The Board shall have the power to hear and decide on applications for dimensional variances whereby reason of the exceptional narrowness, shallowness, or unusual shape of a site on the effective date of the zoning regulation or by reason of exceptional topographic conditions, or some other extraordinary situation or condition of that site, the literal enforcement of the dimensional requirements (height or width of a building or size of yards but no population density) of the zoning regulation would deprive the applicant of reasonable capacity to make use of the land in a manner equivalent to the use permitted other landowners in the same zone. The Board may impose any reasonable conditions or restrictions of any variance it decides to grant.

Note the similarity between this legislation and that of this state.[233] However, the language regarding "unnecessary hardship" and "practical difficulty" has been deleted. In its stead, Kentucky provides that a variance may issue if the applicant is deprived by the zoning regulation "of reasonable capacity to make use of the land in a manner equivalent to the use permitted other landowners in the same zone." The Courts of Tennessee should construe this state's enabling legislation in the same manner. The language is not as highly specific, but the purpose is the same and the conclusion is at least implied from the other sections of the statute.

The California statute is similar.[234]

> Variances from the terms of the zoning ordinance shall be granted only when, because of special circumstances applicable to the property, including size, shape, topography, location or surroundings, the strict application of the zoning ordinance deprives such property of privileges enjoyed by other property in the vicinity and under identical zoning classification.

---

[233] See page 257.

[234] Cal. Govt. Code Section 65906 (1965).

This language makes it clear that a comparison of the uses to which other properties in the vicinity are put is the guide by which to judge whether the owner is actually suffering a hardship.[235]

Again, it must be emphasized that the relationship between the unique physical feature (whatever it might be), the difficulty or hardship, and the factor of causation are all tied up together. It is often difficult to say with any certainty that a particular variance fails because there is no difficulty or hardship or unique physical feature because most often that simply means that the physical feature is not unique (exceptional). Further, sometimes the physical feature is unique but it has no cause or relationship with the alleged hardship. A good example of the latter is a use variance.[236]

(b) Difficulty or Hardship: The Same Standard

A good many states have followed the example of New York in distinguishing between practical difficulty and undue hardship.[237] In *Village of Bronxville v. Francis*,[238] the applicant sought a variance in the floor area ratio provisions of the ordinance. The variance was granted based upon a showing that no conforming building could be constructed which would yield a reasonable profit.[239] The Court held that the

[235] Even though there may be some exceptional physical condition of the property, if the property can be utilized in much the same manner as all the surrounding properties, then no variance should issue.

[236] See page 309.

[237] Section VII of the Standard State Zoning Enabling Act which only speaks in terms of undue hardship. Any state which has adopted verbatim the Standard Act does not encounter this problem.

[238] 1 N.Y.2d 839, 135 N.E.2d 724, 153 N.Y.S.2d 220, aff'g 1 A.D.2d 236, 150 N.Y.S.2d 906 (1956).

[239] 1 A.D.2d at 237, 150 N.Y.S.2d at 908.

variance sought was an area variance[240] and that it would not have as great an impact on the neighborhood as would a use variance. The Court concluded that in order to obtain an area variance, the applicant need only show a practical difficulty; but, if applying for a use variance, the more stringent standard of unnecessary hardship would have to be shown.[241]

As Rohan notes,[242] the use of the disjunctive "supports the view that, as a matter of legislative interpretation, different tests may have been intended to apply to different kinds of requests for relief." The Tennessee Public Zoning Enabling Statutes clearly use the disjunctive form, but as will be demonstrated later, use variances should not be allowed in Tennessee under any circumstances anyway.[243] It is therefore not necessary to use both standards in Tennessee. In fact, evidently, Edward Bassett added the additional language himself and indicated in his writings that there was no deviation intended from the Standard State Zoning Enabling Act.[244] In any case, to distinguish between use and area variances in an attempt to give some definition to the terms "difficulty or hardship" seems ill advised. First, to distinguish between use and area variances can sometimes be difficult. To a great extent, it turns on the design of the local zoning ordinance, and it also depends on the perspective of the decision maker. Is a parking lot variance a use or area variance?[245] Is an application to use an accessory

---

240 Id., 135 N. E. 2d at 725.

241 Id.

242 6 *Rohan*, Section 43.02[2]. Obviously, if the conjunctive form of expression is used, the applicant must meet both the practical difficulty and undue hardship requirements.

243 See page 309.

244 BWBW at 35.

245 See this chapter, Section F.8.c at page 313.

building on a lot as a second single-family dwelling a use or area variance?[246] These questions are difficult to answer.[247]

Furthermore, it is not clear that use variances always offer greater harm to the community at large than an area variance. A 50-story office building in an area zoned for 10-story buildings would probably be considered an area variance, but the impact would be considerable.[248] Additionally, the use of a residence for a part-time beauty shop would normally be considered a use variance, but the impact of that use variance would probably be considerably less than the area variance for the office building.[249]

In practice, given the phraseology of the Tennessee Public Zoning Enabling Legislation, the phrases "practical difficulty" and "undue hardship" are indistinguishable. In *165 Augusta Street, Inc. v. Collins*,[250] the New Jersey Supreme Court, construing a statute which is virtually identical to our own,[251] refused to impose different tests even where both terms were used in the statute and where, like our own statute, the phraseology was phrased in the disjunctive rather than the conjunctive. The Court held that the phrases were for all practical

---

[246] Contrast *Matthew v. Smith*, 707 S.W.2d 411 (Mo. 1986) with *Matter of Hoffman v. Harris*, 17 N.Y.2d 138, 216 N.E.2d 326, 269 N.Y.S.2d 119 (1966).

[247] Although under the Tennessee statutes, neither would be appropriate variance candidates: how could an exceptional physical feature of the property justify the request? There's not relationship between the request and the physical feature.

[248] See *Bienz v. City of Dayton*, 29 Or.App. 761, 566 P.2d 904 (1977).

[249] 6 *Rohan* 43.02[2].

[250] 9 N.J. 259, 87 A.2d 889 (1952).

[251] The statutory language, then N.J.Stat.Ann. Section 40:55-39 (West 1967) is now embodied in N.J.Stat.Ann. Section 40:55D-70 (West 2009).

purposes the same, although the latter was necessarily inclusive of the former.[252]

Thus, in Tennessee, the two phrases, "practical difficulty" and "undue hardship," should also be construed to mean exactly the same thing. Proof of one is proof of the other. This would give effect to Bassett's writing that the addition of practical difficulty was not to change the meaning of the language, is consistent with the fact that use variances cannot be granted given the other language of the statute, and is the same construction given identical language as a very well-known land use planning Court in another state where land use planning controversies are decidedly more frequent.

(c) Types of Insufficient Hardship

Now that "hardship" has been explained in theory, some examples of what are insufficient hardships might be appropriate.

(1) Personal Considerations

Although it may not be necessary to comment upon this, personal difficulties which a property owner may have are simply not a justification for a variance. For example, and it is frequent that this type of request is made, the applicant proves to the board that his mother-in-law is elderly and sick and needs careful attention. He wants to put a mobile home in the back yard so that she can live there and be cared for by his family. The zoning ordinance does not allow a second residence and even if it did, there are setback violations. Hence, the request for a variance. This is not however an appropriate case for a variance: while the intent is admirable, the illness of a family member is not a justification for a variance.

---

[252] 87 A.2d at 891.

(2) Pecuniary Considerations

Perhaps the most relied upon hardship (or difficulty) is financial: The developer contends that if a variance cannot be obtained, the project will not be economically feasible.[253] The Tennessee Supreme Court has already indicated that "the price alone, or financial or pecuniary loss to the applicant, does not, of itself, establish a case of 'unnecessary hardship.' "[254] This is in accord with the majority rule.[255] However, that is definitely not to say that pecuniary considerations are not at all relevant.[256] Assuming that the applicant has crossed the threshold of jurisdiction by offering proof to the Board of unique physical features or conditions, then, and only then, could the Board legitimately consider the financial situation of the project.[257]

This aspect of development is always present: No matter what the size of the project, financial considerations act as a limitation on the plans of the developer. It is a rare applicant indeed who cannot demonstrate to the Board the financial necessity of the variance sought. Because of the ubiquitous nature of this problem, very little consideration should be given it by the Board. If there is some unique physical feature of the property, and it does cause a problem for this developer which would not exist on other properties in the neighborhood, this is prima facie proof that a variance should be granted. If not, then a variance should be denied. Financial considerations in the former are only a makeweight, and actually

---

[253] Virtually every applicant makes this claim. The appropriate response is to suggest that this use or style of use is therefore inappropriate at this location and that the developer should change his plans -- not that the board should grant a variance.

[254] *Reddoch*, 379 S.W.2d at 646. This rule is referred to often frequently in the literature.

[255] Williams at § 143.04.

[256] See, e.g., *Reddoch v. Smith*, 379 S. W. 2d 641 (Tenn. 1964).

[257] Id.

unnecessary. In the second situation, finances are usually an attempt to obscure the fact that the applicant cannot successfully make out a *prima facie* case for a variance. By relying heavily upon the financial problems, the developer (or his attorney) attempts to bluff the Board in the granting of a variance.[258] Neither the Board (nor a Court reviewing the Board's decision) should be bluffed into placing much weight upon such proof. Its probative value is near zero.

---

[258] *Hamilton Bank v. Board of Zoning Appeals*, 11 T.A.M. 21-16 (Tenn.App. 1986). A setback variance was sought for a triangular lot in this case. The property currently was used as a gasoline service station and a repair garage. "The board of zoning appeals held that the property could be used with or without a variance, and, therefore, no variance was needed." Slip opinion at 1. The Trial Court reversed and ordered the issuance of a variance of over 30 feet (66%) on one street and of 10 feet (over 50%) on another. Slip opinion at 2. The Court found that "without the variance, the property would suffer a financial hardship." Id. With the variance, the property value would increase from $50,000 to $60,000. Id. The Court of Appeals reversed. While the result is certainly appropriate, and the Court did give as its first grounds the fact that the property could be used with or without a variance (the conclusion being presumably that there was no hardship or difficulty and quite correctly), it also relied heavily on the fact that the board had denied the variance and had a "wide latitude and great discretion in granting or denying variances . . ." Slip opinion at 3. Essentially the Courts are to defer to the board's judgment unless arbitrary or capricious. Assuming the board was acting under the Tennessee public zoning enabling legislation (the Court did not say in the opinion), its authority should be narrowly, not broadly, construed. Thus, while the decision ultimately is correct, its bases are not. The myth that boards operating under the Tennessee public zoning enabling legislation have great discretion and broad authority must be dispelled. It has been created by virtue of the Memphis triumvirate but as we have seen, that was decided mistakenly under the wrong statute.

(3) Aesthetic Considerations

This is essentially another makeweight argument. While its probative value is near zero, it may be useful in demonstrating compliance with the "negative criteria."[259] Thus, if a developer has offered proof to show that some unique physical feature of the property creates a problem which causes him to be unable to do with his property what others in the same area can do with theirs, evidence of the aesthetic value of the project would not be irrelevant. However, again, as in the case of pecuniary considerations, the evidence is, at best, a make weight. Even without the aesthetic considerations, the variance should probably be granted. All too often, aesthetics are an attempted substitute for an element of the *prima facie* case for a variance. This is intolerable and should not be permitted by the Board or the Court.

In *Topanga*,[260] as part of his case, the developer offered proof tending to show that the property "would be landscaped and terraced to blend in with the natural surroundings."[261] Additionally, "save in places where a wall would be incompatible with the terrain, the plane contemplates enclosure of the park with a wall . . ."[262] Unfortunately for the developer, this proof appears to have been offered to obscure the fact that he could not properly demonstrate a need for a variance. The California Supreme Court considered this proof of aesthetic considerations irrelevant.[263]

> [The developer's] assurances that it would landscape and terrace parts of the property and leave others in their natural state are all well and good, but they bear not at all on the critical issue whether a variance was necessary to

---

[259] See this chapter, Section F 14 at page 320.

[260] See page 265.

[261] 522 P.2d at 20.

[262] Id.

[263] Id at 21.

> bring [the developer] into substantial parity with other parties holding property interests in the zone.

The Board's decision to grant the variance was reversed by the Court.[264]

Another case, this one out of New York, offers the same lesson. In *Devore v. Cazalet*,[265] the developer applied for a large number of "area variances"[266] which were granted by the Board. Virtually no proof was offered by the applicant,[267] except to show that compliance with the zoning ordinance meant a huge block of a building, with little or no open space or green area would be built.[268] The Court concluded that "these aesthetic considerations, while worthy, are insufficient to satisfy the . . . burden of demonstrating the need for an area variance."[269] Tennessee should follow the doctrine as espoused in *Topanga* and *Devore*.[270]

(4) Historical Importance

Another hardship which has at least on one occasion in Tennessee been advanced is the development of a plan which would conform to the perceived historical streetscape of the area in which the building was to

---

[264] *Broadway, Laguna* reached similar conclusions with regard to "attractive architectural features." 427 P.2d at 817.

[265] 68 A.D.2d 17, 416 N.Y.S.2d 282 (1979).

[266] 416 N.Y.S.2d at 283-4.

[267] Id. at 284.

[268] Id.

[269] Id.

[270] Aesthetics may be considered, but are certainly not sufficient if it's the only evidence presented in support of the application. In that instance, the jurisdictional threshold has not been crossed and the variance should be denied without further ado.

be located.[271] "As desirable and laudable as historical preservation may be, it [has] no relevance to the issue before the Board and would not [be] a valid 'hardship' ground for granting a variance for the construction of a new building."[272] Thus, designing a building to take advantage of the historical nature of its surroundings is somewhat akin to designing a building to be aesthetically pleasing: it may be desirable and laudable, but it does not prove hardship.

(5) The Public Good

This is another argument which an applicant may attempt to make in lieu of satisfying the statutory criteria requiring a hardship. It is no better than aesthetic considerations in that respect. Presumably, the public good will be served by precisely applying the statutory criteria, and not by having the Board substitute its judgment for that of the Tennessee General Assembly and the local legislative body.[273] If a developer has already demonstrated that an unnecessary hardship caused by an exceptional physical feature exists on the property, proof that the project will also serve public good is certainly relevant.[274] It cannot, however, serve as a substitute for a true hardship/difficulty. These two concepts are entirely different and if no hardship/difficulty has been demonstrated, the question of the public good need not even be reached.[275] No amount of proof regarding the public good, standing alone, is sufficient to stating an application for a variance.

---

[271] *Metropolitan Historical Commission v. Colony Associates Joint Venture*, 1988 WL 109234 (Tenn. Ct. App. November 1987).

[272] Slip Opinion at 19.

[273] As expressed in the local zoning ordinance.

[274] See page 320 for discussion of negative criteria, including the public good.

[275] The jurisdictional threshold would in that case not have been met.

A number of cases from across the country make this point. *Topanga*[276] is one. In that case, the Court assumed that the particular development would serve the public good.[277]

> The development apparently would partially satisfy a growing demand for new, low cost housing in the area. Additionally, the project might serve to attract further investment to the region and could provide a much needed firebreak.

This assumption had little bearing on the decision.[278]

> The claim that the development would probably serve various community needs may be highly desirable but it . . . does not bear on the issue at hand.

The Court reversed the Board's grant of a variance for the project.

In another California case, the same result was obtained. In *Broadway, Laguna, Vallejo Association v. Board of Permit Appeals of San Francisco,*[279] a developer wanted a variance in the floor area ratio.[280] The Board granted the variance based, in part, upon a finding that since the development would benefit the community, enforcement of the ordinance would work a hardship upon the surrounding neighborhood.[281] The California Supreme Court quite properly pointed out that the hardship must be on the developer, not the neighborhood.[282]

---

[276] See page 238.

[277] 522 P.2d at 20.

[278] Id. at 21.

[279] 427 P. 2d 810 (Cal. 1967).

[280] Id. at 812.

[281] Id at 817.

[282] Id.

In a footnote, the Court explained that the Board was essentially "count[ing] the same factors twice."[283] The point being that community benefit or "the public good" was not relevant if the other factors, such as exceptional physical features, were not satisfied.[284] Even accepting the board's finding of community benefit, "it does not follow that the community would sacrifice [the] benefit if the code were strictly enforced."[285] The Court did not accept that the building would not be constructed without the variance,[286] a claim made by many developers.

> Nothing in the record suggests that if his variance application should be denied, the developer would forego his project or eliminate any of its beneficial features; indeed, the developer has indicated the contrary under penalty of perjury. Although a denial of a variance would cut into the developer's profit margin, the community derives benefit not from his financial gain but from his conforming building.

The public good is sometimes difficult to predict, or analyze. Generally though, the legislative judgment is better than the administrative judgment.

Finally, in a case out of New Orleans, a developer sought "some five variances from the requirements of the Comprehensive Zoning Ordinance for the City of New Orleans."[287] In *State ex rel. Pitts v. Board of Zoning Adjustments of New Orleans*, the Louisiana Court of Appeals began:[288]

---

[283] Id. at note 9.

[284] Id., the board's finding was simply not relevant.

[285] Id.

[286] Id.

[287] *State ex rel. Pitts v. Board of Zoning Appeals of New Orleans*, 327 So.2d 140, 141 (La.App. 1976).

[288] 327 So.2d at 142.

> At the outset it may be well to point out that the true issue here is not whether a project such as the proposed complex can be built at all; but whether this particular structure which exceeds the re-requirements of the Zoning Ordinance, is entitled to a variance from those requirements. To put it another way, the Board was of the opinion that the proposed complex would be beneficial to the growth of this city and to the proper development of the downtown business district and this particular area of St. Charles Avenue. We have no quarrel with that finding. Additionally, the Comprehensive Zoning Ordinance permits the type of usage here proposed, and it is axiomatic that a landowner may use his property in any legal method unless it is restricted in some manner by law. The narrow issue is that this applicant desires to exceed those limitations imposed upon him by law, and only the necessity of relief from these limitations is before us.

Noting that the property was an "almost perfect rectangular shape,"[289] and that the request was for a variance "for almost every requirement of the regulations,"[290] the Court concluded that no appropriate evidence of hardship/difficulty had been presented.

Once again, a Court points out that the mere fact that the development would be beneficial to the community is insufficient to justify the issuance of a variance. It is the specific requirements of the statute and ordinance which must govern. The Louisiana Court reversed the Board's decision.

These cases make it abundantly clear the public good is not a substitute for exceptional physical features. The public good is relevant and will be discussed further,[291] but it simply cannot be substituted for the other elements necessary to justify the issuance of a variance.

---

[289] Id. at 144.

[290] Id.

[291] Section F 14 A of this chapter at p. 320.

(6) Proximity to Inconsistent Uses (Boundary of Zone District; Non-Conforming Use; Property Previously Given Variance or Other Relief).

If the property which is the subject of the variance application is located in close proximity or adjacent to the boundary of a zone district which is less restrictive, this fact will almost certainly be recited. However, it is usually of little or no value.[292] In the vast majority of cases, this factor is absolutely irrelevant. If such a factor is considered, the Board is substituting its judgment for that of the Legislature by, in effect, moving the boundary line of the zone district so that the subject property is now burdened by fewer zoning restrictions. If this goal is desirable, the Legislature should be the body to accomplish it, not the zoning board.

Further, where does it end? There is no logical stopping place. If the property adjacent to the boundary can base its claim of hardship on that alone, then in the future why can't the neighboring party claim hardship based on its proximity to the property granted the original variance, and so on. In the case of a non-conforming use, the law is intended to choke off the use and bring the property into compliance, the provisions of TENN. CODE ANN. § 13-7-208 (the Tennessee Non-Conforming Property Act) allowing expansions notwithstanding.[293] If the presence of a non-conforming use were grounds for hardship, the opposite effect would result: the non-conforming use might very well expand and flourish.[294]

It might be that in an extremely unusual case these factors might come into consideration after a showing of unique physical features and

---

[292] *Williams*, § 142.04.

[293] As explained in Chapter Two, the Tennessee Non-Conforming Property Act may serve as an independent basis for expansion of the non-conformity. The point here is however that no variance should be granted.

[294] *Williams*, § 142.04.

in that way prove determinative. If a small area was totally surrounded by different zone districts, non-conforming uses, or prior valid zoning variances, of course, this might also be a spot zone and unconstitutional. Such an argument might be made; otherwise not.

In an interesting but older case from New Jersey, this very point was commented upon:[295]

> . . . if a municipality is to be zoned for or against various uses, it is inevitable that zones with differing restrictions should abut, and it is likely that a degree of apparent hardship will thus be visited upon the more restricted area along the line of junction. It is not shown to us how this Court may for that, and only that, reason command the allowance of an exception by a board of adjustment without ultimately sounding the death knell of the whole zoning movement . . .

8. Would Result in

Returning now to the analysis of the text of the enabling acts, it is not sufficient simply to have an unusual physical characteristic of the property and undue hardship on the owner; the two must be related. The unusual physical characteristic and the strict application of the ordinance must "result in" or cause the hardship. Without causation, the other elements are not grounds for a variance.

The classic case, mentioned earlier, involving sinkholes on a residential lot, provides a good example. The unusual physical characteristic (the sinkholes) taken in conjunction with a strict application of the zoning ordinance result in or caused the hardship -- the inability of the property owner to use the property in the same manner as his neighbors can use theirs.

[295] *Coriell v Dunellen*, 122 N.J.L. 172, 4 A. 2d 396, aff'd 123 N.J.L. 264, 5 A.2d 576 (1939).

Most variance cases do not (and certainly none of the Tennessee) cases discuss any test for causation. It would seem, however, that a strict "but for" test should be applied both by the board of zoning appeals and any reviewing Court.[296] That is, the applicant should not be entitled to a variance unless he can demonstrate that but for the combined effect of the exceptional narrowness, shallowness, shape, or topographic or other condition of his property, and the zoning ordinance in effect at the time, he would be able to use his property in a manner similar to that to which other property owners in the area are putting their property. This fairly restrictive construction is justified as an effort to minimize the discretion to be exercised by the administrative body.[297] It is important to have this causation requirement in the enabling legislation and the ordinance because otherwise the applicant could argue that so long as he proves some practical difficulty or unnecessary hardship, he may be entitled to the variance regardless if it rationally relates to the proposed relaxation of the zoning ordinance. In fact, this happens in any case. Sophisticated counsel for variance applicants will generally argue strenuously that there is some unique physical feature of the property which justifies the issuance of the variance, and ignore entirely whether the unique physical feature justifies[298] the proposed relaxation of the ordinance. Because so few cases actually involve exceptional physical or topographic conditions of the property, the boards and the courts very frequently do not take the next step to determine whether that exceptional topographic condition causes the alleged hardship or difficulty.

---

[296] This test is borrowed from the well known principle of tort law. See Prosser and Keaton on Torts, § 41 at p. 266.

[297] This "would result in" language does not appear at all in the 1925 Memphis enabling legislation, although it did appear in section 7 of the Standard State Zoning Enabling Act.

[298] That is the feature which causes or results in exceptional difficulties or hardship.

In *Schott v. Metropolitan Board of Zoning Appeals*,[299] the applicant requested a variance of almost 100 percent in the signage restrictions applicable to his property. The property, which was formerly the old governor's residence in the City of Nashville, had been developed for use as a Popeye's Famous Fried Chicken outlet.[300] The applicants argued that there was significant vegetation and slope on the property so as to prevent the ordinary passerby from seeing the signs which were normally permitted by the zoning ordinance.[301] The board of zoning appeals granted the application but the decision was reversed by the Trial Court. On appeal, the Tennessee Court of Appeals, in an opinion written by Judge Henry Todd, affirmed. Judge Todd essentially relied on the conclusion that neither the vegetation nor the slope of the property justified a variance in the signage area.[302] The Court implicitly concluded that the surface area of the signs would not be affected by the suggested exceptional topographic conditions. The location of the signs, by virtue of set-back or side-yard regulations, might be a proper subject of the board's power of variance, but the sheer size of the signs had nothing whatever to do with any topographic condition of the property.

Not only should the Courts and boards of zoning appeals be aware of the necessity of connecting up the hardship and difficulty with the exceptional physical feature of the property, but in addition, they should be aware that certain broad categories of variance requests seem to be inherently unlawful as a result of this requirement.

Those include, under the Tennessee public zoning enabling legislation, variances in the use, floor area ratio, parking, lot size, and sign provisions of any zoning ordinance.

---

[299] 13 T.A.M. 3-4 (Tenn.App. 1985)

[300] It is now part of the site on which the Vanderbilt Plaza Hotel stands, on West End Avenue in Nashville.

[301] Id.

[302] If anything can.

(a) Use Variances

A use variance is a variance which allows the applicant to use his property in a way which the zoning ordinance prohibits.[303] Examples of these are shown by the Memphis Triumvirate. In *Reddoch v. Smith*, for example,[304] the applicant sought to place a gasoline service station in a residential district. This is the epitome of a use variance. Use variances should be distinguished from area variances (or perhaps more accurately, non-use variances)[305] which permit the applicant to deviate from requirements relating to the area of the property which may be used for development. For example, a property owner might seek a variance to invade the front setback because of a sinkhole on the property.[306]

In Tennessee, use variances should be strictly illegal. While no Court has as yet held such,[307] this conclusion is implicit in the text of the public zoning enabling legislation itself. What possible justification, in terms of unique physical features of the property, could justify the placement of a gasoline service station in a residential district? If the slope of the lot is too steep, or if there is a stream cutting through the property, or if it is too narrow, shallow, or unusually shaped, those difficulties or hardships would just as readily apply to a residence as they would to the construction of a gasoline service station. Thus, even

---

[303] 6 *Rohan* 43.01.

[304] 214 Tenn. 213, 379 S.W.2d 641 (1964).

[305] Many times area variances are referred to as bulk or dimensional variances.

[306] 494 S.W.2d 519 (Ky.App. 1973).

[307] See *McClurkan v. Metropolitan Board of Zoning Appeals*, 564 SW 2d 495 (Tenn. Ct. App. 1977); the Court did not go so far as to say that use variances were never permitted but implied that it would be very difficult to justify one based on topographic or other physical characteristics of the property. The case involved a use variance and the Court emphatically rejected it.

though a unique physical feature may be and is assumed for our hypothetical to exist on the property, they do not relate to a variance in the use provisions allowing the construction of a service station. There are no conceivable physical characteristics of the property which would justify a use variance. Thus, while the Tennessee Courts have yet to expressly reach this conclusion, because it is implicit in the terms of the public enabling legislation, any application for a use variance submitted to a board of zoning appeals should be denied by the board, and if granted, should be reversed on appeal by the judiciary. Some local zoning ordinances prohibit the consideration of a use variance.[308] These restrictions would appear to be lawful when construed in conjunction with the interpretation given the variance provision above.[309]

Many other states have also reached a similar conclusion, although their statutes are sometimes not as restrictive as that in Tennessee.[310] A probable majority of the states still permit use

---

[308] Nashville's MetZo at § 17.40.340.

[309] There is a debate among land use attorneys concerning the power of local legislatures to impose more requirements for a variance than those statutorily imposed. See Williams, § 131.02. I tend to disagree with Professor Williams; I think the local government may have no power to impose additional standards (and certainly it cannot relax the statutory standards). However, this type of limitation (concerning use variances) would appear entirely consistent with the zoning enabling statutes in Tennessee.

[310] See *Arrow Transportation Company v. Planning & Zoning Commission*, 299 S.W.2d 95 (Ky. 1956); *Bray v. Beyer*, 292 Ky. 162, 166 S.W.2d 290 (1942); *Town of Hillsborough v. Smith*, 276 N.C. 48, 170 S.E.2d 904 (1969); *Application of O'Neal*, 243 N.C. 714, 92 S.E.2d 189 (1956); *James v. Sutton*, 229 N.C. 515, 50 S.E.2d 300 (1948); Lee v. Board of Adjustment, 226 N.C. 107, 37 S.E.2d 128 (1946); *Livingston v. Peterson*, 59 N.D. 104, 228 N.W. 816 (1930); *Board of Adjustment v. Willie*, 511 S.W.2d 591 (Tex.Civ.App. 1974); *Swain v. Board of Adjustment*, 433 S.W.2d 727 (Tex.Civ.App. 1968); *Board of Adjustment v. Rich*, 328 S.W.2d 798 (Tex.Civ.App. 1959); *Walton v. Tracy Loan & Trust Company*, 97 Utah 249, 92 P.2d 724 (1939); *City of New Orleans*

variances.[311] Inasmuch as there can be no use variance which would result from exceptional narrowness, shallowness, shape or exceptional topographic conditions of a property, Tennessee properly should join those jurisdictions which absolutely prohibit the issuance of a use variance.[312]

---

v. Leeco, 219 L.A. 550, 50 So.2d 490 (1951); State ex.rel Meyer v. Kinealy, 402 S.W.2d 1 (Mo.1966); State ex.rel Nigro v. Kansas City, 325 Mo. 95, 27 S.W.2d 1030 (1930); State ex.rel Tingley v. Gurda, 209 Wis. 63, 243 N.W. 317 (1932); Graves v. Johnson, 75 S.2d 261, 63 N.W.2d 341 (1954); State v. Hull, 65 Wyo. 251, 199 P.2d 832 (1948); Nicolai v. Board of Adjustment, 55 Ariz. 283, 101 P.2d 199 (1940); Wolfe v. Forbes, 217 S.E.2d 889, 906 (W.Va. 1975).

[311] Arant v. Board of Adjustment, 271 Ala. 600, 126 S.2d 100 (1960); Nelson v. Donaldson, 255 Ala. 76, 50 So.2d 244 (1951); Appeal of Blackstone, 8 Del. 230, 190 A. 597 (1937); Wood v. Twin Lakes Mobile Home Village, Inc., 123 So.2d 738 (Fla. 1960); State v. Gunderson, 198 Minn. 51, 268 N.W.850 (1936); Freeman v. Board of Adjustment, 97 Mont. 342, 34 P.2d 534 (1934); Fortuna v. Zoning Board of Adjustment, 95 N.H. 211, 60 A.2d 133 (1948); Oklahoma City v. Harris, 191 Okla. 125, 126 P.2d 988 (1941); Application of Devereaux Foundation, Inc., 351 Pa. 478, 41 A.2d 744 (1945); Alumni Control Board v. City of Lincoln, 179 Neb. 194, 137 N.W.2d 800 (1965); Cook v. Howard, 134 Ga.App. 721, 215 S.E.2d 690 (1975); City of Olaithe v. Board of Zoning Appeals, 10 Kan.App.2d 218, 696 P.2d 409 (1985); see also Matthew v. Smith, 707 S.W.2d 411 (Mo. 1986) overruling State ex rel. Nigro v. Kansas City, supra, in the previous note.

[312] Obviously, this conclusion obtains only in those areas of the state where the public enabling zoning legislation is in effect. If the local governmental entity operates under private enabling legislation which is substantially different from the public enabling legislation, the conclusion may be inaccurate, although the author believes that a use variance should never be granted by a Board of Zoning Appeals; it is an improper legislative action taken by the Board and should only be considered by the local legislative body as a zone change.

(b) Floor Area Ratio

Floor area ratio is a land use planning device used to control the amount of floor area permitted on a given lot. To compute the FAR, the total floor area of an entire building is divided by the area of the lot.[313]

For example, if the FAR is 2, the property may be developed by construction which covers an area equal to an area twice the size of the lot. The development might be of a two-story office building which covers half of the area of the lot, or of a single story which covers the entirety of the lot.[314] "In other words, a structure may have any number of floors within the particular height restrictions of the district so long as the total area of all the floors does not exceed the maximum permissible percentage of floor area as compared with the size of the lot."[315] Some authorities have indicated that if it is difficult for the developer to comply with the FAR, a variance may be applied for.[316]

That may be true in other jurisdictions. It is certainly not true in Tennessee. Inasmuch as some exceptional physical feature of the property must cause the difficulty or hardship suffered by the developer, is there a topographic condition which would cause the developer a hardship under such circumstances? No. The only reason for a developer to seek a floor area ratio variance is to increase the size of his building. In other words, the developer is seeking to put a larger building on the property than the zoning ordinance permits. There is absolutely no reason to permit this kind of a deviation from the zoning regulations. Why should one developer be permitted to have a FAR of 4, when his next-door neighbor, who does not obtain a variance, is restricted to an FAR of 2? Assuming that the successful variance applicant has a unique physical feature on his property, such as, for example, that the property slopes tremendously, or that there is a

---

[313] 6 *Rohan*, Section 42.05 [2][c].

[314] Id.

[315] Id.

[316] Id.

stream running through the middle of it, there is still no reason to increase the floor area ratio of his building. The topographic condition has no effect whatsoever on the amount of floor space which he seeks to use. The topographic impact may affect the location of the building on the property. But it does not have any impact whatsoever on the amount of floor space that he might be able to use. This should be regulated strictly and purely by local ordinance and a Board of Zoning Appeals has absolutely no right to grant a floor area ratio variance.[317]

Because of this lack of a connection between a unique or exceptional topographic condition on the property and the ability of the property owner to use his property as other property owners in the general vicinity could, floor area ratio variances should never be granted in Tennessee.[318]

(c) Parking

For similar reasons, parking variances should be totally unlawful. One commentator has noted that off-street parking is evidently a hybrid involving both use and area restrictions.[319] But under Tennessee law, the classification as either use or area variance

---

[317] I have seen this happen (I represented the applicant), but in that particular case, however, the Trial Court evidently seized upon the exceptional topographic conditions of the property and did not take the second step in an attempt to relate the unique topographic conditions of the property to the alleged hardship. This failure to look at the causal relationship between the hardship or difficulty and the exceptional topographic condition led to an affirmance of the Board's grant of a variance in a case where it should have been reversed.

[318] With the caveat again that this is only considering those jurisdictions operating under the auspices of the Tennessee public zoning enabling legislation.

[319] Comment, *Variances and Partial Rezoning: Relief from Restrictive Zoning in Nebraska*, 60 Nebraska Law Review 81, 92. (1981).

is irrelevant.[320] Exceptional physical and topographic conditions of the property cannot justify and do not cause the developer to either increase[321] or decrease the property devoted to parking. It there is some topographic difficulty which makes it hard for the developer to comply, the solution is to reduce the size of the building to which the parking is incidental. It is not to get a variance which would decrease the amount of parking required. In *Alumni Control Board v. City of Lincoln,*[322] the applicants sought several variances, including one in required off-street parking so as to construct a fraternity house. The enabling legislation involved was much broader than that found in Tennessee. But the Court nevertheless upheld the Zoning Board's decision to deny the variance concluding in part that there was no evidence suggesting that the difficulties facing this applicant were unique to the property involved. But further, how could topographic conditions ever serve as the basis for a variance under such circumstances? They simply cannot.

(d) Signs

The size of the signs permitted (in other words, the square footage of the permitted signage), is also not an appropriate subject for the Board of Zoning Appeals under its variance powers. Once more, the Board or Court should ask what exceptional physical feature of the property can justify the relaxation of zoning regulations concerning the size of signs? Even if there is excessive vegetation or an unusual slope

---

[320] The author considers a variance concerning the size of the parking requirements to be a use variance. Usually, such requirements relate to the size of the structure being proposed on the site. There is no requirement that a developer build a structure which is so big that he cannot place all the required parking on it. Thus, it appears to this author that parking variances (as it relates to size and not location), are in reality use variances.

[321] Ofttimes, in large metropolitan areas, the downtown area has as a permitted use only a small amount of parking and developers typically wish to increase the parking permitted.

[322] 179 Neb. 194, 137 N.W.2d 800 (1965).

to the property, it is not the size of the sign that is affected; it is the location of the sign. It may be that under appropriate cases, the Board of Zoning Appeals could grant a variance in the location of the sign. An example might be where a fairly significant setback requirement exists, along with a height limitation, and there is a severe dropoff in the property. Assume that the slope is such that by the time you get to the end of the setback, the sign is not visible from the street. Let's assume for example that the setback is 50 feet, and that there is a height limitation of 20 feet above the point at which the sign is located. If the slope of the property is such that within 50 feet, it slopes to 20 feet or greater in depth, the sign would not be visible from the street. Thus, a variance in the height provisions might be appropriate. A variance in the setback requirement might be appropriate so as to allow the placement of the sign inside the required 50-foot setback. But to increase the area of the sign would have no effect whatsoever.

In the case of vegetation, once again it appears that the sign could be moved rather than increased in size. The setback or side yard requirements could be modified by the Board given an appropriate finding, so that the signs would be visible from the street. But no increase in the signage area should be permitted. This is simply a disguised attempt by the owner to allow his property to gain increased visibility at the expense of his neighbors. In the commercial setting, this will permit him to increase his profitability; however, those kinds of pecuniary considerations, as previously noted, while relevant, are not sufficient in and of themselves to justify the variance.[323]

(e) Expansion of Non-Conforming Property

For the same reasons, a variance to expand a legally non-conforming property should be denied.[324] There is no possible justification for the expansion of a non-conforming use based on any unique physical feature of the property. In that sense, the non-conforming use

---

[323] See this chapter, Section F 7 c 2 at page 297

[324] See TENN. CODE ANN. § 13-7-208 which allows expansion of non-conforming uses in municipalities and counties in any event.

is just as bad as a use variance and in fact is simply a "variance" on the same theme (and the pun is intended). Many local governments will allow a change in the use of the property from one non-conforming use to another provided that the new non-conforming use is less intense than the old one.[325] That seems a worthy goal and certainly is within the power of the local government. However, a variance to allow such a substitution is simply illegal under the Tennessee public enabling statutes. Granting a variance is not the correct approach.

9. the owner of such property

The Tennessee Public Zoning Enabling Legislation requires that the exceptional physical condition of the property would result in a difficulty or hardship upon the owner of such property. This brings up the interesting, although somewhat academic, question of who has standing to apply for a variance. Notwithstanding the simplicity of the word "owner" in the enabling legislation, it surely cannot be that the applicant must be the owner in fee simple of the property. That would exclude any agent of the owner and also any lessee for a term of years. In the case of the lessee, surely the person in possession of the property under a lease is the real party in interest and should be the applicant. Indeed, while no Tennessee cases appear on any of these issues, Courts from other jurisdictions have so held.[326] The agent of the owner has been held to be an appropriate person to apply.[327] The owner's assignee has also been held to have standing.[328] If there is a contractual

---

[325] See MetZo § 17.40.660 for example.

[326] *Bowen v. Metropolitan Board of Zoning Appeals*, 161 Ind.App. 522, 317 N.E.2d 193 (1974); *Humble Oil and Refining Company v. Board of Alderman*, 284 N.C. 458, 302 S.E.2d 129 (1974) (involving a conditional use permit but treated the same for standing purposes as a variance application).

[327] *Stout v. Jenkins*, 268 S.W.2d 643 (Ky. 1954).

[328] *Cohen v. County Board of Supervisors*, 135 Cal.App.2d 180, 286 P.2d 836 (1955).

obligation to purchase the property, there is also a sufficient interest in the property to apply for a variance.[329]

There has been some difficulty concerning the holders of options and some Courts have held that the optionee does not have standing to apply.[330] This result has been criticized, however.[331]

Rohan suggests that the "critical factor in deciding whether an applicant possesses a sufficient ownership interest to apply for a variance ought to be whether the applicant has a legally enforceable right to use the land."[332] To hold that an optionee has no interest in the property sufficient to apply for a variance personalizes the process, which is contrary to the general thought that a variance should be granted independent of who owns or controls the property. The determination of whether the variance should issue is based on the land, not the person who applies.[333]

Although a person with no connection or interest in the property should not having standing,[334] in those cases where there is some

---

[329] *Shulman v. Zoning Board of Appeals*, 154 Conn. 426, 226 A.2d 380 (1967); *Fail v. Board of Zoning Appeals*, 171 Ind.App. 192, 355 N.E.2d 455 (1976); *Conley Park v. Malone*, 25 Misc. 2d 1072, 205 N.Y.S.2d 166 (1960); *Logden Square Neighborhood Association v. Zoning Board of Adjustment*, 32 Pa.Comnw. 277, 379 A.2d 632 (1977).

[330] *Minney v. City of Azusa*, 164 Cal.App. 12, 330 P.2d 255, 265 (1958); *Conery v. City of Nashua*, 103 N.H. 16, 164 A.2d 247 (1960); *Lee v. Board of Adjustment*, 226 N.C. 107, 37 S.E.2d 128 (1946); *Tripp v. Zoning Board of Review*, 84 R.I. 262, 123 A.2d 144 (1956).

[331] 6 *Rohan*, Section 43.02[7]; 16 Nebraska Law Review at 88; 74 Harv.L.Rev. 1396, 1398 (1961).

[332] 6 *Rohan*, Section 43.02[7].

[333] Id.

[334] Rohan, for example, cites the case of a tenant at suffrage who has been held to lack standing to seek a variance in *Gallager v. Zoning*

property interest, even though remote, the Court should construe this to meet the standing requirement. Ultimately, this furthers the reasonable use of property[335] and would prevent the chicanery which would be obtained by otherwise arbitrary standing rules. For example, the optionee could simply require that the owner apply for the variance himself as a part of the option agreement. There is no policy furthered by requiring the owner instead of an optionee to apply for the variance.

10. to authorize

This language seems a trifle unusual. The original New York legislation said "to vary."[336] But the Standard State Zoning Enabling Act used the same language, "to authorize."[337] It would seem more appropriate to say "to grant" a variance rather to authorize a variance, but perhaps it was meant to imply appellate jurisdiction which is also implied later in the statute. This would not seem to have any particular bearing on the determination to be made by the Board or a reviewing Court.

11. upon an appeal relating to the property

As mentioned in the preceding section, the jurisdiction of the Zoning Board in granting a variance has usually been considered to be appellate. In other words, the zoning administrator denies the application for a zoning permit because it does not comply with the provisions of the zoning ordinance. The applicant may then appeal the decision of the zoning administrator to the Board of Zoning Appeals requesting that it grant a variance relating to the property. It is thus

---

Board of Review, 95 R.I. 225, 186 A.2d 325, 328 (1962).

[335] 16 Nebraska Law Review at 89.

[336] New York City, N.Y. Building Zone Resolution Art. V, Section 20 (1916).

[337] See text of Section VII of the SSZEA.

different from a conditional use permit which is generally thought of as within the original jurisdiction of the Board, and not an appeal.[338]

12. a variance from such strict application

The only noteworthy feature of this phrase is the word "strict." The implication is that the regulations themselves are strict and some latitude must be inherent in the administrative process. Otherwise, it could simply mean that the Board is to allow a deviation from regulations which otherwise would be applied strictly. In any event, again, this phraseology would seem to have little impact on the deliberations of either the Board or a reviewing Court.

13. To relieve the difficulty or hardship

The variance is to be granted so as to relieve such difficulty or hardships that the owner may face. While not expressly stated, this provision at least implies that the relief granted by the Board of Zoning Appeals should be no greater than that which is necessary to enable the applicant to use the land free from the hardship or difficulty which the Board finds to exist on the property. Anything more would be a windfall to the owner of the property and would be detrimental to the public interest.

This requirement is extremely difficult to enforce judicially, however, and in fact there are no reported cases from Tennessee.[339] About five or six years ago, I was involved in a case where the zoning board granted a height variance to a community bank. It was clear that

---

[338] See Chapter 3 at p. 147.

[339] Other states have implied this requirement, *Clark County Board of Commissioners v. Taggert Construction Co.*, 96 Nev. 732, 615 P.2d 965 (1980); and indeed, Ohio, which has enabling legislation fairly similar to that of Tennessee, has implied this minimum variance requirement. *Duncan v. Village of Middlefield*, 23 Oh.St. 3d 83, 491 N.E.2d 692, 696 (1986).

the board wanted the bank to locate in the community and when the bank indicates that it needed only about a 10 foot height variance (from 35 to 45 feet) the board asked if the bank was sure that was enough and granted an additional 5 feet just to makes sure the bank had no problems. There was no evidence of any exceptional physical feature of the property, and the bank's attorney immediately conceded (the bank instead opted for a zoning change, which I had told my clients would be the likely result) and an agreed order was entered overturning the decision of the board. However, the board's insistence that the bank not only get the ten feet it wanted and needed, but an additional five feet, "just in case," is a good example of granting more than the difficulty warranted.

14. The Negative Criteria: Provided such relief may be granted without substantial detriment to the public good and without substantially impairing the intent and purpose of the zone plan and the zoning ordinance.

(a) Without substantial detriment to the public good

The so-called negative criteria get their name from the New Jersey cases.[340] The applicant has the burden of proof and must introduce proof on each of these three issues, as well as the other requirements for a zoning variance. Proving a negative however, is always a bit more difficult.

While the Tennessee Courts have barely, if ever, addressed this issue, the New Jersey Courts[341] have addressed it in a number of different contexts.[342] "When considering the negative criteria, namely

---

[340] See, e.g., *Chirichello v. Zoning Board of Adjustment*, 78 N.J. 544, 397 A.2d 646, 653 (1979).

[341] New Jersey, as noted previously, has enabling legislation remarkably similar to that in Tennessee, including the so-called "negative criteria."

[342] Id. at 653.

the effect upon the public good and impairment of the intent and purpose of the zone plan and zoning ordinance, the parties should direct their attention to that part of the residential area which may reasonably bear on or be affected by the variance." The Court went on:[343]

> We have also adverted to the fact that an impingement of the zoning restrictions may be of varying degrees. The less of an impact, the more likely the restriction is not that vital to valid public interests. Conversely, where the change sought is substantial, the applicant will have to demonstrate more convincingly that the variance will not be contrary to the public good and general welfare expressed in the ordinance.

It seems clear that this clause adds to the Board's power by making it possible to find in favor of the applicant on all of the prior provisions we have discussed, and yet conclude that the applicant has failed to satisfy the negative criteria and deny the variance. "The Board of Adjustment must settle these disputes by engaging in a discretionary weighing, a function inherent in the variance process."[344] Thus, even in the Bettman model variance provision, the inherent discretion so carefully circumscribed in the main portion of the statute appears again in the negative criteria.

The New Jersey approach as to the first of the three negative criteria is to examine the immediate area which may bear the biggest brunt of the proposed variances granted. By analogy, the applicant in Tennessee should do a small inventory of the surrounding land uses, and any irregularities which may show up in the inventory. If the applicant is asking for a setback variance, do all of the properties in the general vicinity comply with the ordinance? If not, to what extent do they not? What other kinds of problems are in the area? It seems obvious that the relevancy of non-conforming uses, other variances,

---

[343] Id. at 654.

[344] Id. at 652, citing *Yahnel v. Jamesberg Board of Adjustment*, 79 N.J. Super. 509, 519, 192 A.2d 177 (App.Div. 1962), *cert. den.* 41 N.J. 116, 195 A.2d 15 (1963).

changes in the zone district and so on are relevant here to prove satisfaction of the negative criteria. However, again, what the Court is looking at is surrounding land uses. Not just any public good. The fact that the project may be aesthetically pleasing may minimize the impact on surrounding properties.

(b) Without substantially impairing the intent and purpose of the zone plan.

The zone plan is most likely the land use component of the comprehensive or master plan adopted by the planning commission.[345] New Jersey has recently made it explicit that the master plan must be considered as part of the analysis concerning the negative criteria. In *Medici v. BPR Co.*,[346] the New Jersey Supreme Court required specific findings by the Board of Adjustment that the variance sought was not inconsistent with the intent and purpose of the master plan and zoning ordinance.[347] The Court made it clear that the Board was to carefully

---

[345] See TENN. CODE ANN. §§ 13-3-301; (regional plan) ("It shall be the function and duty of a regional planning commission to make and adopt a general regional plan for the physical development of the territory of the region . . . the regional plan . . may include . . . a zoning plan for the regulation of the height, area, bulk, location, and uses of buildings, the distribution of population, and the uses of land for trade, industry, habitation, recreation, agricultural, forestry, soil and water conservation and other purposes"); and 13-4-201 (municipal plan). ("It shall be the function and duty of the commission to make and adopt an official general plan for the physical development of the municipality . . . the plan may include . . . a zoning plan . . .") These are however, not mandatory in Tennessee so that in some jurisdictions, there may not be any general plan at all.

[346] 107 N.J.1, 526 A.2d 109 (1987).

[347] 526 A.2d at 110 and 119. The Court was dealing with a use variance here, a different provision from the usual area variance which we have discussed previously. However, the negative criteria in New Jersey applied to area variances, use variances, and conditional use

consider the master plan and the extent to which the proposed variance was inconsistent with that master plan.[348] This means that an applicant for a variance must introduce proof of the zoning element of the master plan for that local governmental unit. The applicant must further demonstrate that there will not be any substantial impairment of the plan as a result of the issuance of this variance. In opposition, naturally, surrounding property owners or other opponents may wish to prove the tremendous harm posed by the particular variance.[349] Absent proof that the proposed variance will not substantially impair the zone plan, the zoning board and/or reviewing Court should not issue or affirm the issuance of the variance.

Tennessee has adopted a Comprehensive Growth Plan Act,[350] but that does not really fit in this context. Section 107 of the Act provides:

> After a growth plan is so approved, all land use decisions made by the legislative body and the municipality's or county's planning commission shall be consistent with the growth plan.

---

permits.

[348] In New Jersey, the adoption of a master plan is now mandatory. N.J.S.A. § 40: 55D-89. The planning board must reexamine the master plan and zoning ordinance at least once every six years and absent such a review, there is created a rebuttable presumption that the zoning ordinance is no longer reasonable. N.J.S.A. 40: 55D-89.1. Tennessee does not have mandatory comprehensive planning and to the extent that the local governmental entity does not have a comprehensive or master plan, then the Board and reviewing Court should simply omit that portion of the analysis.

[349] Of course, regarding area variances, it sometimes seems that the variance is quite minimal. However, as mentioned previously, a large area variance can be as destructive and in many instances much more destructive than an outright use variance.

[350] TENN. CODE ANN. § 6-58-101, et seq. The Growth Plan is mandatory is most areas of the state.

There is no provision for decisions of the zoning board. I would suggest that it can't hurt to submit the Growth Plan for the area in question (if there is one; a few governments are excluded from coverage of the Act), arguing its applicability if appropriate. Unfortunately, most of the Growth Plans have been short on detail and are not likely to be very helpful in this context. The applicant may favor that however; a very general growth plan would be hard to "substantially impair."

(c) Without substantially impairing the intent and purpose of the zoning ordinance.

Finally, the last of the negative criteria examines the extent to which the variance will impair the intent and purpose of the ordinance itself. The Board and reviewing Court should be looking to the magnitude of the variance as compared with what is permitted under the ordinance itself. Obviously, the greater the magnitude of the variance, the more likely a substantial impairment of the zoning ordinance. Further, if the variance seems totally out of harmony with the zoning ordinance, that might also furnish a basis for the denial of the variance.[351]

[351] From my perspective, the board does not really have to articulate a strong reason to deny a variance: it has that power as a matter of discretion. Naturally, the better the reason for a denial the easier it will be upheld on appeal.

G. Burden and Quantum of Proof

The burden of proof is certainly easy to determine: it lies upon the applicant, both with regard to the so-called burden of production and persuasion.[352]

The quantum of proof necessary to shift the burden of production over to the opponents of the application has never been reviewed by a Tennessee Court. However, certain general observations may be made. First, since the Board's actions are usually[353] reviewed pursuant to the common law writ of certiorari,[354] the legal standard should be that established pursuant to that procedure for administrative review.

Under the common law writ, a board's decision may be reviewed only as to its fundamental legality.[355] The board's decision may be reversed only if it was beyond its jurisdiction, illegal, arbitrary, or fraudulent.[356] And while it has sometimes been said that "any material evidence" is sufficient to sustain the findings of an administrative body

[352] *Big Fork Mining Company v. Tennessee Water Quality Control Board*, 620 S.W. 2d 515, 520 (Tenn. Ct. App. 1981). This case is not a land use case, but the legal proposition is the same.

[353] There is a strong argument that a decision of a board denying a property owner non-conforming status might be appealed under the statutory writ of certiorari. So far as the author knows, no court in Tennessee has ever adopted that position. In *Toles v. City of Dyersburg*, 39 S.W.3d 138 (Tenn. Ct. App. 2000), the statutory writ of certiorari was the procedural mechanism by which the case was presented to the court. The Tennessee Court of Appeals ruled against the petitioner without commenting on which writ was proper.

[354] TENN. CODE ANN. §§ 27-8-101, and 27-9-101.

[355] See Chapter Five.

[356] *Hoover Motor Express v Public Utilities Commission*, 195 Tenn. 592, 604-5, 261 S.W.2d 233, 238 (1953).

under the common law writ of certiorari,[357] the better view would be that there must be more than a scintilla or glimmer of evidence.[358] The evidence must be of a substantial and material nature, the type that would require submission of a case to a jury.[359] It is probable that the Tennessee Supreme Court has used the terms "material evidence" and "substantial evidence" interchangeably.[360] The Court of Appeals has on

[357] See *Hoover Motor Express*, 195 Tenn. 592, 604-5, 261 S.W.2d 233, 238 (1953).

[358] *Pace v. Garbage Disposal District*, 390 S.W.2d 461, 463 (Tenn.App. 1965). Several cases have cited *Pace* as defining the terms "substantial and material" in the context of the Uniform Administrative Procedures Act, TENN.CODE ANN. § 4-5-101 et seq. See, e.g., *Big Fork Mining Company v. Tennessee Water Quality Control Board*, 620 S.W.2d 515, 521 (Tenn.App. 1981). *Pace*, however, appears to have been decided under the common law writ of certiorari. First of all, the Uniform Administrative Procedures Act was not enacted until 1974, while *Pace* was decided in 1965. Secondly, *Pace* concerns a utility district which is a municipality under Tennessee law (Tenn.CODE ANN. § 7-82-301) and hence not reviewable under the provisions of the U.A.P.A. See T.C.A. § 4-5-102(2) (agency is defined to include each state board, commission, committee, department, officer, or any other unit of state government).

[359] *Pace*, 390 S.W.2d at 463.

[360] *Tennessee Cartage Company v. Pharr*, 199 S.W.2d 119, 120 (Tenn. 1947). It is somewhat interesting to note that in some ways the law in this state concerning certiorari has come full circle. In the *Tennessee Cartage Company* case, the Court indicated that the presence of substantial evidence expressed "the fact that there was, or was not, a 'rational basis' for the action taken by the administrative board . . ." 199 S.W.2d at 120. The Tennessee Supreme Court, speaking through Special Judge Wade, noted the similarity between the common law writ and the rational basis test commonly utilized to test the constitutionality of a municipal legislative enactment. *McCallen v. City of Memphis*, 786 S.W.2d 633, 640 (Tenn. 1990).

a number of occasions utilized the substantial and material evidence rather than any material evidence standard.[361]

The quantum of proof necessary to meet this substantial and material evidence requirement requires that there must be evidence that "a reasonable mind might accept as adequate to support a rational conclusion and such as to furnish a reasonably sound basis for the action under consideration."[362] As mentioned above, it is akin to the test used on a Motion for Directed Verdict. There must be more than a glimmer or scintilla of evidence, and ultimately it must be evidence which a reasonable board could accept to support a decision. Naturally, this evidence is not limited to direct proof, but may also include circumstantial evidence or inferences reasonably drawn from direct evidence.[363] Thus, under all 14 of the requirements established by the Tennessee Public Zoning Enabling Legislation, the proponent would have to adduce proof sufficient to convince a reasonable mind that the variance should be granted.

While in some zoning cases the quantum of proof is extremely important because the board, once presented with a prima facie case, must grant the permit.[364] In the case of variances, however, the board

---

[361] See *Anderson v. Carter*, 512 S.W.2d 297, 307 (Tenn.App. 1974); *Goodwin v. Metropolitan Board of Health*, 656 S.W.2d 383, 391 (Tenn.App. 1983). Judge Ben Cantrell, in his well-known article, embraces the same test. B. Cantrell: *Review of Administrative Decisions by Writ of Certiorari in Tennessee*, 4 Memphis State University Law Review 19, 30 (1973).

[362] *Pace v. Garbage Disposal District*, 390 S.W.2d 461, 463 (Tenn.App. 1965).

[363] *Wayne County v. Tennessee Solid Waste Disposal Control Board*, 756 S.W.2d 274, 280 (Tenn. Ct. App. 1988) (this is an appeal under the Uniform Administrative Procedures Act, but it would not appear to alter the result).

[364] This is the situation with regard to conditional use permits. The grant of a conditional use permit is not discretionary; if proof as to

has a great deal of discretion to deny. This discretion is inherent in the mechanism itself. For example, even if the property owner puts on evidence that the property is very narrow or very shallow or very unusual in shape, the board could always conclude that despite the narrowness, shallowness or unusual shape, that it is not exceptionally narrow, shallow or unusual in shape. Thus, no variance would be issued.

Even if the board concluded that there was an exceptional physical feature present on the property, it might nevertheless conclude that there was no practical difficulty or undue hardship and again the board could deny the permit. Finally, the board might conclude that the negative criteria were not satisfied, that even though there is a unique physical feature present on the property, and even though there is an undue hardship upon the property owner, to grant the variance would be a substantial detriment to the public good or substantially impair the intent and purpose of either the zoning ordinance or the zone plan. On appeal, any denial of a zoning variance should almost always be upheld by a court. A Court should almost never second guess a Board of Zoning Appeals as to whether or not the alleged physical condition of the property is truly exceptional; or whether the property owner actually does have a practical difficulty or undue hardship; or whether the granting of a variance as requested would substantially impair the public good or the intent and purpose of the zone plan or zoning ordinance. The facts of any case which would justify the reversal of a failure to grant a variance by a board would have to be so extreme as to be almost inconceivable. The board has and properly should have almost absolute discretion to deny a zoning variance. This may result in the taking of property, but there are other remedies for such a taking. The board should not be reversed when it denies a variance.

However, the opposite conclusion obtains when a variance is granted. Variances, being special favors doled out by this administrative body in violation of the standards set for everyone else in the community, should be strictly reviewed by the Courts. And, if there is any hint that the physical condition of the property is not truly

---

each and every requirement of the ordinance is met, the permit must be issued.

exceptional, or that the difficulty or hardship is not practical or undue, or that the negative criteria have not been met, the Board should be reversed. Most variance cases turn on the absence of any exceptional physical condition of the land. In fact, most often, the property owner does not place any evidence of an exceptional physical condition of the land in the record. But the Courts should expect and must require more than just some evidence of exceptional physical condition; the applicant, the board, and the Court should all require proof sufficient to convince a reasonable mind that the physical condition is truly exceptional. If the Court does not require at least that much proof, then there is the possibility of favoritism and similarly situated property owners being treated unequally.

All this really just goes to say that a Board of Zoning Appeals has great discretion to deny a variance, but only a very limited amount of discretion to grant one. When a Court is reviewing the denial of a variance, it can relax. The applicant should almost never be able to overturn the board's decision. But in the case where the board has granted a variance, the Court should search the record to make sure that there is sufficient proof to justify the issuance of that variance. Most of the time there is not.

H. Conditions on the Issuance of a Variance

1. General Relief

The Tennessee Public Zoning Enabling Legislation does not extend any express authority to a Zoning Board to attach conditions to the issuance of a variance. The SSZEA did provide a general grant of authority to "make such order, requirement, decision or determination as ought to be made . . ."[365] and this grant of authority and power would be broad enough to clothe a Zoning Board with the authority to impose conditions upon the approval of a variance. However, that language does not appear in the Tennessee version of the legislation. Nevertheless, the courts have not had any trouble with this issue and it is clear that the boards to have the power to impose conditions upon the issuance of

[365] Section 7 of the SSZEA.

variances (and other forms of administrative relief).[366] Notice however, that the power of the board to grant conditions concerning variances is likely somewhat limited as compared to it ability to impose conditions on conditional use permits where the power is expressly granted.[367]

Any conditions imposed must be related to the land itself and reasonably calculated to achieve a legitimate zoning objective.[368] Perhaps the most typical of these are fencing and screening requirements.[369]

Although very infrequently used in Tennessee, exactions from developers may be imposed if there is a nexus between the issuance of the variance and the condition imposed.[370] Furthermore, the conditions imposed must be sufficiently well defined to allow both the applicant, opposing interests, and the Court to understand what can and cannot be done.

---

[366] *Stevenson v. Palmer*, 448 SW 2d 67 (Tenn. 1969).

[367] See p. 175.

[368] *Spencer-Sturla v City of Memphis*, 155 Tenn. 70, 290 S.W. 2d 608 (1926); *Euclid v. Ambler Realty*, 272 US 365 (1926); *National Black Child Development Institute v. District of Columbia Board of Zoning Adjustment*, 483 A.2d 687 (D.C.App. 1984).

[369] See *Stevenson v. Palmer*, 448 S.W.2d 67 (Tenn. 1969) (this case involves a conditional use permit, but the powers of the Board should be similar in variance cases). *Everson v. Zoning Board of Adjustment of Allentown*, 395 Pa. 168, 149 A.2d 63 (1959).

[370] *California Coastal Commission v. Nolan*, 483 US 85 (1987).

2. Time Limits and Neighborhood Consent

It is clear that the Board may not condition the issuance of a variance upon the ownership of any particular individual.[371] The person owning the property has absolutely nothing to do with whether there is some exceptional physical feature of the property. Conditions must be imposed which relate to the use of the property and not to the ownership of the property. Since variances run with the land,[372] each successive owner is entitled to the benefit of the variance assuming that it was properly issued initially.[373]

In many other jurisdictions, variances conditioned on a certain time limit, such as for a specific term of years, are appropriate.[374] However, in Tennessee, with our very restrictive Bettman model variance provision, it is difficult to understand why any time limit on the duration of the variance is appropriate. Most time limitations relate to use variances and as previously noted, use variances are illegal in Tennessee.[375]

If the variance is truly justified, that is, if it is based upon some exceptional narrowness, shallowness, or shape or topographic or other condition of the property, then no time limitation would be appropriate.

---

[371] *McClurkan v. Metropolitan Board of Zoning Appeals*, 565 S. W. 2d 495 (Tenn. App. 1977).

[372] Id.

[373] *McClurkan* is exceedingly interesting because it suggests that the issuance of a variance which is fundamentally illegal is void and not merely voidable. If that is the case, then many variances granted by our local boards here in Tennessee over the past 75 years are most probably void and of no effect whatsoever. I suspect that most cases would not involve such a holding however.

[374] 6 *Rohan* at Section 43.03[2].

[375] *McClurkan v Metro Board of Zoning Appeals*, 565 SW 2d 495 (Tenn. Ct. App. 1977).

Insofar as the author knows, there is no Tennessee law on this point. But the underlying premise of variance law in Tennessee mandates that Tennessee be in the minority of the states which would not permit a limitation on the time that the variance may be valid.[376]

Many Courts have allowed restrictions on the hours of operation of a particular enterprise.[377] Again, however, these generally are going to be use variances entering into a more restrictive area. Thus, restrictions on the hours of operation may be reasonable and the Courts tend to uphold them.[378] In Tennessee again, such restrictions may be unlawful. Since use variances are illegal, to impose a condition concerning the hours of operation does not reasonably relate to any particular variance which might be granted. However, restricting the hours of operation of a use permitted in the district to accommodate surrounding properties is appropriate.

The consent of surrounding neighbors has, of course, nothing whatsoever to do with whether the statutorily required conditions have been met by the applicant. Therefore, any condition by a Board which would require the applicant to obtain the consent of the neighboring landowners is absolutely unreasonable and illegal.[379]

---

[376] This would also apply to a condition on exercising the variance within some particular period of time. Once the variance is issued by the Board, whether this particular applicant uses it or it is sold five years later to another owner for his or her use, makes no difference. If the underlying bases for a variance were met in the first place, the fact that the variance is not utilized until much later is irrelevant. It would seem, however, that upon a showing of changed circumstances by neighboring and affected property owners, the Board might reconsider at a later date. That standard of proof though is extremely hard to surmount.

[377] See 6 *Rohan* at Section 43.03[6][c].

[378] *Vlahos Realty Company v. Little Boar's Head District*, 101 N.H. 460, 146 A.2d 257 (1958) (closing time restriction held valid on food store).

[379] *Luger v. City of Burnsville*, 295 N.W.2d 609 (Minn.1980).

I. Violations and Modifications

Ordinarily, a violation of a condition imposed by the Board upon the issuance of a variance is not grounds for the revocation of the variance itself.[380] A violation of the conditions, however, may be corrected by seeking injunctive relief against the holder of the variance, or by seeking criminal sanctions usually in City Court.[381]

The Zoning Board may grant a modification of the conditions notwithstanding the general applicability of the doctrine of res judicata to administrative decisions. However, in order to obtain the change, the holder of the variance must show a substantial change in circumstances, otherwise, it should be denied. In addition, obviously, a new hearing before the Board is required along with the attendant notice required of any such hearing.[382] The Board should also be wary of the holder of a variance who asks for a change of condition due to a change of circumstances because the variance holder may now be disputing the original imposition of the condition rather than suggesting a change of circumstances. If the landowner is seeking to get the original condition removed because as imposed it was unreasonable originally, a proper, timely appeal must have been filed and in the absence of such a suit being successfully prosecuted, there is no further remedy. The Board should not remove a valid condition previously imposed simply because the current variance holder believes it to be unreasonable.[383]

---

[380] 6 Rohan Section 43.03[4].

[381] TENN. CODE ANN. § 13-7-208.

[382] The statutory provisions make no express requirement that any notice be given, or for that matter, that any hearing be held. TENN. CODE ANN. §§ 13-7-109 and 13-7-207. However, there may be local ordinance provisions which must be satisfied.

[383] Rohan at Section 43.03[5].

J. Judicial Declaration of Invalidity

If on appeal, the Court concludes that the condition imposed is unreasonable, it would appear that in Tennessee, with our narrow means of administrative review via the writ of certiorari,[384] that the appropriate disposition of the appeal is to reverse the Board's decision of issuing the variance with the condition, and remand it to the Board for further proceedings. At that point, the Board can determine whether the variance should be issued without that particular condition and/or whether it can be issued with other conditions which would protect the public interest. It would also give an opportunity to surrounding property owners to appear and express their sentiments concerning the issuance of the variance without the conditions.

K. Legal Effect: Variance Runs With the Land

Based upon the foregoing, it should be apparent that variances run with the land. The *McClurkan*[385] case makes that clear. Assume for a moment that the use of the variance is discontinued, is the variance still attached to the land? I don't know of any authority on this point: my impression would be that the variance would still be valid so long as the configuration of the property is substantially the same (and with the same zoning restrictions). If the lay-out of the buildings on site changed significantly, the variance may no longer be necessary (and the point would be moot); if the variance is needed, the local government ought to be permitted to review the new lay-out and decide whether a variance under those circumstances is warranted.

---

[384] See the next chapter.

[385] *McClurkan v. Metro Zoning Board*, 565 S.W. 2d 495 (Tenn. App. 1977)

L. Delay in Obtaining Permit or Beginning Construction

Most zoning ordinances provide that if a building permit based upon the variance is not obtained within some specified period of time, such as 6 or 12 months, that the variance lapses.[386] Although the necessity of these requirements is not clear, certainly to the extent that new zoning provisions might remove the need for the variance before the successful applicant obtains the permit, it makes some sense. One must suspect however that this does not happen very often. If the zoning ordinance has not changed, why should the variance lapse merely because the successful applicant has not had time to pick up the permit? There would appear to be no good reason. Even if the ordinance has gotten more restrictive, most of the time there is no reason to prevent the use of the previously granted variance.

M. Void vs. Voidable

On the other hand, variances which have been granted inappropriately, with no discernible basis in law, are void.[387] This means that if the variance seems to have some basis, then a Court probably should not declare the variance void. Only in those circumstances, such as in *McClurkan*, where the circumstances are such that it is abundantly clear that there was no justification whatsoever for the variance should the Court so declare. If there is some minimal justification, then the variance should be sustained.

Naturally, even if the variance is declared void, if the improvements have already been constructed, it is an exercise in futility. Virtually no court will order that the building be removed or modified even where there was no basis for the variance.

---

[386] See MetZo § 17.40.250 (permits must be obtained within two years).

[387] Once again, *McClurkan v. Metro Zoning Board*, 565 S.W. 2d 495 (Tenn. App. 1977), makes this point.

N. Revocation

It might seem that the zoning board should have the power to revoke a previously issued building permit if the variance was improperly granted, but I don't believe that is within the board's power. First, of course, if the decision to revoke is made within 60 days of the original issuance, the board has not yet lost jurisdiction to reconsider the case. Thus, within that short period of time, the board could change its mind.

However, if the variance is older than 60 days and the decision of the zoning board has become final, then most likely the zoning board has no jurisdictional basis to take any action with regard to the issued variance.

Assuming that the board granted the variance with conditions, it still seems inappropriate to revoke the permit. It seems that enforcement in the courts is a better solution. Taking away a variance previously granted and relied upon by the property owner is a very harsh remedy: if that is to happen, a judicial hearing should be required.[388]

O. Res Judicata and Collateral Estoppel

Building on the above, the previous decision of the board granting a variance (or for that matter denying one) should prevent any subsequent change of position with regard to a previous decision as to a variance. Some boards have rules which require that before a new application for a variance can be made after a previous application has been denied, some arbitrary period of time must have gone by, such as 6 or 12 months. Therefore, if the previous application has been denied, no new application of a substantially similar nature may be filed for that period of time.

---

[388] Another question is raised by this issue: if the board does have the power to revoke, can the appeal be under the statutory writ of certiorari? See page 387.

P. Conclusion

Variances in Tennessee are a very complicated topic. Anyone requesting a variance should fully understand the statutory requirements and be certain to demonstrate compliance with each and every part of the statute, as well as the local zoning ordinance requirements.[389] Failure to do so will render the variance, if granted, susceptible to reversal on appeal. On the other hand, the opponents of a variance application have an easier task: they have only to sit back and wait for the applicant to make a mistake, which will almost certainly occur.

[389] This is true even though the local provisions may be irrelevant; surely the local board will think that the local zoning ordinance requirements are important even if at some future point, a court decides that only the statutory requirements are mandatory.

Chapter Five

Judicial Review Of Zoning Board Decisions

A. Introduction

Judicial review of zoning board decisions in Tennessee is accomplished mainly by a procedural device known as the common law writ of certiorari. This is an antiquated method of review of any inferior tribunal and may be filed before any trial court. Although the methodology of the review itself is satisfactory (and will be described later in this chapter), the procedure by which certiorari is obtained is not well understood, often varies in practice from county to county, and most likely should be discarded in favor of a more modern statutory approach. Perhaps at some point an amended version of the Uniform Administrative Procedures Act[1] will be passed so that those procedures are made applicable to local government administrative agencies.[2] This would be a great help, because at least the process by which decisions of these administrative agencies are reviewed will be more clearly understood by everyone and the same rules will apply everywhere. Currently, that is simply not the case.[3] In addition, the rules governing

---

[1] TENN. CODE ANN. § 4-5-101 et seq

[2] Part of the difficulty is that certiorari is countenanced by the constitution. Section 10 of Article VI of the Tennessee Constitution provides:

> The Judges or Justices of the Inferior Courts of Law and Equity, shall have power in all civil cases, to issue writs of certiorari to remove any cause or the transcript of the record thereof, from any inferior jurisdiction, into such court of law, on sufficient cause, supported by oath or affirmation.

[3] Perhaps the clearest explanation of the procedure and substantive review provisions may be found in Judge Ben Cantrell's

the issuance of the writ have become more stringent, and a failure to follow the rules often will result in a lack of subject matter jurisdiction and dismissal of the petitioner's case. The decision of the board may be upheld solely on procedural grounds, perhaps resulting in an erroneous decision being upheld by the court, mainly because the attorney for the appealing party did not know the rules governing certiorari.

B. The Common Law Writ of Certiorari

Generally speaking, the procedure governing the common law writ of certiorari is very similar to the procedure employed under the provisions for the statutory writ of certiorari. As a result, most of the observations below are also applicable to the statutory writ. In a separate section of this chapter we will describe the most important procedural differences between the two writs.

1. Petition for Writ of Certiorari

Instead of filing a complaint as would be customary and required under the Tennessee Rules of Civil Procedure, the document which initiates review under either of the writs of certiorari is a petition for writ of certiorari.[4] Just as attorneys are accustomed under the Tennessee Rules of Civil Procedure to provide a "short and plain statement of the claim"[5] the petition must "state briefly the issues involved in the cause, the substance of the order or judgment complained of, the respects in which the petitioner claims the order or judgment is erroneous, and pray for an accordant review."[6] However, distinctly dissimilar are the technicalities which have made the use of

---

authoritative work, *Review of Administrative Decisions by Writ of Certiorari in Tennessee*, 4 Memphis State University Law Review 19 (1973). The thoughts expressed in this chapter have been heavily influenced by that article as well as by my own practical experience.

[4] TENN. CODE ANN. § 27-9-102.

[5] Tennessee Rules of Civil Procedure 8.01.

[6] TENN. CODE ANN. § 27-9-102.

this petition exceedingly dangerous: failure to observe those technicalities may result in dismissal.[7] A sample petition is appended to the end of this chapter.

Before getting along too far in our discussion of procedure, it is important to note that although Chapter 9 of Title 27 of the Tennessee Code purports to apply procedurally to both the common law and statutory writs of certiorari, there are important differences in the manner in which the two writs are handled procedurally. As mentioned above, these will be discussed shortly, but it is never safe to presume that simply because the statute says it is so that it actually is so with regard to the common law writ of certiorari.

(a) Where to file

The case may be filed in either Chancery[8] or Circuit Court[9] in any county in which any one or more of the petitioners or any one or more of the material defendants reside, or have their principal office.[10] As a practical matter of course, in an appeal from a local zoning board, the case almost always is filed in the county in which the local zoning board is found. There is the interesting question as to whether a local zoning board could be required to defend a case in another county where one of the parties resides in a county other than where the zoning board has jurisdiction. Ultimately, such a result seems unfair; the local zoning board should be permitted to defend on its home turf, so to speak.

---

[7] *Blair v Tennessee Board of Probation*, 246 SW 3d 38 (Tenn. App. 2007)

[8] TENN. CODE ANN. § 27-9-102.

[9] TENN. CODE ANN. § 27-9-103. The petitioner is given an option to choose between chancery or circuit court jurisdiction. As a practical matter, the cases have historically been filed in Chancery Court and as a result, the Chancellors are generally more familiar with the procedure.

[10] TENN. CODE ANN. § 27-9-102.

(b) What to allege and verification

There several tricky aspects concerning the petition for writ of certiorari, as mentioned above. First, the petition must be verified (that is, sworn to before a Notary Public or other appropriate official).[11] A failure to verify the petition may result in dismissal for lack of subject matter jurisdiction. Furthermore, if the petition is not sworn at the time of filing, it may not be amended to permit verification unless the order is entered before the statute of limitations runs[12] (60 days from the date of decision to be safe). This then becomes very important because a failure to verify the petition ultimately results in a lack of subject matter jurisdiction. Since this defense cannot be waived, it may be brought up at any time (even on appeal) and the petitioner loses.

It may seem that this is not a trap that licensed members of the bar would fall into, but I have seen it happen several times. I don't particularly like the rule, but it now seems part of the jurisprudence of the state.

Another note on verification: merely indicating that the affiant or petitioner is familiar with the allegations, and signing before a notary public, does not equal a sworn petition.[13] The affiant must state that

---

[11] TENN. CODE ANN. §§ 27-8-104 and 106, and the Tenn. Constitution Article VI, Section 10. The statute only requires that the petition be sworn; it does not specify who must swear to it.

[12] "A trial court has subject matter jurisdiction to extend the sixty-day time period of § 27-9-102 if the order granting the extension is entered within the sixty-day period. After the sixty day period has expired, however, the trial court no longer has such jurisdiction. In other words, 'to grant time in which to file a petition for certiorari after the expiration of the original term is a power not given to this court.'" *Blair v Tennessee Board of Probation*, 246 SW 3d 38 (Tenn. App. 2007).

[13] *Montague v State, 2001 WL 1011464.*

Discussion of verified documents usually arises in the

the allegations are true to the best of his knowledge, information, and belief. Merely swearing to having knowledge of the allegations contained in the petition is insufficient to qualify as a verification under oath. Having knowledge of the allegations does not mean that those allegations are true to the knowledge, information and belief of the affiant. While it would not seem that an attorney would be caught in this kind of trap for the unwary, it has happened to attorneys and others.[14] This procedural trap seems to overlook the essence of the

---

> context of analysis of properly acknowledged documents. In Tennessee, acknowledged documents are ones which have been notarized by a notary public or acknowledged in the presence of an official. As defined in Black's Law Dictionary, "verify" means "[t]o prove to be true; to confirm or establish the truth or truthfulness of." Black's further explains, as an example of verification, that "a verified complaint typically has an attached affidavit of plaintiff to the effect that the complaint is true." Id. There is no doubt that the essence of a verification is truthfulness of the document's contents. As Judge Koch explained in an opinion from the Court of Appeals, "[a]n acknowledgment establishes the proper execution of the document while a verification establishes the truth of the document's contents." D.T. McCall & Sons v. Seagraves, 796 S.W.2d 457, 463 (Tenn. Ct. App.1990) (recognizing a distinction in Tennessee between an acknowledgment and a verification); see also Varner v. Brown, No. 03A01-9405-CV-00171, 1994 WL 666902, at *2 (Tenn. Ct. App.1994) (discussing the difference between an acknowledged document and a verified document for purposes of self-authentication pursuant to Rule 902(8) of the Tennessee Rules of Evidence).

See also *Underwood v Tennessee Department of Correction*, Court of Appeals, January 20, 2005.

[14] These arcane requirements have cropped up with more regularity now that the common law writ is used by prison inmates to appeal adverse administrative corrections decisions. It is perhaps

judicial process: did the board act arbitrarily or beyond its jurisdiction? Surely, that is the determination that should be resolved. Procedural irregularities have become too important and the underlying merits of the cases are getting lost.

Another issue which occasionally comes up is the propriety of the attorney for the petitioner verifying the petition. Before addressing this, it surely seems safer to simply have the client (or some other person with knowledge) verify the complaint. However, my personal view is that there is nothing wrong with this the attorney signing the verification. Certainly where the attorney attended the zoning board meeting s/he has personal knowledge of the events. Even where the attorney was not present for the hearing, it may be appropriate for him or her to verify the complaint. In most cases the attorney will have a copy of the order of the administrative agency and surely that is personal knowledge of the decision,. What does the affiant have to have personal knowledge of? The actual hearing? Why is that necessary? Or is it most important to have some educated basis for concluding that the decision was wrong? How can a lay person (the client for example) satisfy that requirement? Further, many administrative bodies maintain video records of the proceedings, and if the attorney watches the recordings before filing, there would seem to be very little to complain about concerning the verification of the petition. I have had courts criticize this practice on the grounds that the attorney could be called to testify and that places the advocate in a difficult (and perhaps unethical) position as a witness. However, the common law writ of certiorari does not normally allow testimony: the proof is restricted to the record before the administrative body. It would seem therefore that there is little risk that the attorney could become a witness with the attendant ethical difficulties that implies.

Furthermore, the facts alleged in the petition are usually very straight forward. For example, the petition for a neighbor challenging a variance might allege that the application for the variance was

---

understandable that the appellate courts are desirous of avoiding cases which often have little basis in fact, brought by pro se petitioners. Unfortunately, the rulings are working to the detriment of licensed members of the bar as well.

submitted on January 10; notice by publication was on January 20; the board meeting took place on February 15; the proof presented by the applicant did not demonstrate that there was any exceptional physical feature or condition of the property in any respect; the board acted illegally and arbitrarily in granting the variance because there was no such proof required by the statute. Who has the best knowledge of these items? Surely the lawyer, not the client. The date of the application, and the date of notice by publication or otherwise are usually admitted. The lack of proof (the client ordinarily has not idea what proof is needed), and the conclusion that the decision to grant the variance was arbitrary and capricious are all items that are peculiarly within the training of the attorney. So who really is the best person to verify?

Even if the attorney was not present at the zoning board hearing, all meetings must now be recorded so as to allow for a transcript of the evidence to be produced in the case of an appeal[15] and many meetings are now recorded by video. So the attorney, even if s/he is retained after the zoning board decision only has to obtain the recording to verify what took place. Nevertheless, given some objections from various courts, it may be best to have the client verify the petition even though the client may not clearly understand the allegations, and may not really be familiar with all of the facts; often first hand knowledge is questionable. But this eliminates the risk that a Judge will conclude that the attorney's verification was somehow tainted and thereby void after the 60 day statute of limitations has run. At that point the court would lack subject matter jurisdiction and the case would be over without ever getting a hearing on the merits.

In summary then, the petition must be notarized and the affiant must swear or affirm that the allegations are true. Failing such may result in dismissal.

---

[15] *Lewis v. Bedford County, Lewis v Bedford County BZA,* 174 S.W.3 d 241 (Tenn. Ct. App. 2004), expressly ruled that the board had the obligation to produce and file the transcript of the proceedings.

Perhaps even more obscurely, the petition must state that it is the first application for the writ[16] and that there is no other plain, speedy, or adequate remedy.[17] There is at least one old case which suggests that the petition for writ of certiorari may be dismissed in the absence of such statements[18] and several newer ones where that result has been argued for and threatened. While certainly the courts do not want to have multiple applications for this type of relief pending before them, it is unclear why such a statement is necessary especially when it is certainly true that any administrative agency which is a respondent would point out to a court if multiple requests truly were pending. But the statute does demand it, and failing to allege it may be perilous to the case. In any event, out of an abundance of precaution, this statement should be made either in the body of the petition or immediately below it.[19]

One other allegation or statement which must be included in the petition is an allegation that the petitioner is "aggrieved" by the action of the administrative tribunal. The statute requires that the petitioner be "aggrieved"[20] and although this may also seem somewhat hypertechnical, an allegation to that effect in the petition seems the easiest way to avoid a motion to dismiss.

---

[16] TENN. CODE ANN. § 27-8-106; *Bowling v Tennessee Board of Paroles*, 2002 WL 772695

[17] TENN. CODE ANN. § 27-8-101; *Bowling v Tennessee Board of Paroles*, 2002 WL 772695. In the case of the zoning board, planning commission, or local legislative bodies (exercising administrative functions), there is no other way to appeal at all so far as the author is aware.

[18] *Jones v. Williams*, 32 Tenn. 105 (1852).

[19] In my practice, I have never seen a petition for writ of certiorari dismissed for lack of this statement. Of course, if a motion is filed, and the petition is the first application for relief, it is certainly a simple matter to amend the petition to include the statement.

[20] TENN. CODE ANN. § 27-9-101.

In summary, the petition must:

* state the factual basis of the appeal;
* be notarized;
* the affiant must swear or affirm that the allegations are true to the best of his/her knowledge, information and belief;
* allege that this is the first application for the writ;
* allege that there is no other plain, speedy or adequate remedy; and
* allege that the petitioner is aggrieved by the decision of the administrative tribunal

(c) Attorneys' Fees

In addition, although certainly not required by the statutory scheme[21] it is definitely worthwhile for the petitioner to include[22] a request for attorneys fees pursuant to the Tennessee Equal Access to Justice Act.[23] The legislative intent of the chapter is to offer "small-business an opportunity for adequate representation in any administrative hearing involving the operation of such business and,

---

[21] It is certainly an ironic twist to this entire procedure that the name of the judicial device is the common law writ of certiorari and yet it is governed almost entirely by statutory provisions.

[22] The petitioner may be able to ask for fees and expenses at a later time after the decision of the court concerning the central issue in the case, that is, the legality of the decision of the zoning board. TENN. CODE ANN. § 29-37-104 (c)(2) seems to indicate that a later filed notice is appropriate. However, it may be that the statute limits recovery to fees and expenses incurred after the notice has been filed. Out of an abundance of precaution, it would seem natural to file the request for expenses and fees as a part of the request for relief in the petition for writ of certiorari itself.

[23] TENN. CODE ANN. § 29-37-101, et seq.

where necessary, in the resulting appeal process."[24] The term "small business" is defined in such a way as to include any neighborhood or homeowners' association which is not-for-profit, supported by contributions and does not employ more than 10 persons on a full-time basis.[25] The statute is fairly complicated and it is beyond the scope of this chapter to consider it in detail. However, it certainly provides a mechanism by which a petitioner[26] who is able to demonstrate that the decision of the local zoning board was "arbitrary and capricious"[27] is able to recoup his attorneys' fees up to a maximum of $40,000.[28] This is particularly apt because generally in order to reverse a zoning board under the standard of review associated with the common law writ of certiorari, the petitioner must prove in order to prevail at all that the actions of the zoning board were illegal or arbitrary and capricious. As a result, ordinarily, any petitioner who qualifies under the terms of the Tennessee Equal Access to Justice Act, and who can prevail on appeal from a decision of the local zoning board, will likely be entitled to fees

---

[24] TENN. CODE ANN. § 29-37-102.

[25] TENN. CODE ANN. § 29-37-103 (3) (B).

[26] The statutory scheme also has various restrictions on the size of the business which may utilize this statute in order to recover its attorneys fees and expenses. See TENN. CODE ANN. § 29-37-103(3)(A).

[27] TENN. CODE ANN. § 29-37-104 (b)(2) & (c)(2). Please note that this statutory scheme allows for recovery of attorneys fees against both state agencies and local governments. For example, TENN. CODE ANN. § 29-37-104 (b)(1) sets the standards by which a small business may obtain an award of attorneys fees and expenses against a state agency. Unfortunately, the statute is not drafted extraordinarily clearly and it takes some reading to decipher its meaning.

[28] TENN. CODE ANN. § 29-37-104 (a)(2)(A). In addition, the Tennessee Supreme Court ruled in 2006 that the $10,000 maximum was the cap on each stage of litigation, not for the entire case. The stages include the administrative hearing, the trial level, an appeal as of right, and an appeal by permission, according to the court. *State v Thompson*, 197 SW 3d 685 (Tenn. 2006).

and expenses. The "arbitrary and capricious" standard which was probably chosen by the Tennessee General Assembly because it is an extremely high standard and difficult to surmount, is not in the case of local zoning disputes because it is that very standard which you must ordinarily overcome anyway.

Finally, another means of accomplishing the same objective is to sue the local government under the terms of the Federal Civil Rights Act and its associated attorneys fees provision.[29] Again, a thorough discussion of the Civil Rights Act and its applicability to zoning disputes is certainly well beyond the scope of this chapter. However, assuming that there may be a claim based on the Civil Rights Act,[30] it is clear under Tennessee law, that a request for attorneys fees pursuant to the Civil Rights Act is appropriate as a part of the certiorari petition. In *Wimley v Rudolf,*[31] the Tennessee Supreme Court looked at a case that is very much the same as many zoning disputes. In that case, the petitioner in an administrative appeal joined a claim of a Civil Rights violation in an effort to obtain attorneys' fees. The underlying claim was the denial by the state of Tennessee of the petitioner's claim for Aid to Families with Dependent Children. The Chancery Court of Davidson County found for the petitioner and awarded the fees. The issue in that particular case was whether the § 1988 attorneys' fees could be

---

[29] 42 USC § § 1983 & 1988.

[30] The federal courts generally do not welcome litigation under the Civil Rights Act generated by local zoning disputes. For example, in *Pearson v City of Grand Blanc*, 961 F.2d 1211 (6th Cir. 1992), the Court of Appeals makes clear how difficult it is to successfully prosecute a local zoning dispute in the federal courts. There are however, certainly several exceptions and one possible exception involves a situation where the applicant would ordinarily be entitled to the permit but the administrative agency arbitrarily and capriciously denied it anyway. *Woodwind Estates v. Gretkowski*, 205 F. 3d 118 (3rd Cir. 2000) (a case in which a planning commission arbitrarily and capriciously denied approval of a subdivision plat). Often, that is a principal contention championed by the petitioner in zoning appeals cases.

[31] 931 S.W. 2d 513, 515 (Tenn. 1996).

requested in the same action as the administrative review, to which the Supreme Court replied in the affirmative. There is, therefore, no reason why a request for such fees could not also be made and granted in a zoning dispute, assuming that the Civil Rights Act provides for a recovery.[32]

One further observation on the applicability of the Civil Rights Act as a means of recovering attorneys fees in a zoning dispute is perhaps in order. It seems to easiest for a property owner seeking to develop his property but who is arbitrarily denied permission to do so to recover fees and expenses under the Act. It is perhaps more difficult to construct an argument that neighboring property owners should be entitled to their attorneys fees where the applicant was illegally granted the relief he sought. For example, in a situation where an applicant for a zoning variance is granted that relief by the zoning board notwithstanding the fact that the evidence presented by the applicant clearly falls short of the standard required by zoning law, it is more difficult to contemplate the surrounding property owners recovery of attorneys fees even though the grant of the zoning variance would appear to have been clearly arbitrary. The Civil Rights Act allows a recovery where a citizen has been deprived of some federally protected right. It is hard to construct a scenario under which the neighboring property owners have a federally protected property right which requires that their neighbor not be granted a variance where he is not entitled to one or a right which requires the local zoning board to make the proper decision and not act arbitrarily in granting a variance. If the zoning board affirmatively acts illegally, that may qualify. If the board refuses to allow the opponents to speak at the hearing; if a member discusses the case ex parte with the developer; these types of procedural due process

[32] For example, a developer who requests a conditional use permit but is denied for an invalid reason (such as opinion testimony of neighboring property owners) should arguably be entitled to recovery of fees and expenses pursuant to the act. On the other hand, it is clear under federal law that a zoning change which satisfies the rational basis test is certainly not a proper candidate

It is for that reason that where the neighborhood organization is the petitioner, appealing a decision of the local zoning board which granted permission to develop an adjacent property, that recovery of fees and expenses is perhaps best left to the state Equal Access to Justice Act.

(d) Statute of Limitations

Another area of extreme concern as regards the writ of certiorari is the statute of limitations. If the order is not appealed within that time frame, then it is final and no appeal may be taken. Furthermore, the board should have no further jurisdiction to reconsider the matter either. The case is closed. The petition for writ of certiorari must be filed within 60 days "from the entry of the order or judgment,"[33] in order to preserve an appeal.

The question then becomes when was the order or judgment entered? Based upon an older case,[34] it appeared that the proper date on which to focus was the date that a writing memorializing the decision of the zoning board was approved or filed. In that case, *Carter v. Nashville Board of Zoning Appeals*, the zoning board met on February 11, 1963 and decided to grant the application. However, the petition (filed on April 25, 1963) alleged that no order or judgment was entered at that time. Several months later, on April 24, 1963, the board did issue an order. The transcript of the proceedings before the board indicated that the order was entered on February 11, 1963, but the Supreme Court of Tennessee ruled that because the 60 day time frame runs from the entry of the order or judgment and not from the rendition of the judgment, that the trial court's decision dismissing the case, should be reversed so as to give the petitioner an opportunity to demonstrate that in fact the order was entered on April 24. The court held that the entry of the judgment is the ministerial act by which

[33] TENN. CODE ANN. § 27-9-102.

[34] *Carter v. Nashville Board of Zoning Appeals*, 377 S.W. 2d 914 (Tenn. 1964).

enduring evidence of the judicial act of rendition [of the judgment] is afforded."[35]

In another interesting case, bearing on the same issue, *Brannon v. County of Shelby*,[36] an application for a "special use permit"[37] was submitted to the Shelby County Board of Commissioners. On Dec. 7, 1992 the Board voted to approve the application, 9 to 2.[38] A zoning resolution was signed by the mayor of Shelby County on December 14, 1992.[39] Approximately one month later, on Jan. 25, 1993, the Board entertained a motion to reconsider approval of the application. The motion to reconsider failed by a vote above 5 to 5.[40] On February 23, 1993 a petition for writ of certiorari was filed in seeking to have the special use permit declared invalid on the basis that it was arbitrary and capricious and not supported by substantial evidence.[41] Obviously, if the entry of the order was completed on or before December 14, 1992, the petition for writ of certiorari filed on February 23, 1993 was over 60 days and too late. The petitioners argued that the motion to reconsider was a part of the administrative process and that by filing within 60

---

[35] Id. at 916. "To render judgment is to return or give judgment; and it can not be said, in our opinion, that the phrase, in any of its forms, includes the idea of making a written entry or record of a judgment." Id.

[36] 900 S.W. 2d 30 (Tenn. App. 1994).

[37] Generally speaking, a "special use permit" is ordinarily thought of as a conditional use permit (otherwise known as a special exception) and is normally considered by the Board of zoning appeals. Frequently, local zoning processes are somewhat different from jurisdiction to jurisdiction oftimes because local enabling legislation is different from the public enabling legislation.

[38] 900 S.W. 2d at 31.

[39] Id.

[40] Id at 32.

[41] Id.

days of that motion, they complied with the statutory requirement. The Tennessee Court of Appeals, relying upon a provision of the Shelby County Charter which indicated that any ordinance or resolution submitted to the mayor and signed by the mayor becomes effective on the date of signature. The court concluded that the motion to reconsider was a nullity[42] and that the petition for writ of certiorari was filed outside the time frame required by statute.

As a result of these cases, I have for years recommended that attorneys need not file a petition for writ of certiorari from a decision of the zoning board until after either an order has been filed by the board or the minutes approved at some subsequent meeting. Think about what this means for a moment. Most zoning boards act through their minutes[43] and as a result, after a meeting is over where an application has been, for example, approved, some member of the administrative staff writes an entry for each of the cases heard by the zoning board on that particular day. Most boards meet approximately once each month.

---

[42] There is an interesting question as to whether a local zoning board has the power to reconsider a decision it has previously made in light of this case and the general enabling legislation. As I have previously noted (see page 68), I believe that the most flexible and convenient answer to this question is to allow a zoning board, so long as it is within sixty days of the date of the original action on the application, to reconsider or rehear the case. By analogy, this would be similar to a court granting a motion to alter or amend within 30 days of the entry of its judgment. However, once 60 days have gone by, in my opinion to zoning board loses jurisdiction to consider any additional action on the case without the submission of another application and even then, there must be some change in the factual circumstances to justify any different result.

[43] "The official record of a governmental board's or commission's actions is customarily its minutes. The courts have repeatedly observed that boards and commissions, like the planning commission in this case, speak or act officially only through their minutes and records made at duly called meetings." *B & B Enterprises v. City of Lebanon*, 2004 WL 2916141, at *3 (Tenn. Ct. App. Dec. 16, 2004)

As a result, the minutes will not be approved and signed off on by the Secretary until the following meeting approximately one month later. It is only after that date, once the zoning board has approved the minutes as written up by the staff member, that the 60 day time frame within which to file a petition for writ of certiorari begins to run. As a result, if you represent a neighborhood group, your strategy might be to delay as long as possible before filing the petition for written certiorari. Most often, an applicant who is trying to develop his property wants to get the development under way as soon as possible. The longer that the neighbors can delay the project, the more likely the project may be defeated.

This advice has been called into serious question by the case of *Advanced Sales v. Wilson County.*[44] Judge Ben Cantrell wrote the opinion for the Tennessee Court of Appeals and reversed the advice that I formerly gave. In that case, the hearing before the zoning board took place on December 20, 1996. The petition for writ of certiorari was filed on February 19, 1997, some 61 days later. Although the petitioner alleged that the "order or judgment" of the board was not entered until January 24, 1997, when the minutes of the December 20, 1996 meeting were approved, Judge Cantrell found no support for this in the record.

> What does appear is the application dated December 3, 1996 reflecting a hearing date of December 20. Various notices to the public and to affected landowners appear in the record announcing a hearing date of December 20. The petition itself has a section on which to show the action of the Board. That section reflects that the petition was presented to the Board on December 20, 1996, and the entry, "Relief Denied," is circled on the form. It is true that the place on the form showing how the members voted is left blank, but there is no dispute that the Board voted unanimously to deny the petition. The form is signed by the Board secretary.

The Court distinguished in the *Carter* case holding that *Carter* simply indicated that under the factual circumstances presented there, the

[44] 1999 WL 336305 (Tenn. App. 1999).

order had not (or may not have) been entered at the time of the hearing before the zoning board. In the case before the Court of Appeals here however, the factual circumstances were different. Because the petition itself contained a section showing how the board had acted, that was sufficient to trigger the sixty day time frame within which the petition must be filed.

It is important therefore, for any attorney representing any party before any municipal administrative tribunal to assume that the administrative body will make some kind of a notation or entry at the time of the hearing which will be sufficient to trigger the sixty day window of opportunity for an appeal. The petition for writ of certiorari must therefore be filed within sixty days of the date of the hearing before the local administrative agency. If you wait beyond that time frame, you hesitate at your peril.

There is nothing to lose by filing within 60 days. Even if the local zoning board did not make some notation sufficient to trigger the sixty-day time limit, it would appear that nothing is lost by filing the petition for writ of certiorari too early. It might get dismissed (say, because to official decision has been made and entered), but it can be filed again at a later and more appropriate time if necessary.

Advanced Sales certainly presents no insurmountable difficulty to the practitioner. However, there is one area of concern. Zoning boards are not noted for their lengthy and detailed orders under any circumstances;[45] the net effect of the decision in *Advanced Sales* is to encourage a zoning board to simply make a quick note concerning its judgment and leave it at that. At the hearing on any zoning case, it is virtually impossible for the zoning board to record any logical reasons for the decision.[46] In *Advanced Sales* itself, all the zoning board did was

[45] Unfortunately, the contrary is more often the case.

[46] Think how difficult it is for a Judge to rule from the bench and contrast it with zoning board procedure. Although ruling from the bench is a practice encouraged by many, it is nevertheless difficult. And remember of course, that one of the attorneys then writes up the order and submits it at a later date for entry. Zoning boards would surely find

indicate that relief was denied. There was no reasoning; without some rationale given by the zoning board for its decision, judicial review becomes extremely difficult.[47] Furthermore, as we have discussed in Chapter One, it would seem possible that a zoning board could issue the perfunctory denial at the time of the hearing, and if a petition for writ of certiorari is filed, it could thereafter adopt minutes explaining its decision in great detail based on the fact that suit had been filed. This would seem to give the board a great advantage in defending itself against suit. The minute entry could even be drafted to refute the allegations of the cert petition. The zoning board already has a huge advantage in terms of the standard of judicial review; to increase that advantage seems ill-advised.

Of course, to the extent that the administrative body does not use a checklist as in *Advanced Sales*, the 60 days would run beginning on the date of the entry of the minutes. In *McMurray Drive Area Residents Association v Metro Planning Commission*, [48] a revision to a residential planned unit development was granted by the local planning commission on July 8, 2004. An administrative assistant took notes and later prepared the minutes of the meeting based on those notes. The minutes were adopted at the next meeting on July 22, 2004.

On September 17, 2004, the neighbors filed a petition for writ of certiorari, but the petition was dismissed on motion under the *Advanced Sales* doctrine, the lower court holding that the petition should have been filed by September 7 (60 days after the hearing where the decision was made and noted by the administrative assistant).

---

this a difficult proposition under the best of circumstances.

[47] *Weaver v Knox County Board of Zoning Appeals*, 122 SW 3d 781, 785 (Tenn. Ct. App. 2003).

[48] 2006 WL 1026428 (Tenn.Ct.App., April 18, 2006). This is an appeal from a planning commission.

On appeal, the decision was reversed. The Court first noted that "something more" is needed to elevate a vote to a entered decision:[49]

> The case law beginning with the Supreme Court's decision in *Carter* certainly shows that something more than simply a vote taking place is required before a judgment or order will be considered as having been entered pursuant to TENN.CODE ANN. § 27-9-102. In *Brannon* the Board's judgment was entered when the special use permit was signed by the mayor, and in *Advanced Sales* the Board's judgment was entered when the petition was marked 'Relief Denied' and signed by the Board Secretary. It is this "something more" which elevates a judgment from one which has simply been rendered, to one that also has been entered. It is this 'something more' which is the 'enduring evidence of the judicial act of rendition of judgment ....' Carter, 377 S.W.2d at 916.

The appellees argued that the notes were "something more" but[50]

> the decision by the Tennessee Supreme Court in *Carter* . . . clearly establishes that "[t]he 'entry' of judgment is the ministerial act by which enduring evidence of the judicial act of rendition of judgment is afforded." Ms. Brooks' notes can hardly be said to be "enduring" as they were not even present in the record. Furthermore, in *Advanced Sales*, and *Brannon*, the Tennessee Court of Appeals found that the existence of an authoritative signature on a paper writing, containing a recordation of the action taken was indicative of a ministerial act sufficient to trigger the sixty-day time limitation. Here, the record is void of any

---

[49] *Grigsby v City of Plainview*, 2005 WL 1330845.

[50] *McMurray Drive Area Homeowners Ass'n v. Metropolitan Government of Nashville and Davidson County,* 2006 WL 1026428, 5 (Tenn.Ct.App.,2006)(citations omitted).

> evidence indicating a signature on Ms. Brooks' notes by any member of the Planning Commission or anyone else.

The court then clearly distinguished the officially adopted minutes of the Planning Commission:[51]

> Unlike Ms. Brooks' notes, the typed official minutes from the July 8, 2004, were signed by both the Chairman and the Secretary of the Planning Commission. The minutes also indicated the resolution number for the revision and the specific conditions of the approval. These minutes were not presented to nor approved by the Planning Commission ***until the July 22, 2004, meeting***. The Court finds that these official typed minutes, signed by the Planning Commission Chairman, contain the "something more" which elevate the decision from a mere rendition of judgment to an entry of judgment, and create the "enduring evidence of the judicial act of rendition of judgment" contemplated in the Carter decision.

At its heart, this case presents an argument that a set of contemporaneous notes recording the votes taken by the planning commission is an "entered" decision of the body. Surely, the court correctly rejected this contention in favor of the officially approved minutes, properly prepared, voted on by the commission, and signed by the chair. Remember, however, that it doesn't take much of a "something more" to change the result and hence the benefit of filing within 60 days of the public meeting where the vote is taken (and the decision rendered): the attorney doesn't have to worry about that "something more."

Ultimately, the question in *Advanced Sales* is whether a brief notation "relief is denied" is an order or judgment within the meaning of the statute. As of now, we know that it is, and it is surely important to file the petition for writ of certiorari within sixty days of the actual hearing to avoid being surprised by such a document. But for my part, it certainly would be nice to get a reasonably thought out order from the

---

[51] Id.

zoning board to form the basis for later judicial review. If all the zoning board has to do is circle the word "denied" or mark a checkbox indicating that the application has been granted (or denied), on appeal it will be extraordinarily difficult to understand the reasoning of the zoning board and ultimately this will lead to more delay in the process. Certainly, most judges will wind up throwing a case like *Advanced Sales* back to the zoning board and requiring that it supply the reasons for its action. It would seem preferable to require that the zoning board do that prior to the time that the appeal is taken, if possible.

(e) Parties to the Litigation

The petition for writ of certiorari must name the (1) zoning board (or other Board or commission) and (2) "such other parties of record, if such, as were involved in the hearing before the board or commission, and who do not join as petitioners."[52] In years gone by, the practice was to name the individuals who comprised the board of zoning appeals, I believe on the theory that the zoning board was not a suable entity. Rather than suing the individuals, my approach usually is to name the city or county government, "acting by and through its board of zoning appeals." In this way, if there is a question about the susceptibility of the zoning board to suit, clearly the city or county government is suable and this method of bringing the respondent before the court seems very reasonable. I don't know of any case in any event dismissing a petition for failure to use the proper name of the defending board.

The second set of potential respondents, "such other parties of record," presents the attorney for the petitioner with a distinct problem in many cases. It is not unusual in any zoning case before a zoning board to represent a property owner against a significant number of surrounding neighbors. Often, some of the neighbors will have banded together in a neighborhood association which may be incorporated. The attorney for the petitioner must decide whether to name the neighborhood association, and/or some or all of the individual neighbors, as respondents. Strategically, of course, most often the attorney for the petitioner does not want anymore respondents allied against him then

[52] TENN. CODE ANN. § 27-9-104.

is absolutely necessary. In addition, many neighbors who appear before a local zoning board have no idea that by merely appearing and voicing opposition to a particular project they may put themselves in harm's way with regard to potential litigation (even though no damages are sought by the petitioner, most people are not happy to be named in a lawsuit). While it is certainly true that becoming a respondent in a case brought under the common law writ of certiorari is not an onerous obligation; in fact, there is no obligation that any respondent actually file an answer in response to the petition. Tenn. Code Ann. § 27-9-110 provides that: "all defendants named in such petition, desiring to make defense, shall do so by answer . . ." Therefore, if a neighboring property owner whose only connection to the process was the fact that he or she appeared in opposition to the application before the zoning board winds up as a respondent in the litigation, he or she can, by the simple expedient of failing to answer, avoid any further involvement in the litigation. It would seem of course that this would imply that the neighbor has no further opposition to the proposal and that may be in fact incorrect. However, by opting not to answer the petition, any neighboring property owner would thereby relieve him or herself from further participation in the litigation and any financial obligations (his attorneys' fees, and costs) which might thereby otherwise attach.

Another concern which the attorney for the petitioner frequently has is the possibility that a respondent might sue for malicious prosecution. Practically, I have seen this happen only once, but if one of the named respondents felt that he or she was improperly included in the litigation, there might be grounds for a malicious prosecution lawsuit.

On the other hand, the statute seems to require that all other parties of record be named. The real question then is what does the term "of record" mean within the context of the statute. Fortunately, we do have some guidance in this area.

One case which arguably may provide some guidance comes out of the Tennessee Administrative Procedures Act, Tenn. Code Ann. § 4-5-101 et seq. Section 322 (b) provides for judicial review by filing a petition for review and serving copies of the petition upon the administrative agency and "all parties of record." In *HRA, Inc. v Tennessee Department of Commerce and Insurance*,[53] the Tennessee Court of Appeals held that the failure of the petitioner to serve a party who was instrumental in the decision-making process barred the application for judicial review. While this case has been overruled subsequently by the Tennessee Supreme Court,[54] based upon the language of the statute which is specifically applicable to the State Administrative Procedures Act, the *HRA* case may nevertheless be good precedent for cases brought under the writ of certiorari.

The *HRA* case is probably most similar to a zoning appeals case where a neighbor files the petition for certiorari and neglects to name the property owner who filed the application before the zoning board itself. For example, if the WatchMeRun Day Care Center files and application for and obtains a conditional use permit before the Metropolitan Board of Zoning Appeals, and a neighboring property owner files and a petition for writ of certiorari naming the zoning Board but omitting the WatchMeRun Day Care Center, the statute (and *HRA*) presumably would require dismissal.[55] That much appears reasonably certain. However, in a case brought by WatchMeRun Day Care Center, where its application for a conditional use permit was denied by the zoning board, it is not as clear that every neighboring property owner who opposed (and how about neighboring property owners who may have supported) the application must be made a respondent, and served with process. As a rule of thumb, my practice has been to name as respondents the principal opponents including any neighborhood association, but not to name everyone who spoke against the application at the hearing before the zoning board.

Fortunately, there is another savings grace in the procedure. TENN. CODE ANN. § 27-9-110 (b) provides that "Any other person who may be affected by the decision to be made by such court may, upon leave given, intervene and file such an answer in the cause." As a

---

[53] 914 S.W. 2d 512 (Tenn. App. 1995).

[54] *Jaco v. Tennessee Department of Health*, 950 S.W. 2d 350 (Tenn. 1997).

[55] TENN. CODE ANN. § 27-9-104.

result, it would seem that the failure to name a party "of record" is reasonably easily corrected by a judicial policy of liberally granting leave permitting intervention by parties who may have not been included originally in the litigation. This is not altogether a satisfactory answer to the problem. Certainly, a party who has been omitted might simply lobby one of the parties who was included to seek a dismissal because of the failure of the petitioner to include the omitted party. However, this approach does seem a reasonable compromise between suing every neighboring property owner who appears before the zoning board and not naming anyone. As a practical matter, a number of cases involve neighboring property owners who move for leave to intervene and generally it has been my practice to agree to such motions. Most likely, the trial court will grant the motion in any event. Clearly, if I knew on the front end that those neighbors desired to be included in the case, I would have named them as respondents in any event.

In 2001, the Tennessee Court of Appeals took a little of the guesswork out of this problem, at least with regard to neighbors' suits appealing a decision. In *Levy v. Williamson County Board of Zoning Appeals*,[56] a case where two neighbors fought over the location of a storage shed and a swimming pool. Mr. Levy objected to the location of a storage shed and a variance for a swimming pool, apparently as a part of an on-going dispute with Mr. Franks, his next-door neighbor. Levy filed a petition for a common law writ. Levy however did not name the Franks as respondents in the lawsuit; he named only the county board of zoning appeals.[57] The county board moved to dismiss on the grounds that the applicant had not been named. Mr. Levy then moved to amend the petition, to add the applicant as a respondent.

---

[56] 2001 WL 1141351 (Tenn. Ct. App. September 27, 2001).

[57] This is the worst case scenario: here, a neighbor doesn't name the property owner requesting development approval. In this type of situation, there seems to be no reason not to name the party who requested the zoning relief. It is far more difficult to make the determination if you are the party making the application and a large number of neighboring property owners show up. Do you sue one? Do you sue them all? This case implies that you can make a reasonable judgement and the others, if they wish to join, can do so.

The trial court dismissed the petition, characterizing the requirements of TENN. CODE ANN. § 27-9-104 as jurisdictional.[58]

The Court of Appeals reversed. Analogizing to both appellate court procedure and to the Administrative Procedures Act, TENN. CODE ANN. § 4-5-322, the court ruled that a timely filed petition for writ of certiorari naming a local board as a defendant is sufficient to invoke the court's jurisdiction and that a failure to name one of the parties to the proceeding before the local board could be cured by a later amendment. The court did characterize the applicant (Mr. Franks) as a necessary party and indicated that he should have been named in the original petition. The court found no prejudice to Mr. Frank or the board by allowing the amendment.

This case goes a long way then to reassuring the lawyer for the petitioner that a failure to name a party, even a necessary party, will not result in the case being tossed out of court, at least in the absence of some showing of prejudice. Granted, when a neighbor sues the zoning board arising out of an application concerning a nearby property, the petition should name the applicant before the zoning board as a respondent. But even that omission is not fatal under this case. From my perspective this is an eminently reasonable result; these cases should not be decided by procedural niceties; the merits should be addressed and the case should rise or fall on the real issues.

(f) Standing[59]

The law requires that any time a plaintiff or petitioner is bringing suit against another party that there be some reasonably close connection between the petitioner's position or situation and the

---

[58] This is what every land use attorney worried about before the decision in this case: the failure to name a party might wind up getting the case dismissed. And as we have seen with regard to several of the other jurisdictional prerequisites, the concern was definitely not unfounded.

[59] Standing issues were also discussed in Chapter One, at page 8.

concern he is expressing in the lawsuit. In land use planning law, generally the problem is that a petitioner may live or own property so far away from the area where the proposed land use development is located as to make his or her complaints unjustifiable or sufficiently insignificant that the courts will not entertain them. This is normally referred to as a lack of standing. In short, the petitioner must have a legally recognized interest exceeding the interest in the community shared in common with all other citizens.

Zoning appeals especially can bring this problem to the forefront very quickly. Ordinarily, most zoning boards do not inquire other than in the most general ways about the relationship of a person speaking in favor or in opposition to any particular request pending on its agenda. Certainly, many boards ask that each speaker identify him or herself, and specifically state an address. Practically however within my experience, I have never seen any citizen who has asked to speak at such a hearing be denied the opportunity to speak based on the fact that he or she lives too far away from the property which is the subject of the application.

On appeal however, the standards may be more discerning. The petitioner may be challenged by either the zoning board itself or any other defendant or respondent by way of a motion to dismiss. Technically, the petitioner should be able to demonstrate both that he has a close connection to the property which is the subject of the litigation as well as some type of special damage which might accrue to him or her as a result of the action of the administrative body. Special damage might include a decrease in the value of the property, an increase in noise or traffic or any other substantial annoyance, inconvenience, discomfort, harm, or injury to the plaintiff, to plaintiff's personal comfort or to the plaintiff's free use, possession or occupation of the property.

My experience in practice is that the requirement of special damage is usually less significant especially if the petitioner owns or occupies property immediately adjacent to or in close proximity to the property in dispute. To put it another way, an adjacent neighbor rarely has to demonstrate significant special damage; most courts will assume special damage arising out of a change in the land use regulations or the manner in which those regulations are applied to a particular piece of property.

A good case in point is *Citizens for Collierville v. Collierville.*[60] In this case, a nonprofit corporation sued the town and a number of its officials both for damages and injunctive relief based on the approval of a planned development for a hospital and medical center.[61] Before the court reached the substantive issues under the writ of certiorari, it considered whether the nonprofit corporation lacked standing.[62] The court concluded that a nonprofit corporation, even in the absence of any injury to its self, may have standing solely as a representative of its members.[63] The court pointed out that representational standing does not eliminate the constitutional requirement that one or more of the organization's members must suffer an immediate or threatened injury as a result of the challenged action. The court concluded that many members of the nonprofit organization did have standing to sue based upon their status as adjacent property owners. The court pointed out that many of the members of the nonprofit corporation owned single-family residences within 2000 feet of the proposed development. As a result, the court concluded that the nonprofit corporation had standing to sue.[64]

---

[60] 977 S.W. 2d 321 (Tenn. App. 1998).

[61] The court appears to have treated the sued for damages as a request for judicial review of the planned development pursuant to the common law writ of certiorari. 977 S.W. 2d at 323.

[62] Technically, the court appears to have considered this matter of standing under TENN. CODE ANN. § 13-7-208. Whether the issue is presented pursuant to that statutory proviso (which generally allows for the enforcement of zoning ordinances) or under the terms of a common law writ of certiorari seeking judicial review, the legal issues would appear to be the same or at least very closely related.

[63] *Collierville*, 977 S.W. 2d at 323.

[64] Id.

In a case tried approximately 20 years ago, a department of the local government, a nonprofit corporation interested in historical preservation, as well as a number of private citizens opposed the grant of a variance to allow the construction of a high-rise office building with a parking garage on second Avenue in downtown Nashville.[65] The difficulty was that insofar as we could ascertain, none of the officials who made up the Metropolitan Historical Commission and none of the members of the nonprofit corporation (Historic Nashville, Inc.) owned property in the area of the proposed development. Members of both organizations conducted a search to try to locate someone who owned property in the immediate vicinity and ultimately, after several abortive attempts, a proper petitioner was found. A number of the possible parties were interested in pursuing the litigation until they realized that there was some possibility even if a small one, that a lawsuit could be filed back against them presumably for malicious prosecution.

In practice, I always try to get a property owner who owns property within approximately one-quarter to one-half mile of the location of the subject property. This is not based upon any case law[66] but is just a rule of thumb which I have used for many years. A little further out probably would not be any real harm, but certainly the closer the better. In addition, given a choice, and I would prefer to have a property owner as opposed to a lessee or some other occupier of the premises. Sometimes, you have very little choice about the parties; however, it is possible to structure the way the parties are presented to the court, the attorney certainly wants a petitioner who has a significant interest in a property which is as close as possible to the property which

---

[65] *Metropolitan Historical Commission v. Colony Associates Joint Venture*,1988 WL 109234 (Tenn. App. 1988).

[66] The court in the *Collierville* case seemed to hold that the fact that some members of the nonprofit corporation lived within 2000 feet (about 4/10ths of a mile away) of the subject property gave both the individuals and the corporation standing. Perhaps that distance is a better indication of how close a neighbor must reside in order to have standing without showing some specific vestige of injury. 977 S.W. 2d at 323. Suppose that the neighbor only owns or leases the property but does not live there, does that effect the standing issues? Presumably not.

is the subject of the litigation. The owner or occupier of the property next door is naturally the best of all worlds.

Another question which comes up from time to time in this area of standing is whether a petitioner must have attended the public hearing before the zoning board in order to qualify as a proper party plaintiff. There are now a couple of cases here in Tennessee, but they seem to conflict. In *McRae v Knox County*,[67] the Court of Appeals held that the mere failure of the petitioners to appear at the zoning board hearing and present proof was not fatal to the case.[68] Frankly, how would the court or anyone else know for sure if the petitioners were at the hearing?[69] Do the petitioners have to testify (speak at the hearing)? Suppose the neighbors were there and only held up their hands as opposed to the project? Why need they do anything more? Unless there is a video recording, there will likely be no way for the developer or the zoning board to dispute an allegation that they were present at the hearing (assuming that there were a number of opponents otherwise present).[70]

---

[67] 2004 WL 1056669 (Tenn. Ct. App. May 7, 2004) (perm. app. den. November 15, 2004).

[68] The Court in that case seemed to believe that the standing issue could be addressed in the trial court by the introduction of additional proof. Because of the *Hoover* decision, that seems unlikely

[69] Sometimes, boards have a sign-in sheet, but often they do not. Even if there is a sign-in procedure, does a neighbor have to sign in? Some people may feel it an invasion of privacy to require such information. Further, now many zoning hearings are broadcast live on television, and the neighbor could watch from home and/or submit email or letters in opposition. Attendance at the hearing seems unnecessary.

[70] An attorney representing the entire group of neighbors would likely want to select as representatives neighbors who were there and who did speak. But suppose an elderly couple choose not to speak, did raise their hands in opposition, and later after the hearing decided they wanted to appeal on their own. Is there any reason that they should not be permitted to do so? Seems to me that assuming they lived reasonably

However, in *City of Brentwood v Metro Board of Zoning Appeals*, the Court of Appeals held to the contrary. " . . . [the landowners] do not have standing to join [in the] petition because they were not parties to the original hearing before the Board of Zoning Appeals."[71] The Court went on to say that the landowners could petition to intervene in the proceedings as "affected parties" under TENN. CODE ANN. § 27-9-110(b). In making such a motion, the moving parties would need to demonstrate standing. I have never seen an evidentiary issue made when another group of landowners attempts to intervene, but it may be necessary and it could get a little difficult. The moving parties would likely need expert proof of the impact of the future project. Once again, lay witnesses likely cannot testify to such concerns.

I have never seen this raised and believe that most judges would not be very concerned by the fact that the petitioner did not attend the public hearing. There are just too many reasons for missing a public hearing which have nothing whatsoever to do with the position of the petitioner with regard to the merits of the application. As a result, I would suggest that a motion to dismiss for lack of standing based upon the fact that the petitioner did not attend or speak at the public hearing should not be granted.

The Brentwood case also addressed waiver in another way. The issue was whether there was any proof of standing on the part of the neighbors; the defense was that the applicant failed to object to a possible lack of standing during the zoning board hearing and the court agreed.

> Parties to administrative proceedings must raise all objections to procedural errors during the hearing in order to preserve these questions for later appellate review. Thus, to raise the issue of [petitioner's] standing to file the petition for common-law writ of certiorari, [respondent] must have argued to the Board that [petitioner] did not

---

close to the project, that they should be allowed to appeal.

[71] 149 S.W.3d 49, 60 (Tenn. Ct. App. 2004).

> have standing to request the Board to review the zoning administrator's decision.[72]

Therefore, a developer should in all cases, include in the letter brief or other informational materials[73], some request that any neighbors who testify be required to demonstrate standing. It may be difficult to remember in the heat of the moment, but by including the request in the letter (or other materials) presented to the board, the developer may avoid waiving the defense.

How do these issues come up procedurally? Should the petitioner (a neighbor or neighborhood organization) allege special damage in the petition for writ of certiorari? Because of the waiver argument discussed above, if the issue was not brought up at the Board of Zoning Appeals by the developer, then it is probably waived. Even if it is not, generally, the neighbor will have given his/her address at the time of the zoning board hearing and using the address, the petitioner should be able to demonstrate that s/he lives in close proximity to the project. That alone is usually enough.

If the petitioner alleges more in the petition by way of raising standing issues, I fear that s/he may be obligated to prove those. Since new evidence is not usually allowed in a common law writ proceeding, unless standing was demonstrated before the zoning board, there may not be a way to demonstrate such standing after the appeal is filed. In a sense, the neighbor petitioner has alleged too much. Usually, I simply allege the address of my client and that it is in the immediate vicinity of the project. I fear that by alleging that the project will decrease property values or increase traffic that my client may have to prove that.[74] Notice that the lay witness cannot prove such matters, it takes

---

[72] *City of Brentwood v Metro Board of Zoning Appeals*, 149 S.W.3d 49, 60 (Tenn. Ct. App. 2004)

[73] A slide inserted into a PowerPoint presentation may be particularly effective.

[74] The court could order evidence on the sole issue of standing. The petitioner might then have trouble proving special damage.

an expert witness to prove that in the future, the project, once built, will have those effects. That's why my lay client cannot testify as to those effects: they will take place in the future and therefore, s/he has not witnessed the harm being suggested. I believe it is far better to keep the allegations of the petition very short and succinct, relying on the waiver doctrine to protect against dismissal based on standing.

In an interesting case from Indiana, the Supreme Court there concluded differently.[75] The zoning board granted a special exception for a confined animal feeding operation (CAFO), 2000 cows on 27 acres. A neighbor who lived about 1/3 of a mile from the farm appealed under a writ of certiorari; the farmer moved to dismiss the appeal for lack of standing. The trial court ordered an evidentiary hearing on the standing issue, and ultimately concluded that the petitioner had failed to demonstrate standing and dismissed the petition.

The Court of Appeals reversed on procedural grounds and the case was accepted for review by the Indiana Supreme Court. The definition of standing under Indiana law may be more restrictive than here in Tennessee ("the petitioner's resulting injury must be pecuniary in nature") but the Supreme Court considered that the trial court's evidentiary hearing was an appropriate method of determining standing. The evidence was conflicting at the hearing but the trial court concluded that the petitioner had not carried her burden of proof that the farm would significantly impair the value of her home and the Supreme Court upheld the trial court's decision.

In Tennessee, this process would seem misplaced. The zoning board is to make these factual judgments; to the extent that a trial court holds a separate evidentiary hearing it is considering new proof that the zoning board did not have before it and is substituting its judgment for that of the zoning board, a result forbidden by Tennessee law of the common law writ. Thus, under Tennessee law, the result in *City of*

---

[75] *Thomas v Blackford County BZA*, June 16, 2009 (Indiana Supreme Court).

Brentwood seems appropriate: unless raised at the zoning board, the standing issues are waived.[76]

However, before we assume that is true in all cases, some reality should be considered: if the petitioner lives several miles away, the failure of the defending party below to object or raise the standing issue may not be viewed as a waiver. In other words, the lack of a discussion about standing at the zoning board, may not be waiver if the petitioner in the lawsuit lives a considerable distance away from the project. Thus, the petitioner should live or own property fairly close (within 2000 feet as in Collierville seems a safe bet) to the project. If s/he does not, the standing issue may arise, notwithstanding *City of Brentwood.* Quite frankly, most courts will not want to review a case where the petitioner lives far away, even if the issue was not raised below.

On the whole, my feeling is that courts should be lenient about standing issues where the petitioner lives nearby (within 2000 feet or so), requiring very little to accept the fact that the new use of the property may have an impact on the neighbors. On the other hand, if the petitioner lives two miles away, the court should require something more to demonstrate standing, some real injury threatened to the land owner.[77]

---

[76] *City of Brentwood v Metro Board of Zoning Appeals*, 149 S.W.3d 49, 60 (Tenn. Ct. App. 2004).

[77] *Roten v City of Spring Hill*, 2009 WL 2632778 (Tenn. Ct. App., August 26, 2009) involves a planning commission but the court adopts just such a lenient posture concerning standing. "Petitioners reside in the 'immediate vicinity' of the project and participated in the Planning Commission's public hearings regarding the project's site development plan approval. Given their proximity to the project as well as the scale of the project and its economic and environmental impact on the neighboring area, Petitioners have a special interest in the project's development that is not common to the public generally."

(g) Prevents Further Proceedings Below

Finally, it is important to note that once the certiorari petition is granted, there should be no further proceedings in the administrative forum (the zoning board) below.[78] The board, once the certiorari petition has been granted, no longer has any jurisdiction over the case and should cease any further proceedings until the judicial proceedings are concluded.[79] This makes perfect sense: "proceeding simultaneously in both the administrative and judicial forums on the same matter is fraught with the dangers of inconsistency and duplication of effort."[80] Once the cert has been issued, the zoning board should not proceed on any other facet of the matter.

2. Writ of Certiorari

The writ of certiorari is normally issued by the trial court clerk requiring that the administrative tribunal return to that office a true and complete copy of the record of the proceedings before it. There is no requirement in the statute with regard to the time frame within which the administrative tribunal must make a return.[81] It is a good idea therefore to require as a part of the writ itself that the return be made within some specified time period, perhaps 30 or 60 days. In that

---

[78] *Stone Man v Rutherford County Regional Planning Commission*, 1985 Tenn. App. Lexis 2607.

[79] Id.

[80] Id.

[81] TENN. CODE ANN. § 27-9-109 requires that "immediately upon the grant of a writ, the Board or commission show cause to be made, certified and forwarded to such court a complete transcript of the proceedings in the cause, containing also all the proof submitted before the Board or commission." The meaning of this word "immediately" in the context of judicial proceedings is sometimes hard to ascertain. In addition, local zoning disputes are most likely not the most pressing matters that any judge has before him or her.

way, if the return is not made within the specified time, the petitioner can move the court for some type of relief, perhaps a reversal of the decision based simply upon the failure of the zoning board to respond to the order of the court, but certainly an order giving a deadline for the record which, if not met, will result in dismissal. More frequently what happens is that the attorney for the zoning board requests an extension which is usually agreed to by the attorney for the petitioner. My normal practice is to liberally grant such requests from opposing counsel except if my client is in a tremendous time crunch. In that case, I try to let opposing counsel know that I may have trouble agreeing to time extensions, as a courtesy. Usually that makes it easier for everyone.

The reason for specifying that time frame however is because in some cases I have seen six months, 12 months, and even up to two years go by before return has been made in response to the writ of certiorari. Certainly, neither side is pursuing the case in a timely manner; however, if you do represent the petitioner, and there is no specified time frame for a return of the record, it makes it more difficult to move the court for relief. By placing a specific time period in the writ of certiorari itself, the attorney for the petitioner retains control of the manner in which the administrative record is produced.

It is also important to specify as precisely as possible what elements of the record you believe are necessary for appropriate judicial review. Even today, some zoning boards have two different phases of their proceedings, public hearings, and executive session. Of course, pursuant to the Tennessee Open Public Meetings Act[82] all parts of the hearing are open to the public. However, sometimes the zoning board believes that the deliberations in executive session, although open in public hearing, should not be made a part of the record submitted to the trial court. Some zoning boards believe that if you specify all of the proceedings relating to a certain case number, that all that needs to be transcribed are the proceedings where the board took final action and as a result omit the discussions of the application at the prior to meetings. Precision in the drafting of the writ of certiorari is highly desirable. An example of a writ is attached at the end of this chapter.

---

[82] TENN. CODE ANN. § 8-44-101 et seq.

Another reason to specify the contents of the records precisely is that there may have been several hearings on the same or related issues over a period of serval months or more. The board may prepare and submit only the last of those hearings, and it may be important to have all the material available for the court to review. A specific request for the hearings by date may eliminate any difficulty on such issues.

In some case I have had particular documents which were of such importance that I have specified those documents by name and date in the writ of certiorari. For example, in *Cost v City of Lebanon*,[83] I specifically requested an engineering letter I thought critical to the case. Most likely the letter would've been included anyway (and of course the attorney for the petitioner should always check once the record is filed) but in that case the record was very long, and the letter very short. The specific request was I thought an easy way to make sure that the document was included. Another common element to specify in the record is the zoning ordinance itself, although I believe the board should include this as a matter of course.

3. Fiat

This is simply an order of the court directing the clerk to issue the writ of certiorari. Typically, the clerical procedure in the court clerk's office is that the Chancellor or Judge reviews the petition for writ of certiorari, signs the fiat, and the clerk issues in the writ of certiorari pursuant to the judicial fiat. The clerk is also required to send by registered return-receipt mail, a notice of the filing of the petition and a certified copy of the petition. The clerk must also send a similar notice to the last known address of each party named as a defendant (respondent).[84]

---

[83] 2009 WL 856643 (Tenn. Ct. App., March 31, 09). This is an appeal from a city council decision regarding a planned unit development, and not a cert petition from a zoning board decision but the principle is the same.

[84] TENN. CODE ANN. § 27-9-107. The failure of the clerk to properly send notice pursuant to this statutory provision evidently does not affect the filing date of the petition for writ of certiorari. *Washshukru Al-*

4. Bond

The statute does require a cost bond for costs.[85] This is an administrative requirement not significant in the overall evaluation of the procedure. Distinguish this requirement from the bond for the issuance for a writ of supercedeas, which can be significant.

5. Writ of Supersedeas

The writ of supersedeas is an injunctive companion to the writ of certiorari. In essence, the cert petition complains of some administrative error, and the supersedeas requests that no change in the status of things take place until after the court has had an opportunity to review the legality of the decision. Depending upon the size of the project and hence the amount of any bond which might be required, requesting supersedeas may be a good strategy. On the other hand, if a group of neighbors asks for judicial review of a permit given to a Wal-Mart SuperCenter, the bond is likely to be so much that only Bill Gates could afford it. In that kind of situation, it is generally better to omit any request for supersedeas and bank on the fact that the developer may not want to risk construction even if the respondent's assessment of risk is very low.[86] If the developer does begin construction but loses the case,

---

Jabbar A'La v. Tennessee Department of Corrections, 914 S.W. 2d 914 (Tenn. App. 1995).

[85] TENN. CODE ANN. § 27-9-105.

[86] In fact, I have had a number of large developer clients simply refuse to proceed even though my evaluation of our chances of success were very high, in the 95 to 98% range. If the construction is going to involve millions of dollars, even if there is only a 2% chance of loss, it's too high. It is very rare that those kinds of numbers can be used in any kind of litigation and I am always surprised when my client decides not to proceed in the face of that type of risk. However, almost never will the developer of a large project proceed in the fact of virtually any kind of risk.

presumably any improvement already installed would have to be removed.

TENN. CODE ANN. § 27-9-106(a) provides:

> If the order or judgment rendered by such board or commission made the basis of the petition for certiorari shall make any material change in the status of any matter determined therein, the petitioner may, upon reasonable notice to the board or commission and other material defendants, apply to the chancellor, at the time of filing such petition, for a supersedeas, and the chancellor, in the chancellor's discretion, may grant a writ of supersedeas to stay the putting into effect of such order or judgment or any part thereof.

Clearly, the decision of the board or commission must have authorized a material change in the status of the property at issue. This provision allows the petitioner to request that the Chancellor issue a supersedeas or stay, so that during the pendency of the litigation, no construction can take place. If the neighbors sue over an approval of a variance for example, they would need to name the developer or property owner as well as the zoning board as respondents. Generally speaking, the Chancellor will usually issue a stay (a temporary restraining order under the terms of the Tennessee Rules of Civil Procedure[87]) and then set the request for a hearing after notice to the zoning board and other respondents.

The statute clearly leaves the decision about the issuance of a supersedeas to the discretion of the judge, but the law should I submit be similar to the analogous area of preliminary injunctions. The legal tests in that area have evolved over the years so that there is now a reasonably uniform approach to the issuance of such an injunction.

---

[87] Rule 65 of the Tennessee Rules of Civil Procedure.

Borrowing heavily from federal case law, there is a four part test which the court should consider in deciding whether to issue the supersedeas.[88]

First, if the supersedeas is issued, what will be the harm to the property owner?

Second, if the supersedeas is not issued, what will be the harm to the neighbors?

Third, what is the probability of success on the merits of the case?

And finally, what is in the best public interest?[89]

Generally speaking, with regard to the first issue, if the supersedeas is issued, the property owner may stand to lose significant sums of money as a result of the delay. There is then the possibility of significant harm to the property owner. The second issue also suggests the possibility of significant harm: if the supersedeas is not issued, and the construction project is begun, and then later is declared illegal for whatever reason, the neighbors will have had to live and suffer with the project for quite some time. Most courts would probably believe that the harm in factor 1 more egregious than the harm in factor 2, but nevertheless, these two factors standing alone do not generally suggest a clear cut answer to the question of a stay.

The last two issues are more helpful. The third factor is the probability of success on the merits of the case; that is, who will win? I would suggest that in most zoning cases, particularly those brought under the writ of certiorari, the probability of success is not hard to

---

[88] Frankly, while this standard has not been routinely applied in Tennessee, it is a quick and simple means of assisting the court in evaluating the request.

[89] This test has been employed many times over the years in the federal courts. *Southwest Williamson County Community Association v. Slater*, 243 F. 3d 270 (6th Cir. 2001); *Nightclubs, Inc. v. City of Paducah*, 202 F. 3d 884 (6th Cir. 2000).

determine.[90] If the developer is probably going to win, then there is very little reason to grant the stay. On the other hand, if the neighbors are probably going to win, then the stay should be granted.

In many other kinds of cases, the issue of the public interest is almost a throw-away: it is too difficult to determine the public interest and as a result, the court cannot easily interpret the factor. However, of course, many, if not most issues before a local zoning board require that the board consider the public interest at least in some oblique way: as a result, it is fair to say that if the board has, let's say, granted a variance, it has determined that the variance "may be granted without substantial detriment to the public good."[91] Frequently, zoning boards become even more enthused and conclude that a particular project is beneficial to the public good. Under those circumstances, it is not hard for a reviewing court to conclude that the project is in the public interest as found by the local zoning officials. Suppose for a moment that the court has concluded that the merits of the case are most likely with the neighbors, but that the project is definitely in the public interest: what result? Of course, different judges will view that issue differently, but I would suggest that most courts would issue the stay. If the neighbors will win, the fact that the public will benefit overall from the project is really not all that important.

TENN. CODE ANN. § 27-9-106(b) provides:

> No such supersedeas shall be granted until a good and sufficient bond, in an amount to be fixed and approved by the chancellor, shall have been given by the petitioner, conditioned to indemnify the defendants named in the petition from any injury that may result by reason of the granting of such supersedeas.

---

[90] Hopefully, our discussions in the previous chapters have demonstrated some ability to predict the ultimate outcome of zoning cases decided under the writ of certiorari.

[91] TENN. CODE ANN. § 13-7-207(3).

As is perfectly clear, ordinarily in the zoning context, the delay in construction is the injury that the supersedeas might cause. As suggested in the introduction to this section, if the case involves a large project, the neighbors should entirely omit any request for supersedeas. The bond might be huge. From their perspective, it is better to take the risk that the developer will not begin the project without knowing for sure that it is legal. And generally, that is correct.

A smaller project on the other hand, may not require a large bond and its impact may be just as inconvenient or even worse. Under those circumstances, it may be worthwhile to ask for supercedeas. Bear in mind, that once the bond amount has been set, a bond must be filed in order for the supersedeas to be effective. A failure to file a bond in the amount set by the judge is just as if no supersedeas had been granted at all. Remember also, that in the event that the neighbors lose, the amount of the loss by the respondent may be more than the bond amount and the neighbors would be responsible for that overage as well as the bonded amount.[92]

There is of course no need for a supersedeas when there is no action that must be stayed to preserve the status quo.[93] Mostly this is true when the developer applicant loses the appeal before the zoning board or where the neighbors have won the appeal in front of the board. The status quo is not threatened under those circumstances.

---

[92] While slightly beyond the scope of this chapter and the book, SLAPP lawsuits have become more common in the last 10 or 15 years. These are "strategic litigation against public participation" suits and mainly are brought as an offensive weapon by developers to scare neighbors into accepting without further review whatever result was obtained at the administrative (or other, possibly legislative) level. These cases are really not worth pursuing and I always strongly recommend against them. My advice is not always taken.

[93] *Stone Man v Rutherford County Regional Planning Commission*, 1985 Tenn. App. Lexis 2607.

C. Practice in the Trial Court

1. Filing of the Record

As soon as this record is filed, the appellant should examine it carefully.[94] Just as the record in an appeal from a trial court needs to be reviewed to make sure it includes everything necessary for the successful prosecution of the appeal, so too should a transcript from a board of zoning appeals be examined to make sure that everything is in the record which is sent to the court. The earlier any errors or omissions can be isolated and identified, the more likely they can be successfully remedied.[95] Of course, it is particularly important to ensure that the portions of the record critical to the appeal are present.

It is also important to have a copy of the zoning ordinance in the record unless there is a good reason to avoid it. Sometimes it is not critical to the case; but in those instances where it is important, it is worthwhile to make sure it is there. In my opinion, I don't think that the applicant or the opposition needs to request a copy before the zoning board to make it a part of the record. Although there is no case law on

---

[94] TENN. CODE ANN. § 27-9-109 (b) and requires that the clerk promptly notify each party named as a defendant in the petition of the filing of the transcript. Presumably, the clerk will also notify the petitioner.

[95] Much like the tape recordings of zoning board meetings, the omissions which I have discovered in various records typically hurt the board's position as much as or more than the opposing parties. In one case, the appeal concerned an interpretation of the code by the Metro Zoning Administrator. When the record was filed with the court, the letter from the zoning administrator evidencing his position concerning the case, had entirely been left out of the record. While certainly this omission was quickly and easily remedied by a stipulation between counsel, if the omission is not identified until the time of the hearing before the judge, it may be more difficult to remedy the situation.

this issue to my knowledge, the board should include the entirety[96] of the ordinance as a matter of course in the record, whether requested or not. If the ordinance is not included, usually counsel can agree and if not, most trial court judges will order its inclusion.

2. Discovery

Generally, discovery is unnecessary in these cases. However, in my practice, upon request I have generally permitted discovery of my clients and the proposed land use based on my experience that most courts are accustomed to our wide open discovery practice under the Tennessee Rules of Civil Procedure. As a result, even though discovery makes little sense in most types of certiorari proceedings, judges are unlikely to quash discovery requests.

There is one circumstance where discovery does make good sense in the context of certiorari proceedings. As described above, most certiorari cases are not factual disputes but are rather legal arguments that based upon the facts as found by the zoning board, a different legal result must obtain. There are however a few kinds of cases where factual controversies can arise. These are cases where proceedings which are not included ordinarily in the record before the court may have had some impact on the deliberations of the zoning board. For example, if a zoning board member was inappropriately approached on an ex parte basis by the opposing attorney, or if the petitioner believes he has proof that one of the zoning board members has accepted a bribe, discovery concerning these types of allegations would certainly be appropriate. Certainly, if one of the board members was to accept a bribe, he or she would not be foolish enough to place that fact upon the

[96] I recommend the entirety of the ordinance to be included because it is difficult to know which parts of the ordinance may become important. There are usually a large number of cross-references in zoning ordinances and it is sometimes difficult to understand fully the section under consideration without the referenced material. Also, definitions are important and those are often forgotten (left out) if the ordinance is submitted piecemeal.

record. Other proof of the fact of the bribe would need to be developed and discovery is one mechanism by which such proof can be adduced.

Fortunately, only rarely are such allegations made. Most cases which appeal a decision of the zoning board simply allege that the board reached the wrong result based on the facts which were presented to it.

3. Hearing

Procedurally, these cases are handled in many different ways across the state. Davidson County provides in its local rules that the petitioner must prepare and file a brief, much like an appellate brief, within 30 days of the filing of the record. An answer is required to be filed by the defendant,[97] but the answer is largely irrelevant and frequently the requirement is entirely ignored. The respondent, the board (and any other parties to the appeal), must file a brief in opposition to the brief submitted by the petitioner. Again, in essence this is a form of appellate procedure, but the appellate court in this instance is a trial level court, instead of the Court of Appeals. Ordinarily, no proof will be permitted.[98] Thus, the proceeding before the trial court is simply an oral argument by the two attorneys representing the diverse parties. Again the analogy to a hearing before the Court of Appeals is relevant. Errors of law are the only things which will be

---

[97] TENN. CODE ANN. § 27-9-110. The statute indicates that "all defendants . . . desiring to make defense, shall do so by answer . . ." This sounds ominous, but it has been frequently ignored in practice, perhaps at the peril of the defendants. On the other hand, an answer technically in these cases in not helpful.

[98] Contrary to the provision of TENN. CODE ANN. § 27-9-111(b) which provides that "The hearing shall be on the proof introduced before the Board or commission contained in the transcript, and upon such other evidence as either party may desire to introduce."

considered by the court.[99] The court is not interested in reweighing the evidentiary issues brought before the board.

Another means of accomplishing the same result is to dispose of the case on cross-motions for summary judgment. Each side files a motion and brief, and the courts rules. One difficulty here is the admission of additional proof through affidavit; again, ordinarily, additional proof is not admitted and many times parties will attempt to get proof into the record by affidavit which should not properly be considered by the court.

4. Standard of Review

The standard of review on appeal pursuant to the common law writ of certiorari has been well defined over the years. Traditionally, the courts say that the board may be reversed only if it acts arbitrarily, fraudulently, illegally, or beyond its jurisdiction.[100] The findings of fact made by the board, if supported by the proof in the record, may not be

---

[99] Once again, this observation is generally contrary to the provision not TENN. CODE ANN. § 27-9-111 (d) which provides "In making such findings of fact, the judge shall lay the evidence and determine the facts by the preponderance of the proof."

[100] *Hoover Motor Express Company v. Tennessee Railroad and Public Utilities Commission*, 195 Tenn. 593, 604, 261 S.W. 2d 233, 238 (1953). As the Tennessee Supreme Court stated in that case, "... the common law writ does not bring up for determination, any question accept the question of whether the inferior board or tribunal (1) has exceeded its jurisdiction, or (2) has acted illegally, arbitrarily, or fraudulently." Id. The zoning cases are similar. *Reddoch v. Smith*, 214 Tenn. 213, 379 S.W. 2d 641, 645 (1964); *Glankler v. City of Memphis*, 481 S.W. 2d 376, 378 (Tenn. 1972); *McClurkan v. Metro Board of Zoning Appeals*, 565 S.W. 2d 495, 497-8 (Tenn. App. 1977); *McCallen v. City of Memphis*, 786 S.W.2d 633, 639 (Tenn. 1990); *South Harpeth Farms v. Metro Zoning Board*, 2001 WL 327908 (Tenn.Ct.App. April 05, 2001)

disputed or set aside by the court.[101] The court cannot substitute its judgment for that of the board of zoning appeals.[102] Essentially, the court may only look at the record, determine if any errors of law have been made,[103] and if not, it must affirm the decision of the board, regardless of whether it would have reached the same conclusion upon the proof in the record.

The articulation of the standard of review is however, sometimes a little confusing. In *Hoover Motor Express v. Railroad and Public Service Commission,*[104] the Tennessee Supreme Court held that the Court could not substitute its judgment for that of the administrative body because the administrative body (the Public Service Commission), acted in a legislative and administrative capacity and was a part of a co-equal branch of government.[105] The scope of review therefore had to be quite limited because the court was dealing with a legislative body or a body which exercised executive or administrative functions. Constitutional questions arise when the judiciary interferes in those areas.

On the other hand, the court made it clear also that if the full power of the board was to exercise quasi-judicial powers, those kinds of powers similar to those exercised by a court of law itself, there would be

---

[101] *Whittemore v. Brentwood Planning Commission,* 835 S.W.2d 11, 15 (Tenn. Ct. App. 1992).

[102] *Hoover, Inc. v. Metropolitan Bd. of Zoning Appeals,* 924 S.W.2d 900, 904 (Tenn. Ct. App. 1996)

[103] *Hoover Motor Express Company v. Tennessee Railroad and Public Utilities Commission,* 195 Tenn. 593, 605, 261 S.W. 2d 233, 238-9 (1953) ("Under the common law written of certiorari, questions of law only will be reviewed by the courts.")

[104] 195 Tenn. 593, 261 S.W. 2d 233 (Tenn. 1953).

[105] Id at 239.

no problem with the court reviewing in detail, and substituting its judgment for a quasi-judicial body.[106]

The difficulty arises in the case of *Reddoch v. Smith.*[107] In *Reddoch*, the board of zoning appeals was, in fact, characterized as a quasi-judicial decision-maker.[108] It would appear, therefore, that rather than the common law writ, the statutory writ of certiorari would be appropriate with its de novo hearing, the introduction of additional evidence, and the court substituting its judgment for that of the board by making up its own mind as to whether the requested relief should be granted. The case law makes it clear that this is not appropriate. But it has never been sufficiently explained as to why a board of zoning appeals, characterized by the *Reddoch* court as a quasi-judicial administrative body, should not be reviewed pursuant to the statutory writ of certiorari instead of the common law writ of certiorari.[109]

Even if the reasoning of the courts was not clear, the result is generally appropriate. What would be the use of having a board of zoning appeals if every case could be entirely reheard by the courts? There would be no sense in having the administrative body at all. It is possible to make a strong case that the local zoning boards have not operated very effectively and that as a result very little deference is deserved by the local zoning boards. But there are better ways to

---

[106] Id.

[107] 379 S.W. 2d 641, 645 (Tenn. 1964). A fuller discussion of the merits of the case is found at page 244.

[108] Actually, the board was said to be both quasi-judicial and administrative. 379 S.W. 2d at 645.

[109] One reason is that the Memphis private enabling legislation specifically provided review pursuant to a mechanism that appeared to be very similar to the common law writ of certiorari (although the court may have been able to make its own decision de novo on appeal). 1925 Tennessee Private Acts, Chapter 428, at 1623-4. There has never been any similar proviso in the Tennessee Public Zoning Enabling Statutes, TENN. CODE ANN. § 13-7-101 and following.

ensure that the boards act appropriately without totally rehearing the case before the trial court. The board's attempted adjustment of local land use planning problems should be given the deference which is inherent in the common law writ of certiorari except possibly in the area of non-conforming uses,[110] and that the common law writ of certiorari is the appropriate vehicle by which to review these decisions.

In an interesting case in a related area of the law, Judge Cantrell, writing for the Court of Appeals in a case where a lower court had issued a statutory writ of certiorari to review a decision of the Tennessee Department of Environment and Conservation granting a landfill permit concluded that only the common law writ was applicable.[111] "We are of the opinion that the decision to grant the solid waste disposal permit involves an essentially administrative function; i.e., the administration and enforcement of the solid waste act." As a result, only the common law writ of certiorari was applicable. Certainly, the majority of the functions performed by a local zoning board may aptly be characterized as administrative, much as the Department of Environment and Conservation. The common law writ is ordinarily the only avenue of appeal which may be pursued.

5. Judicial Remedies

Ordinarily, the Court has only limited remedies in certiorari cases. The typical remedy is to remand the case to the administrative body to carry out the conclusion of the matter in accord with the court's ruling. The Courts will vary from this rarely; one instance is when the board has demonstrated an unwillingness to follow the Court's direction.[112]

---

[110] See the next section (D) on the statutory writ of certiorari.

[111] *Town of Dandridge v. Tennesse Department of Environment and Conservation*, 1992 WL 12189, Tenn.Ct.App., January 29, 1992

[112] *B & B Enterprises v. City of Lebanon*, 2004 WL 2916141, at *3 (Tenn. Ct. App. Dec. 16, 2004)

D. The Statutory Writ of Certiorari

The statutory writ of certiorari is a much different mechanism for review of administrative decisions. The most important differences can be summarized simply: any additional evidence which any party desires to submit to the court on appeal may be admitted and considered by the court under the statutory writ of certiorari; in addition, and building significantly upon the rule concerning additional evidence, the court may substitute its judgment for that of the local administrative body and decide the case in the manner in which the court believes most appropriate. In other words, under the statutory writ of certiorari, the court is not examining the essential legality of the decision to ensure that the local administrative tribunal did not act arbitrarily and capriciously; to the contrary, under the statutory writ, the trial court sets aside altogether the decision of the lower tribunal and makes its own decision on the facts presented to it.

1. Procedural Considerations

The procedural devices which were discussed earlier in this chapter regarding the common law writ of certiorari apply to the statutory writ as well. The aggrieved party must file a petition for writ of certiorari, a costs bond, and the trial court must issue a writ of certiorari requiring that the record of the administrative tribunal be brought before it.

2. Standard of Review

As mentioned earlier, under the statutory writ, judicial review is de novo. This means that the proceeding is entirely open for the judge to do whatever he or she believes is correct. There is no presumption that the zoning board acted properly; there is no deference paid to the administrative proceedings. The court hears the case (usually the judge will read over the transcript from the lower body plus allow any additional proof that anyone would like to offer) and renders its decision. This approach makes the court a super zoning board and for that reason, there are few, if any, instances where the statutory writ applies. Most of the time, the zoning board is given broad deference and its decision upheld unless clearly arbitrary or capricious, reviewed under the common law writ of certiorari. Only in those areas where there is some fundamental right at issue is this process appropriate. Most of the areas of zoning law which come up do not involve fundamental rights. However, there is one area of inquiry here.

So far as the author is aware, no one has raised this issue[113], but a non-conforming use appears to involve a property right which might be denied if the zoning board is reviewed only pursuant to the common law writ. It seems therefore, that the statutory writ with its less deferential standard of review is more appropriate. Judge Cantrell, in his landmark certiorari law review article tries to make some sense of the cases (although he notes they "defy precise classification"):[114]

> A second class of cases where some coherence is discernible involves rulings on applications by individuals for licenses or permits to conduct certain businesses. Included in this class of cases are proceedings to revoke or rescind licenses previously granted to such individuals. These proceedings tend to be classified as "judicial" in nature on the grounds that a license to practice a profession, or a permit, or the right to public office, is some species of private property right.

Judge Cantrell concludes:[115]

> Apparently the court will sanction the granting of review by the statutory writ with its trial de novo only where the

---

[113] *Toles v. City of Dyersburg*, 39 S.W.3d 138 (Tenn. Ct. App. 2000), did involve a statutory writ of certiorari in the context of a non-conforming use, but the Court of Appeals did not address the issue of its propriety. See also page 131.

[114] Cantrell, *Review of Administrative Decisions by Certiorari in Tennessee*, 4 Mem. St. U. Law Rev. 19, 23 (1973)

[115] Id at 26.

> administrative tribunal is acting as to the petitioner much like a court would; namely, the individual petitioner has something like a private property right (e.g., a license, a permit, an office) which by its order, the administrative body may take away.

Non-conforming property cases are much like these "private property right" cases noted by Judge Cantrell. The owner/operator may have a vested right which the decision of the zoning board may effectively take away. I'm not suggesting that the board not be given an opportunity to review the factual components, but why not de novo review under the statutory writ? It is a property right at issue; one that has vested or may have vested. Judicial oversight seems warranted under those circumstances.

Notice that this situation is much different from the customary appeal from a zoning board. A variance is a special relaxation of the rules; there's no species of property right involved. A special exception is an application to use property for a particular type of use; but again, the use has not started, there is only an application to use the property for that purpose in the future. Finally, an interpretation of the ordinance again usually arises in the context of a permit application. The use is not established: the issue is whether that use may be permitted in that area. These three zoning board actions usually deal with whether a permit should be issued, not revocation of a previously issued permit.[116] If no permit has been issued, it is certainly difficult to argue that there is any kind of property right involved.[117] Thus, as to the

---

[116] Even after the issuance of a building permit, ordinarily no rights are vested, at least until substantial construction has been done. *Howe Realty v. City of Nashville*, 114 SW 2d 904, 906 (Tenn. 1940). But in the case of a non-conforming property, substantial construction has been done (the building or structure is entirely complete!) and it has been used for usually many years. It is this existing non-conforming property which I suggest is entitled to more rigorous judicial scrutiny to ensure appropriate protection of the property interest.

[117] In some circumstances, the NCFP may not have a permit either, but that is usually because it has been there so long that a

3 major types of customary zoning board action, they clearly fit under the common law writ; the actions are administrative and de novo review would be inappropriate.

But a non-conforming property is very different. It may well be a vested property interest which has everything to do with the livelihood of the owner or operator. Given its difference from the other zoning techniques we have reviewed, the statutory writ may be most appropriate when appealing a decision denying (or granting) non-conforming status.

E. Conclusion

The writ of certiorari in Tennessee is a cumbersome and antiquated device for administrative review and needs to be changed. Failing that, greater understanding of the basic concepts by the attorneys working in this field can go a long way towards making judicial review of zoning decisions easier and faster. The basic methodology concerning substantive review is sound; but frequently the process is misunderstood and misapplied. It is also helpful for codes officials staffing zoning board (and other administrative bodies) to be somewhat familiar with the writ because they will most often be given the task to construct the administrative record in a manner suitable to judicial review under the writ. A basic understanding of the writ and its process makes that much easier.

---

permit was not needed when it began operations. The key is the long use of the property; it is almost always present with a non-conforming property and almost never present with a variance, CUP, or interpretation.

Appendix: Petition for Writ of Certiorari

IN THE CHANCERY COURT OF WILSON COUNTY
At Lebanon

COST ENTERPRISES LLC

Petitioner,

v DOCKET #

THE CITY OF LEBANON, TENNESSEE

Respondent

PETITION FOR WRIT OF CERTIORARI

The petitioner, Cost Enterprises, LLC, hereby petitions this Court for a writ of certiorari, and alleges the following as the basis for the issuance of the writ:

1. The petitioner, Cost Enterprises, LLC has a contract to purchase 116 acres of land located on Bethlehem Road (Parcel 13 on Lebanon City Map 69), in Lebanon, Tennessee.

2. The respondent, the City of Lebanon, is the duly incorporated regulatory authority exercising jurisdiction in the City of Lebanon with regard to land use planning and zoning.

3. The petitioner's property is zoned R-1A, low density residential.

4. The petitioner applied to the Lebanon Planning Commission for approval of a planned unit development so as to permit the residential development of the property. The application included a traffic study and stormwater management engineering analysis demonstrating that the application would comply with local requirements.

5. A hearing concerning the planned unit development was held by the Lebanon Planning Commission on February 28, 2006. The Planning Commission approved the application with conditions at that time.

6. As required by the Lebanon Zoning Ordinance, the preliminary master plan for the planned unit development was submitted to the City Council. On March 21, 2006, the council deferred the matter because of concerns regarding stormwater and traffic.

7. The planned unit development was again considered by the City Council on April 4, 2006 and again deferred because of stormwater issues.

8. On May 16, 2006, the planned unit development was again on the agenda before the City Council. The city engineer explained that an independent engineer had been retained to review the plans submitted by the project engineer and that the plans as submitted comply with the city's requirements. Notwithstanding this compliance, the planned unit development was deferred for the third time.

9. On July 18, 2006, the petitioner withdrew the application from consideration of the City Council believing that the application would be deferred once again.

10. The planned unit development was placed back on the agenda at the request of the petitioner on November 21, 2006. The Council denied the application at that time.

11. The decision of the respondent on November 21, 2006, was illegal, arbitrary, and/or capricious.

12. The petitioner is aggrieved by the decision of the City Council denying approval to the planned unit development.

PREMISES CONSIDERED, Petitioner requests the following relief:

1. That a Writ of Certiorari issue, requiring the Respondent, the City of Lebanon, to certify and file with the Clerk and Master of this Court, the entire record in this case, including all exhibits and all entries made in connection therewith, and in particular, including the transcript of the hearing held before the Lebanon City Council on November 21, 2006; the application of the petitioner (including both the stormwater study and the traffic study); the stormwater study done by Ragan Smith engineers (including the letter from Jeffrey Ballard of that firm dated November 15, 2006); the minutes of the City Council dated March 21, April 4, May 16, and July 18, 2006; as well as the planning commission minutes dated February 28, 2006.

2. That process or notice issue to the Respondent pursuant to Tennessee Code Annotated, § 27-9-107, and should Respondent elect to answer, the answer be filed within 30 days of the filing of the transcript;

3. That upon the hearing of this cause, the Court set aside the action of the City Council denying approval and further, that the Court reverse the decision of the Council, and remand to the City Planning Commission for final consideration of the master development plan;

4. That attorney's fees be awarded pursuant to 42 U.S.C. § 1988 for a violation of the Petitioners' constitutional rights, and pursuant to the

Tennessee Equal Access to Justice Act of 1984, as amended, TENN. CODE ANN. § 29-37-101 et seq., and

5. That the Court grant such further general relief as the equities of this case may require and as the Court deems necessary and appropriate.

THIS IS THE FIRST APPLICATION FOR A WRIT OF CERTIORARI IN THIS CAUSE. (T.C.A. § 27-8-106)

Respectfully submitted,

ROCHELLE, MCCULLOCH & AULDS PLLC

By: ______________________________
Jere N. McCulloch
109 Castle Heights Ave N
Lebanon, TN 37087

PARKER, LAWRENCE, CANTRELL & DEAN

By: ____________________________
George A. Dean
200 Fourth Avenue North
Suite 500, Nashville, TN 37219
Attorneys for the Petitioners

STATE OF FLORIDA)
COUNTY OF *******)

I, Robert Parker, having been first duly sworn, make oath, that I am Managing Member of Cost Enterprises LLC, and that I am familiar with the allegations made in the foregoing petition, and that those allegations are true to the best of my knowledge and belief.

____
Robert Parker

Personally appeared before me, the undersigned, a Notary Public in the aforesaid county and state, the within named Robert Parker, with whom I am personally acquainted, and who acknowledged that he executed the within instrument, and that the facts stated therein are true to the best of his knowledge and belief.

Witness my hand and official seal, this ____ day of November, 2006.

____

My Commission Expires:

____

Writ of Certiorari

IN THE CHANCERY COURT OF WILSON COUNTY
At Lebanon

COST ENTERPRISES LLC

Petitioner,

v DOCKET #

THE CITY OF LEBANON, TENNESSEE

Respondent

WRIT OF CERTIORARI

TO: THE CITY OF LEBANON

WHEREAS, Cost Enterprises LLC has filed a Petition, under the above-styled caption, asking that a Writ of Certiorari issued to you, the City of Lebanon and a Chancellor of this Court, having endorsed the Fiat directing that the Writ issue requiring you to make, certify, and transmit to the Court for examination and review the entire record, including all exhibits and entries made in connection therewith, and in particular, including the transcripts of the hearing held before the Lebanon City Council on November 21, 2006; the application of the petitioner (including both the stormwater study and the traffic study); the stormwater study done by Ragan Smith engineers (including the letter from Jeffrey Ballard of that firm dated November 15, 2006); the minutes of the City Council dated March 21, April 4, May 16, and July 18, 2006; as well as the planning commission minutes dated February 28, 2006; as is all more fully set out in the Petition to which reference is herein made;

YOU ARE, THEREFORE, HEREBY COMMANDED to make, certify, and transmit to the Court the entire true and correct record of the aforementioned proceedings, had before you and on file in your office, and make return of this Writ showing how you have obeyed the same within 30 days of issuance.

WITNESS, the Clerk and Master of the Chancery Court for Wilson County this _____ day of December, 2006.

CLERK AND MASTER

By:______________________________
Deputy Clerk and Master

Table of Cases

Index

Made in United States
North Haven, CT
05 November 2026

21760262R00237